Introduction to Early Childhood Education

a Canadian Perspective

INGRID CROWTHER

ATHABASCA UNIVERSITY

NELSON / EDUCATION

NELSON / EDUCATION

**Introduction to Early Childhood Education:
A Canadian Perspective**

by Ingrid Crowther

**Associate Vice-President,
Editorial Director:**
Evelyn Veitch

**Publisher for Social Sciences
and Humanities:**
Joanna Cotton

Marketing Manager:
Rosalind Wright

Developmental Editor:
Alwynn Pinard

Senior Production Editor:
Natalia Denesiuk

Copy Editor:
Valerie Adams

Proofreader:
Kelli Howey

Indexer:
Christopher Blackburn

Senior Production Coordinator:
Hedy Sellers

Creative Director:
Angela Cluer

Interior and Cover Designs:
Sarah Battersby

Cover Image:
Anthony Marsland/Image Bank/
Getty Images

Compositor:
Brenda Prangley

Printer:
RR Donnelley

**Library and Archives Canada
Cataloguing in Publication Data**

Crowther, Ingrid, 1944–
    Introduction to early childhood
education : a Canadian perspective /
Ingrid Crowther.

Includes bibliographical
references and index.
ISBN 0-17-641564-5

1. Early childhood education.
2. Early childhood education—
Canada. I. Title.

LB1139.3.C3C76 2004   372.21
C2004-905697-2

CONTENTS

PREFACE

Introduction to Early Childhood Education: A Canadian Perspective introduces the novice learner to the ECE field. You will learn about children, their families, and child-care settings through photographs and scenarios. I have taken care to accurately represent the diversity of Canadian culture, and the photographs are inclusive of most cultures in Canada (including visible and non–visible minorities) and of urban, rural, and isolated locations throughout the country. The use of scenarios and photographs will introduce you to

- dynamic aspects of the early years—infants, toddlers, preschoolers, and school-aged children;
- the joys of working with children;
- the joys of partnerships in learning;
- creative aspects of children's learning environments; and
- the excitement of interactions with children and their families.

You will learn about the relevant skills needed to work with children. In order to make skill development easier to understand and apply, I have presented these skills in the context of children, their families, children's environments, and legislative requirements through scenarios, photographs, and interactive Web-based exercises. These skills include learning about children's needs at various ages; building partnerships with families, other professionals, and community members; communicating effectively with all partners, including children and other staff members; building advocacy skills; gaining knowledge about legislative requirements; and fitting early childhood education into the context of society.

Various philosophical approaches, such as High/Scope, Reggio Emilia, Montessori, and the Head Start program, are presented from a Canadian perspective. Canadian childcare facilities that utilize these approaches are described through the use of floor plans, photographs of the environment, and photographs of children engaged in activities.

I have taken care to ensure that the information presented is at an introductory level. *Introduction to Early Childhood Education: A Canadian Perspective* has been written in recognition that learners are novices in the field and need to remain excited about this choice of profession. The text identifies introductory concepts that are critical to students' success in the field and that can subsequently be built upon. Care has been taken to help students to see the relevance of what they are learning and continue to enjoy their studies by ensuring that any theoretical content is easy to understand, that terms are defined clearly, and that real scenarios and photographs of children support and enrich the content. Materials covered in other core courses in the program have been kept to a minimum to avoid repetition. Information is presented in a format to encourage students to find relevant material quickly and easily through tables, charts, figures, lists, and bulleted points.

You will become actively involved in learning through the use of exercises at the end of each chapter and interactive exercises on the Web site. Numerous pertinent, up-to-date Internet references may be used as a forum for discussion and research, and as a source of new ideas.

The interactive exercises on the Web may be used to

- support in-class learning;
- encourage self-evaluation of your progress;
- identify knowledge or skills that you need to review; and
- support your independence in the learning process.

Throughout the text, the Web exercises symbol shown here in the margin is used to indicate a connection between the text material and the interactive Web-based exercises. You can find all of these exercises on the Nelson ECE Resource Centre at **www.ece.nelson.com**.

In addition to the Web exercises icon, a World Wide Web icon will also appear beside various items in the text. This icon tells you that this feature is available for download from the Nelson ECE Resource Centre at **www.ece.nelson.com**. Students and instructors alike can then print off and/or modify these forms for learning and instructional purposes.

ANCILLARIES AVAILABLE

An Instructor's Manual (0-17-640748-0) and Microsoft® PowerPoint® Slides (0-17-640747-2) are available to accompany the text. These items can be ordered from your sales representative or through Thomson Nelson customer service. They are also available for download on the password-protected Instructor's portion of the Nelson ECE Resource Centre.

The purpose of the Instructor's Manual is to guide instructors in creating learning environments based on the principles of adult learning. Through PowerPoint presentations, instructors are able to build an interactive curriculum based on active participation and application of learning. Activities are presented that help to foster long-term retention of learning and focus on the coordination of information from the text, photographs, Web site, and interactive activities on the Web.

ACKNOWLEDGEMENTS

I would like to acknowledge the children and the families who have participated in helping to create this text—in particular, Lara, Lauren, Jacob, and Christopher and their families. I would also like to thank the children, families, and staffs of Aakuluk Day Care Centre, BC Aboriginal Child Care Society, Brite Beginnings Day Care, Capilano College Child Care Centre, Cedar Road Aboriginal Head Start Program, Family Space Ontario Early Years Centre, Kitsilano Area Childcare Society, Loyalist College Curriculum Lab Preschool, Sheridan Child Care Centre, Village Day Care Society, Westcoast Child Care Resource Centre, and Whispering Hills Child Care Centre.

In addition, I would like to acknowledge the assistance of the reviewers: Carol Anderson, Durham College; Diane Bergeron, George Brown College; Louisa Dyck, Conestoga College; D'Anne Epp, University College of the Fraser Valley; Mabel Higgins, Lambton College; Kathryn Lockwood, Humber College; Claude Painter, Langara College; and Cheryl Taylor, Institute for Human Services Education.

THE MAGIC OF CHILDHOOD

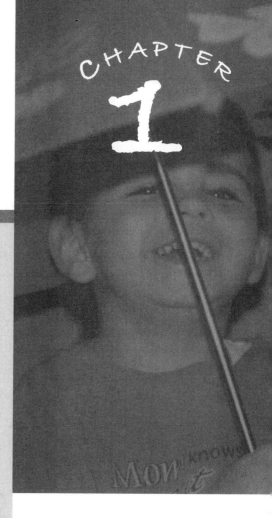

CHAPTER 1

"[W]e are living in the presence of a new kind of child. A child that lives in a state of wonder, which is our natural state and which we are still recognizing if we know where to look for it. For we have only forgotten it, lost along the way somewhere."
(Lorie, 1989, p. 20)

Chapter Outcomes

After reading this chapter, the reader will

1. Describe the main characteristics of each of the following age groups:

    a) infants,

    b) toddlers,

    c) preschoolers, and

    d) school-aged children.

2. Describe why quality experiences in the early years are of critical importance.

3. Identify various family backgrounds.

4. Identify and discuss factors that impact on the development of young children.

5. Identify how young children learn best.

6. Identify and describe what experiences are needed to support children's learning.

7. Discuss experiences that children need to learn appropriately.

THE MAGIC OF CHILDHOOD

Childhood is a magical time of life. It is a time when children learn the most that they will ever learn. It is the foundation of *all* future learning—physical, social, emotional, communicative, and cognitive (Nash, 1997; McCain & Mustard, 1999; Lefrancois, 1999). Children embrace learning enthusiastically, creatively, and full of joy and vigour. As adults we are privileged to share, learn, and remember. As adults we once again share the beauty of learning through the eyes of the child. "No matter what your experience with children, you have one thing in common, with all other adults: You will never again directly experience the 'magic time' of childhood. Once we become adults, we can no longer see the world through children's eyes. We trade that vision for a more rational understanding of how things work, an understanding that allows us to function competently in the world" (Schickedanz et al., 2001, p. xix).

Observe and Remember

Learning becomes more powerful if we can relate what we have learned through linking our learning with remembered experiences and by applying that learning to new situations. It is important to recognize how we learn and what we remember. Research shows that after one month we remember

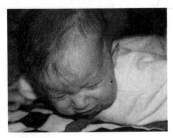

Photo 1.1

*   14 percent of what we hear;
*   22 percent of what we see;
*   30 percent of what we observe others do—demonstrated or modelled;
*   42 percent of what we repeat through seeing, hearing, and doing;
*   72 percent of what we link to remembered or imagined experiences;
*   83 percent of what we do that is a first-time activity or what we do that demands action that applies new meaning; and
*   92 percent of what we teach others (Robinson, 1994, p. 62).

The reflection exercises in this section will help you to remember experiences to help you to apply those memories to your work with children.

Infants communicate with their caregivers in a variety of ways. Lauren had been lying on her stomach. She became most unhappy about lying on her stomach (photo 1.1). She was immediately picked up. Her mother said, "You don't like to be on your stomach anymore." After cuddling Lauren for a while, she asked, "Do you want to sit in your chair?" Lauren looked toward her chair. She smiled and continued to look at her chair. Her mother placed her in her chair. Lauren quietly started to play with the toys in front of her. Lauren cannot express her feelings verbally. She needs to have her signals, such as crying, facial expressions, and eye contact, interpreted by her caregiver. When infants' signals are understood and responded to, they develop a sense of trust in their caregivers. Do you remember a time when you were unhappy and a caring adult in your life gave you the positive attention you needed at this time? Do you remember how good it felt to have someone understand you, listen to you, and care for you? These interactions early in life lead to long-term positive social interactions (McCain & Mustard, 1999; Watson et al., 2000).

Photo 1.2

When working with children, there are times when the only important moment is that moment. Notice the intense interaction of joy between Lauren and her mother (photo 1.2). They are totally absorbed in each other. They react to each other's smiles, sparkling eyes, close body contact, and eye contact. Do you remember a time when you were held close as a child by someone special in your life? Do you remember that special feeling—a feeling of being safe, snuggly, warm, and content? Such early interactions build strong neurological connections that enhance all future development (Greenspan, 1997; Machado, 1999).

Photo 1.3

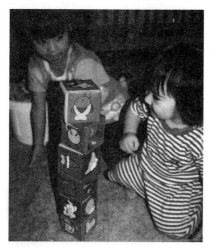

Photo 1.4

Children are naturally curious. They embrace learning in a multitude of ways. Jacob had been lining up the plastic animals in the sand area. He noticed a book that had been placed in that area. He was fascinated to see the pictures of the animals he had been playing with. He traced the picture with his fingers and quietly named some of the facial features (photo 1.3). Do you remember being fascinated by certain books? You could look at them over and over again. You liked the look of the pictures and enjoyed gently touching the pages. Children who are exposed to books earlier set positive life-long patterns associated with communication—reading, writing, and speaking (Machado, 1999; Sawyer, 2000).

Photo 1.5

Children in every culture in the world enjoy building. Lara was particularly fond of the small cube blocks. She took great delight in creating towers of the small blocks (photo 1.4). She is totally absorbed in her task and smiles each time she manages to place a block on top of another block. She especially enjoys Christine's comments about how high the tower is getting. Do you remember the joy of accomplishing something by yourself? How proud you felt when you could make something and improve upon it? How happy you were when someone noticed your effort? When given the opportunity to explore materials in the environment freely, children will gain pride in their accomplishments and self-confidence in their actions. These children will grow up to feel free to try new challenges (Gestwicki, 1999).

Children seek out opportunities to play and work together. By playing together we learn tolerance for others, gain understanding about others, and learn to socialize appropriately. Mackenzie and Reghan are creating a picture together (photo 1.5).

Photo 1.6

Photo 1.7

Photo 1.9

Notice the joy expressed on Reghan's face. Notice the quiet contentment on Mackenzie's face. The girls are sharing a precious moment in time, when they can cooperate together to share space, time, and materials. Do you remember when you shared a task with a friend? Do you remember how good it felt to be able to accomplish something together? Children who learn to play together learn life-long skills in how to form friendships, how to maintain friendships, and how to behave around others (Gestwicki, 1999).

Children seek out quiet time, times when they can indulge in sensory and pleasurable experiences. Yasmine loved to find a quiet spot in the sandbox. She would run her fingers through the sand, trickle sand through her fingers, and pat the sand she had placed in her hand smooth (photo 1.6). At these times she was oblivious to what was going on around her. She was simply enjoying the feel and texture of the sand. Do you remember the luxury of stopping what you were doing and simply enjoying the moment? Do you remember the feel of sand on your bare hands as it trickled through your fingers? Children who are given opportunities to engage in quiet sensory activities learn to gauge their own needs. They will learn to value all moments of the day (Crowther, 2003; Shipley, 2002).

As adults, we must cherish and protect these moments for our children. In our hurried times, it is too easy to get trapped in the routines of everyday life. The danger of this is that we forget what it was like to be a child. In forgetting, we risk doing the very things that make the child's world a less pleasurable one. We need to continue to be in touch with our own pleasurable memories and build new ones through every child we meet. We need to be in touch with the core values that we all need—nurturance, acceptance, freedom, and trust.

Photo 1.8

WHO ARE THE CHILDREN?

Infants

Web exercises

Lara is an active and curious infant. Her caregiver is very astute in reading Lara's signals in order to respond appropriately. When Lara heard someone come into the room, she quickly raised her body up from the mat and looked for that individual (photo 1.7). Her father immediately noticed that she was looking at him. He understood that Lara had heard him come in and wanted him to respond to her. He smiled at her and talked to her. Lara immediately smiled and relaxed her body.

Lara can make choices if given the opportunity. Her caregivers carefully observe Lara in order to understand and facilitate her choice. When toys are placed within her reach she can actively pick the one she wants to grasp, shake, or put in her mouth (photo 1.8). Lara indicates what she wants by directing her gaze to the object wanted or by reaching out and grabbing it. Her mother held out several toys within reach to Lara one at a time. She paused each time and inquired, "Do you want this one?" When Lara wanted one of the toys, she reached out to grasp the toy (photo 1.9).

Lara shows her excitement in a variety of ways—by smiling, by waving her arms and legs around, by gurgling, and by reaching. She will cry if upset, hungry, or uncomfortable. It is important not to assume that Lara is all right because she has just eaten or has just been changed. It may be something totally different. She may simply need to feel the closeness of someone she is secure with.

Photo 1.10

Photo 1.11

Photo 1.12

Photo 1.13

In just a few weeks, there are some rapid changes. Lara's skills seem to grow daily. Lara has learned to crawl. She straightens her legs behind her (photo 1.10), and then jumps forward to place her legs under her body (photo 1.11). This activity gives her much more opportunity to explore the environment on her own. She is not as dependent on her caregiver to provide for her. She can actively choose what she wants to get (photo 1.12).

Lara has also learned to **imitate** certain behaviours—sticking out her tongue and clapping. She shows great delight to have someone clap so that she can clap back (photo 1.14). This is one of the ways that infants learn—by imitating. Another way is by early exposure to different types of activities and experiences. Lara enjoys looking at books (photo 1.13). She may not want to have a story read to her, but enjoys looking at the pictures as someone talks about what she is looking at or pointing to.

Lara will grow and increase her skills in many ways over the next months. Observing her change, helping her master new skills, watching her grow, and enjoying each step of this process is truly a rewarding experience for all caregivers.

imitate
Copy an action, expression, idea, or symbol.

Toddlers

Photo 1.14

Jacob is an active curious toddler. He loves to explore things by himself. His explorations often lead to unpredictable behaviours as judged by adults. They are perfectly logical to him. Dishes and boxes are wonderful items to stack (photo 1.15). Unfortunately the adult may only see the "mess" created when the items in the containers were dumped out rather than Jacob's need to find meaning in his world. He is learning about how things fit together.

Jacob spends a lot of his time organizing his world. Much of his time is spent in **solitary play**—playing by himself. One of his favourite activities is to line up blocks (photo 1.16) or to stack them. When finished, he will take them apart or knock them down, then repeat this activity again. Toddlers spend a lot of time doing things over and over and over again. It is through this repetition that neural connections are made and reinforced. By this "wiring" of the brain, learning becomes efficient and is retained (Shore, 1997).

Jacob is easily attracted by other children's behaviour. He had been busily stacking blocks when he heard Benjamin call out excitedly, "Look it fits, it fits!" He immediately stopped what he was doing and ran over to see what Benjamin was doing. Benjamin had found that he could fit the small plastic bugs into a bottle. Benjamin allowed Jacob to try to fit one in too (photo 1.17). Toddlers are often attracted by activities or events going on around them. Their natural curiosity will

Web
exercises

solitary play
Play alone doing one's own thing.

Photo 1.15

Photo 1.16

Photo 1.17

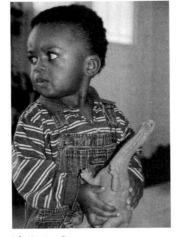

Photo 1.18

parallel play

Play beside one or more children, engaged in similar activity with similar toys but doing own thing.

symbolic play

Using one thing to represent another, such as using a stick to represent an airplane.

attract them to come and see, interact, or watch from a distance. Learning through observation is another way that learning occurs.

Jacob had seen and heard Rashawn play with the dinosaurs. He decided to go over and play with Rashawn. Unfortunately, there was only one large triceratops available. Jacob picked it up. Rashawn immediately grabbed the dinosaur and said, "Mine!" (photo 1.18). Toddlers have not yet developed the concept of sharing. If they see something and want it, they will attempt to get it. Often this will result in an argument between them. An astute caregiver will ensure that there is more than one of each toy available. This avoids the situation altogether and acknowledges the toddler's stage of development.

Some of the toddlers had set up a horizontal row of blocks. One of the toddlers, Kayla, started to crawl along the top of the blocks (photo 1.19). Soon most of the toddlers were involved in the activity. Toddlers are very active. They explore the environment to develop their gross motor control. Some toddlers, like Timmy, have developed a great deal of control in their physical abilities. Timmy loves to run and jump from various heights (photo 1.20). Toddlers also use riding toys to propel themselves along by pushing with their feet (photo 1.21). It is extremely important to allow toddlers the freedom to explore their environment through physical activity. Large open areas are required that allow for running, jumping, and building.

Derrick and Venice are pasting and gluing using similar materials. Both are totally absorbed in their own activity (photo 1.22). Toddlers often play beside each other, known as **parallel play**. They play by themselves without interacting with each other as long as ample similar materials are available.

Jacob found a house that someone else had built with blocks and left. He got into the house and proceeded to make a car-like sound (photo 1.23). He was pretending to be driving a car. This is an example of **symbolic play**. Toddlers' play is abundant in symbolic play. Toddlers start to imitate what they see around them and start to adapt their actions to what they see. For example, a toddler might have seen a digger in action at a construction site. The child then imitates the digger's actions "symbolically" by using his or her arm and hand to duplicate the action previously seen.

Caregivers of toddlers must recognize the toddlers' endless curiosity, abundant physical energy, and emergent independence. Working with toddlers is always challenging and rewarding. Toddlers challenge our ingenuity, test our patience, and inspire our awe. Working with toddlers is a uniquely satisfying experience.

Photo 1.19

Photo 1.20

Photo 1.21

Preschoolers

Josh enjoys all aspects of the learning environment. He is often found working alone, with other children, or observing others at play and commenting on what they are doing. Gabrielle was trying to put powder on the baby doll. It would not work. She showed the powder puff to Josh. Josh told her, "Too wet" (photo 1.24). He then prompted her where to find a new puff. Josh loves to help others solve their problems.

Web exercises

Photo 1.24

Hannah, Benjamin, Damon, and Reghan enjoy activities that can be played together. They had been listening to the song, "Pop Goes the Weasel." They decided to hide in a box together and pop up at the appropriate prompt—"POP" (photo 1.25). Josh stopped what he was doing. He watched the children from a distance, smiled when they "popped" up, but continued with his own activity. As you notice, the children enjoyed the activity together, were able to share a small space, and were able to follow through by listening and following simple directions. Preschoolers spend much of their time playing together. They are learning to enjoy each other's company and to share ideas, space, and materials. They also make personal choices based on their desire to participate actively or simply enjoy the activity from a distance.

Autumn actively explores the environment. She loves to try to do things in different ways. Autumn is often at the water centre. She loves to pour from one container to

Photo 1.22   Photo 1.23

Photo 1.25

another. Autumn had tried a variety of materials—measuring cups, bottles, ladles, small pitchers, and a water wheel. She experimented by using different sizes of containers to pour into the water wheel. She was delighted when she could make the wheel turn faster. She was able to pick a container that made it easier to pour without spilling and control the speed of the water pouring into the water wheel (photo 1.26). If appropriate choices and materials are provided, preschoolers will experiment with these materials to solve their own problems. In the process they discover many new and exciting skills. These skills are later applied to other areas—watering plants or pouring a drink from a pitcher into a cup, measuring how much one container holds, and solving the problem of using the appropriate containers for a task.

Photo 1.26

Michael and Colin participated in a dramatic corner of the room that had been collaboratively set up between the children, their families, and the early childhood educators in the program. Several pet cages had been brought in. Colin and Michael thoroughly enjoyed pretending to be dogs (photo 1.27). They both loved acting out the situation—to be locked in a cage, howl to be let out, growl or bark at individuals, pretend to eat and drink, and be put on a leash to go for a walk. This scenario was repeated many times. Through this type of play, the children were able to talk about what they knew about pet care; try out various roles (owner, dogs, vet); share ideas, space, materials, and equipment; and practise and improve upon the role they were engaged in.

Autumn, Yasmine, and Matthew are all engaged with activities that have a distinct purpose. They use the materials and equipment in the environment creatively with little prompting or help. Autumn (photo 1.28) was putting together an insect puzzle.

She noticed a large book of insects on the table near the puzzles. She looked through the book and was delighted to be able to match the insect pieces to the pictures in the book. She not only gained knowledge about what insects looked like in different types of media, but also gained some prereading skills—finding information in a book, associating written words with the pictures, and using left-to-right progression.

Photo 1.27

Yasmine (photo 1.29) was using the rainbow gems. She had been pouring them from one container to another. When she went back to the shelf, she noticed the coloured dishes on the shelf. She brought out all the dishes and started to sort the gems into the appropriate coloured dishes. **Sorting** activities are important as they lead to later skills in almost all cognitive areas. Sorting leads to recognition of similarities and differences and classification skills. Recognition of similarities and differences is of primary importance in learning to read, write, and distinguish how letters are the same or different, and how words are the same or different. **Classification** skills require children to group and regroup ideas, quantities, or objects. These skills are primary requirements in language development, science, and math skills.

Matthew was trying to roll the cars through the unit blocks. He was frustrated when he increased the length of the unit blocks and found that the cars got stuck inside. Jennifer noticed his frustration. She asked him what the problem was. He answered that the cars always got stuck. She asked him what he could do about it. He said that the cars needed to go faster. She asked him what he could do to make them go faster. He thought about it and said that he could build a ramp. He started to look around for appropriate materials. At first he used the hobbyhorses and planks. This was partially successful. It worked if the cars stayed on the ramp. He thought that the ramps needed to have curbs, so that the cars would not fall off. He looked around and spied the large cardboard carpet rolls. His eyes lit up and he said, "Built-in curbs!" This activity was very successful (photo 1.30). In fact, he found that he could increase the length of the unit blocks and still be successful. Matthew learned to effectively think through a problem and try different solutions.

Benjamin and Jenna share many similar interests. Their play is often very creative and imaginative. Both children had been on a nature walk and were fascinated by a spider and its web that they observed outside. They decided to create their own spider web. Notice that the two children were creating a similar structure, but each child was still doing his or her own thing—**associative play** (photo 1.31). Both children talked about the web they were creating, but continued with their own activity. Jenna was fascinated with her activity of winding the yarn around the hobbyhorses. Benjamin had also wound the yarn around initially, but then was more concerned to make the web look more realistic. He added natural materials to the web to make it look more realistic. He also found plastic spiders to put on the web. Benjamin tried to interest Jenna in the problem of how to attract insects to the web for the spiders

sorting
Putting things or ideas together based on a common characteristic—such as all the same size, all the same shape, or all the same colour.

classification
Grouping and regrouping of objects or ideas along more than one characteristic; for example, find all animals together that have horns.

Photo 1.28

Photo 1.29

associative play
Playing together, sharing materials and ideas, but engaged in individual activity.

to catch. However, although Jenna answered him, she continued to work on creating her web. Both children had used past experiences to re-create something that they had seen. Preschool children often play together in order to re-create experiences. Through this process they solve problems, communicate together, and learn to cooperate in order to complete a project.

Photo 1.30

Sarah and Braelyn often engage in activities that continue to expand and improve their gross motor skills. Sarah (photo 1.32) has become quite proficient in using the rings and bar. She is also involved in gymnastic activities during the week. Braelyn is exploring different ways of jumping off a platform that she had built (photo 1.33). Stephanie is often in the carpentry area. She is starting to build a house (photo 1.34). This is a project that continued over time. All three children demonstrate how much both fine and gross motor skills have improved in the preschool years. Preschoolers need many opportunities to continue to improve fine and gross motor skills. The environment must be set up to encourage safe risk-taking and provide challenging activities for children to engage in over time. Caregivers must learn how to facilitate children's activities, rather than to set up activities that they feel children should do.

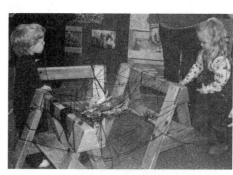

Photo 1.31

Chelsea likes to build structures. She often selects specific blocks to use and then transports these to her building site. She continues to refine skills that she has developed during an earlier stage. She has become very proficient in her ability to find methods of transporting heavy blocks from one location to another (photo 1.35).

Josh also likes to create structures. He is creative in using materials and supplies. He has built a dough structure by using all the items for moulding the dough. He is explaining to Miranda that there is no more room to "stick things on" (photo 1.36). When children are left to use the materials in innovative ways, they learn about the properties of those materials. Josh learned that he can stick items onto dough. He has also developed a concept of space. He is able to explain that there is no space left.

Christine had been actively involved in the morning program. She went over to the book area, chose a book, and asked to have an adult read it to her (photo 1.37). Christine has learned to recognize her own need to slow down and relax. She also

Photo 1.32

Photo 1.33

Photo 1.34

Photo 1.35

Photo 1.36

Photo 1.37

knows what an appropriate relaxing activity should be. Preschoolers are starting to gain greater knowledge about themselves, are beginning to gain self-control of their own feelings, and have developed the ability to express what they wish to do.

The preschool years offer children many opportunities to practise and consolidate skills. Preschoolers are continually experimenting to test and develop their skills and ideas. They continue to be curious about the world around them. Ideas and activities are expressed from their particular viewpoint about the world around them and are based on the experiences they have had in the past and the new ones they are empowered to engage in. Caregivers of this age group are challenged to continue to provide experiences that expand the children's skills and knowledge, encourage children to solve their own problems, and transfer knowledge and skills from one setting to another.

Photo 1.38

School-Aged Children

Christopher is rapidly increasing his motor dexterity. He enjoys challenging activities that test his abilities (photo 1.38). This increased motor dexterity provides Christopher with many opportunities to participate in sports activities. He actively participates in sports for enjoyment (photo 1.39) and in formal competitive individual and team sports—swimming, skiing, biking, track and field, baseball, and hockey. He has gained understanding of the rules of games and the physical skill necessary to participate effectively. Through these activities he is learning to gain greater control of his body, work together with others as a team, follow a set of rules, and win and lose.

Christopher also enjoys many structured activities. He enjoys the outdoor group activities that the boy-scout movement provides (photo 1.40). He is learning to play the piano and is increasing his ability to creatively represent items of interest through art (Figure 1.1).

Photo 1.39

Christopher is learning to apply the skills and knowledge he has gained to new tasks such as building a fire and learning to play the piano. These types of activities encourage children to participate in well-rounded learning experiences—physically, socially, emotionally, and cognitively.

Christopher is very curious about other cultures and historical events. He loves to visit a local restoration project about Native cultures and try some of the activities with friends (photo 1.41). It is most important that children learn about

■ Figure 1.1

Child's Illustration

other cultures and gain an understanding of the past and the experiences that have led to our society today. When children gain understanding of other cultures, they start to understand their own cultural origins. Eventually, this leads to a greater tolerance and understanding of the world and people around them. This growth enables children to learn to accept themselves and others.

This is a period in children's lives when they wish to emulate others. It is a time for hero worship. Often movie actors, sports stars, other important figures (as portrayed by the media), family members, friends, community members, or teachers become important role models. Christopher strongly admired Wayne Gretzky. He got an original Oilers' hockey shirt with Gretzky's number on it for Christmas. He wore this shirt constantly, for all activities (photo 1.42). Children need strong role

Photo 1.41

models to emulate. Some of these models will come from their own family life and others will be more distant—from stories, sports, music, movies, or cartoons. Role models will allow children to incorporate common societal mores—values, achievements, morality, and beliefs—into existing ones.

Christopher forms strong friendships during this time (photo 1.43). Often friendships formed during this age last for a lifetime. Most often, the friendships that are formed are with children of the same gender and with individuals who are interested in similar activities. Children learn about how to interact with each other, how to form and maintain friendships, and how to cooperate with each other.

Photo 1.40

Christopher has gained many skills. He is an avid reader. He loves to write and illustrate stories (Figure 1.2). He loves to participate in school activities—sports, drama, music, and art. He has developed many of the skills he will need for life, and he will continue to expand and refine his skills as he gets older. He needs adults who offer opportunities to engage in a multitude of learning experiences in a variety of

Photo 1.42

■ Figure 1.2

Child's Dinosaur Picture

Photo 1.43

diverse settings, and he needs to interact with other children to continue to learn to cooperate and work together to achieve common goals. He needs to be exposed to experiences that are diverse in all aspects of his life—gender, race, religion, beliefs, abilities, and age.

School-aged children are able to solve problems in increasingly more complex ways—through reading, computation, and writing. They are able to handle abstract concepts, although they still need to approach such tasks through concrete manipulation. School-aged children are increasingly more aware of themselves as individuals. Adults working with these children must respect the increasing complexity of their skills. It is easy to forget that individuals in this age group are still children as they become more independent and increasingly more able to solve abstract problems. Adults need to be sensitive to provide guidance to nurture and respect the abilities, interests, and individuality of the children they interact with.

WHO ARE THE FAMILIES?

The Vanier Institute defines the family as ... any combination of two or more persons who are bound together over time by ties of mutual consent, birth and/or adoption or placement and who, together, assume responsibilities for variant combinations of some of the following:

- Physical maintenance and care of group members
- Addition of new members through procreation or adoption
- Socialization of children
- Social control of members
- Production, consumption, distribution of goods and services, and
- Affective nurturance/love (The Vanier Institute of the Family, 2004).

economic family
Any group of individuals sharing a common residence, related by blood, marriage, common-in law, or adoption.

Most recently, the term **economic family** has been used for the Canadian census (Mooney et al., 2001). The economic family may be defined as "a group of individuals sharing a common dwelling unit who are related by blood, marriage (including common-in law relationships), or adoption" (Mooney et al., 2001, p. 138). The children you have met in the preceding examples come from diversified family backgrounds. These family backgrounds include

- *Lone-parent families.* Families that have a single parent figure (male or female) and one or more children.
- *Grandparents raising children.* Grandparents raising one or more of their grandchildren as a result of the death of the natural parents or grandparents who have been granted legal guardianship of their grandchildren.
- *Extended families.* Other family members, such as grandparents, uncles, aunts, siblings, and cousins, are involved in raising the children along with the parent or parents.
- *Blended families.* The combination of remarried spouses or common-law spouses and the children of a previous relationship.
- *Culturally diverse families.* The backgrounds of the families include partners from different cultural or ethnic groups, such as a combination of French Canadian and English Canadian partners raising children.
- *Mixed families.* Family members are from different racial groups—for example, a Native mother and a French Canadian father, a combination of black and white parents, or Chinese and white parents raising children.

FACTORS THAT IMPACT ON CHILDREN'S DEVELOPMENT

The early years—birth to age six—have a profound influence on children's growth and development:

> New knowledge has changed our understanding of brain development and complements what has been learned about the early years from developmental psychology. We know that early experiences and stimulating, positive interactions with adults and other children are far more important to brain development than previously realized. (McCain & Mustard, 1999, p. 52)

The children identified in the previous examples were fortunate enough to have had experiences that research defines as critical for optimal development (McCain & Mustard, 1999; Doherty-Derkowski, 1994; Gestwicki, 2003; Childcare Resource and Research Unit, 2003). All of their families

- read to their children at home;
- are involved in the learning program of their children;
- have post-secondary education;
- use positive reinforcement to guide their children's behaviour;
- demand a balanced learning environment for their children;
- provide a variety of additional educational experiences at home (such as music, dance, art, and gymnastic lessons, enriching learning environments and family activities); and
- are able to provide for their children's physical, emotional, cognitive, communicative, and social needs.

Not all children are as fortunate. Many children in Canada are raised in conditions that are less than ideal. There are many factors that impact on children living in conditions that are less than optimal. Factors that influence children and their families living in Canada are reported annually in *The Progress of Canada's Children*. The 2002 edition (Hanvey, 2002) reports on the following factors:

- family life;
- economic security;
- physical safety;
- community resources;
- civic vitality;
- health status;
- social engagement; and
- learning.

Each of these factors will be analyzed to identify specific factors that impact the well-being of children. Table 1.1 outlines some of the features relating to family life.

How Do These Factors Impact on Children?

Most of the factors identified in Table 1.1—lone parents, parental age, parental education, and parents in the work force—directly influence the income level of that family. There are some predictable consequences for families with less disposable income. However, it is important to remember that the children raised under these circumstances may still thrive if the parental interactions are positive and nurturing. Here are some factors to consider for children of families with less disposable income:

- *Higher stress levels associated with trying to make ends meet.* Young children exposed to stress respond to stress in a variety of ways. "Babies may be at risk for a variety of difficulties if their mothers experience emotional stress during pregnancy" (Schickedanz et. al., 2001, p. 78). Children who live in environments that have

Family Life

Factor	Description
Children living in **lone-parent** families	• 16.3% of children under 12 • gradual increase over the years
Parental age	• 7.7% of children under 12 have parents under age 30 • relatively constant over time
Moving three or more times in one year	• the lower the family income, the greater the likelihood of multiple moves • one in five children in families with income under $30 000 moved at least three times
Parental education	• most children live with parents who have some post-secondary education • half of children under 11 had fathers with degrees or diplomas • 43% of children under 11 had mothers with degrees or diplomas
Parents in the work force	• 63% of children under 15 had parents employed full-time • as children get older, they are more likely to have both parents employed full-time • average income of both parents working full-time: $78 425 • average income of parents working part-time or less: $29 205

Source: Adapted from Hanvey, 2002, pp. 8–14.

higher stress levels may suffer from some physical symptoms such as stomachaches, ulcers, and asthma attacks. They may also suffer from emotional problems such as being fearful, having high anxiety levels, having sleeping or eating disorders, being listless, and possibly showing signs of depression (Lefrancois, 1999; Honig, 1993; Craig, Kermis, & Digon, 2001).

• *Less money to provide for adequate nutrition and clothing.* Good nutrition is paramount in developing healthy bodies, healthy growth patterns, positive self-concepts, and healthy ways of interacting. However, poor nutritional dietary patterns in early childhood have been shown to lead to later adult obesity, cardiovascular disease, and cancer (Sayre & Gallagher, 2001). More directly, children may have weight problems—either underweight or overweight. This may influence the child's ability to participate in physical activity or affect how alert the child may be (Pimento & Kernested, 1996).

Appropriate clothing is equally important. Children need to be protected from the elements—snow, rain, wind, and sun. Clothing needs to fit properly in order for children to maximize their ability to be involved in active play. Children who lack the appropriate clothing may not wish to participate or may be unable to participate. For example, ill-fitting shoes may lead the child to avoid certain activities such as running, as the shoes may be too big and fall off or too tight and therefore hurt. Older children may become self-conscious about their clothing and therefore may become shy or withdrawn.

Proper nutrition and clothing is also a first defence against disease and injury. A healthy body is much more ready to battle infections and disease than a poorly nourished one. A child well protected against the elements is less likely to suffer from the effects of sun or wind burns.

- *More likely to spend money on "filler" foods such as pop, chips, and higher-sugar-content cereals.* "Foods that contain large amounts of added sugar, salt and fats often supply calories but few essential nutrients" (Duyff, Giarratano, & Zuzich, 1995, p. 171). These types of foods are often cheaper to purchase, but also give the feeling of a full stomach. The danger of consumption of too many of these foods is that this is not a balanced diet. Children exposed to this type of a diet for extended periods may suffer from **malnutrition,** eating too much or too little of one type of food. This may lead to below or above averages in height and weight; tooth decay; anemia; and associated behaviours such as listlessness, irritability, lack of motivation, shorter attention spans, and less coordination (Duyff, Giarratano, & Zuzich, 1995; Marotz, Cross, & Rush, 2001).

- *Less money to spend on "educational items" such as books, library memberships, and recreation.* Children will thrive in conditions that provide positive interactions. Caregivers who spend time talking to their children, reading to their children, and who stimulate their children in many ways tend to have children who become well-adjusted individuals (McCain & Mustard, 1999). Parents who may not have the financial stability to provide children with books or other nurturing experiences may have children who have some developmental lags in domains such as language or motor development.

- *Less time to spend with their families.* "[M]others working full-time outside the home have consistently lower levels of engagement than mothers working part-time or mothers staying home" (McCain & Mustard, 1999, p. 63). Children who live in situations where all family members work full-time will have less quality time to spend with their caregivers. This may lead to children that are not as securely attached to their caregiver. These children may have greater difficulty interacting with other adults and other children.

- *Less money to spend on accommodation.* With less money to spend on living accommodations, families may be forced to move more frequently in an effort to find affordable housing. Children who move often have fewer opportunities to form lasting friendships or establish supportive networks. They may feel more disconnected from the world around them.

malnutrition
A condition that occurs over a period of time. Individuals consume either too much of one food or too little of another.

EFFECT OF FAMILY DYNAMICS ON YOUNG CHILDREN

1. Parental Health

When parents have health problems it can affect their ability to adequately care for their children. Notably, 10 percent of children under 12 live with parents who have some disabling condition. For example, depression is one common condition, and parental depression is most often associated with poverty (Hanvey, 2002).

2. How Families Are Able to Function

"Research has shown a significant connection between family dysfunction and mental health problems among children" (Hanvey, 2002, p. 10). The lower the income, the more likely it is that the family will be dysfunctional. Twenty-three percent of children in families whose annual income is under $20 000 are living in a dysfunctional family setting. Only 9 percent of children living in households earning above $20 000 per year live in dysfunctional families.

■ TABLE 1.2

Economic Security

Influencing Factor	Descriptions of Factors
Poverty	<ul><li>18.5% of children live in poverty</li><li>highest poverty rates in lone-female families</li><li>social assistance in *all* provinces below the poverty line</li><li>more than 4 in 10 children living in employed lone-female households live in poverty</li><li>26.8% of children living in two-parent households with one wage earner live in poverty (increase of 7.4% since 1984)</li><li>low-income families are forced to spend a higher proportion of their income on the basic necessities of food, shelter, and clothing</li><li>35% of the cost of raising children is child-care outside the home</li></ul>

Source: Adapted from Hanvey, 2002, pp. 16–32.

3. Family Support

In all social systems, support for family members comes from within the family and from the community the family lives in. "Children in families with low incomes are more likely to have parents who report low levels of social support" (Hanvey, 2002, p. 11). These families also tend to move more often. Thus the support system is further weakened.

4. Parenting Styles

All parents, regardless of income levels, are aware of the importance of positive interactions with their children. Most parents are more likely to use positive interactions with younger children than with older children. Over the years, there has been a decrease in the use of physical punishment with young children.

Overall, it would appear that families seem to be aware of how to raise young children. The use of more inappropriate childrearing practices is, therefore, linked to other factors, especially poverty. Table 1.2 describes the factors of **economic security**, which refers to an assured standard of living that can provide families with the level of resources and benefits necessary to participate economically, politically, socially, culturally, and with dignity in their community's activities (Hanvey, 2002, p. 16).

How Do These Factors Impact on Children?

Effect of Continued Poverty

Compared to children who are not poor, children who live in poverty

- have fewer support systems;
- are twice as likely to live in dysfunctional families;
- are twice as likely to live with violence;
- participate less in recreational activities;
- have poorer scores when tested on verbal language and cognitive scales;
- may have poorer mental health; and
- are more likely to experience emotional problems such as anxiety, aggressive behaviours, and hyperactivity.

economic security
An assured standard of living that can provide families with the level of resources and benefits necessary to participate economically, politically, socially, culturally, and with dignity in their community's activities (Hanvey, 2002, p. 16).

These factors lead children to become excluded from many social activities—specialized programs such as gymnastic programs, attending children's concerts, or going away on family vacations. "What is particularly troublesome about all of these

Physical Safety

Influencing Factors	Descriptions of Factors	Impact on Children
Environmental air quality	Children are more vulnerable to air pollution because • they spend more time outside in physical activity • they take more breaths than adults do • they are closer to vehicle pollutants at ground level • they are more susceptible to indoor contaminants as they tend to spend 80% of their time indoors	Children may be affected in the following ways: • increased number of asthma attacks, and asthma is the most common chronic childhood illness • coughing and wheezing • more visits to the doctor or hospital • permanent decreased lung capacity • increased respiratory infections and allergies • increased incidence of sudden infant death syndrome
Pesticides	Recent decisions by the Supreme Court of Canada have led to new pesticide regulations.	Pesticides have been linked to leukemia, brain cancer, neurological disorders, and developmental disorders in children.
Climate change	Average temperatures in Canada have risen steadily. Temperature is anticipated to rise 1.5 to 5°C in the south and 5 to 7°C in the north over this century. Increased temperatures have the following effects: • changing weather patterns: more tornadoes, hurricanes, floods, winter storms • increased harm from pollution: smog is intensified by warmer temperatures • increased illness: heat stroke and dehydration; migration of insects carrying diseases such as malaria, yellow fever, and dengue fever	Children are affected by • trauma of severe weather conditions • greater risk of heat stress, as children have lesser capacity to regulate own body temperature and children do not recognize the danger signs • increased respiratory problems due to increased pollution • contamination of water supply (drinking and recreational) due to heavy rains and flooding • greater risk of illness from insects carrying disease

Source: Adapted from Hanvey, 2002, pp. 21–27.

indicators of social exclusion and their relationship to poor children in Canada is that, throughout the 90s the poor became poorer while the rich got richer—forcing these children even further away from full participation in society" (Hanvey, 2002, p. 20). Table 1.3 describes some aspects of **physical safety**, which refers to "the quality of children's natural environments and threats to their personal safety and well-being" (Hanvey, 2002, p. 20). These factors can have a major impact on the development of young children.

"At the dawn of the 21st century, Canada stands at a crossroads. The 1990s were marked by reductions in education, health care and social services—all things that are crucial to the healthy development of children and families" (Hanvey, 2002, p. 2). According to *The Progress of Canada's Children* (Hanvey, 2002), the following barriers must be removed in order to ensure that Canada's children and families thrive:

- Governments must stop taking families for granted. Governments need to support healthy family functioning.
- Businesses need to become more flexible. Individuals should not be placed in a conflict situation between work and family.
- Economic growth should not be at the expense of spiritualism.
- The political system at all levels—municipal, provincial, and federal—needs to become more aware and accountable about issues in Canada, rather than blaming global economic trends.
- The educational system at all levels—early childhood, elementary, and secondary—must be strengthened. There must be a re-emphasis on creativity and imagination.
- Public policies must be scrutinized and renewed to ensure that quality practices can be implemented.
- More women must be empowered to participate in decision making at all political levels.
- The well-being of families should be a priority in setting public policies.
- A safe world needs to be created for children.

HOW DO CHILDREN LEARN?

Children learn best when

- They actively explore the environment by using all of their senses and by manipulating real objects (see photo 1.6 on page 4).
- They are encouraged to make choices, make meaningful plans, and make their own decisions (see photo 1.30 on page 9).
- Learning experiences are provided that build upon what they already know (see photo 1.31 on page 9).
- There are opportunities to explore and play alone (see photo 1.29 on page 8) and explore and play with other children and adults (see photo 1.2 on page 3).
- They are in environments that provide safe risks and physical and psychological safety (see photo 1.32 on page 9).
- The learning experiences respect each individual child and his or her family (see photo 1.42 on page 11).
- All individuals involved with the child—including the family and the teachers—become partners in providing quality experiences for that child (see photo 1.30 on page 9).
- All experiences are developmentally appropriate, based on the child's abilities, interests, and background experiences (see photo 1.40 on page 11) (Gestwicki, 1999; Kieff & Casbergue, 2000; Shipley, 2002; & Crowther, 2003).

Children learn through play. All the points presented in the above description of how young children learn are aspects of learning through play. Play as a primary mode of learning for young children is supported by all theorists: "Because the nature of children's play is so complex, no single theory completely explains its value to children's growth and development. Viewed together, these theories offer insights into the multiple purposes and values of play in the lives of both children and adults" (Kieff & Casbergue, 2000, p. 4).

Recent neuroscience research indicates that early experiences are critical to the developing child. "There is powerful new evidence from neuroscience that the early years of development from conception to age six, set the base for competence and coping skills that will affect learning, behaviour and health through life" (McCain & Mustard, 1999, p. 5). The experiences that children have in the early years are crucial to brain development. When Lauren interacted with her mother (see photo 1.2 on page 3, her senses were stimulated. She felt the closeness of her mother's touch. She saw the joy in her mother's face. She heard what her mother was saying. All these stimuli serve to "wire" or make connections within the brain. As these connections are formed and strengthened, the functions of the brain, such as arousal, emotional control, and thinking, become established:

> Play is a critical element in early childhood because it provides the context for experiences that are vital to the development of neural pathways. Connections among neurons are formed when children explore their environment, play, and develop attachments to family members and other care-providers. In fact, warm responsive care and positive interactions between children and care-providers are critical to healthy neurological development. (Kieff & Casbergue, 2000, p. 7)

What Experiences Are Needed to Support Children's Learning?

All children need experiences that support learning through play. Gestwicki (1999) identifies four such experiences: physical context of play, real-world experiences, adult intervention, and intervention strategies.

1. Physical Context of Play

Children need a learning environment that is set up to meet their needs. Each age group will have needs that support their development. However, all children need an environment that provides the following:

- *Real choices.* Lara was given a choice when her caregiver placed various objects within her reach and gave her the opportunity to make her own decision (see photo 1.9 on page 4). Jacob was encouraged to use the materials in his environment as he wished (see photo 1.15 on page 5). Hannah, Benjamin, Damon, and Reghan could create their own activity to support their play (see photo 1.25 on page 7). Christopher could engage in activities that provided him with opportunities to challenge and refine his skills (see photo 1.38 on page 10).
- *Flexibility.* Children need the flexibility to move between indoor and outdoor environments, change their existing environments, and visit alternative environments. Lara could safely explore her environment by sitting in her chair (see photo 1.8 on page 4) or explore by crawling (see photo 1.10 on page 5). The children could create a block path within their environment to crawl along (see photo 1.19 on page 6). Autumn could find a place where she could be by herself (see photo 1.28 on page 8). Christopher was able to explore a variety of alternative environments to enrich his concept about the world (see photo 1.42 on page 11).

- *Realistic equipment and materials.* Lara had opportunities to look at real books (see photo 1.13 on page 5). Derrick and Venice could paint and glue items on a box to decorate it (see photo 1.22 on page 7). Michael and Colin had real props to help them with their role-play (see photo 1.27 on page 8). Christopher used a real setting to start a fire and cook his hot dog (see photo 1.40 on page 11).
- *Time.* Children need appropriate time blocks that encourage participation in activities for longer blocks of time during the day and also over several days. All of the children in the examples provided could dictate their own time involvement in the activities (see photo 1.33 on page 9). Some of the activities continued for longer than one day. Stephanie's creative carpentry activity continued over several days (see photo 1.34 on page 9). First she researched through several books to look for an idea to build her house. Next she cut the pieces. She then had to put the pieces together, and lastly she decorated her house.

2. Real-World Experiences

Children need real experiences to help them to understand the world around them. Lara was able to view her world from different perspectives—on the floor (see photo 1.7 on page 4), in her chair (see photo 1.8 on page 4), and from her mother's arms (see photo 1.14 on page 5). Logan was able to ride his three-wheeler outside (see photo 1.21 on page 6), and Christopher could engage in a variety of sport activities (see photo 1.39 on page 10).

3. Adult Intervention

Adult interactions enrich the quality of play (Gestwicki, 1999). Lara's interaction with her father gave her the satisfaction of having her signals observed and responded to (see photo 1.7 on page 4). When Jacob and Rashawn's caregiver noticed that the two toddlers had a problem sharing (see photo 1.18 on page 6), she immediately drew the children's attention to additional dinosaurs in the area. This prevented further arguments. Jennifer noticed that Matthew was frustrated (see photo 1.30 on page 9), so she helped him to verbalize and solve his own problem. Successful adult intervention should include the following:

- *Provide realistic props.* The remote control (see photo 1.12 on page 5), the watering can (see photo 1.26 on page 7), the books and insect puzzles (see photo 1.28 on page 8), and the materials to build a fire (see photo 1.40 on page 11).
- *Intervene only when needed.* Providing choices to Lara (see photo 1.9 on page 4), helping to solve problems (see photo 1.30 on page 9), and letting children create their own activity without intervention (see photo 1.20 on page 6).
- *Provide props to extend play.* Coloured dishes for sorting (see photo 1.29 on page 8), the book of insects with a puzzle of insects (see photo 1.28 on page 8), and baby bath materials (see photo 1.24 on page 7).

4. Intervention Strategies

The following intervention strategies can be useful:

- *Helping children plan and organize.* The environment was set up in ways that encouraged children to use space effectively (see photo 1.19 on page 6), find materials they needed (see photo 1.8 on page 4), and jointly plan what was needed for the dramatic area for pets (see photo 1.27 on page 8).
- *Prompting.* Lara's mother provided her with choices. Each time she prompted Lara by asking her if this was the toy she wanted (see photo 1.9 on page 4). Jennifer prompted Matthew to solve his own problem (see photo 1.30 on page 9).

- *Modelling.* The environment was set up to model organization (children could find what they needed), flexibility (children could make changes as needed), and positive interactions (Lauren's mother immediately recognized her need and responded positively to her).
- *Providing props.* Some of those used were logs (see photo 1.38 on page 10), cardboard rolls (see photo 1.30 on page 9), and boxes (see photo 1.25 on page 7).

Shipley (2002) identifies some additional components. These include providing informal settings, helping children transfer knowledge from one context to another, and helping children build upon what they already know:

- *Provide informal settings.* Much of the learning of children occurs spontaneously. Often this learning is not anticipated by the adults. The astute adult will recognize many powerful aspects of this type of learning and provide opportunities to encourage it further. Lara's mother observed Lara's interest in the remote control. She encouraged Lara's interest by placing the remote control on the floor where she could get to it. Lara learned that she could get the object herself. She also manipulated the object with her fingers and her mouth (see photo 1.12 on page 5). She learned about the texture of the object—hard case and soft pliable buttons, and if the buttons were pushed, they moved. Benjamin and Jacob (see photo 1.17 on page 6) learned about relative size. They were able to fit the insects into a small opening. They also had to discover how to get them out again. Eventually they needed help. The caregiver was directed to cut the bottle open to get the plastic insects out.
- *Transfer knowledge from one context to another.* Children need to use the knowledge they have gained from one situation to another. This allows brain connections to become reinforced. Additionally, children learn to use information in a variety of settings. This encourages them to make connections between various types of activities. Autumn (see photo 1.26 on page 7) had learned to pour water efficiently. A logical next step for Autumn would be to provide opportunities to practise this skill in other settings—watering plants and pouring her drink. Josh was interested in making sculptures with dough and sticking objects into this creation (see photo 1.36 on page 10). Another natural adaptation might be to collect items on a field trip outdoors to create structures using clay and natural products.
- *Build upon what children already know.* The children who engaged in the "Pop Goes the Weasel" activity (see photo 1.25 on page 7) had previous knowledge about a jack-in-the-box and the song. They were able to apply these skills to use an existing box and to follow the simple directions of the song. Colin and Michael (see photo 1.27 on page 8) already had knowledge about dogs. They knew how they acted, what they could eat, and about some of their routines. They were able to use this information to develop a role-playing scenario.

Kieff and Casbergue (2000) identify the following additional points as important considerations of play—process/product orientation, intrinsic motivation, nonliteral quality, experimentation with rules, and mental activity:

- *Process/product orientation.* As young children engage in activities their attention and interest are on what they are doing, not on what they will eventually create. Notice the enjoyment of Mackenzie and Reghan as they paint (see photo 1.5 on page 3). They have put several layers of paint on their paper. They enjoy the flow of the paint on the paper, the changing colours created, and the interactions between the two of them. As Jacob was using his blocks to create the horizontal

Photo 1.44

rows (see photo 1.16 on page 6), he was more interested in lining up the blocks than creating a specific structure. He was learning about placement—side by side, next to each other, and in a row. Benjamin and Jenna (see photo 1.31 on page 9) had a product in mind. However, as they were involved in creating their web, the process became more important. Jenna enjoyed creating the strands of the web. She continued to create the web using the yarn. Benjamin became much more intent on role-playing the role of the spider. He was more concerned about how the spider could catch the flies.

Notice the difference in Christopher's art (see photo 1.44). Older children become more interested in the product—what the artwork will be like when finished. Christopher went through an interesting process. He experimented using different techniques to create the feathers on the body of the bird, and on the wings. He used different types of materials until he found the tools that satisfied him.

- *Intrinsic motivation.* Children engage in play because they enjoy what they are doing. Notice how Yasmine continues to sift through the sand, touching it, feeling it, manipulating it. She is enjoying the sensory soothing experience (see photo 1.6 on page 4). Timmy (see photo 1.20 on page 6) enjoyed the feeling of jumping from the blocks. Each time he jumped, he seemed to jump a little higher. He always had a smile on his face. Lara (see photo 1.4 on page 3) enjoyed creating her vertical structures. She enjoyed all aspects of her activity—stacking, watching it fall, and building the structure again.

- *Nonliteral quality practices.* When children play, objects may magically become something entirely different: a hand may become a digger, a crack on the pavement a road, or a box a car. Notice Jacob's transformation of the house that had been built into a car (see photo 1.23 on page 7) and Matthew's use of the cardboard roll as a ramp with "built-in curbs" (see photo 1.30 on page 9).

- *Experimentation with rules.* "Children's play is often simultaneously rule-bound and rule-free. That is, the play is bound to the implicit rules the players bring to it: rules of role requirements and rules of social negotiation. These rules are dependent on the players' prior knowledge, cultural background, and experience" (Kieff & Casbergue, 2000, p. 20). When the children were engaged in the "Pop Goes the Weasel" activity (see photo 1.25 on page 7), they established their own rules about how to play the game. Each child followed the rules that they had set and the rules were based on their experiences with a jack-in-the-box and the song they were listening to.

- *Mental activities.* "When children explore, probe, experiment, investigate, and inquire during their play, their minds are active in the process of constructing and reconstructing meaning and understanding about their world" (Kieff & Casbergue, 2000, p. 21). Notice how Matthew worked through the process of propelling his cars through the hollow blocks (see photo 1.30 on page 9). He started by pushing the cars through the blocks. He evolved to using a ramp system to create enough momentum to propel the cars through the hollow blocks without needing a push.

In summary, children play in every corner of the world. Play is a pleasurable experience, an open-ended activity, imaginative, creative, satisfying, and a superb learning experience. As adults, we also need to play. Think of all the things that you enjoy doing. If you could apply that enjoyment to every task you do, think of how much more enjoyable life and learning would be.

KEY POINTS

WHO ARE THE CHILDREN?

- All children: curious, active, able to make choices, communicative, observant, sociable, engage in manipulative activities, creative
- Infants: rapid growth and development, imitative, dependent
- Toddlers: unpredictable, inventive, and solitary; parallel, repetitive, and symbolic play; learning to share
- Preschoolers: enjoy learning, help others, associative play, solve problems, independent, engage in familiar role play, share materials/ideas/space, imaginative, engage in pre-operational skills, practise and consolidate skills, increased skills level
- School-aged children: curious about others, self-reliant/independent, forming friendships, increasing complex skills, playing musical instruments, active, cooperative and competitive play

WHO ARE THE FAMILIES?

- Economic family: includes common-law families, lone families, grandparents raising children, extended families, blended families, culturally diverse families, mixed families

FACTORS THAT IMPACT ON CHILDREN'S DEVELOPMENT

- Family life: parental age, parents in the work force, health, stress, support, and parenting style
- Economic security: poverty, continued poverty
- Physical safety: air quality, pesticides

EFFECT OF FAMILY DYNAMICS ON YOUNG CHILDREN

- The types of family dynamics that impact on the development of young children include parental health, family function, family support systems, parenting styles, and poverty

HOW DO CHILDREN LEARN?

- Play: developmentally appropriate experiences, materials, and equipment; active involvement; develops neural connections

WHAT EXPERIENCES ARE NEEDED TO SUPPORT LEARNING?

- Appropriate physical space, flexibility, time, real-world experiences
- Build upon what children know
- Process orientation

EXERCISES

1. Reflect on your memories. What types of quality interactions do you remember about your childhood? Why were these important? Share and discuss similarities and differences with your peers. How are your memories similar? Different? How does this influence how you think about children?
2. a) Describe what you know about the development of infants, toddlers, preschoolers, and school-aged children.
   b) Compare your description to the description of infants as presented in the text. How are your thoughts similar or different?
3. In a small group, identify key quality experiences that are important. Explain why each of these experiences is important.
4. Survey members of your class. What types of families do the individuals in your group come from? Refer to the guidelines on pages 12–18. Discuss how the various families might have influenced the way you were brought up. How has this affected how you think about children (infants, toddlers, preschoolers, and school-aged children)?
5. Identify the key factors that impact on the development of children. Describe how each factor might affect the children—infants, toddlers, preschoolers, and school-aged children—and their families.
6. Look at the pictures and accompanying scenarios in Chapter 1. For each picture, list at least one aspect of play that is represented by that scenario.
7. In a small group discuss the importance of play. Compare your answer with the information in Chapter 1. Compare your list with the large group.
8. Interview a parent of an infant, toddler, preschooler, or school-aged child. Find out what the families think are the most important characteristics of their child at this age. Compare the family's response with your own perceptions. How are they similar or different?

REFERENCES

Childcare Resource and Research Unit. (2003). *Building a Firm Foundation for Lifelong Learning: The Importance of Early Childhood Education and Care*. Toronto: ON: Childcare Research and Research Unit.

Craig, G., & Digdon, N. (2001). *Children Today*. Toronto, ON: Prentice Hall.

Crowther, I. (2003). *Creating Effective Learning Environments*. Scarborough, ON: Nelson Thomson Learning.

Doherty-Derkowski, G. (1994). *Quality Matters Excellence in Early Childhood Programs*. Toronto, ON: Addison-Wesley.

Duyff, R., Giarratano, S., & Zuzich, M. (1995). *Nutrition, Health and Safety*. Princeton, NJ: Glencoe/McGraw-Hill.

Gestwicki, C. (1999). *Developmentally Appropriate Practices* (2nd ed.). Scarborough, ON: Nelson Canada.

Gestwicki, C. (2003). *Developmentally Appropriate Practices* (3rd ed.). Scarborough, ON: Nelson Canada.

Greenspan, S. (1999). *The Growth of the Mind and the Endangered Origins of Intelligence*. Reading, MA: Addison Wesley.

Hanvey, L. (2002). *The Progress of Canada's Children*. Ottawa, ON: Canadian Council on Social Development.

Hanvey, L. (2003). *The Progress of Canada's Children*. Ottawa, ON: Canadian Council on Social Development.

Honig, A. (1993). Mental Health for Babies: What Do Theory and Research Tell Us? *Young Children, 48,* 69–78.

Kieff, J., & Casbergue, R. (2000). *Playful Learning and Teaching. Integrating Play in Preschool and Primary Programs*. Needham Heights, MA: Allyn and Bacon.

Lefrancois, G. (1999). *The Lifespan*. Toronto, ON: Wadsworth Publishing Company.

Lorie, P. (1989). *Wonder Child*. Switzerland: Labyrinth Publishing S.A.

Machado, J. (1999). *Early Childhood Experiences in Language Arts Emerging Literacy* (6th ed.). Scarborough, ON: Delmar Thomson Learning.

Marotz, L., Cross, M., & Rush, J. (2001). *Health, Safety, and Nutrition* (5th ed.). Albany, NY: Delmar.

McCain, M., & Mustard, F. (1999). *Early Years Study Final Report*. Toronto, ON: Publications Ontario.

Mooney, L., Knox, D., Schacht, C., & Nelson, A. (2001). *Understanding Social Problems* (1st Canadian ed.). Scarborough, ON: Nelson Thomson Learning.

Nash, M. (1997). Fertile Minds. *Time, 149,* 48–56.

Pimento, B., & Kernested, D. (1996). *Healthy Foundations in Child Care*. Scarborough, ON: Nelson Canada.

Robinson, R. (1994). *Helping Adults Learn and Change*. West Ben, WI: Omnibook Co.

Sawyre, N. (2000). *Growing Up with Literature* (3rd ed.). Scarborough, ON: Delmar Thomson Learning.

Sayer, W., & Gallagher, J. (2001). *The Young Child and the Environment*. Toronto, ON: Allyn & Bacon.

Schickedanz, J., Schickedanz, D., Forsyth, P., & Forsyth, G. (2001). *Understanding Children and Adolescents* (4th ed.). Needham Heights, MA: Allyn & Bacon.

Shipley, D. (2002). *Empowering Children*. Scarborough, ON: Nelson Thomson Learning.

Shore, R. (1997). *Rethinking the Brain*. New York, NY: Families and Work Institute.

The Vanier Institute of the Family (2004). Family Facts. The Vanier Institute of the Family [On-line]. Available: http://www.vifamily.ca/.

Watson, L., Watson, M., Cam Wilson, L., & Crowther, I. (2000). *Infants and Toddlers* (1st Canadian ed.). Scarborough, ON: Nelson Thomson Learning.

THE WORLD OF
THE CHILD

CHAPTER OUTLINE

"Children have the right to be recognized as subjects of individual, legal, civil, and social rights; as both source and constructors of their own experience, and thus active participants in the organization of their identities, abilities, and autonomy, through relationships and interactions with their peers, with adults, with ideas, with objects, and with the real and imagined events of interconnecting worlds."
(Malaguzzi, 1997, p. 214)

Chapter Outcomes

After reading this chapter, the reader will

1. Explain why play is the best way for young children to learn.
2. Describe how early forms of play are similar at the fetal stage and in the newborn.
3. Describe how play changes during the infant years.
4. Define the various ages and stages of play.
5. Compare how play develops and changes from infancy to the school-aged child.
6. Define developmentally appropriate practices.
7. Identify the 12 principles of developmentally appropriate practices.
8. Identify the core elements of any learning environment.
9. Identify and describe the key differences between infant, toddler, preschool, and school-aged learning environments.
10. Identify and describe adaptations that should be made in an inclusive setting.
11. Explain why the child's total experiences must be considered when planning a learning environment.
12. Explain how individual differences might affect planning learning environments for young children.

LEARNING THROUGH PLAY

The natural way that all children play occurs in all cultures and with all children. Play as a way of learning is supported by all philosophical approaches and all theorists (Gestwicki, 2003; Crowther, 2003). It is essential that any adults working with young children recognize and support the importance of play, as it is through play that children gain skill and knowledge. Through play children

- learn about the world around them;
- develop and practise emergent skills—physical, emotional, social, and cognitive;
- gain skills in socialization with peers and adults;
- learn to learn;
- learn to solve problems;
- learn to collaborate; and
- are empowered to make decisions about their learning.

1. Early Types of Play

Learning through play is the fundamental way all children learn. Play is found at all age levels, and it is an essential component for healthy brain development (Nash, 1997). Early types of play observed in very young children involve:

- solitary activities—involvement in activities alone;
- tactile activities—touching own body parts, tasting by mouthing things;
- motor activity—moving various body parts; and
- observing through watching and listening.

sensorimotor activity
Learning about the world through sight, touch, hearing, tasting, smelling, and motor movement.

This type of play is often referred to as **sensorimotor activity**. "Babies begin to learn about their world through their senses and muscle movements of their bodies.

This information is organized mentally for use later" (Gestwicki, 1999, p. 212). The sensorimotor stage begins in the prenatal stage and continues through to toddlerhood.

2. Sensorimotor Activity in the Womb

There is mounting evidence that the fetus is involved in some of these early forms of play: "Awake or asleep, the fetus moves 50 times or more each hour, flexing and extending its body, moving its head, face, and limbs and exploring its warm wet compartment by touch" (Hopson, 1998, p. 75). The fetus develops hearing by 25 weeks and starts to listen to various sounds around him or her. The fetus can be calmed by the soothing sounds of his or her mother's voice. The fetal heartbeat slows when the fetus hears the voice.

The fetus also moves as a result of the actions of the mother:

> "When we're watching the fetus on ultrasound and the mother starts to laugh, we can see the fetus, floating upside down in the womb, bounce up and down on its head, bum-bum-bum, like it's bouncing on a trampoline," says [Janet] DiPietro [a psychologist at Johns Hopkins University]. "When mothers watch this on the screen, they laugh harder, and the fetus goes up and down even faster. We've wondered whether this is why people grow up liking roller coasters." (Hopson, 1998, p. 46)

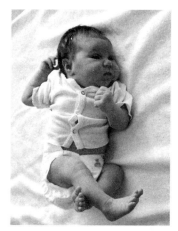

Photo 2.1

Within the womb, the fetus can be observed sucking his or her thumb, can be felt kicking or elbowing the mother, and will react differently to various types of auditory stimulation. "[William] Fifer [a psychologist at Columbia University] has found that fetal heart rate slows down when the mother is speaking, suggesting that the fetus not only hears and recognized the sound, but is calmed by it" (Hopson, 1998, p. 47). These early activities already build memories that will be used after birth to build upon experiences in the womb. Infants are born with memories such as mothers' and fathers' voices, the smell of the mother, and soothing, familiar music. These early activities also bear a remarkable similarity to early play activities that newborns engage in. Young infants relax with familiar sounds or startle to strange sounds, just as the fetus did; they flay their limbs and kick in their wakeful periods. They listen—and stop motion—to things that they like to hear.

Photo 2.2

3. Play and the Newborn

Aleah is two weeks old (photo 2.1). She has come into the world with many skills already in place. "When a baby is born, it can see and hear and smell and respond to touch, but only dimly" (Nash, 1997, p. 49). She needs caregivers who will play with her, talk to her, hold her close so that she can see them, let her see their facial expressions, and provide opportunities for solitary activity. As a result, Aleah, during her **alert states** (times when the infant is awake and ready to engage in activity), will interact with the adults around her. She is especially attentive to the expressions on her father's face. She will gaze intently at the face in front of her and watch and listen to the expressions and soft words spoken to her.

alert states
Times when the infant is awake and ready to engage in activity.

When placed on her back, she will kick and move her arms and legs. In fact, during her alert state she spends a lot of time kicking and flaying her arms. She will turn toward sounds she hears, especially her mother's voice (photo 2.2). When fingers are placed near her hand, she will grasp them (photo 2.3).

Aleah's play shows attentiveness to the auditory signals around her. She is combining what she has learned about the voices she heard prenatally with the sense of sight. She is marvellously prepared to interact with her caregivers. She seems fascinated by their voices and changing facial expressions. This, in turn, predisposes the

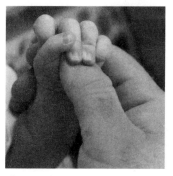
Photo 2.3

Photo 2.4

Photo 2.5

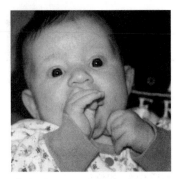

Photo 2.6

Photo 2.7

caregiver to spend more time interacting with her. After all, it is hard to resist a newborn's total fascination and responsiveness to the caregiver's actions.

4. Play and the Infant

As infants mature and grow, their play also changes. They become increasingly more interested in their own body parts. Lara is fascinated by her hands and arms. She continually waves her hands in front of her face. She delightfully wriggles her fingers. As she watches them move, she giggles and laughs (photo 2.4). She is engaged in solitary play. She is learning to control her actions, what her different body parts look like, and what happens when she moves them.

Lara also learns through imitation. Lara loves to watch facial expressions. When an adult sticks out his or her tongue, Lara will imitate this behaviour (photo 2.5). She is learning to take turns.

Infants use all their senses when they play. They may be playing by themselves in their cribs or in a room close to their caregivers. Lauren has learned to control her hand movements. She is still fascinated by her fingers and hands, but after watching them, they are often put into her mouth (photo 2.6). A few months later, she is able to sit by herself. She can now reach for and grab objects that are within her reach (photo 2.7). These, too, are placed into her mouth. Lauren is learning about the world through her play activities. She is learning about what the object looks like and what it feels like, both by touching and mouthing the objects. She is learning how to refine her grasping skills, and she is learning about what sounds objects make.

Lauren uses her hands and feet in play. She will grab her feet and often pull them to her mouth. She is easily distracted from activities. She hears her mother come in. She immediately turns toward her mother, looks at her, and smiles (photo 2.8). Her mother

Photo 2.8

spoke to Lauren. Lauren gurgled and smiled at her mother, then stretched out her arms. Her mother recognized the signal and picked her up. Just as Aleah was fascinated with her father's face and voice (see photo 2.1 on page 29), Lauren is fascinated with her mother's face and voice. Lauren and her mother play together within a close physical space. Lauren not only imitates her mother's expression, she also imitates some of the sounds her mother makes. Lauren and her mother take turns at making and copying sounds or expressions (photo 2.9). Through this type of play, the infant learns more about turn taking, and practises and uses everexpanding vocalizations and body language to express feelings and intent. The infant also learns to play with others.

As infants mature, their attention spans increase and their play changes from play with their own bodies or objects near them, to more

Photo 2.9

intentional play with objects that they choose to play with. Lara has learned to crawl. She is on the floor in the living room at home. She sees an object on the floor at the other side of the room (photo 2.10). She crawls over to the object, stretching out to reach and grab the remote controller (photo 2.11). Once she has it in her hands, she rolls over onto her back and looks at it intently. She turns the object over and over

Photo 2.10

Photo 2.11

Photo 2.12

repeatedly, pushing the buttons and looking at all the details (photo 2.12), an example of **functional play** (repeated manipulation of an object). At this stage, caregivers are not needed as much to interact directly with the child. The caregiver is needed to create an environment safe from harm and to supply safe materials for the child to use and play with. Lara's parents realized Lara's fascination with the remote controller. They ensured that the object was safe for her to use by removing the batteries from the controller and checking it to see that none of its parts were in danger of coming out.

Much of infants' play becomes dictated by what they have observed and by the type of toy they are using. Lara is now in a daycare. She is using the phone to talk to her caregiver (photo 2.13). She is involved in the initial stages of dramatic play—prop-dependent, imitative play. During this type of play, children's play is influenced by the experiences they have had and by the type of prop used. Lara has seen individuals use a telephone. She has talked to her father on the telephone. She is imitating a known behaviour using a prop that looks like a telephone correctly (Crowther, 2003). This type of behaviour is known as **deferred imitation**—imitating an action or event that has been seen previously. As infants grow and develop, this type of behaviour increases dramatically.

functional play
Repeated manipulation of an object.

Photo 2.13

deferred imitation
Imitating an action or event that has been seen previously.

Web
exercises

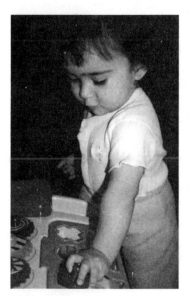
Photo 2.14

Play behaviours change dramatically with the increased ability to walk with control and the ability to balance the body in various positions. Children are now able to explore the environment more thoroughly in order to find activities to engage in. Lara is intent on seeing how things fit together. She loves to fit small pieces into slots. She engages in this activity over and over again (photo 2.14). This is **repetitive play**—play that is repeated over and over again. Through this type of play children practise **emergent skills**—skills that are beginning to appear.

Rashawn is very curious about things in his environment. He likes to do things by himself. He finds a new book, sits down, and opens the book. He enjoys looking at books, touching things that are novel (photo 2.15). He has opened the book many times, attracted to the shiny surface of the foil. Rashawn is also engaged in repetitive play. However, he is also easily distracted by other activities. His mother had brought out his musical toy. He immediately stopped looking at the book. He started to push the buttons to activate the music and listened (photo 2.16). Rashawn continued to switch from reading his book to listening to the music and back to reading his book. Although his attention shifts, he comes back to tasks that have interested him previously.

repetitive play
Play that is repeated over and over again.
emergent skills
Skills that are beginning to appear.

Photo 2.15

Photo 2.16

Photo 2.17

Web
exercises

parallel play
Playing beside another doing similar things with similar materials.

onlooker or observer play
Watching others without obvious personal involvement.

Web
exercises

imitative play
Copying a behaviour that is being observed exactly, or copying the behaviour to obtain a similar result.

Play materials can become anything and are limited only by the child's imagination. Rory is able to open cupboard doors, and has learned to remember where things are kept. He searched through the cupboard to bring out various plastic utensils. He then filled a large waffle block by trying to fit the plastic utensils through the various holes in the block (photo 2.17).

5. Play and the Toddler

The various types of behaviours seem to increase as the young child grows and becomes more confident. This gives rise to the expression "the terrible twos," as the toddlers enthusiastically and actively explore the environment. In actual fact, the stage should be renamed "the wonderful twos." During this time, the toddler is learning about the environment and the things within that environment. They are learning to make sense of their world. As adults we need to appreciate and delight with toddlers in their new learning.

Toddlers are intensely curious. They are continually exploring, touching, and trying to make sense of their world. Lindsay is at the water table, and she is repeatedly turning the frog around to look at it from different viewpoints (photo 2.18). She alternates this activity with letting her frog fall into the water. She is oblivious to what is going on around her. Lindsay is involved in solitary functional play. She is learning about what a frog looks like and what happens when it drops into the water.

Toddlers are also curious about each other. They spend a lot of time in **parallel play**—play beside each other doing similar things with similar materials. Kayla had been dumping the beads from one

Photo 2.18

container to another. She delighted in the sound that the beads made when they clattered into the bowl. Kai heard the noise and immediately came over to also pour the beads. He grabbed Kayla's container. Kayla shouted, "NO, mine!" Jennifer, the early childhood educator, immediately came over and gave Kai another similar container. Both children poured the beads into the larger container, and then scooped them back into the smaller container over and over again (photo 2.19). It is typical of the toddler to see something and want to do it now. The toddler sees the world from his or her own perspective. Thus, the toddler has not yet learned to share. It is important to have similar materials available for toddlers so that the play is not interrupted.

Jesse had heard the children pouring the beads into containers. He watched this activity from a distance for a while, which is known as **onlooker** or **observer play**. He saw a bin of large pegs on the floor. With a smile he ran over to the bin, stepped in it, and moved his feet around. The pegs clattered within the tub. Jesse looked over to the children playing with the beads and bowls (photo 2.20). He smiled and continued to move his feet to create his own sound. Often toddlers' play is influenced by what is going on around them. They will then imitate the behaviour either by using similar techniques or by creating their own adaptation of the activity. Jesse was learning through **imitative play.**

Photo 2.19

Photo 2.20

Toddlers' play is full of imitative play. Jesse had observed one of the preschool children use the snap-on beads. She had put them on her finger and then counted them. A little while later, Jesse decided to use the beads in a similar way (photo 2.21). Jesse was using deferred imitation to recreate a situation he had seen earlier. Through these types of activities, toddlers increase their memories of objects, actions, and events. This will ultimately help the toddler learn to communicate and interact more effectively in order to play with other children.

Photo 2.21

6. Play and the Preschooler

The preschool years can be described as actively exploring and learning together with peers (photo 2.22). Braelyn had decided to climb a tree. She encouraged Taylor to also join her. As the girls climbed, they talked about what they were doing. Braelyn said that she needed to use both her hands to "balance myself, so I won't slip and fall." Taylor responded that she also needed to support herself but only with one hand, occasionally. Olivia watched the girls for a while. Both Braelyn and Taylor encouraged her to join in. "It's easy if you use your hands," said Braelyn. Olivia finally also decided to climb the tree. She climbed standing up holding onto the trunk of the second tree and stopped when she could no longer hold onto the tree trunk. Braelyn, Taylor, and Olivia were involved in **associative play**. Each of the girls was doing a similar activity—climbing a tree. Each girl climbed the tree using the techniques that were most comfortable and at the appropriate skill level. As a result, each girl approached the task in a slightly different way. As they were engaged in their activity, the girls shared ideas and comments about what they were doing.

Photo 2.23

Preschoolers also engage in solitary activity. Often the type of activity engaged in lends itself to solitary play such as reading, puzzles, or painting. Preschoolers' play may also reflect parallel play and deferred imitation. HoSeok had been attracted to the activity at the drawing table. He proceeded to draw the potato head that he had seen other children create at another table (photo 2.23). Bowen saw

Photo 2.22

HoSeok drawing. He immediately went to the drawing table. He retrieved a picture that a friend had given to him. Bowen picked out the various colours of markers he wanted to use and sat down by himself to colour the picture (photo 2.24). Note that both boys were doing similar tasks. Both boys were influenced by a past activity and by an ongoing activity, and both boys approached the task differently in accordance to their abilities. HoSeok was still using a **palmar grasp** (using the whole hand to grasp the utensil, Figure 2.1) to draw, whereas Bowen was using a **tripod grasp** (grasping the utensil between forefinger and thumb, Figure 2.2) to colour in his picture.

Web exercises

associative play
Play together, doing a similar task, using similar materials, and sharing ideas and materials, but engaged in the activity in individual ways.

palmar grasp
Using the whole hand to grasp the utensil to manipulate with; usually combined with movement of the whole arm to control the activity engaged in (see Figure 2.1).

tripod grasp
Grasping the utensil between forefinger and thumb, usually used to write or draw; the activity is controlled by wrist action with little whole arm movement (see Figure 2.2).

Photo 2.24

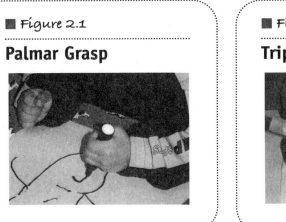

■ *Figure 2.1*

Palmar Grasp

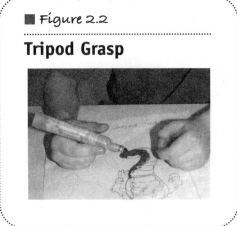

■ *Figure 2.2*

Tripod Grasp

symbolic play
Substituting one object to represent another object during play activities.

constructive play
Using materials, space, or objects to build or create specific ideas or structures.

dramatic play
Practising skills, roles, social interactions, and communication strategies.

cooperative play
Two or more children working together toward a common goal.

Web exercises ☞

Photo 2.25

Preschoolers' activities reflect what they understand about the world around them. The children had been outside exploring the winter environment. Jacob found a frozen puddle. He stepped into it and the ice broke. He picked up a piece of ice, looked through it and said, "Look I found some glass" (photo 2.25). Jacob had experience with what glass looked like and therefore made the connection from ice to glass. When the ice was brought indoors and it eventually melted, Jacob made a new connection. He learned that glass and ice might look the same, but that they are two different things.

Preschoolers start to increasingly use objects **symbolically**—substituting one object to represent another object. This type of play is also referred to as **constructive play**. Children in this stage become very innovative in finding objects that can be substituted to support their play. Dillon liked to use the vehicles. He especially liked to drive the vehicles under tables and chairs. A cardboard tube had been left out. He used the tube to create a tunnel to drive his vehicles through (photo 2.26).

Preschoolers begin to use materials for different purposes. A piece of paper can become a lake, a piece of string a snake, and a hat may be used to represent a variety of purposes—firefighter, construction, dress up, and so on.

Photo 2.26

Role-play becomes an important part of play. Children are involved in **dramatic play** to practise skills, roles, social interactions, and communication strategies. Dramatic play may be as simple as dressing up to go for a walk or preparing a meal for a "family" (photo 2.27).

As children approach the school-aged years, their play becomes increasingly more cooperative. Kristy and Sarah had decided to create an apartment building with a fountain at the front. They decided on which blocks they needed, how high the building should be, how to transport the blocks efficiently, and where to build so that the structure would not be destroyed (photo 2.28). **Cooperative play** involves working together toward a common goal. The two girls decided what to build, what materials were needed, and how and where to find the materials, and finally, they worked together to build the structure.

7. Play and the School-Aged Child

School-aged children are involved in increasingly more complex cooperative activities. One of the children had become ill and needed to be hospitalized for a longer period

Photo 2.27

of time. The group of children decided that they should make a wall hanging for him to cheer him up. One of the children had visited Tim in the hospital. He thought that Tim needed more colour in his hospital room. They discussed the matter and recorded what they needed. One of the children created a list on the computer (Figure 2.3). The children posted a notice on the door requesting a donation of a large white sheet (Figure 2.4). First the children thought that they should paint a scene. Then they decided that it should be "Abstract, so it can hang any way you want to hang it." They also decided it would be more personal if they added handprints and footprints of everyone. The children worked on this project over several days (photo 2.29). When the project was completed, it was decided that only a small group should go to present it to Tim, as a large group would be too big for the hospital room.

As skills to write, read, and complete mathematical computations increase, so do children's ability to cooperate on ever-increasingly intricate projects.

Cooperation among individuals leads to being able to play together in games that are competitive (photo 2.30). The children involved in this ball game need to understand the rules of the game and need to play together in pairs to score. The result of this activity leads to winners and losers. **Competitive play** is evident in most board games, in sports such as baseball or soccer, in contests such as spelling bees, and in individual interactions. Jerimya and José were comparing their artwork. Both boys insisted that their work was the best. A heated argument followed that involved many of their peers. Finally the group took a vote to decide which painting was the best.

Competition may not always be between children. It may also be within one individual who continually strives to complete a task that is continually improving. Children involved in activities such as learning to play an instrument or involved in individual or team sports often continually practise to improve their own abilities.

The creations of school-aged children become increasingly more complex and realistic (photo 2.31). They are able to use a greater variety of materials with a greater degree of skills. They become more independent in finding needed materials or substituting other materials as needed.

8. Play and the Child with Special Needs

Often programs for children with special needs focus on developing specific skills. For example, Jamie entered a junior kindergarten program at four. Jamie found it difficult to maintain attention on one task, was non-communicative with his peers, and often would retreat to a corner of the room and start to rock. A teacher assistant was hired

■ Figure 2.3

The List

```
Sheet
Sign
Paint—yellow,
green, blue,
purple, red
Brushes
Soap and water
Towels
```

Photo 2.28

competitive play
Individual or group striving towards superiority in an activity; the products are superior or inferior; activities lead to winning or losing.

Photo 2.29

■ Figure 2.4

The Notice

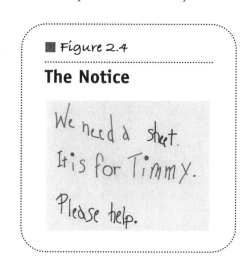

We need a sheet.
It is for Timmy.
Please help.

Photo 2.30   Photo 2.31

inclusive setting
A setting that provides children with special needs opportunities for active participation with children who are developing typically; includes support services and adaptations to the environment.

specifically for Jamie. Much of Jamie's afternoon program was spent in one-to-one interactions with his teacher assistant. She would supply materials and activities to improve his eye contact, verbalizations, and ability to stay on task. While Jamie was working on individualized tasks with his teacher assistant, his peers were engaged in free play activities. Children with special needs need the same opportunities as all other children. They also need to learn through play.

In an **inclusive setting** (Hope et al., 2000), there are four main features:

1. active participation of young children with special needs and typically developing children in the same setting;
2. support services to children to accomplish goals set by families and a team of professionals;
3. collaborative effort of the total team of professionals from different disciplines (speech and language, pediatrician resource consultants, early childhood educator); and
4. evaluation of the effectiveness of the inclusion on the progress of the child with special needs.

All children learn through play. However, children who have special needs may require additional supports. Appropriate adjustments should be made to the learning environments and the learning materials, rather than depriving the child with special needs of opportunities to participate fully in the activities within the learning environment. When children of various abilities learn to play together, there are many advantages. Children learn to:

• respect others;
• recognize that everyone has unique abilities and talents;
• develop empathy and compassion;
• help each other; and
• accept individual differences.

cumulative play
Types of play that emerge in a predictable order, at a predictable age, and each type of play builds on the previous stage.

9. Summary of Play

Play emerges in predictable stages. These stages of play are **cumulative** (i.e., play types emerge in a predictable order, at a predictable age, and each type of play builds on the previous types) (Craig, Kermis, & Digdon, 2001; Parten, 1932; Play, 1962). As children grow and mature, they may use various types of play selectively. Children may decide to play alone or in a group. They may decide to compete or withdraw from competition (Figure 2.5). All types of play share the following characteristics:

Cumulative Levels of Play

Note: Ages are based on normative data and may change with individual or cultural differences.

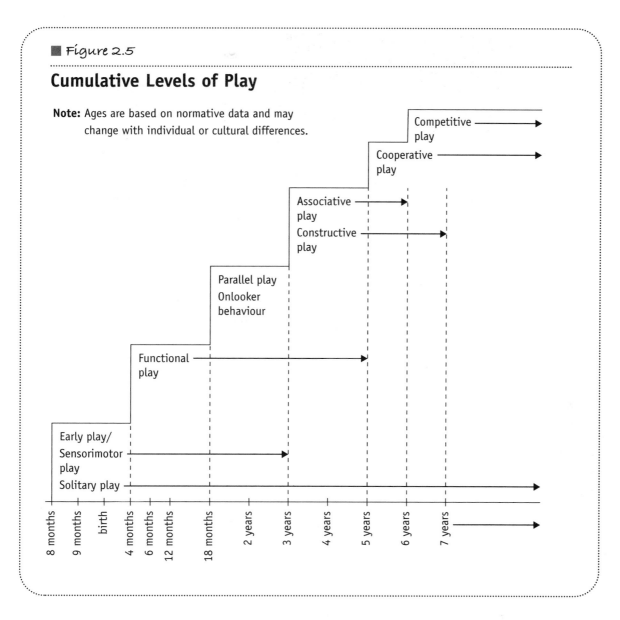

- active involvement;
- spontaneous;
- intrinsically motivating;
- self-satisfying and rewarding;
- **process oriented** (i.e., the play itself is rewarding, and there may not necessarily be a product or the product is not as important as the process in getting to the product);
- symbolic representations;
- self-directed; and
- pleasurable.

Web
exercises

process oriented
The play itself is rewarding; there may not necessarily be a product, or the product is not as important as the process in getting to the product.

DEVELOPMENTALLY APPROPRIATE PRACTICES

"Developmentally appropriate practice is based on knowledge of how children develop and learn. All early childhood teachers must understand what occurs in the first eight years of life and how best to support growth and development." (Gestwicki, 1999, p. 6)

The following 12 principles for **developmentally appropriate practices** were established by the National Association for Early Childhood Educators (NAEYC). Knowledge of and implementation of these principles will help the early childhood educator develop and maintain a quality program and learning environment for children and families. The 12 principles (adapted from Gestwicki, 1999, pp. 8–11) are that:

1. *Children's physical, social, emotional, and cognitive development are closely related.* For example, as Lara (see photo 1.10 on page 5) gained the skill of crawling, she could explore the environment more freely (physical); find things of interest to her (emotional); and explore objects, such as the remote controller, using all her senses to discover what the object is and how it functions (cognitive). Each area of growth and development has a decided effect on other areas.

2. *The sequence of how children grow and develop is predictable.* There is an ordered sequence. Infants learn to roll over, push themselves up (see photo 1.7 on page 4), sit with support (see photo 1.8 on page 4), and sit by themselves (see photo 1.13 on page 5). All healthy infants follow this sequence of development. The skills, abilities, and knowledge the child gains are used as stepping-stones to future learning. Note how Lara has learned to refine and use her grasp. In photo 1.8, Lara is able to grasp and shake things within her reach. In photo 1.12 (page 5), Lara can now manipulate the object by transferring it from hand to hand, turning it around to look at its various aspects, and push the buttons.

3. *Not all children develop at the same rate.* Timmy enjoys gross motor activities. He has developed greater control and self-confidence in gross motor activities (see photo 1.20 on page 6). Jacob enjoys organizing and sorting things within his environment (see photo 1.16 on page 6). He has gained greater control and self-confidence in fine motor activities. Additionally, the rate of development is uneven within different areas of the child's functioning. Timmy expresses little interest in fine motor activities at this stage. He rarely paints, writes, or draws. Jacob is more hesitant to try gross motor activities. He will watch other children engage in these tasks before he will try them himself. Both boys do not hesitate to initiate activities in the areas that they are self-confident in, but rarely initiate activities in those areas they are not.

4. *Lack of certain early experiences may lead to later developmental delays.* In a study conducted in Jamaica, the importance of appropriate nourishment and stimulation was clearly identified. "The children who received neither stimulation nor good nourishment developed poorly and may have been permanently handicapped" (McCain & Mustard, 1999, p. 43). Additionally, there are **critical periods** for optimal development. For example, for optimal development of the visual connections to occur, there must be early visual stimulation. "When visual stimulation is not available in the critical period, and deficits occur in the cortex responsible for vision, they are not correctable at later stages of development" (McCain & Mustard, 1999, p. 29). There are also **sensitive periods** of development. These are times when learning, such as language development, occurs more easily (McCain & Mustard, 1999).

5. *Development is predictable.* It moves from simple to complex, from reflexive to controlled, from disjointed to organized, and from concrete to abstract. When Lara (see photo 1.8 on page 6) first learned to grasp, her efforts were hit and miss. It seemed almost by chance that she could grasp the object. As her skills increased (see photo 1.13 on page 5), not only could she grasp objects of choice by intent, but she could also use her fingers to point to items of interest. Jacob

spent time organizing his small puzzle blocks into rows (see photo 1.16 on page 6). He later used this skill to help organize an obstacle course (see photo 1.19 on page 6). Christopher no longer needed any help to build the fire to cook his hotdogs (see photo 1.40 on page 11). He had internalized the process and could call it to mind when needed.

6. *Development and learning are influenced by social and cultural contexts.* Olivia was encouraged by her peers to try a new skill—climbing a tree (see photo 2.22 on page 33). Autumn is Native American. She has been taught to appreciate nature around her. Autumn was most fascinated by the books and puzzles within the learning environment that depicted things that she had seen in nature (see photo 1.28 on page 8). Christopher is of German and Canadian descent. He could communicate both in German and English from the time he could talk. When he entered the school system, he decided that it was no longer "cool" to speak German. He was influenced by peer pressure to conform to the norms around him and sadly lost much of his earlier German language skills.

7. *Children create their own understanding about the world around them through a variety of active physical, social, and cultural experiences.* Christopher and Katrin (see photo 1.41 on page 11) developed greater understanding about how Native cultures lived in the past. Aleah (see photo 2.1 on page 29) is increasing her understanding about her father—the sound and tone of his voice, the expressions he uses, and the comfort of his touch.

8. *Development is a combination of the interaction between heredity and environment.* "It is generally believed that some human behavior can be easily changed because it is learned, whereas other behavior resists modification because it is part of our biological heritage" (de Waal, 1999, p. 97). Learned behaviour could include such things as preferences for certain types of play activity, food, toys, interaction patterns with others, or type of learning stressed (verbal or written). Hereditary factors include such things as innate cognitive abilities, certain conditions such as Down syndrome, or certain learning disabilities.

9. *Children learn best through play.* All the children portrayed in the examples learned through various types of play. "Play is instrumental in stimulating and shaping child development and learning. Development and learning occur throughout constructive processes in which the child's previous knowledge, brought to the play experience, is modified by new experiences and discoveries that are initiated by the child" (Shipley, 2002, p. 20).

10. *Children need to practise new skills and be challenged to try new skills.* Lauren (see photos 2.6, 2.7, and 2.8 on page 30) is practising manipulation skills. She is learning about her fingers and hands and learning how to grasp objects. Her parents provided her with various challenges. They have placed her in different positions to allow her to practise her skills in different ways—holding her, in a support seat, and on her back on the floor.

11. *Children show in different ways what they have learned or how they are learning.* Lara (see photo 2.13 on page 31) is indicating through deferred imitation that she remembers not only what a telephone is, but also what it is used for. She cannot tell you this yet, but she can show you. When Kayla and Kai (see photo 2.19 on page 32) poured the beads, they showed that they had gained greater fine and gross motor control. It also tells you that they are involved in repetitive play by practising their motor skills. Both children are learning by being actively involved with the materials.

12. *"Children learn best in the context of a community in which they are safe and valued, their physical needs are met, and they feel psychologically safe"* (Gestwicki, 1999, p. 11). Lauren (see photo 1.1 on page 2) immediately had her needs met by her mother. This helps her develop a sense of psychological safety in knowing that she is being listened to and her needs are being met. Another way to meet psychological safety is to make sure that the environment is a safe place to explore. Lara's parents made sure that the remote control was safe to use by removing the batteries from the controller (see photo 2.12 on page 31). Lauren's parents provided her a safe place to sit with support to free her hands (see photo 2.7 on page 30). The children (photo 2.30 on page 36) were provided with materials to allow them to safely engage in competitive play. The work of the children was acknowledged—the artwork was displayed in the hospital room, children's written efforts were encouraged and posted (see Figure 2.4 on page 35), and Chris's artwork was framed and posted for display.

In summary, practitioners who utilize developmentally appropriate practice make decisions about the well-being and education of young children based upon:

- what they know about how children develop and learn;
- what they know about the strengths, needs, and interests of individual children; and
- what they know about the social and cultural contexts in which children live.

INDOOR AND OUTDOOR LEARNING ENVIRONMENTS

Children may spend as much as eight hours of their day within a child-care facility. It is of critical importance that the learning environment ensures that the children feel comfortable, safe, and nurtured. The learning environment must afford children opportunities to:

- be involved in active play;
- explore the environment and the materials and equipment within that environment;
- interact with peers and adults;
- find a place to be alone or be with others;
- make real choices;
- manipulate a variety of objects;
- involve all their senses;
- solve problems by themselves or with others; and
- build upon what they already know (Crowther, 2002).

It is of equal importance that the adults who work within the child-care settings also work in an environment that provides pleasure, comfort, privacy, and opportunities for personal growth. The learning environment must afford adults the opportunities to:

- interact with children individually or in groups;
- find adult space to be alone;
- store personal belongings safely;
- interact with other adults;

- utilize a variety of professional resources; and
- provide meeting spaces to meet with other adults (families, other professionals, and staff) (Harms, Clifford, & Cryer, 1998).

1. Elements of the Learning Environment

All spaces within the child-care environment, whether these are indoor or outdoor spaces, should have certain commonalities in order to provide quality care. These commonalities include:

- *Physical safety*. Children must be free to explore in an environment that is free from physical danger. This includes checking all equipment and materials for loose or broken parts, maintaining a sanitary environment, providing surfaces that are safe to traverse both on foot and with riding toys, setting up learning areas that encourage children to move easily from area to area, ensuring that all equipment and furniture is sturdy and splinter-free, and providing appropriate soft surfaces under play equipment.
- *Psychological safety*. An environment that encourages children to interact to their fullest potential also includes psychological safety. "Children must feel secure in order for positive mental processes to develop and for positive feelings and behaviors to dominate their lives" (Sayre & Gallagher, 2001, p. 94). Psychological safety includes meeting social and emotional needs; having sensitive caregivers who observe, listen, and respond to the signals children give; providing an environment that encourages children and families to express themselves freely and openly; and providing an environment that acknowledges cultural and gender-related differences and similarities.

2. Infant Environments

Infants have very specific needs. Meeting these needs is the responsibility of the caregiver. The interactions that encourage infants to participate actively are a reflection of the sensitivity of the caregiver to listen, observe, and react to the signals the infant gives. As infants gain more control over their movements and begin to navigate around the environment by themselves, the caregiver strategies must change to reflect the growing competence of the infants. Factors that should be considered in any quality infant environment that supports active play during all routines are outlined in Table 2.1.

3. Toddler Environments

Toddlers also have unique needs. The toddler is continually on the move, very curious, and examining everything within the environment. Toddlers become increasingly more independent. They want to do things by themselves. They are much less dependent on the caregiver for help than infants. The main factors to consider in setting up toddler environments that encourage active play during all routines are listed in Table 2.2.

Considerations for an Infant Environment

Factors	Nonmobile Infants	Mobile Infants
Sleeping area	• Comfortable sleeping cribs in separate area to encourage individual sleeping patterns. • Mobiles hanging from crib with features face-down over infant to encourage choice in sleeping or quiet activities. • Soft music (see the Resources section at the end of the chapter).	• As the infant approaches the toddler stage, beds should be low to the ground with railings or cots can start to be used. Also include personal bedding. • Mobiles should change to include crib toys that can be pushed, prodded, and pulled.
Toileting area	• Change area—soft, no sharp edges, constant supervision to prevent falling. • Mobiles or mirrors hanging over area (see listing in References). • All materials organized within reach of caregiver (see Figure 7.8 on page 200).	• As infants gain more skill to do things for themselves, add steps to change area to encourage infants to climb up themselves (this also helps prevent back strain for caregiver). • Post familiar pictures or photographs around the area to encourage dialogue
Learning areas	• Soft area in room protected from intrusion by more mobile infants. • Large pillows or pads to provide supportive sitting area. • Surrounded by hanging mobiles and pictures on the wall. • Comfortable chair or comfortable pillows on floor for caregiver. • A variety of soft toys to grasp when placed in or near hand within reach of caregiver, and in later months within reach of infant.	• Sturdy furniture that encourages pulling self up into standing position and walking around with support. • Large clear area free from obstruction to encourage crawling, walking, pulling, or pushing toys. • Low sturdy shelves (non-tipping) with toys infants can retrieve/put back. • Duplicate toys. • Labelled shelves with picture/outline/words.
Eating areas	• Quiet corner with comfortable furniture for breast-feeding or bottle feeding. • Encourage mothers to come in to feed their infants.	• High chair (once infant can sit and is starting to eat solid foods). • Small table with supportive chairs that infants can climb into unassisted to feed themselves when ready. • Create social setting for meal times.

Factors	Infants
Outdoor area	• Protected area from other children. • Shaded area, protected from wind. • Soft surface to crawl on. • Sturdy equipment to encourage climbing and sliding. • Area free from obstruction to run, use riding toys, and push or pull toys. • Area for quiet activities; place to be alone.

Considerations for a Toddler Environment

Factors	Toddlers
Sleeping area	• Low beds or cots that toddlers can climb onto by themselves, with personal bedding. • Toddlers are more likely to have common sleep time, so common sleep area can be set up—low lights, good ventilation, adequate spacing. • Soft music—similar to mobile infant music. • Comfortable floor space for adults to interact with toddlers trying to sleep. • Area set up for quiet play to accommodate early risers.
Toileting area	• Change table that toddlers can climb up to by themselves. • Child-sized toilet, sink, and step stool for smaller toddlers. • Hooks for personal-care items that toddlers can reach. • Photos or pictures of toddlers engaged in self-care routines.
Learning areas	• Large clear area free from obstruction to encourage crawling, walking, running, and pulling or pushing toys. • Low, sturdy, open shelves with duplicate toys that toddlers can retrieve or put back by themselves, labelled by picture/outline/word (see Figure 2.6). • Large and small containers to fill and dump. • Greater variety of learning areas to encourage greater choice. • Area for quiet activities; place to be alone.
Eating area	• Small tables and chairs to encourage independence and socialization. • Utensils to encourage serving, eating, and clean-up routines.
Outdoor area	• Protected area from other children. • Shaded area protected from wind. • Soft surface to crawl, walk, sit, and run on. • Sturdy equipment to encourage climbing, sliding, and role-play. • Paved area for riding toys. • Area for quiet activities such as puzzles and drawing; place to be alone.

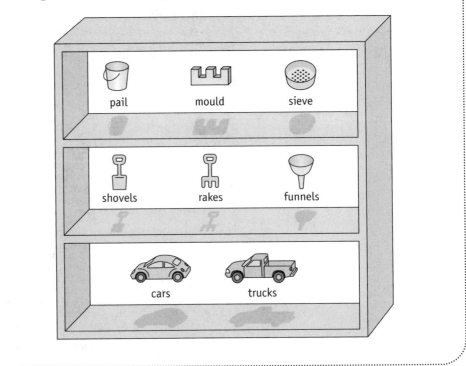

Storage and Labelling

4. Preschool Environments

During the preschool years, children in quality settings continue to gain self-confidence in their abilities and greater independence. Preschoolers enjoy social settings. They will interact with peers in group play situations. The learning settings should encourage individual and group activity. Preschoolers are also much more skillful at making choices, planning their activity, and solving their own problems. The environment needs to encourage preschoolers to be involved in a full range of choices to engage in appropriate learning situations and learn to solve their own problems. Table 2.3 outlines some important considerations for preschool environments.

5. School-Aged Environments

Children in this age group usually attend a child-care centre in a before- or after-school program. This program may be within the elementary school setting or in the daycare setting near the school. Children may attend the program for half days if in junior or senior kindergarten. These children usually fit into the regular daycare program or may be in a separate kindergarten room. The environmental considerations are similar to those for preschoolers, as identified in Table 2.3. Children may attend the program before school starts and after school is over (see Table 2.4 on page 46 for some environmental considerations).

Considerations for a Preschool Environment

Factors	Preschoolers
Sleeping area	• Cots or mats on the floor with personal bedding; common sleep time, so common sleep area can be set up—low lights, good ventilation, adequate spacing (see page 204 in Chapter 7). • Soft music. • Comfortable floor space for adults to interact with preschoolers trying to sleep. • Area set up for quiet play to accommodate nonsleepers and early risers.
Toileting area	• Increased ability to be independent in toileting routines. • Child-sized toilet and sink. • Hooks for personal-care items preschoolers can reach. • Photos or pictures of preschoolers engaged in self-care routines.
Learning areas	• Full range of learning areas set up to encourage choice and socialization (sand, water, woodworking, music, creative arts, reading/writing, blocks, manipulatives, drama). • Space set up to encourage ease of movement and supervision between learning areas. • Materials arranged on open shelves and clear containers labelled with pictures/outlines and words. • Mobile storage units available to transport materials from centre to centre. • Provision for soft quiet areas and places to be alone.
Eating area	• Small tables and chairs to encourage independence and socialization. • Utensils to encourage serving, eating, and clean-up routines.
Outdoor area	• Shaded area, protected from wind. • Soft surfaces to walk, sit, and run on. • Sturdy equipment to encourage climbing, sliding, role-playing, swinging, and hanging. • Paved area for riding toys. • Quiet area for relaxation and quiet activities such as drawing and puzzles.

■ TABLE 2.4

Considerations for a School-Aged Environment

Factors	School-Aged Children
Quiet area	• Children will need a soft quiet area with quiet activities such as reading or puzzles to encourage rest and relaxation.
Personal care area	• Privacy for toileting—individual cubicles. • Personal self-care items stored in personal containers such as zippered bags or small overnight bags.
Learning areas	• Set up in interest centres with increasing emphasis on opportunity to engage in collaborative tasks, solve problems together, and make individual and group decisions; reading and writing activities; and opportunities for group play including sports activities.
Eating area	• Age-appropriate tables and chairs to encourage socialization. • Children may need breakfast or snacks. • Children are independent.
Outdoor area	• Shaded area, protected from wind. • Soft surface to walk, run, and relax on. • Sturdy equipment to encourage climbing, sliding, and role-playing. • Large open areas to encourage sport activities and team efforts.

6. Considerations for Children with Special Needs

In an inclusive setting, all children should have equal access to the materials and choices within the environment. Children with special needs should be able to use the environments as described for their respective age groups. Adaptations that might need to be made for children are listed in Table 2.5. Adaptations should emphasize independence for individuals. At times these may contravene safety requirements such as controlled entry into the setting. Strategies should be discussed and put in place to meet the requirement of individual settings and the need for independence of the children.

Adaptations for Children with Special Needs

Condition	Possible Adaptations
Physical impairments	• Wheelchair access (access by wheelchair usually accommodates most other physical disability aspects such as crutches, leg-braces), ramps into centre and on outdoor equipment, smooth entry through doorways or from rug areas to tile areas, automatic door openers at child height, larger cloak room space and toilet area, bars around toilet, lower sink and fountain, tilt mirrors, longer handles on taps or automatic water flow, room within all centres to move around, adjustment of all furniture to accommodate wheelchair, basket on wheelchair to transport items. • Placement of materials such that all children can safely reach materials on open shelves—may mean duplication of similar materials on lower and higher shelves.
Mobility limitations **communication boards** Boards that are set up with symbols and pictures to encourage children to communicate by pointing.	• Adaptive switches to operate computers, CD players, or any other electrical equipment, turn lights on and off. • Wrist straps to help hold utensils such as spoons, brushes, pens, and crayons. • Standing frames to encourage free use of hands to paint, draw, build, or manipulate materials. • Sturdy chairs with seatbelts to provide support and opportunities to socialize and create. • **Communication boards**—boards that are set up with symbols and pictures to encourage children to communicate by pointing. • Sturdy carts that will assist walking, collecting materials, and pulling oneself to a standing position. • Foam and cardboard blocks to lighten weight of wooden blocks to make manipulation of blocks easier. • Table tops to build on. • Table-top easels, or easels on the floor to draw, paint, and write on. • Nonslip surface on all floors. • Adaptive equipment, such as special cutlery to eat with, suction cups on plates, and nontilt cups and glasses.
Visual handicaps	• Stable set-up of environment to give individual security to move freely. • Tactile clues such as felt strips on walls to guide individual from place to place; bliss Braille symbols included in labelling system. • Braille writing utensils. • Braille books. • Moving equipment or materials with sound-making devices to attract attention, such as bells on carts or in balls. • Auditory alarm system such as a whistle.
Hearing handicaps	• Sound barriers such as carpeting, padded dividers or padding attached to back of shelves, and cloth-covered furniture. • Flashing lights to indicate time changes or emergencies. • Sign language symbols and cue cards. • Sufficient lighting to promote visual acuity.
Cognitive/language impairments	• A wide range of materials should be available to provide opportunities for all children. • Facilitative communication devices. • Age-appropriate materials as well as developmentally appropriate materials. • Representation of all conditions within materials—dolls with braces; posters, books, and puzzles about children with special needs.

RESPECTING THE CHILD'S TOTAL EXPERIENCES

The Early Childhood Environmental Rating Scales (Harms et al., 1998; Harms, Cryer, & Clifford, 1990; Harms, Vineberg Jacobs, & White, 1996; Harms & Clifford, 1989) clearly identify the core areas that are needed to lead to a quality program for infants and toddlers, preschool children, school-aged children, and children in family daycare settings. The core areas that are identified include the following experiences that children need:

- *Manipulative*—beading, puzzles, small blocks, Lego, Duplo, peg boards, sorting, and classifying.
- *Creative art*—both two-dimensional (drawing, painting, colouring, cutting and pasting, weaving, sewing) and three-dimensional (dough, sculptures, sewing).
- *Blocks*—unit blocks, foam blocks, cardboard blocks, planks, accessories such as people, animals, vehicles, and signs.
- *Drama*—housekeeping; familiar roles such as medical, firefighter, police officers.
- *Nature and science*—field trips, simple experiments, collections, using items for nature in creative activities, observing weather, animals, plants.
- *Math and numbers*—counting materials such as an abacus, beads, small vehicles, dominoes; counting experiences such as counting cutlery on the table, stairs; counting books, posting of numbers, number cards.
- *Water*—experiment, skill development such as pouring, filling, measuring, and smoothing.
- *Sand experiment*—skill development such as pouring, filling, measuring, moulding, sculpting, building, and smoothing.
- *Audiovisual materials*—TV, computers, videos.
- *Reading and writing*—picture books, easy reading books, books to read aloud, poetry, dictionaries, books in languages supported within environment, writing utensils and appropriate paper, letters, numbers.
- *Music and movement*—musical instruments, listening to music, moving to music, using props with music, and singing.
- *Gross motor activities both indoors and outdoors*—opportunities to run, jump, climb, ride, balance, hang, and swing.
- *Promoting and accepting diversity*—representation of cultural diversity, gender, and special needs in all aspects of the environment, including pictures, books, materials, eating utensils, dress-up clothing, and so on.

Children need to practise emergent skills in different settings. For example, Kayla came to her preschool experience already seemingly able to "count to ten." She would often be heard counting. Her skill of counting varied as sometimes she would miss numbers and other times she might backtrack to recite numbers again—"one, two, three, four, three, four, five." There were several practice-teaching students in the daycare at the time. They were quite amazed when she did not seem able to relate her apparent counting skills to actually counting objects. When she was asked how many objects she had counted, she could not answer that question. She had not really learned to count yet. She had simply learned to rote count—reciting numbers without actually counting objects. Jennifer, the early childhood educator, noticed Kayla's interest in counting. Whenever possible she would model counting by counting the stairs as they walked up or down the stairs, pointing to the blocks and counting the stack of blocks created, or pointing to and counting the number of beads on a string. Kayla started to imitate the behaviour at the water table. She counted the splashes made as she dropped objects into the water. She said "Three splashes." Her skill in counting real objects gradually increased. She counted objects in a variety of areas, thus transferring and confirming her counting skill in different settings.

It is critical that children learn to transfer skills and knowledge from one setting to another. Some skills change dramatically depending on the materials used. For example, you can pour beads, water, or sand. The skill is similar, but you might use different equipment such as containers, funnels, pitchers, or watering cans for the task. In each instance the materials react quite differently. It is to exposure in various settings that the connections can be made between an action such as pouring, the language involved with the action, and the result of the action. Through this process children learn language, learn about the cause and effect between actions and materials, and learn about the world around them.

INDIVIDUAL DIFFERENCES

Individual differences are common within our society. Our society has a number of ethnic and racial differences. "Due to variation in its ethnic makeup, each province has a unique cultural mosaic" (Broderick, 2003, p. 48). Ethnic variation is usually classified in terms of visible minorities or non–visible minorities. Visible minorities include individuals who look different from the majority group because of obvious differences such as skin colour or the shape of eyes. Non–visible minorities include individuals who look the same as the members of the majority culture. Table 2.6 identifies some of the ethnic and cultural variations in Canada.

Too often we infer that cultural diversity is something that is always observable. Skin colour or facial features are the obvious ones. Often, differences are not noticed because the child may already speak English, may be dressed like everyone else, and may behave the same as everyone else. We may miss differences of religion, language, and customs totally, and fail to represent these in the classroom. For example, Kate was three years old when she started in the daycare centre. She had dark brown hair, big greenish-blue eyes, and a light olive complexion. She seemed to fit into the setting extremely well. It was not until mealtime that a difficulty was discovered. Kate

■ TABLE 2.6

Ethnic and Cultural Variations

Ethnic Variation—Non–Visible Minorities		Ethnic Variation—Visible Minorities	
North America	Italian	Chinese	Métis
Danish	Jewish	East Indian	North American First Nations
English (United Kingdom)	Norwegian	Filipino	Inuit
French	Polish	Jamaican	Spanish
Dutch	Portuguese	Japanese	Vietnamese
German	Russian		
Greek	Swedish		
Hungarian	Ukrainian		

refused to eat the food placed in front of her. The meal was spaghetti in meat sauce. After checking her records, it was discovered that Kate's father was Indian and her mother Canadian. The caregivers had only met the mother. Somehow the information that the family ate only vegetarian food had been forgotten. Neither Kate's physical appearance, nor her name, nor her behaviour gave a clue to any potential problem. Kate's experience was short-lived. Her caregivers checked the information and adjusted the mealtime accordingly.

There are other differences that need to be paid attention to. Individual differences can arise because not all children develop at the same rate, nor is the rate of development consistent for one individual across all areas of development. Christopher at 12 months was not yet walking independently, but he could climb to the top of a five-foot climber with ease and he could swim the width of a pool. Christopher had started a physical activity program at six months that included swimming.

Individual differences may also be caused by a disabling condition at birth, such as cerebral palsy. Mark could not control his muscles to walk or talk at four years old. He could use a communication board effectively to indicate his desires. He could use his hands and arms with brace supports to engage in manipulative activities. He could already use the computer to write simple sentences. He could answer questions asked of him after reading to him on the computer. Some other disabling conditions may be temporary. A child with a broken leg or arm may need to have temporary adjustments made to the environment.

We also have differences that arise from the values families place or stress while growing up. Some family values stress verbal communication over written communication. These children may enter daycare or the educational system with excellent listening and oral language skills, but may be disinterested in the written word. Other children may come from value systems that encourage children to be active listeners. These children often appear to be shy to speak out or express an opinion and they may be reluctant to try new things.

Gender differences also need to be acknowledged. Some of these differences are obviously physical. Boys tend to be a bit bigger and longer at birth than girls. However, there are many research findings that point to the fact that some differences may be taught:

- "Children learn some aspects of gender roles by modelling themselves after significant individuals in their lives and by being reinforced for gender-appropriate behaviour" (Craig et al., 2001, p. 356). These behaviours can be observed in children's play preferences. Girls may tend to be more interested in playing with dolls and engage in art and music activities. Boys may tend to be more interested in building with blocks, engaging in rough play, and playing with cars and trucks (Craig et al., 2001).
- In North America, "Boys under two years of age are already provided with more sports equipment, tools, and large and small vehicles than are girls. Girls on the other hand have more dolls, toys representing fictional characters, and child's furniture" (Schickedanz et al., 2001, p. 540).
- "Cross cultural studies show that parents in many societies also dress boys and girls differently and assign them different chores" (Schickedanz et al., 2001, p. 540).

In summary, according to Schickedanz, Schickedanz, Forsyth, and Forsyth (2001), many families clearly assign gender by the way they dress, by their hairstyle, by body decorations, and by the status assigned to the work they do. Children are raised in these traditions, and conform to them at an early age. It is up to daycare providers to represent genders in fair and equitable ways. This should be done through

- Assigning helping tasks equally to boys and girls.
- Providing representational dress-up clothes for both genders.
- Providing illustration examples, books, and pictures of diversity in gender roles.
- Inviting guest visitors from diverse role backgrounds.
- Encouraging children to utilize all areas by careful observation of interests of the children and subsequent selection of appropriate materials. For example, a small group of boys is observed in the block area playing with the large construction vehicles and trains. Jennifer brought a roll of newsprint, crayons, pencils, scissors, glue, and construction paper and left it in the area. The boys noticed these when they came in the next day. They used the newsprint to create a road. They drew a dotted line down the middle of the road, and they used the construction paper to create traffic signs.

KEY POINTS

LEARNING THROUGH PLAY

- Early types of play include activities that are
    - solitary, tactile, and involve the use of fine and gross muscles, and
    - include opportunities to observe and listen.

- Sensorimotor activities at the fetal stage involve
    - solitary motor activities,
    - listening, and
    - reacting to sounds, movement, and stimulation.

- Play activities with the newborn include
    - solitary motor activities, and
    - observing, listening, and reacting.

- Play activities with the infant include
    - solitary and interactive activities with caregivers,
    - tactile, sensory experiences, and
    - functional, imitative, and repetitive play.

- Play activities with toddlers include
    - solitary, functional, observer, and parallel play,
    - active exploration, and
    - imitative behaviour.

- Play with the preschooler includes
    - solitary, symbolic, dramatic play and role play,
    - associative play, and
    - cooperative play.

- Play with school-aged children includes
    - solitary, cooperative, and competitive play both within groups and with self, and
    - increased skill during play—reading, writing, and mathematical computations.

- Play with the child with special needs includes
  - active participation of all children,
  - support and adaptation for individual needs, and
  - collaborative efforts of all individuals involved.

- Play is
  - active, spontaneous, intrinsically motivating, and pleasurable;
  - process oriented; and
  - self-directed.

DEVELOPMENTALLY APPROPRIATE PRACTICES
- Developmentally appropriate practices include principles about
  - interrelatedness of children's physical, social, and cognitive development;
  - sequence and predictability of development;
  - varied rates of development between different children;
  - influence of the social and cultural contexts on learning; and
  - the interplay of heredity and environment

INDOOR AND OUTDOOR LEARNING ENVIRONMENTS
- Nonmobile infants—creating learning opportunities that foster safe choices and foster growing independence.
- Mobile infants—creating safe learning environments to foster increased independence and growing ability to make choices.
- Toddlers—creating safe environments that foster growing autonomy.
- Preschoolers—increased independence and protection to support making choices and decisions.
- School-aged children—increased independence of choices and decisions in personal care, learning, and socializing.
- Children with special needs—individual accessibility and independence; adaptations to the environment to meet needs of all children.

INDIVIDUAL DIFFERENCES
- Respect for cultural diversity.
- Varied rates of individual development.
- Varied interests and background experiences.
- Gender differences.

EXERCISES

1. For this activity you should work in small groups of four to six individuals. You will need to cut recipe cards into four equal pieces. Each group member should have eight small cards. Using the text, find eight aspects of why children learn best through play in Chapter 2. Learners should look at all the points they have written and make sure that each point is repeated at least twice. Place all cards face down on the table and play the game of concentration (try to find two matching cards by turning up cards two at a time). When the game is finished, put the cards away and ask each learner to write down at least five points explaining why play is the best way of learning for young children. Discuss your results. Did you learn better this way?
2. Using the following chart, compare the early play of the infant and toddler.

Early Play Characteristic	Behaviour of the Infant	Behaviour of the Toddler
Motor Movements		
Tactile Exploration		
Play		

3. Observe infants of at least two different ages. Ages observed in the whole group should represent at least one observation of each of the following age groups—birth to four months; four months to eight months; eight months to 14 months; and 14 months to 18 months. You should observe and record the following:

   a) What kinds of toys does the child play with?
   b) Who does the child interact with? Describe what happens during the interaction.
   c) Where is the child playing?
   d) How does the child use his or her hands and fingers to grasp objects?

   When everyone has completed the activity, record all information on a master chart so that a visual progress of play is provided for the various age groups.

4. In small groups:

   a) Identify the various play types.
   b) Define each play type.
   c) Give a specific example of the behaviours a child might use when involved in each play type.
   d) Identify at what age each play type first emerges.

5. In small groups discuss how each play type (solitary, onlooker, parallel, associative, cooperative, competitive, functional, symbolic, and dramatic) might be used in various age groups (young infant, mobile infant, toddler, preschooler, and school-aged child).

6. In small groups, define what is meant by developmentally appropriate practices. Develop a questionnaire that reflects the 12 principles of developmentally appropriate practices. Share the questionnaire with classmates and discuss necessary improvements. In small groups, interview various daycare directors using your questionnaire. Bring back the results and compare them. How similar were the responses? What items were missed?

7. List the core requirements of any learning environment for an age group of choice. Develop a floor plan that clearly indicates how you plan to address each requirement.

8. Try to observe an infant, toddler, preschool, and school-aged environment. Duplicate the chart below for each age group, and record your observations. When completed, bring back the charts to discuss in class. What aspects did you find that met the general guidelines in the text? What changes might need to be made? Be sure that you keep the information confidential. You should not be able to identify the setting that the observations were made at.

9. Using the information presented in Table 2.5 (page 47), explain how each of the adaptations listed:

   a) leads to greater independence for the child with special needs, and
   b) helps the early childhood educator be more effective in offering an inclusive program.

10. What individual differences in children might affect how a learning environment is set up? How would you ensure that you respect all individual differences? List at least three strategies that might help you reach this goal.

w w w

Observation of .... **Environment**   **Date:** ....

Sleeping	
Eating	
Toileting	
Learning Areas	
Outdoor Area	

RESOURCES

Baby's Best Quiet Time Songs (2003). Laurent, QC: Madacy Kids.

Baby Reflections (2000). *Nature's Lullabies*. Don Mills, ON: Baby Reflections.

Baby Reflections (2003). *Bach for Baby's Brain*. Don Mills, ON: Baby Reflections.

Daquioag, W. (2002). *Hawaiian Lullabies: Volume II*. Waipahu, HI: Entertainment Music Enterprise & Tami Records.

Musical Reflections (1999). *Lullabies: Cherished Bedtime Classics*. Don Mills, ON: Musical Reflections.

Stone, J. (1998). *Baby Needs Mozart*. Hollywood, CA: Delos International, Inc.

Walker, T. (2000). *Heartbeat Pacifier*. Don Mills, ON: Baby Reflections.

REFERENCES

Broderick, Michelle. (2003). Demographic Trends in Canada. In P.U. Angelini (Ed.), *Our Society: Human Diversity in Canada* (2nd ed., pp. 33–58). Scarborough, ON: Nelson.

Craig, G., Kermis, M., & Digdon, N. (2001). *Children Today*. Toronto, ON: Prentice Hall.

Crowther, I. (2002). Guardians of the Critical Years: Infant and Toddler Caregivers. *Interaction, 16, No. 3,* 17–20.

Crowther, I. (2003). *Creating Effective Learning Environments*. Scarborough, ON: Nelson Thomson Learning.

de Waal, F. (1999). The End of Nature versus Nurture. *Scientific American,* December, 94–99.

Gestwicki, C. (1999). *Developmentally Appropriate Practices* (2nd ed.). Scarborough, ON: Nelson Canada.

Gestwicki, C. (2003). *Developmentally Appropriate Practices* (3rd ed.). Scarborough, ON: Nelson Canada.

Harms, T., Clifford, R., & Cryer, D. (1998). *Early Childhood Environment Rating Scale* (rev. ed.). New York: Teachers College Press.

Harms, T., & Clifford, R. (1989). *Family Day Care Rating Scale*. New York: Teachers College Press.

Harms, T., Cryer, D., & Clifford, R. (1990). *Infant/Toddler Environment Rating Scale*. New York: Teachers College Press.

Harms, T., Vineberg Jacobs, E., & White, D. (1996). *School-Age Care Environment Rating Scale*. New York: Teachers College Press.

Hope Irwin, S., Lero, D., & Brophy, K. (2000). *A Matter of Urgency: Including Children with Special Needs in Child Care in Canada*. Weck Cove, NS: Breton Books.

Hopson, J. (1998). Fetal Psychology. *Psychology Today, 76,* 44–48.

McCain, M., & Mustard, F. (1999). *Early Years Study, Final Report*. Toronto, ON: Publications Ontario.

Nash, M. (1997). Fertile Minds. *Time, 149, 5,* 48–56.

Parten, M. (1932). Social Participation Among Preschool Children. *Journal of Abnormal and Social Psychology, 27,* 243–269.

Play, D. A. I. I. C. (1962). *Piaget, J.* New York, NY: Norton.

Sayre, N., & Gallagher, J. (2001). *The Young Child and the Environment: Issues Related to Health, Nutrition, Safety, and Physical Activity*. Toronto, ON: Allyn & Bacon.

Schickedanz, J., Schickedanz, D., Forsyth, P., & Forsyth, G. (2001). *Understanding Children and Adolescents*. Toronto ON: Allyn & Bacon.

Shipley, D. (2002). *Empowering Children* (3rd ed.). Scarborough, ON: Thomson Nelson.

ROLE OF THE FACILITATOR

"Educators working with young children between the ages of 3 to 8 recognize that young children's learning differs significantly from that of older children and adults and approach their work with that understanding in mind. Thus the application of developmentally appropriate practices places the nature and well-being of children as the central focus of professional practice." (Kostelnik, Solderman, & Whiren, 1999, p. 45)

Chapter Outcomes

After reading this chapter, the reader will

1. Describe the characteristics of a facilitator.
2. Discuss the characteristics of partnerships.
3. Discuss how the facilitator might develop partnerships with families.
4. Compare the difference between direct instruction and facilitated learning.
5. Discuss why facilitative teaching is an effective practice to encourage the learning of young children.
6. Discuss the role of the facilitator in setting the stage for learning.
7. Describe the characteristics of positive child–adult interactions.
8. Describe when it is important to leave children's play alone and when it is important to step in to guide the play.
9. Describe what and how adults learn from their interactions with children and families.
10. Identify and describe the planning cycle.
11. Identify and describe the steps in planning activities.
12. Identify and describe the core areas of a learning environment for young children.
13. Describe the aspects of setting up a learning environment to encourage active participation.
14. Identify aspects of safety in setting up a learning environment.
15. Identify and discuss factors in evaluating the effectiveness of a learning environment.
16. Define the role of the facilitator in the community.

WHAT IS A FACILITATOR?

Photo 3.1

Kaya, the early childhood educator, observed Yasmine in the sand area. Yasmine had brought a large grey flat rock into the sand area. She was using some of the jungle animals and dinosaurs in dramatic play activities. As the dinosaur flew on the rock she said, "I am looking around to find a more appropriate place to live. This is too bare" (photo 3.1). Yasmine added a log round to the sand area and built "mountains" for her animals to climb. She trekked her animals around the sand box. Finally she sighed, "We just can't find a good place to live. We are soooo tired." Kaya went over to Yasmine and asked her why her animals were tired. Yasmine explained the situation. She said that she wished she could help her animals find a better place to live. As it was toward the end of the day, Kaya said that they could both think about it and maybe work on this tomorrow.

The next day, Kaya added a few things to the sand area. She put a natural log into the area, and she added some natural materials to the labelled containers on the shelves. When Yasmine came in, she immediately went to the sand area. Her eyes lit up. She spent an hour creating an environment that might please her dinosaur (photo 3.2). Yasmine continued with the play in the sand area over the next few days. Her scenarios became more intricate and soon included other children in collecting materials that could be used and actively supporting the dramatic play. At one point there were ten children carefully manipulating objects and actively engaged in role-play of the dinosaurs and other animals. Kaya observed and recorded the children's interactions, took photos to document their play, and posted the photographs within the sand area.

Photo 3.2

During this play scenario, the facilitator did the following:

1. *Set up the learning area to encourage play.* The sand area was set up on the floor, with a variety of materials (rocks, dinosaurs) available for children to choose. The new materials were organized in a way to increase the children's independence. All materials could be easily found as the materials were clearly labelled.
2. *Observed children's play.* Kaya observed Yasmine's play in the sand area. She also observed and documented the play as it progressed.
3. *Knew when to step in and when to leave the play uninterrupted.* Kaya knew when to step in to interact with Yasmine and when to leave Yasmine's play undisturbed. Yasmine had already indicated that she could solve her own problems. She had retrieved the appropriate rock and had created "mountains" to support her play. Kaya was also sensitive enough to recognize that Yasmine was giving her a gentle hint that she could no longer maintain her play. She verbalized that her dinosaur was frustrated. Kaya listened and responded by asking Yasmine to verbalize what was troubling her.
4. *Encouraged children to solve their own problems.* Kaya encouraged Yasmine to verbalize her problem. She offered a suggestion that encouraged Yasmine to continue her play the next day. The children collected other materials to add to the play situation. Kaya observed the larger group of children. She realized that the children interacted with each other appropriately and used the materials respectfully. The children had solved the problem of a larger group of children within a confined space themselves.
5. *Provided additional materials to extend the play.* Kaya brought additional materials to the area that could encourage Yasmine to continue to build her play drama with the dinosaur. The materials were put on the shelf so that Yasmine could pick her own materials to continue to build with.
6. *Recognized that learning can occur without direct intervention.* The children were learning how to use the materials effectively, what materials to use, how to solve their own problems, how to interact with each other, how to maintain an activity over time, and that they needed to respect each other's efforts.
7. *Reflected upon what has been observed and adapted strategies as needed.* Kaya reflected upon how difficult it had been for Yasmine to verbalize situations that bothered her. Subsequently, she carefully observed and listened to Yasmine. She carefully structured her interactions to give Yasmine confidence to express her concerns.

In summary, a **facilitator** sets the stage for learning to occur, observes and monitors the children's activity, reflects upon the situations, provides additional resources when needed, and is sensitive to guide children's behaviour only when guidance is needed. These are developmentally appropriate practices. In the example above, the facilitator

- applied knowledge of child development to interact with children and set up appropriate learning experiences;
- based decisions about children's learning and activities on observations of children's skills, knowledge, and abilities; and
- provided a structure of learning experiences that was flexible and sensitive to the needs of young children.

facilitator
A person who sets the stage for learning to occur, observes and monitors the children's activity, provides additional resources when needed, and is sensitive to guide children's behaviour only when guidance is needed.

ROLE OF THE FACILITATOR IN ESTABLISHING PARTNERSHIPS WITH FAMILIES

The children represented in the scenarios in this book come from very diverse backgrounds. The beliefs and values that the families of these children hold are quite different. These differences include

- various religious belief systems,
- ethnic differences in eating and sleeping habits,
- various beliefs on how children should be raised,
- beliefs and values on how and what children should be taught, and
- values on how children should behave.

Child development teaches us that children's learning is based on the experiences and knowledge that they bring with them to any setting. It is critical that early childhood educators pay attention to the experiences and backgrounds that the children come from. Learning grows from the roots that the learning came from. Healthy development acknowledges those roots and expands upon them. "To feel whole and integrated, children need to grow up in a stable community. This means a continuity of values in family, peer groups, religion and culture, as well as exposure to diversity" (Brazelton & Greenspan, 2000, p. 35).

The early childhood educator, therefore, needs to develop sensitivity and knowledge about the children under his or her care. The easiest way to accomplish this objective is to form partnerships with families. Partnerships may be defined as "Relationships among different groups in which each group has equal influence on decision making" (Barbour & Barbour, 2001, p. 39). There are many types of partnerships. Roberts, Rule, and Innocenti (1998, p. 21) identify five basic patterns of interactions. These patterns vary in the degree that the relationship is dominated by one of the partners or by the degree of equality between the partners. Partnerships may be

- dominated by the professional;
- dominated by the family;
- a battle between families and professionals for control;
- shared control and decision-making; or
- neither the family nor the professional asserts control.

Research indicates that the optimal pattern of interactions develops when families and professionals share the control and decision-making:

> As families and professionals meet and begin to form relationships based on the assumptions that they bring to their interactions, they form the reality of their present circumstances and the possibilities for their future interactions. This joint construction of the activity setting begins to define the relationship over time. The activity setting is most likely to produce optimal family well-being when the family and the service providers are able to forge a partnership that is based on mutual respect, an understanding of each other's strengths and a gradual emergent sense of a common purpose. (Roberts, Rule, & Innocenti, 1998, p. 25)

Quality in early childhood education programs has also been strongly linked to partnerships with families (Dechillo, Koren, & Schultze, 1994; Canadian Childcare Federation, 1991; Friendly, 1994; Roberts et al., 1998).

In order to build partnerships with families, the facilitator sets the tone for positive interaction patterns. Interactions that are built on mutual respect, trust, and cooperation require that facilitators

- become knowledgeable about the families of the children they serve;
- develop a system of clear, open communication with all families;
- engage in **active listening** (listening to the content and feelings expressed without bias or prejudice);
- show empathy and understanding towards families;
- avoid any labelling or blaming;
- be accessible to respond to parents' inquiries or suggestions; and
- be honest and trustworthy in all interactions with families.

active listening
Listening to the content and feelings expressed without bias or prejudice.

The facilitator must also take on a leadership role to ensure that the interactions with families become meaningful and involve meaningful activities for all participants. Some of these activities are listed in Table 3.1.

TABLE 3.1

Meaningful Partnership Activities

Activities	Suggestions
Setting of mutual goals	• Include goals families have on application form. Review all goals, pick out common ones, and combine with centre goals.
	• Post all goals on bulletin board with room for response.
	• Send home a paper copy for review and comment.
	• Discuss with families individually when families come to centre.
	• Post and distribute final copy when agreed upon.
	• Have a goal-setting meeting.
Shared planning	• Identify ministry requirements for planning. Post and send home for review.
	• Establish a routine for sharing planning information
	– committee of interested families to help with planning process,
	– newsletter of planned ideas with feedback request, and
	– bulletin board that staff and families can record on
Shared decision-making	• Invite board participation of families.
	• Inform families of decisions that need to be made and invite input.
	• Set up a collaborative system that encourages input, discussion, and decision-making.
	• Ensure that decisions are reached with full consensus of all partners.
Mutual contributions	• Share information both ways regularly—sharing boards, books, and charts.
	• Brainstorm and post possible contributions all partners can make.
	• Develop possible roles for all participants.
	• Agree upon roles for all participants.
	• Respect roles once assigned.
	• Respect contributions by all partners.
	• Recognize families as key resources.

Another important function of a partnership is to share information individually with families about their child. The early childhood educator will be more effective in guiding the child if he or she knows how the child has fared at home. Did the child have a good night's sleep? Did anything happen that should be reported? How is the child feeling today? Similarly, the families will want to know how their child's day has been. This can be shared in writing on daily charts and individual sharing books, and should also be discussed verbally. This time can become a personal time between the facilitator and family member to share information about the child's development, day, learning, and exciting experiences. In this way, the task of caring for the child is shared and nurtured.

ROLE OF THE FACILITATOR WITH CHILDREN

Web exercises

Facilitating learning of children can be very difficult. It is much easier to direct learning than it is to guide learning. There is a comfort level in knowing what you think you have taught a group of children or an individual child. You know what you have told them, you can see what they have done, and you can quickly identify who understood and who didn't by the children's interactions. What you cannot tell is what has actually been learned. Sometimes the learning is not what was anticipated, nor may it be what was wanted.

In a directed learning situation the following might happen. Tessa was painting at the easel. She had painted curved lines of various colours in the corner of her paper. The early childhood educator, Maryann, observed her efforts and said, "Tessa

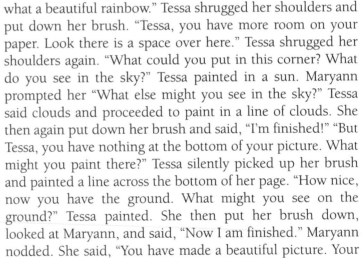

what a beautiful rainbow." Tessa shrugged her shoulders and put down her brush. "Tessa, you have more room on your paper. Look there is a space over here." Tessa shrugged her shoulders again. "What could you put in this corner? What do you see in the sky?" Tessa painted in a sun. Maryann prompted her "What else might you see in the sky?" Tessa said clouds and proceeded to paint in a line of clouds. She then again put down her brush and said, "I'm finished!" "But Tessa, you have nothing at the bottom of your picture. What might you paint there?" Tessa silently picked up her brush and painted a line across the bottom of her page. "How nice, now you have the ground. What might you see on the ground?" Tessa painted. She then put her brush down, looked at Maryann, and said, "Now I am finished." Maryann nodded. She said, "You have made a beautiful picture. Your mother will be very pleased" (photo 3.3). Later in the morning, Tessa took her painting off the drying rack, crumpled it up, and threw it in the garbage. When her mother arrived, Maryann told her about the "beautiful" picture Tessa had painted. When they couldn't find the picture, they asked Tessa if she knew where it was. She said that she had thrown it in the garbage. Her mother asked her why she would do a thing like that. Tessa just shrugged her shoulders. For the next few days, Tessa did not get to the painting easel again, even when she was asked.

What had Tessa learned through this experience? She learned that

- painting was not a pleasant experience;
- her efforts were not appreciated;
- she needed to listen and do as she was told;

- her creativity was not valued;
- self-expression was not important; and
- painting was an activity to avoid.

Tessa had a very negative learning experience. She was deprived of the opportunity to explore and create without direction. Maryann did not realize the value of the activity. She interpreted Tessa's behaviour from an adult perspective and proceeded to enhance this activity. She did not take into account that sometimes children paint for the sheer joy of painting, without creation of an end product. Children also need to explore the use of space—where to place things, what fits into a particular space, and how much of a space to fill. These are all important skills that will later help develop writing and reading skills.

Photo 3.4

In contrast, Jessica, Christine, and Alicia decided that they wanted to paint. They wanted to paint a picture together. They asked for a big piece of paper. Michael encouraged the children to measure the length they wanted. The children rolled out the paper until it reached the desired length. Christine cut off the paper from the roll. The children discussed what they might want to create. It was finally decided that they would paint an underwater scene. Jessica went to the book corner and retrieved books that had underwater scenes in them (photo 3.4). Christine and Alicia gathered the materials. Christine carefully poured the colours of choice into a paint tray. Alicia got the brushes out. As the children worked, they discussed what they were doing. Michael became an active partner in the discussion. At one point, Alicia could not decide what to paint. She asked Michael to read a book that she had found about life in the sea. One of the scenes had pictures of dolphins. She decided to paint a dolphin. Jessica was busily painting the lava from an underwater volcano. She told Michael that it looked like hot jam. Michael responded that he didn't want to taste it—it looked too hot and was probably salty.

Jessica decided to get more books. She found the book about the rainbow fish. She said, "The scales are very shiny, this fish is beautiful." Michael responded that he thought that the scales were iridescent. Christine asked what that meant. Jessica said she thought it meant shiny. Alicia decided to make her mermaid "iridescent." She asked Michael how she could do that. Michael asked her to look to see if she could find something. She went to the shelves and came back with glitter. "This will work," she said. Michael asked her how she could make them stick. She thought that the paint was still wet so that they would stick. She also said, "We can lift the paper after to see if all the glitter is attached to test it. We might need some glue too."

Photo 3.5

Christine added glitter to her water and shapes (photo 3.5). Her glitter did not stick. She decided to try a glue stick. All the glitter stuck to her glue stick. Michael asked her how she might get it off. She looked into the box and found a stick. She scraped off the glue with the little stick. Alicia watched and indicated that she thought that the stick would be a key for her treasure chest. She asked Christine if she could have it. Christine agreed, and Alicia stuck it onto her treasure chest.

Photo 3.6

Alicia wanted to add scales to her fish. She found some small pieces of green bark to stick on. She also decided to add seashells to the bottom of the sea (photo 3.6). She lifted the paper to see if they stuck and was pleased to note that they did. After this, she decided that she was done. The other two girls agreed. Michael reminded the girls that they should clean up. Christine and Alicia cleaned up the paint tray. As they were cleaning, they discovered that they could change the colours of the paint every time they dipped their brush into a new colour. They stopped cleaning and mixed the colours. Alicia asked Michael to come to see the new colour that they had created, "a mauvey green."

The mural was left to dry, then placed on the wall. The girls came back to the mural over time to finish it.

What did Alicia, Christine, and Jessica learn through this experience? They learned that

- their efforts were appreciated and valued;
- their creativity was valued;
- they could control what they wanted to;
- they could work together to create a mural;
- self-expression was important;
- each person in the group could set her own pace;
- each person did not need to do the same thing; and
- painting and creating is an enjoyable experience.

The difference between the two early childhood educators is that one valued the end product, whereas the other valued the process. It is during the time that children are actively engaged in activity that most of the learning takes place. They gain in all areas. Tessa learned how to follow someone else's instructions, whereas the other three girls were able to interact together to plan and execute their plans. How Tessa used her materials was controlled by someone else. Alicia, Jessica, and Christine controlled their own choices and their own actions. Maryann controlled the situation and Tessa's actions, whereas Michael encouraged the children to control their own situation and actions. Tessa destroyed her work and avoided painting for a while. Alicia, Christine, and Jessica continued to work on their creation over time. These girls had a very positive, broad learning experience. Tessa's learning experience was limited. She did not enjoy the experience.

What is the facilitator's role? According to Crowther (2003), the facilitator sets the stage to encourage learning. Setting the stage requires the facilitator to do the following:

- *Organize the environment and routines to encourage active learning.* Michael had materials available to allow the children to make choices and he organized adequate space to encourage a small group activity.
- *Establish a climate for positive social interactions.* The children were comfortable interacting with each other and Michael. Michael listened to the children and responded appropriately.
- *Encourage children's intentional actions, problem solving, and verbal reflection.* Michael encouraged the children to complete the activity in their own way. They could choose the materials they wanted and could reflect their own ideas in their artwork. He encouraged active problem solving—to measure and cut the paper and apply glitter in various ways. He responded to their thought—Jessica remarked on the shiny scales. Michael offered a new word—*iridescent*. Jessica thought that the

red in her painting was like hot jam. Michael responded to her by indicating that he did not want to eat this jam and why.

- *Plan experiences that build on the child's action and experiences* (Hohmann & Weikart, 1997). Michael had set up the learning environment with appropriate materials based on his knowledge of what this group of children was interested in and what skills they had.

Another characteristic of a facilitator, positive child–adult interactions, was identified in a Canadian study on quality aspects in child-care (Doherty-Derkowski, 1995). Positive child–adult interactions include that the facilitator do the following:

- *Set up the learning experiences in the environment based on his or her observations of the children and their abilities, needs, and background experiences.* Michael had observed previously that Jessica, Christine, and Alicia liked to work together and liked to work in the creative area. He set up the learning area to reflect this interest. He also knew that Jessica liked to look at books. This encouraged her to look in the animal section of the book centre to find the books that she was interested in.
- *Use positive interactions with children.* Michael showed his interest in what the children were doing by offering comments and suggestions as needed and by prompting the children as appropriate (e.g., his reminder to clean up the area).
- *Engage in verbal interactions.* Michael expanded the children's vocabulary by offering new words. He also encouraged Jessica's sense of humour by responding to her comparison of the red painted area to jam.
- *Respond to children appropriately.* Michael continually interacted with the children. He offered suggestions only when needed. He became part of the play when he was invited by a comment. He helped when he was asked to help.
- *Set up a rich learning experience.* Michael provided books, a variety of different-sized brushes, different colours of paint, different types of glue, a variety of different types of scissors, and a variety of decorative materials such as shells, coloured bark, sticks, glitter, and ribbons.
- *Provide an atmosphere of mutual respect and support.* Jessica felt free to leave the activity to find books that could be used. All children asked for help. Michael did not interfere with the activity. He supported it by his comments and facial expressions.

How does the facilitator know when to step in to support the children's play or when to leave the play of the children alone? This is a critical skill. When an adult steps in to interact in the play of children, it should always be to support the children's play, never to direct the children's play. A facilitator needs to have trust in the children's ability to direct their activities and their learning (Hohmann & Weikart, 1997; Malaguzzi, 1997). Following are some guidelines to help the facilitator understand when the play of children should not be interfered with and when it is important to step in (Crowther, 2003). A facilitator should leave play uninterrupted when

- children are gainfully employed;
- children are interacting with each other and the materials and equipment provided;
- children are solving their own problems;
- play extends over a longer period of time; and
- materials and equipment are being used appropriately.

The facilitator should always step in before the play becomes

- harmful either to the child or to the other children; or
- destructive of the materials or equipment.

The facilitator should always interact positively with the children when

- help is asked for, or when he or she notices that help is needed;
- arguments erupt among children;
- the noise level starts to escalate;
- children exhibit signs of stress, such as raised voices, tense body language, withdrawal, or tears;
- children interfere with each other's activity; and
- children seem to flit from one activity to the next.

In summary, a facilitator places trust in the learners to construct their own learning and their own experiences: "In effect, the teacher is removed from the centre stage, and many of the functions of the teacher are taken up by the group members. However, the teachers are not less involved or less accountable for the children's learning" (Gestwicki, 1999, p. 280).

Web exercises

ROLE OF THE FACILITATOR AS A LEARNER

Alexandria's parents owned a gardening business. She often went to the sandbox to create her own garden using the dried and fabric flowers available (photo 3.7). A student early childhood educator, Jenny, was watching her create her garden. Alexandria asked her what kind of flower she was planting. Jenny replied that it was a purple flower. Alexandria promptly picked up another flower and asked her what kind of flower this was. This time Jenny replied that it was a pretty yellow flower. This dialogue was repeated two more times. Each time Jenny responded by identifying another colour of flower. Finally, Alexandria put her hands on her hips and said, "Don't you know any other word than flower? I KNOW the colours of the flowers."

The next day Jenny was more prepared. She had brought in some flower books that had pictures of the various flowers in them. When Alexandria arrived, she again went to the sand area and started to create her garden. Jenny watched her. As Alexandria placed flowers in the sand, Jenny looked in her book, identified the flower, and said, "You are planting a daffodil." Alexandria listened. She brought over a flower to Jenny and the two both identified what flower it was before Alexandria planted it. At the end, Alexandria pointed to her flowers and named each one. When she could not name one, she asked Jenny to name it. When Jenny could not name it she said, "I don't remember the name, let's look it up."

Photo 3.7

This is an obvious example of learning together. It is impossible to know all the answers to children's questions. It is, however, important to be able to find the answers. Jenny had planned an excellent experience for Alexandria. She carefully noted Alexandria's interest and took into account her background experiences. She provided the materials that captivated Alexandria's attention. She failed to realize that Alexandria would be curious to know and learn the names of the various flowers that had been collected. Jenny quickly learned that she needed to be better prepared. She also recognized that she could learn alongside Alexandria. They could both look up the names of flowers together.

Adults continually learn from the children they teach. Learning comes from observing the children. Observing children as they interact and are engaged in various activities gives the early childhood educator critical knowledge about aspects of child development. This knowledge includes

- what skills the children have;
- what milestones have been reached;
- what developmental level the children have attained;
- the capabilities of the child in various domains (cognitive, language, social, emotional, and physical); and
- what aptitudes have emerged.

Observing children also gives the early childhood educator valuable information on what experiences and materials to provide. Information from these types of observations includes

- knowledge about the child's interests;
- details about background experiences the child brings to the setting;
- understanding about the personality of the child, such as the shy or outgoing child; and
- knowledge about the child's routines—washroom, sleeping, eating, and so on.

Adults also learn by interacting with children and their families. These interactions may be verbal or may be documented in photographs or written formats such as forms or questionnaires that families fill in. The early childhood educator learns about

- the values that families hold;
- the cultural differences that need to be respected;
- different types of lifestyles and belief systems; and
- expertise of families (e.g., families may bring experiences to draw upon such as music, cultural, meal preparation, woodworking, biology, artistic talents, etc.).

The role of the facilitator as a learner implies that the adult no longer looks upon himself or herself as the expert in all areas. It means that he or she can learn from the children, from families, and from other professionals. It means that learning is shared among all partners. This not only acknowledges and nurtures all partners, but also opens up innovative new directions and understandings about each other, about who we are, and about what we are doing and learning: "Working together, guiding the children in their projects, teachers and I have repeatedly found our selves face to face—as if looking in the mirror—learning from one another, and learning from the children. This way we were trying to create paths to a new educational approach, not tried before" (Malaguzzi, 1997, p. 141).

ROLE OF THE FACILITATOR IN OBSERVING, PLANNING, AND IMPLEMENTING

All planning should start with the observation of the children. When the facilitator observes the children carefully, he or she gains information about the children to help plan appropriate learning activities. According to Gestwicki (1999, pp. 61–62), planning an overall child-care program requires the following skills:

1. Flexibility in planning—developing forms that document emergent interests of children (see Figure 3.1).
2. Observing children—listening, answering questions, documenting observations using several methods (such as taping or recording information), and reflecting on what they have seen, heard, and documented.

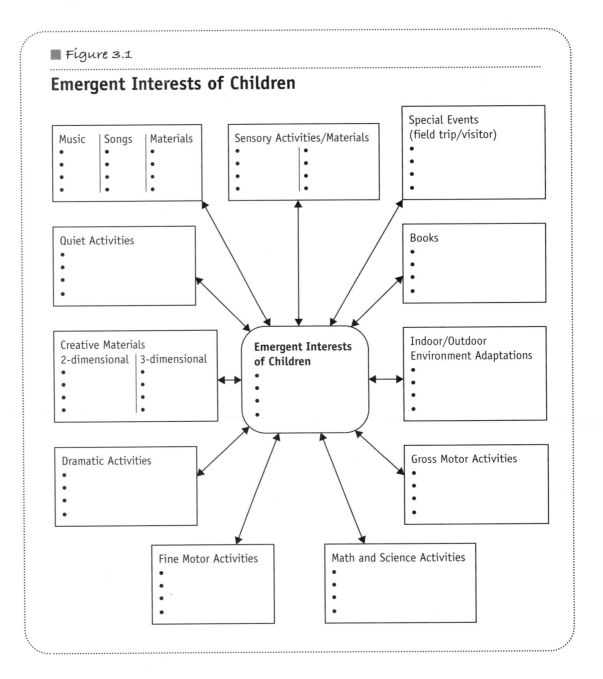

■ Figure 3.1

Emergent Interests of Children

3. Planning around what is actually happening in children's lives—for example, important events such as a new sibling.
4. Observing and interacting with children to identify how materials are used, what skills are used, and how to enhance or enrich the area.
5. Observing to identify the developmental tasks that are being used by children—documenting the development in various domains (e.g., cognitive, physical, emotional, social, and language) to ensure that all areas are developed.
6. Observing children's interests and expanding the curriculum around these interests.
7. Brainstorming and collaborating with all partners—other staff, children, and families.

Planning is a never-ending spiral—it's continually emerging and changing (see Figure 3.2). This leads to the development of an **emergent curriculum**—a curriculum that is sensitive and responsive to all children. The following example gives a practical overview of how such a planning process might emerge.

emergent curriculum
A curriculum that is sensitive and responsive to all children.

Web exercises

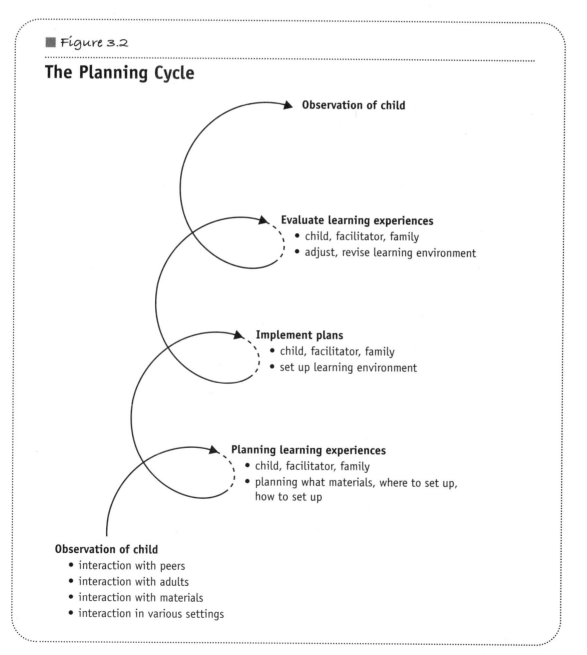

■ Figure 3.2

The Planning Cycle

Observation of child

Evaluate learning experiences
• child, facilitator, family
• adjust, revise learning environment

Implement plans
• child, facilitator, family
• set up learning environment

Planning learning experiences
• child, facilitator, family
• planning what materials, where to set up, how to set up

Observation of child
• interaction with peers
• interaction with adults
• interaction with materials
• interaction in various settings

Autumn came from a family background that highly valued creative activities. Much of this creative activity involved using beads. There were many beads in the learning environment that children could use. Autumn liked to create "necklaces," but expressed a wish to take the necklaces home. Rachel talked to Autumn and asked her what would happen if Autumn took her necklaces home:

Autumn:	There wouldn't be no more beads.
Rachel:	Yes, we would soon run out of beads to use. What do you think we could do about this?
Autumn:	Buy more.
Rachel:	If we spend all our money on beads, we couldn't buy some of the other things.
Autumn:	Maybe we could make some. My grandmother could help.

Rachel and Autumn then discussed how they could make beads. Autumn thought that maybe she could make them out of play dough. Autumn made her own salt dough with the guidance of Rachel. She formed some of the beads and then discovered that she needed an instrument to poke holes. She went to the shelf and

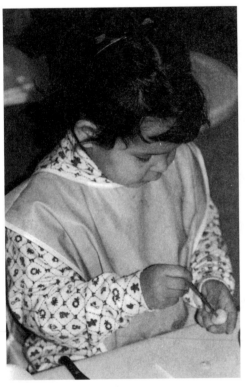

Photo 3.8

selected a large plastic straw. When Autumn's grandmother came to pick her up, Autumn excitedly indicated that she was making her own beads and that her grandmother could help. The two decided to take more dough home to make beads.

Rachel anticipated that this might become a popular activity. She had observed interest from several other children. She made sure that she had enough ingredients and enough bowls to encourage children to make their own dough. She also checked to make sure that the oven could be used to dry the beads the next day. She tried to make her own beads in order to anticipate some of the problems. She noticed that air-drying was not as good as drying in the oven at a low temperature. She also noticed that the straw no longer fit into the hole after the bead had dried. She found that stir sticks were sturdy and held the bead steadily. If the children wanted to paint the beads, this would make it easier.

When Autumn returned the next day, she proudly presented a bag of beads to Rachel: "My grandmother and I made them. We dried them in the oven, but it was too hot so now they are brown. Could I paint over the brown?" Rachel was pleased that she had anticipated the problem and had set out the materials that might be needed.

Autumn soon found the appropriate materials to use and started to paint her beads (photo 3.8). She was joined by other children who wanted to make their own beads, or who wanted to simply paint beads. Again Rachel was thrilled that she had prepared some beads ahead of time for this activity. This activity lasted for several days. Once the children had painted their beads, they strung them into necklaces and bracelets to wear home. Autumn wore her necklace for many days.

One of the parents noticed the activity. She indicated that she had a kiln and wouldn't mind expanding the children's activity to use clay to create beads. Rachel and the parent discussed how they would do this. They decided to create a working corner in the room for her, so that the children could observe her work. The children became very enthusiastic about the activity. The beading activity lasted for many weeks. The children became very skilled at creating various types of jewellery. The activity soon also expanded to creating animals of various types. Christopher, a four-year-old, created a rabbit that could also be a dinosaur (photos 3.9 and 3.10).

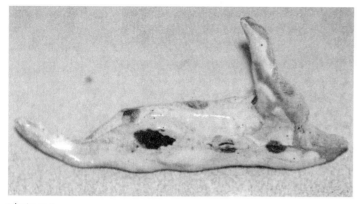

Photo 3.9

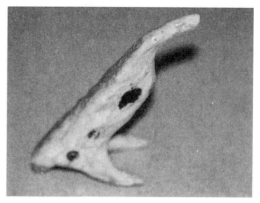

Photo 3.10

Some of the school-aged children who had siblings in the program expressed a desire to participate. As with the younger children, the school-aged children created jewellery (photo 3.11) and animals (photo 3.12).

How was this activity planned and implemented? The planning was done in several steps:

Step 1: Observation—Rachel observed Autumn's interest in creating beads that she could take home.

Step 2: Brainstorming—Autumn and Rachel created a chart of what was needed. Autumn dictated a list of items that she needed. The initial list included salt, water, bowl, spoon, flour, and a recipe. This step was revisited several times and items were continually added—straws, paint, brushes, plates, markers, stir sticks, oven, drying rack, clay, rolling pins, knives, modelling tools, flat boards, kiln, and glaze.

Step 3: Collecting the materials, posting a sign to encourage family help and input, and posting a sign that included the recipe.

Step 4: Setting up the space—organizing the materials with labels, pictures, and words. This step was revisited many times during the project. The space had to be increased, and new materials were added as needed.

Step 5: Creating a **documentation board** of the children's activities—photographs and descriptions of the work in progress that continued to grow over time (see Figure 3.3).

Step 6: Creating the parent corner.

documentation board
Photographs, drawings, and written descriptions of the children's activities that are mounted and displayed in a central location that all partners can view.

Photo 3.11

Photo 3.12

Documentation Panel

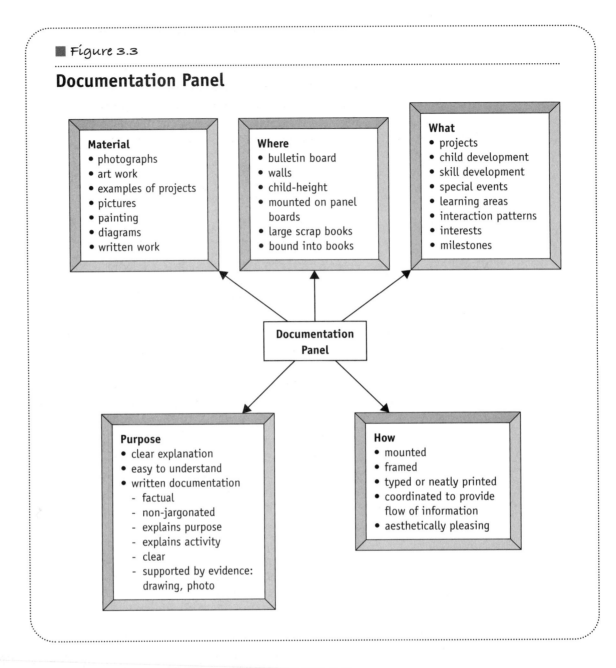

Material
- photographs
- art work
- examples of projects
- pictures
- painting
- diagrams
- written work

Where
- bulletin board
- walls
- child-height
- mounted on panel boards
- large scrap books
- bound into books

What
- projects
- child development
- skill development
- special events
- learning areas
- interaction patterns
- interests
- milestones

Documentation Panel

Purpose
- clear explanation
- easy to understand
- written documentation
  - factual
  - non-jargonated
  - explains purpose
  - explains activity
  - clear
  - supported by evidence: drawing, photo

How
- mounted
- framed
- typed or neatly printed
- coordinated to provide flow of information
- aesthetically pleasing

In summary, this planning and implementation process involved all of the children and included all of the partners in varying degrees. It emerged from the interest of one child and quickly expanded to include the varying interests of other children. It was dynamic and changed as the needs and interests of the children changed.

Web exercises

ROLE OF THE FACILITATOR IN THE ENVIRONMENT

The primary role of the facilitator in the environment is to organize the learning materials and learning spaces in order to maximize the learning and independence of all individuals within that setting. These settings should be represented both indoors and outdoors. Most early childhood settings organize the learning environments into core curricular areas. These include

- *creative art activities*—painting, drawing, sculpting, cut and paste, decorating, working with mixtures, working on projects that are three dimensional or two dimensional;
- *quiet activities*—place to be alone, puzzles, book corner, writing corner, computer, concentration activities;
- *science and math activities*—measuring, counting, comparing, matching, sorting, experimenting, predicting;
- *sensory activities*—sand, water, finger painting;
- *music and movement activities*—singing, dancing, playing instruments, listening, moving;
- *fine motor activities*—stringing, building, fitting things together or taking them apart;
- *gross motor activities*—climbing, balancing, swinging, sliding, riding, running, walking, crawling, hopping, turning;
- *constructing activities*—using large and small blocks, sand, Lego, Duplo, wood; and
- *role-playing activities*—drama, using accessory materials in other areas to encourage role-play.

Often these core areas are arranged into **learning areas** or **interest centres**—areas that are arranged for a common purpose such as building with blocks: "Thus, adults organize play space into specific interest areas to support preschool children's abiding interest in such activities as sand and water play, building, pretending and role play, drawing and painting, 'reading' and 'writing,' counting, sorting, climbing, singing, and dancing" (Hohmann & Weikert, 1997, p. 7).

learning areas or interest centres
Areas that are arranged for a common purpose such as building with blocks.

Storage of materials becomes a critical factor. In order for children to be independent, they must be able to find and return materials. Storage needs to be arranged so that materials are accessible both visually and physically. Dress up clothes in a box are accessible neither visually (children cannot see what is inside the box) nor physically (they cannot readily find what they want without dumping). "Adults arrange storage of materials using low shelves, clear boxes, and picture labels children can 'read' so all children can independently find, use, and return the items they need" (Hohmann & Weikert, 1997, p. 7) (photo 3.13).

The facilitator must also ensure that the learning spaces are set up in such a way as to encourage active participation by the children. In such an environment children are encouraged to do the following:

- *Solve problems.* Christine (see photo 3.5 on page 63) solved the problem of how to make the glitter stick to her creation.
- *Make choices and decisions.* Christine, Jessica, and Alicia could decide what project they wanted to be engaged in, what materials they wished to use, and how long they wanted to continue this activity.
- *Interact in small or large groups.* The environment was flexible enough to encourage Autumn (see photo 3.8 on page 70) to work by herself or in a larger group as the interest of the beading activity attracted other children.
- *Practise these skills in both indoor and outdoor environments daily* (photo 3.14).

Photo 3.13

Photo 3.14

Another important task for the facilitator is to ensure that all learning spaces both indoors and outdoors are checked continually to make sure that children are safe from physical harm. To provide safe learning spaces in both indoor and outdoor spaces, the following should be part of daily routines:

- cleaning floors and other surfaces as needed—sweep floors, keep riding paths clear of stones or other obstructions, and wipe down table tops;
- disinfecting washroom areas as needed and as a daily routine—toilets, sinks, taps, and floors;
- disinfecting the diapering area after every diaper change;
- disinfecting toys that have been mouthed or sneezed on or are simply dirty;
- scanning the learning areas to remove materials that are not safe—broken pieces, furniture/equipment that is not stable, hidden objects in sand; and
- establishing healthy routines for children—personal-care routines such as washing hands.

The facilitator needs to observe carefully to identify how learning areas and materials are being used. When children use the same materials over time, they become bored and may either stop using these materials or may start to use them inappropriately. The facilitator should reflect and act on the following questions:

- Are the materials being used appropriately?
- Are all learning areas used effectively?
- Are activities extended over more than one day?
- Are the children enjoying the learning activities?
- Is there a balance between individual and small-group activities?
- Are children able to solve their own problems?
- Are enough choices available to meet the needs of all children?
- Are social interactions appropriate?

The learning activities should remain flexible so that changes and/or adaptations can be made as needed based on the reflections of the facilitator. Additional materials should be available to rotate materials to maintain interest.

Facilitators need to create culturally responsive and inclusive environments: "Many teachers are faced with limited understanding of cultures other than their own and the possibility that this limitation will negatively affect their students' ability to become successful learners" (Montgomery, 2001, p. 78). Montgomery further identifies that teachers working with children must reflect and assess themselves in order to accommodate the growing diversity in individual settings. Self-assessment that leads to greater diversity awareness includes

- knowledge of the types of diversity represented in the setting;
- awareness of personal feelings/assumptions about various groups;
- researching personally to become more aware of cultural diversity; and
- providing appropriate displays, materials, and equipment to represent diversity within the setting.

All environments need to display children's work appropriately. Children should be involved in the process. It is up to the facilitator to initiate and model appropriate ways of displaying children's work. Aesthetically pleasing displays not only build feelings of pride in accomplishments, but also model various other aspects. When displays are pleasing, individuals are motivated to stop and look. This is one way to share the joy of the children's creation with their families. These displays give important information about the children's activities, skills, abilities, and interests. Children learn to appreciate different aesthetic values, especially if they become involved in setting up these displays.

In conclusion, there is mounting evidence from the research that the role of the facilitator in the environment is critical. Much of this research arises from recent brain research and supports philosophical viewpoints of many earlier theorists such as Vygotsky, Dewey, and Piaget.

> How space is organized and used influences how comfortable children feel and how they work, contributing to a challenging and satisfactory learning environment. Because children's activity patterns change as they gain new skills and mature, and because spatial organization influences other behaviours, the physical facilities must be flexible enough to change to accommodate the children. Similarly, the arrangement of learning materials determines their level and use. How well materials are arranged also affects the ideas and connections children can make with the materials. (Moyer, 2001, p. 103)

ROLE OF THE FACILITATOR AS A LEADER

Web exercises

According to the *Family Word Finder* (Flexner, 1986), a leader can be described by the following words: forerunner, pacesetter, pioneer, guide, pathfinder, and trailblazer. Each of these words describes particular characteristics that a facilitator has and uses:

- *Forerunner*. Early childhood educators by their training have gained knowledge and skills that make them leaders in the field of early childhood education. When one views the exhibit of the *One Hundred Languages of Children* (Malaguzzi, 1997), one is in awe of the artwork that young children can and do produce. Invariably, when this art show travels across the country for public viewing, a broadening of awareness occurs about children and their capabilities.
- *Pacesetter*. Within the early childhood environment, the facilitator must manage a schedule that includes all the components of a child's day—routines such as sleeping, eating, and toileting, and organizing learning activities for varying-sized groups of children that maximize each child's potential.
- *Pioneer*. At times the facilitator will meet roadblocks that seemingly prevent appropriate learning experiences. Many programs still teach young children through large group instruction for much of the day. The early childhood educator must take the lead in showing that alternative ways not only work, but also are better ways of learning for young children with far more positive results.
- *Guide*. The facilitator continually guides children in their learning. Rachel guided the process of "bead-making" with her group of children.
- *Pathfinder*. It is sometimes very discouraging to work in settings that are unable to afford all the materials and equipment that young children should have. When Nancy worked for a daycare that had limited funds, she organized a group of family and community members to find free donations in the community. The group was able to collect a variety of free resources within their neighbourhood,

such as the ends of newsprint rolls from the local newspaper; material scraps, odd buttons, and leftover yarn from a craft store; and shoe boxes from a shoe store, which were turned into building blocks. As the community grew aware of the problem, donations continually increased. Eventually, the centre became very well equipped with the help of the community.

- *Trailblazer.* Sometimes the facilitator is faced with a situation that requires changes within the daycare setting. Many jurisdictions in Canada demand that daycare must be *inclusive.* When some daycare centres received the news that they must accept all children—including children with special needs—within their daycare, there was some concern. Did the staff have the training needed to accept all children? Were the materials and environment suitable for all ability levels? Would the children and families accept these children? Many of these centres found not only that their fears were unwarranted, but also that their programs became much richer and fuller. With their example, other staff could visit, discuss, and share experiences in order to help them make the transition to an inclusive setting much easier and more effective.

In summary, the facilitator of an early childhood program is often the central focus to ensure that the children under his or her care receive the best possible program within the structure of that community. The facilitator must coordinate all the individual pieces—the families, children, community, and learning environment (see Figure 3.4).

ROLE OF THE FACILITATOR IN THE COMMUNITY

There are many ways that the facilitator establishes a role within the child-care community. Some of these roles may be very formal, such as a presentation to a municipal office, or very informal, such as information boards at the daycare centre. All of these roles play a significant part in how the early childhood field is viewed by the outside community. The facilitator is in a central position to become an advocate for the children entrusted to his or her care. Some of the roles that a facilitator holds are as follows.

1. *Expert on children's development.* The initial training that early childhood educators receive gives them a good start to building expertise in the field of early childhood education. A facilitator continues to learn (as previously discussed) with the children, families, and other professionals. The expertise of the facilitator is evident in

   - the materials and equipment found in the environment;
   - the daily and weekly routines of the children;
   - the organization of the environment;
   - the interactions established with the children and families;
   - the atmosphere of the learning environment;
   - the empathy and understanding of the facilitator; and
   - the communication system established with all partners.

2. *Expert within the community.* The facilitator is often in a position that encourages information sharing about new initiatives, innovative or new research, changing ministry guidelines, innovative approaches, and common requests for information from various sources. There are a variety of ways information may be shared, including

- parent workshops—on site or at local facilities, libraries, recreational programs, continuing education programs;
- information boards—on site, in stores, within public facilities (libraries, town hall, schools);
- displays—on site, in stores, or within public facilities (libraries, town hall, schools);
- documentation boards—within learning spaces, as part of a conference or workshop session, or on site;
- conference presentations—local or regional;
- articles in journals (e.g., *Canadian Children* and *Interaction* from the Canadian Child Care Federation), newspapers, and provincial and territorial association publications;
- newsletters—sent home monthly or bimonthly; and
- pamphlets—at medical offices.

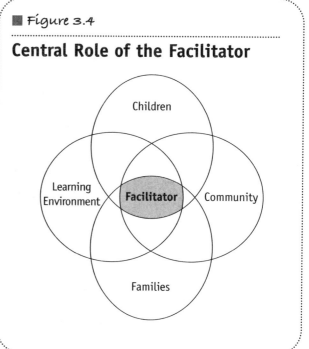

■ **Figure 3.4**

Central Role of the Facilitator

3. *Advocate.* At times political action—locally, provincially, or nationally—may be warranted. An example of a local political action was in Trenton, Ontario. The municipal government had decided to cut the number of subsidized spaces. The early childhood community put together a presentation that clearly showed that cutting spaces was not a viable option. Subsidized spaces were ultimately not cut.

   Sometimes it is important to raise the political awareness of child-care issues. Issues such as quality aspects in early care are often addressed through articles in newspapers or magazines. *Maclean's* magazine will accept articles on current children's issues. In the past, articles on children and television, public education concerns, and home schooling have been published. Interviews with early childhood educators are often published in local and national newspapers.

   Advocacy can also be very effective when an early childhood educator serves as a representative on a local board. Often there is a need for the expertise of such educators on boards involving speech and language pathology, community development, and sports and recreation.

4. *Fundraiser.* Often funding is required for special events, trips, equipment, and materials. The facilitator needs not only to have knowledge of effective fundraising activities, but also be able to delegate some of the tasks involved to others.

5. *Counsellor.* The facilitator is often asked to advise families on issues such as how and where to find resources for their child, how to find alternative ways of interacting with their child, how to decide what types of toys to buy, how to determine if their child is at the appropriate developmental level, and how to guide their child's behaviour. The facilitator must listen carefully in order to advise in an appropriate manner. The facilitator must also recognize when he or she does not have the expert knowledge required and needs to refer the family to other experts in the community.

6. *Organizer of community functions.* Each community has a variety of events that can help to raise public awareness of the early childhood field. These may include events such as the March of Dimes, Festival of Trees, Community Awareness Week, garden shows, Week of the Family, and Week of the Child. When early

childhood educators help organize these events, they often facilitate an awareness of young children and their families through their professional interactions with the individuals involved in these events. At times this may also involve setting up appropriate play spaces for children, providing parents with opportunities to participate with their children in common events, or planning programs such as appropriate summer activities for children.

In summary, advocacy for the children and their families is an ongoing activity that not only attracts varying levels of expertise and commitment but also offers the early childhood educator many opportunities to interact and learn in partnership within a larger social setting.

KEY POINTS

WHAT IS A FACILITATOR?
- The facilitator sets the stage; observes and monitors; provides additional resources; and guides children's behaviour.

ROLE OF THE FACILITATOR IN ESTABLISHING PARTNERSHIPS WITH FAMILIES
- Develop partnerships with families—goal setting, planning, decision-making, and making contributions.
- Show sensitivity to the cultural values and beliefs of families.
- Develop a communication system built on mutual respect, trust, and cooperation.

ROLE OF THE FACILITATOR WITH CHILDREN
- Organize the environment and routines; encourage active learning; and establish a climate for positive social interactions.
- Set up rich learning spaces based on observations of children's abilities, needs, and background experiences.
- Respond to children sensitively and appropriately.

ROLE OF THE FACILITATOR AS A LEARNER
- Learn about children's skills, milestones, and capabilities.
- Learn about children's experiences.
- Learn about families.

ROLE OF THE FACILITATOR IN OBSERVING, PLANNING, AND IMPLEMENTING
- Required skills in planning, observing, and recording.
- Steps in planning with children.
- Review plans and observations to revise and adapt.

ROLE OF THE FACILITATOR IN THE ENVIRONMENT
- Organize the environment into core learning areas.
- Arrange core areas into interest or learning areas.
- Store materials to increase independence and to encourage active participation, problem solving, making choices and decisions, and interacting in small or large groups.

- Provide daily activity in all areas both indoors and outdoors.
- Provide safe, sanitary learning spaces and establish healthy personal-care routines.
- Evaluate the effectiveness of learning and learning areas.
- Create a learning environment that respects diversity.
- Research to gain greater understanding about aspects of the environment.
- Create appropriate display areas of children's work.

ROLE OF THE FACILITATOR AS A LEADER
- Forerunner—knowledge and skills to lead.
- Pacesetter—manage daily schedules and routines.
- Pioneer—advocate for appropriate activities for young children.
- Guide—learning and behaviour.
- Pathfinder—find alternative resources, activities, and methodologies.
- Trailblazer—lead the way to foster and encourage new directions and new knowledge.

ROLE OF THE FACILITATOR IN THE COMMUNITY
- Expert on children's development.
- Create ways to share expertise in the community.
- Advocate on behalf of children and families.
- Raise funds for special events.
- Counsel and advise parents.
- Help organize and attend community functions.

EXERCISES

1. Recall a teacher that you thought was a great teacher. Record some of the characteristics that made that teacher excellent. Compare your answer to the answers of your classmates. Develop a definition of a facilitator from the list. How is your definition similar to and different from the one in Chapter 3?

2. Describe three characteristics of a good facilitator that, in your opinion, are most important when working with young children. Compare your answers in a small group. Discuss the similarities and differences. Each member of the small group should explain their reasons for their choices. At the end of the discussion, identify how many people changed their minds and, if so, why.

3. In a small group, discuss the characteristics of a good partnership. Compare your answers to the ones found in Chapter 3.

4. In a small group, discuss how the facilitator might develop partnerships with families. Create a list of important points. For each point, discuss strategies that might be used to encourage partnership activities.

5. Create a chart that compares the difference between direct instruction and facilitated learning. For each point compared, discuss what effect that type of instruction has on an infant, toddler, preschooler, and school-aged child. Post the group chart. Compare the various charts. Discuss why facilitative teaching is a more effective practice to encourage the learning of young children.

6. Discuss how a facilitator sets the stage for learning using the following points:

   a) Organization of the environment.
   b) Establishing a climate for positive social interactions.

c) Encouraging children's independence.

d) Encouraging children to problem solve.

e) Planning activities that reflect children's experiences and backgrounds.

WWW

7. Using the format shown below, develop a chart to identify and describe the characteristics of positive child–adult interactions.

CHARACTERISTIC	DESCRIPTION OF INTERACTION	EXAMPLE

8. Identify why it is sometimes important to observe children's play without interruption and why it is sometimes important to interrupt the children's play. Identify the guidelines that will help you know when to step in and when to leave children's play uninterrupted.

9. In small groups discuss why it is important to interact with the families of the children. Identify the following:

a) benefit to the child;

b) benefit to the facilitator; and

c) importance to setting up learning experiences.

10. Using the scenario about Jessica, Christine, and Alicia (see photos 3.4, 3.5, and 3.6 on pages 63–64), discuss and fill in the information in the chart below. Identify how you might expand this activity over time to maintain interest. Use Figure 3.2 (page 69) to help you.

Development of a Planning Cycle

Category of Planning Cycle	Documentation/Description
Observations—What information do you have about Jessica, Christine, and Alicia?	
Planning—What additional materials would you need? How and where would you set up the activity? How would you display the children's efforts?	
What information might you share with the families and how?	
What information would you need to evaluate this learning experience?	

11. In small groups, pick one core learning area identified in this chapter. Visit a toy store and consult a child-care equipment catalogue such as Wintergreen. List appropriate materials that could be used for this learning area for infants, toddlers, preschoolers, and school-aged children. You might organize your information in a chart form, as shown below. Share and discuss the information with other classmates by posting the information around the classroom.

Materials and Equipment for .... Area

Age Group	Materials/Equipment
infants	
toddlers	
preschoolers	
school-aged children	

12. What do you need to consider in order to set up a learning area to encourage

   a) active participation?
   b) safety from physical harm?
   c) evaluation of the learning experiences?
   d) respect for diversity?
   e) pride in children's efforts?

13. Identify what leadership roles you might take with children, families, and within the early childhood community.

14. Identify one of the roles of the facilitator in the community as outlined in this chapter. In small group discussions, identify some strategies that could be used to establish and enhance the facilitator's role in the community.

REFERENCES

Barbour, C., & Barbour, N. (2001). *Families, Schools, and Communities: Building Partnerships for Educating Children*. Upper Saddle River, NJ: Merrill Prentice-Hall Inc.

Brazelton, T,. & Greenspan, S. (2000). Our Window to the Future. In K. Paciorek, J. Munro, and M. J. Paciorek (Eds.), *Annual Editions 2002/03*. Guilford, CT: McGraw-Hill/Dushkin.

Canadian Childcare Federation (1991). *National Statement on Quality Childcare*. Ottawa, ON: Health and Welfare Canada.

Crowther, I. (2003). *Creating Effective Learning Environments*. Scarborough, ON: Thomson Nelson.

Dechillo, N., Koren, P., & Schultze, K. (1994). From Paternalism to Partnership: Family and Professional Collaboration in Children's Mental Health. *American Journal of Orthopsychiatry 64*, 564–576.

Doherty-Derkowski, G. (1995). *Quality Matters: Excellence in Early Childhood Programs*. Don Mills, ON: Addison Wesley.

Flexner, S. (1986). *Family Word Finder*. Pleasantville, NY: Reader's Digest.

Friendly, M. (1994). *Childcare Policy in Canada: Putting the Pieces Together*. Don Mills, ON: Addison-Wesley.

Gestwicki, C. (1999). *Developmentally Appropriate Practice* (2nd ed.). Scarborough, ON: Nelson Canada.

Hohmann, M., & Weikart, D. (1997). *Educating Young Children*. Ypsilanti, MI: High/Scope Press.

Kostelnik, M., Solderman, A., & Whiren, A. (1999). *Developmentally Appropriate Curriculum: Best Practice in Early Childhood Education*. Upper Saddle River, NY: Prentice-Hall, Inc.

Malaguzzi, L. (1997). *The Hundred Languages of Children* (2nd ed.). Via Guido Da Castello, Italy: Reggio Children.

Montgomery, W. (2001). Creating Culturally Responsive, Inclusive Classrooms. In Karen Menke Paciorek & J. Huth Munro (Eds.), *Early Childhood Education* (2002/03 ed., pp. 78–83). Guilford, CN: McGraw-Hill/Dushkin.

Moyer, J. (2001). The Child-Centered Kindergarten—A Position Paper. In K. Paciorek & J. Huth Munro (Eds.), *Annual Editions* (2002/03 ed., pp. 101–105). Guilford, CN: McGraw-Hill/Dushkin.

Roberts, R., Rule, S., & Innocenti, M. (1998). *Strengthening the Family–Professional Partnership in Services for Young Children*. Baltimore, MD: Paul H. Brookes Publishing Co.

CRITICAL SKILLS
FOR FACILITATORS

"Child care practitioners work with one of society's most vulnerable groups—young children. The quality of the interactions between young children and the adults who work with them has a significant, enduring impact on children's lives. The intimacy of the relationship and the potential to do harm call for a commitment on the part of child care practitioners to the highest standards of ethical practice." (Doherty, 2003, p. 26)

Chapter Outcomes

After reading this chapter, the reader will

1. Describe an effective communication cycle.

2. Describe appropriate communication strategies with children.

3. Describe appropriate communication strategies with adults.

4. Discuss why observation skills are a critical component of working with young children.

5. List the characteristics of good observation skills.

6. List appropriate guidance techniques for infants, toddlers, preschoolers, and school-aged children.

7. Identify the importance of positive behaviour guidance techniques.

8. Identify the skills needed to build collaborative learning experiences.

9. Describe various types of advocacy activities.

10. Discuss strategies to develop advocacy skills.

11. Discuss the importance of understanding what the legislative requirements are in your area.

12. Explain how societal factors affect early childhood settings.

BUILDING EFFECTIVE COMMUNICATION SKILLS

Web exercises

1. Communicating Effectively with Children

Emily had been trying to put shapes into the correct slots in the shape sorter box. Hannah saw the activity and immediately went over to help. Emily responded by saying, "I am doing it. I can do it." Hannah continued putting pieces into the slots.

Photo 4.1

Emily started to frown. She reached over to grab the box (photo 4.1). Sarah had observed the interaction. She quickly retrieved another shape sorter box and took it over to Hannah before Emily pulled the box away. She sat down on the floor with the children and said, "I think Emily wants to do this by herself. Here is another box for you, Hannah. Now you each have a shape sorter." Emily looked up at her and smiled. Sarah returned the smile and continued to watch the two children for a while.

Sarah was communicating effectively with a great deal of sensitivity. She not only listened to the dialogue, but also observed Emily's body language. Without looking at Emily's body language the message might have been misunderstood. Emily might have been sharing her thoughts on the activity with Hannah. However, when you look at her facial expression and notice that she is ready to pull the box toward her, a different message is received. Sarah understood that toddlers are not likely to share. She quickly averted a problem by giving each child her own sorter box.

Communication is an interactive process that requires a message to be created by an individual (**encoded**), sent to another individual or individuals (verbally, physically, symbolically, or in writing), and understood by the receiver (**decoded**). Emily verbalized her feelings by trying to tell Hannah that she wanted to do it alone. This message alone was not understood. Hannah was too busily concentrating on her own activity to pay attention to Emily. She reinforced her message by her facial expression. This was also not understood by Hannah. She had not been watching Emily. Her final strategy was to take the box away (see Figure 4.1). It is easy to see that Emily had tried to communicate what she wanted. It is also easy to understand that she might have been getting frustrated.

Sarah, on the other hand, heard the message, saw the body language and action, processed the information, understood what had happened, and was able to react (see Figure 4.2). Sarah was able to complete the communication process satisfactorily. Sarah listened to the content of the message, observed Emily's body language, correctly interpreted the messages, and responded appropriately.

Many of the communication skills needed to communicate effectively were demonstrated by Sarah. Communication is a critical skill for a facilitator to develop. Appropriate communication skills are critical to children's future development. "Communication and language skills are critical to children's social, emotional, and cognitive well-being. Throughout the early childhood years, we encourage children to develop increasingly sophisticated language skills through social interactions, dramatic play, and age-appropriate activities" (Firlik, 2003, p. 76).

communication
An interactive process that requires a message to be created (encoded), sent to someone else (verbally, physically, symbolically, or in writing), and understood by the receiver (decoded). The receiver then may respond to the message to continue the process.

encoding
Creating a message (verbal, in writing, using body language, or in sign language) in order to start a communication interaction.

decoding
Making sense of or understanding a message that has been sent.

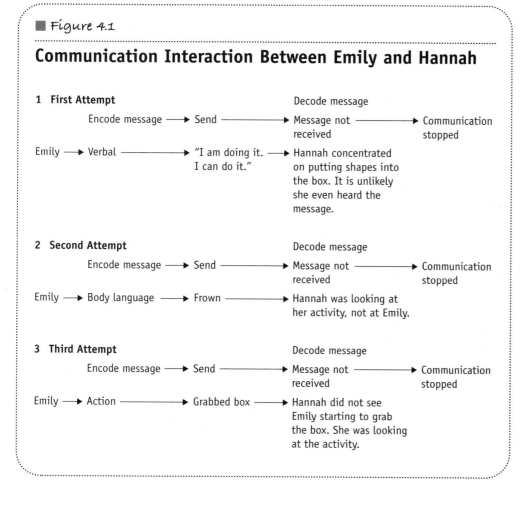

■ Figure 4.1

Communication Interaction Between Emily and Hannah

1 First Attempt

Encode message ——▶ Send ——————▶ Decode message
Message not ————▶ Communication
received   stopped

Emily ——▶ Verbal ————————▶ "I am doing it. ——▶ Hannah concentrated
I can do it."   on putting shapes into
the box. It is unlikely
she even heard the
message.

2 Second Attempt

Encode message ——▶ Send ——————▶ Decode message
Message not ————▶ Communication
received   stopped

Emily ——▶ Body language ——————▶ Frown ————————▶ Hannah was looking at
her activity, not at Emily.

3 Third Attempt

Encode message ——▶ Send ——————▶ Decode message
Message not ————▶ Communication
received   stopped

Emily ——▶ Action ————————▶ Grabbed box ——▶ Hannah did not see
Emily starting to grab
the box. She was looking
at the activity.

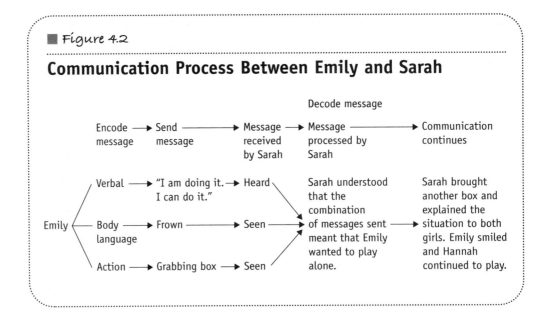

■ Figure 4.2

Communication Process Between Emily and Sarah

Decode message

Encode → Send → Message → Message → Communication
message   message   received   processed by   continues
                        by Sarah   Sarah

Verbal → "I am doing it. → Heard   Sarah understood   Sarah brought
            I can do it."   that the   another box and
                                      combination   explained the
Emily ← Body → Frown → Seen   of messages sent → situation to both
        language   meant that Emily   girls. Emily smiled
                                      wanted to play   and Hannah
Action → Grabbing box → Seen   alone.   continued to play.

Developing appropriate communication skills with children involves

- *Listening to children.* Sarah had listened to Emily's verbal message. However, she needed more information to be able to respond effectively.
- *Watching what children are doing.* Often it is necessary not only to listen to the verbal message, but also to look at the child's actions and behaviours. These will give a clue as to the meaning of the message. Sometimes what children say and do may not be the same. Sarah needed to listen and watch Emily and Hannah in order to respond appropriately.
- *Interpreting what has been seen and heard.* Sarah had to use her knowledge of child development in order to accurately interpret the message received. She knew that when young children are involved in an activity, they may be so intent on that activity that they do not hear what is going on around them. She also knew that toddlers are not yet ready to share.
  - *Clarifying the message.* Sarah listened and watched Emily and Hannah. She put into words what Emily had been trying to say.
  - *Responding to children verbally.* Sarah gave both children valuable information. She acknowledged Emily's feelings—to be alone. She also explained what was happening to both girls—they could both have a sorting box.
  - *Responding to children physically.* Sarah sat down with the children. She was at their level. She acknowledged and smiled at the children as appropriate.
  - *Taking turns.* All communication requires that individuals take turns—listening, responding, thinking, and reacting. Maryam was looking at a book with Lara (photo 4.2). She would watch to see what Lara was looking at. This prompted her to point to the picture that Lara was looking at in order to verbally identify what Lara had seen. She would wait for Lara to respond. Lara gazed at the page. Eventually she looked up at Maryam. Maryam looked back down to her, repeated what she had said, and again pointed to the picture. Lara smiled.

Photo 4.2

Photo 4.3

Photo 4.4

- *Waiting to give the child a chance to respond.* Children may need to think about what they are doing. It is important to wait to see if the child will respond before continuing with the conversation. Rashawn had been playing with a shape sorter. He got up and wandered around the room. Dwayne noticed that Rashawn was wandering around. He knew that Rashawn enjoyed looking at books. He asked Rashawn to bring a book to him. Rashawn continued to walk around. He saw a drum on the floor. He sat down and played with the drum. After a few minutes, he walked over to the bookshelf and found a book. He sat down and opened the book (photo 4.3). When he found a page he liked, he looked up and smiled. Dwayne sat down beside Rashawn. Rashawn promptly climbed on his lap (photo 4.4). The two of them looked at and talked about the pictures in the book.

- *Using the words that are appropriate to the age of the child.* When Sarah interacted with the infants in the infant room, her voice changed. It became softer; she used higher tones and was more expressive. She talked about what she was doing: "I am taking off the diaper. Let's clean your bum." She asked questions: "Does this feel good?" She waited for a minute, looking at Alana. Then she answered the question based on the smile on Alana's face. "Yes you like it. You are smiling." She also copied and initiated **babbling** (stringing consonants and vowel sounds together in different intonation patterns—loud, soft, high, low) with Alana.

  When Sarah was in the toddler room, she listened and responded by labelling their actions, experiences, or materials as needed. She also expanded the toddlers' expressions. As Sarah was watching Emily and Hannah putting shapes into the shape boxes, she observed carefully. Sarah noticed that every time Hannah picked up the oval shape, she would try to put it into the circular hole. When it did not fit, she would turn the object around in her hand, and look at it carefully before trying to place it in the circular spot again. Sarah quietly told her that she was holding an oval shape. Sarah picked up the circular shape and told Hannah, "I am holding a circle." Hannah looked at the oval and said "oval shape." Sarah **expanded** (added more relevant detail to an expression) by saying, "Yes that is a little oval shape."

  Sarah's dialogue with preschoolers changes to become much more adult-like to model appropriate language structures. She still uses expansions, but she also

babbling
Stringing consonants and vowel sounds together in different intonation patterns—loud, soft, high, low, and so on.

expansion
Adding more relevant detail to a verbal expression.

Chapter Four Critical Skills for Facilitators

models correct language usage. Jamie told her he had "hurted his finger at home." Sarah provided the correct model by responding, "Oh no, you hurt your finger at home? Tell me what happened."

2. Communicating Effectively with Adults

Similar strategies are used with adults. June, Arianna's mom, came in earlier than usual to drop off her daughter. Johanna, the early childhood educator, noticed that June seemed agitated. Her left hand was continually rubbing her right arm. When she bent down to kiss Arianna, Arianna threw her arms around her neck. June stiffened. As June straightened, she noticed Johanna watching them. She quickly looked away, and said that she was in a hurry and had to leave. Johanna smiled and said that she would talk to her later. June nodded and left. Johanna was puzzled by her behaviour and decided to make sure she was there when June came back to pick up Arianna. When June returned that afternoon, she had her arm in a cast. Johanna promptly went over to June and asked her what happened. June's eyes filled with tears. She said, "It is just too awful," and started to cry harder. Johanna said, "Something major has happened to you. Would you like to go somewhere more private to talk about it?" June simply nodded yes. Johanna quickly arranged to have the supervisor take over her role on the floor and led June to the office. She gave June some Kleenex and waited until June was ready to talk. June told her that she and her husband had been in an automobile accident. Her husband was in critical condition in the hospital. She had not realized that her arm was broken. She had been too worried about her husband. Johanna indicated that she was shocked to hear the news. She asked how the centre could be of help. June indicated that Arianna's grandparents would be taking care of her and would drop her off and pick her up. She also indicated that Arianna was too young to understand how serious the situation was. She simply knew that her daddy was very sick and in the hospital. Johanna agreed that toddlers did not have such understanding. Johanna filled in the appropriate forms for June and added the pertinent information about the grandparents to the centre's records. She told Johanna not to worry about Arianna. The staff would make sure that she would be given as much support as she needed.

This scenario describes some excellent communication strategies that are effective techniques to use with adults:

- *Listening actively.* Johanna did not jump to conclusions about June's strange behaviour in the morning. She knew something was wrong, but decided to wait until she could get more information. "Active listening serves several important functions. For one thing, it enables you to check on your understanding of what the speaker meant. When you reflect back to the speaker what you perceived to be the speaker's meaning, he or she can confirm or deny your perceptions. Future messages will have a better chance of being meaningful" (DeVito, Shimoni, & Clark, 2001, p. 100).
- *Building relationships.* Before interpersonal communication can take place, the partners involved in the process must build a relationship with each other. "Interpersonal communication is a transactional process that takes place between two people who have a relationship" (DeVito et al., 2001, p. 35).

    Johanna had built a relationship with June in the past. She realized that June's behaviour was not normal. She also realized that June was not ready to talk to her. She respected June's choice.

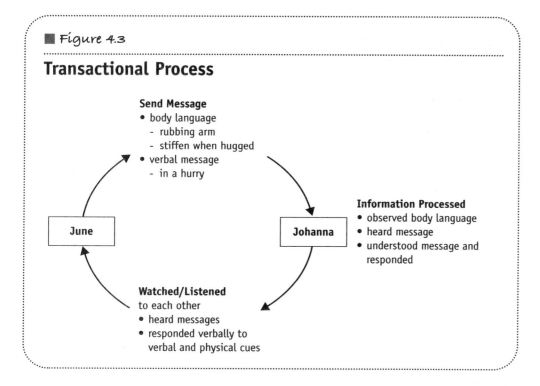

■ Figure 4.3

Transactional Process

Send Message
- body language
  - rubbing arm
  - stiffen when hugged
- verbal message
  - in a hurry

June

Johanna

Information Processed
- observed body language
- heard message
- understood message and responded

Watched/Listened
to each other
- heard messages
- responded verbally to verbal and physical cues

- *Paraphrasing the message.* Johanna repeated what June had stated in her own words to make sure that she understood the message.
- *Expressing understanding and empathy.* Johanna expressed her shock at the news. She also offered realistic help. She helped fill in the required forms and reassured June that her daughter's needs would be met.
- *Asking questions.* Johanna asked pertinent questions about what help could be offered.
- *Choosing an appropriate setting.* Johanna realized that June needed privacy to express herself. Had she remained in the room with the children, the children might have been very upset too, especially Arianna.
- *Taking the cue from the speaker.* Johanna waited patiently until June had sufficient composure to speak to her.
- *Eliminating background noise.* All environments have background noise that can distract individuals from clearly understanding each other. In a children's environment, there is a continuous hum of voices and the noises made by the interactions of the children with the materials in that environment. It was much more appropriate to use the office space, which was much more quiet, for Johanna and June to talk to and understand each other.

In summary, communication is a **transactional process** (see Figure 4.3). In a transactional process, the speaker and the listener both act as a speaker and a listener. "At the same time that you send a message, you're also receiving messages from your own communication and from the reactions of the other persons. At the same time you are listening, you're also sending messages" (DeVito et al., 2001, p. 6).

transactional process
Process in which the speaker and the listener both act as a speaker and a listener simultaneously.

BUILDING EFFECTIVE OBSERVATION SKILLS

Web exercises

Observation of children and their behaviours is one of the critical skills an early childhood educator must develop. Observation skills help the facilitator provide excellence in planning activities and experiences, setting up appropriate learning areas for young children and their families, and discussing the progress of the children with families and other professionals (see Figure 4.4).

Good observation skills require practice and knowledge of child development. Observation skills should follow these criteria:

- *Reliability*. Individuals often judge what they see rather than observing what they see. For example, when several individuals were asked to record their observations about Rashawn (photo 4.5) the following comments were made:

  – Rashawn does not want to share his dinosaur.
  – He does not like his dinosaur.
  – He is unhappy.

  This example shows that there is not complete reliability among the different observers. All recordings of the observations are different. It is difficult to use this

Web
exercises

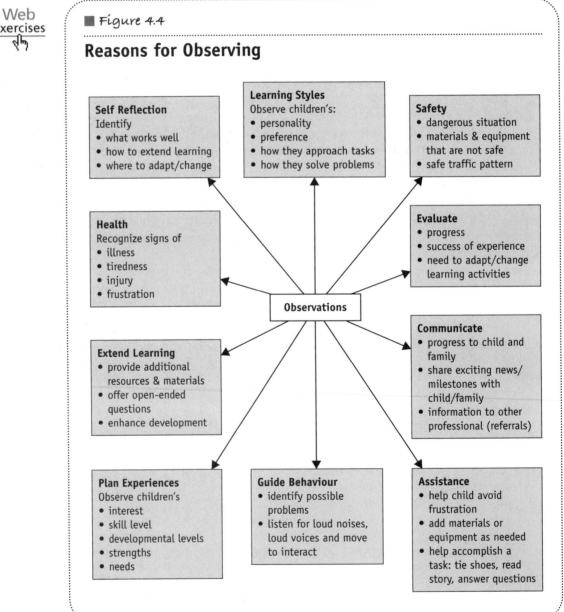

■ Figure 4.4

Reasons for Observing

Self Reflection
Identify
• what works well
• how to extend learning
• where to adapt/change

Learning Styles
Observe children's:
• personality
• preference
• how they approach tasks
• how they solve problems

Safety
• dangerous situation
• materials & equipment that are not safe
• safe traffic pattern

Health
Recognize signs of
• illness
• tiredness
• injury
• frustration

Evaluate
• progress
• success of experience
• need to adapt/change learning activities

Observations

Communicate
• progress to child and family
• share exciting news/ milestones with child/family
• information to other professional (referrals)

Extend Learning
• provide additional resources & materials
• offer open-ended questions
• enhance development

Plan Experiences
Observe children's
• interest
• skill level
• developmental levels
• strengths
• needs

Guide Behaviour
• identify possible problems
• listen for loud noises, loud voices and move to interact

Assistance
• help child avoid frustration
• add materials or equipment as needed
• help accomplish a task: tie shoes, read story, answer questions

information effectively because you have no way of knowing which one is accurate. In order to use observations effectively, each of the observers should be recording the same or similar information. **Reliability** therefore refers to the consistency of the observations among different people.

reliability
The consistency of the observations among different people.

- *Validity*. Individuals often have preconceived notions about the behaviours of children. For example, a group of individuals indicated that they thought that infants have a very short attention span. The group knew that Lara liked books. Several books were put out on a low shelf. During the observation period, Lara played with a variety of toys. She stacked blocks and knocked them down. As she was involved in this activity, one of her blocks landed near the shape sorter. She immediately tried to fit it into one of the slots. Her activity switched from stacking to placing shapes into the shape sorter. When the shape sorter was filled, she dumped out all the pieces. This delighted her. She changed the activity from sorting shapes to filling and dumping. As one of her shapes rolled near the bookshelf, she looked at the books, picked up a book, and put it on the floor. She saw a shape that was on the floor in front of her and returned to her other filling and dumping activity. She had been playing for 20 minutes. The group decided that they had been correct in judging that infants did have a low attention span.

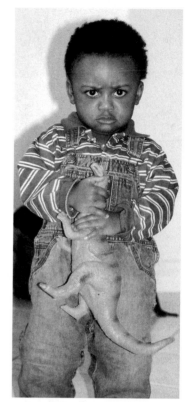

Photo 4.5

This is not a valid observation to test attention span. Lara was given a variety of choices. At her age, she is easily distracted by things around her. Notice how her attention switched from one activity to another as she noticed something new. This observation might be better to look at her interests, her learning styles, or her ability to maintain her own activity over a period of time.

Later that morning, Maryam picked up the book that Lara had looked at briefly. She sat down at the table and read the book aloud. Lara quickly came over and sat on her lap. She listened to the story being read to her. She then took the book and looked at it herself (photo 4.6). Next Maryam labelled the pictures of what Lara was looking at. This activity lasted for 22 minutes. As you can see, the conclusion made by the group was incorrect. Lara does have a lengthy attention span at this task.

In order for an observation to have validity, the purpose of the observation must be met. Validity is important to ensure that

- appropriate information is collected,
- reliable information is collected, and
- accurate understanding of the information can be made.

- *Freedom from bias*. Everything we see and hear is open to our personal viewpoints and interpretations. Additionally, our perceptions are influenced by

Photo 4.6

- our physical well-being;
- our understanding of what we see or hear;
- our personal feelings toward the situation;
- our beliefs (religious, political, and spiritual);
- our background experiences;
- our knowledge about what we see and hear;
- our mood; and
- the situation itself.

In order to observe, we must become aware of our personal biases. We must try to observe with an open mind, using language that is clear and precise.

Chapter Four Critical Skills for Facilitators **91**

Photo 4.7

• *Objectivity (freedom from judgment and interpretation).* When describing a situation or setting, most individuals tend to do so using many descriptive and judgmental terms. This is a logical way of talking or writing. Consider the following description of photo 4.7: "Christine loves to paint. She is very creative and imaginative. Her painting is very neat and colourful. She has excellent fine motor control."

Using this type of description about Christine's artwork is very subjective. The observer has already drawn conclusions about what has happened. How do you know that Christine loves to paint, that the artwork is creative or imaginative, that the work is neat or colourful, and that Christine has excellent fine motor skills? In order to be reliable and valid, the observer should record only factual observations.

All interpretative words such as *loves, creative, imaginative, colourful,* and *excellent* should be left out. These words lead to a different interpretation and therefore Christine's behaviour may well be misinterpreted.

• *Conciseness (to the point).* When observing children, the observer does not have the time to write long descriptive passages about all the children. Nor does the facilitator have the time to read long narratives. The facilitator will be busy interacting with all the children within the environment. Therefore, recordings of observations should include pertinent information including the context and setting of the observation. This information can then be used later to interpret or make sense of what has been observed in order to plan learning experiences for the children.

Thus, the observation about Christine when changed to be objective and concise might look something like that presented in Figure 4.5.

• *Preparation beforehand.* Required background information can be prepared and duplicated ahead of time. This makes it simple to fill in the relevant information and saves a lot of time. Note that the boldface headings in Figure 4.5 can be produced ahead of time (as well as the child's name and the date).

WWW

■ Figure 4.5

Objective, Concise Recording of Observations

Individual: Christine   **Date:** Feb. 14

Setting: Painting on previously started mural (see photo 4.7) on the floor

Context: Continuing to paint by herself on the underwater mural

Observation:

❑ Right hand, tripod grasp (using thumb, middle finger and forefinger to hold brush—see photo 4.7) to paint.

❑ Used pink paint

❑ Controlled hand, wrist, and arm movement to paint pink around shape already completed without overlap of colours.

Collaborative Process

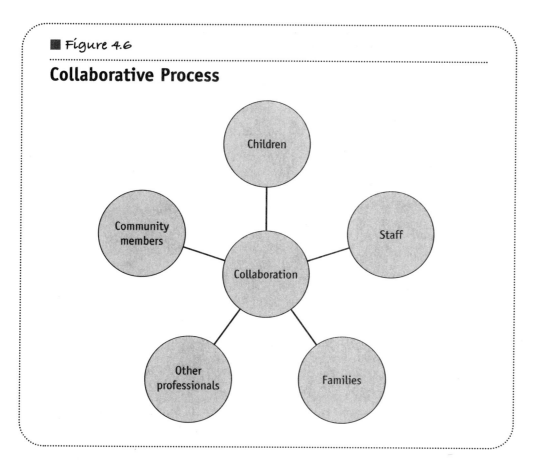

- *Participant observations.* Daily observations need to be made on children's interests, skills, behaviours, and development. When working with children, one rarely gets time to sit back and just observe. This requires the early childhood educator to observe and interact with children at the same time. This is a harder skill to develop as it requires an individual to do two things at once. However, you can learn this skill and you can become quite proficient. Some tasks that you might engage in to make this easier include the following:

  - Practise writing without looking at your paper—it is hard at first but it does become easier. Remember, you can learn to type or play the piano without ever looking at the keys.
  - Prepare your recording forms ahead of time.
  - Focus on particular skills, behaviours, and development or individual children at a time. This allows you to focus your attention on a specific task without getting overwhelmed.
  - Keep your recording forms in a pocket, on a clipboard at a convenient spot, or posted in a cupboard or on a wall for easy access.
  - Develop recording tools that are easy to use and gather information for different purposes (see Table 4.1).
  - Engage families and peers and other individuals involved with the child to help in the process. Collect information collaboratively (see Figure 4.6).

- *Knowledge of child development and the background experiences of children.* Without the knowledge of child development, it is hard to interpret the information about Christine (see photo 4.7). At what age might her fine motor skills be considered

Various Types of Observation and Recording Methods

Type of Tools	Description of Tool
Portfolio	• Collection of information and interpretation about one child in all domains—physical, social, emotional, cognitive, language. • Information is gathered from a variety of sources (see below) and over time. • It is a collaborative process between all partners—families, children, staff, and other professionals.
Photographs	• Actual snapshot of a moment in time. • If combined with setting and context may give valuable information about interests, skills, and developmental levels. • Quick to use. • Easy to use in documentation panels and portfolios. • Way to preserve information about an activity that will disappear when finished.
Video	• Accurate record of a particular episode in the child's life. • May be viewed again to interpret the situation. • Less pressure to get all the pertinent information in writing. • Especially useful for behaviours that occur over longer time periods or behaviours that occur less frequently. • Requires individual's continuous attention to videotape.
Audio taping	• If context and setting are added—gives valuable information about child's verbal communication. • Samples should be taken over time in various situations. • Gives information about language development over time.
Collection of materials— art, drawings, written work	• Identifies skills/developmental levels. • Identifies progress over time. • Identifies preferences and interests
Checklists	• Easy to use, and little time involvement. • Useful for developmental milestone information and presence of skills or interests. • Useful as a tool to evaluate what centres children are using.
Duration counts	• Useful to identify how long a behaviour is occurring. • Easiest to use in form of graph. • Gives information about attention span or behavioural responses of child in various activities.
Frequency counts	• Useful to count how often a behaviour is occurring. • Useful information about interests of children, types of behaviours observed (e.g., separation anxiety), health-related issues (e.g., number of bowel movements), and how often the child engages in certain activities.
Anecdotal records	• Written record that captures additional information to add to other information collected. • In-depth written information about a behaviour that needs more detail (e.g., illness, suspected child abuse, unusual behaviours such as fears, anxieties, frustration).

excellent? What materials should be provided to her based on her skill level that might increase her competency? How often should you see her engaged in an activity to conclude that this might be one of her interests? Is she involved in this activity at home? Does her family support and encourage this type of activity?

- *Observation over time.* More than one observation is needed to confirm or deny that the observations about a child's interests, skills, development, or behaviour are accurate. A child who cries the first day when dropped off in the morning may exhibit this behaviour again the following day or never again. Additionally, it is important to observe the skill in different settings. Does the child exhibit the same behaviours during indoor or outdoor play, at home and at the preschool, and with different individuals?

- *Interpretations of observations.* At this point, the early childhood educator looks at all of the information gathered and tries to make sense of this information based on his or her knowledge of

  - child development;
  - background experiences of the child;
  - observations in more than one setting and confirmed over time; and
  - interactions with family members, the child, and other professionals.

- *Use of the observations and interpretations.* Interpretations are the final step in the observation process. The information gathered and interpreted may be used to

  - adapt/change existing learning opportunities,
  - create new learning experiences,
  - adapt/change the environment,
  - enhance skills,
  - provide opportunities to practise emergent skills,
  - gain insight into development and skills of children,
  - share information with families,
  - collaborate with families, and
  - refer children to other professionals.

In summary, observation is a method to collect pertinent, reliable information about young children. "Reliable research demands hard data. It is necessary to preserve in writing what has been observed and to substantiate it. Recording methods that include facts rather than inferences along with date and time of the recording are essential to meaningful documentation. The details must be preserved to see progress, trends, and correlations" (Nilsen, 2001, p. 6).

Observing is a process that involves identification of a behaviour to observe, choosing an appropriate documentation process or tool, interpreting the information gathered, and using the information for a specific purpose (see Figure 4.4 on page 90).

BUILDING DEVELOPMENTALLY APPROPRIATE GUIDANCE SKILLS

Web exercises

A guidance approach to discipline fosters the growth and development of the individual child in the socialization process. Adults and children interact with one another and the environment as part of an interdependent system. (Gordon & Browne, 1996, p. 22)

Guiding children's behaviour follows a number of principles. These principles include guidance techniques such as

1. dependency on knowledge of child development;
2. varying guidance strategies with ages and stages of development;
3. influence of various other factors on behaviour;
4. fostering individual problem-solving skills;
5. fostering self-respect and respect toward others; and
6. guidance as a process.

1. Dependency on Knowledge of Child Development

Web exercises

In order to know how to appropriately guide young children, the adult needs to have knowledge of child development. Louise understood that Lauren could make choices. She carefully selected toys that she thought Lauren might enjoy. She held these toys out to her and watched for Lauren's body language to see which one she wanted (photo 4.8).

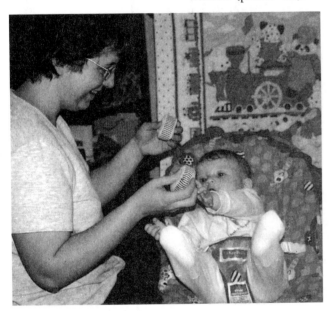
Photo 4.8

Emily and Hannah (see photo 4.1 on page 84) are both toddlers. Telling Emily or Hannah that they need to share is not developmentally appropriate. Children at this age do not share (see Figure 4.7). Toddlers focus on their own needs. They are not yet aware that others have their own or similar needs. Sarah realized that toddlers do not share. She quickly brought a second similar toy to the two children. In this way she avoided a conflict between the two children by encouraging both children to continue to play.

In contrast, older children like Alicia, Jessica, and Christine (see photos 3.4, 3.5, and 3.6 on pages 63 and 64) are well able to share the materials they use. These girls have many more skills to bring to a situation that will allow for a greater ability to work together and share. They have the language skills to ask each other for things they want. They have the cognitive skills to know that they can use other materials—such as a different colour to paint with while they wait for the one required. They can use alternative materials if the one desired is not available—

W W W

■ Figure 4.7

Toddler's Creed

If I want it, it's mine.

If I give it to you and change my mind later, it's mine.

If I can take it away from you, it's mine.

If I had it a little while ago, it's mine.

If it's mine it will never belong to anyone else, no matter what.

If we are building something together, all the pieces are mine.

If it looks like mine, it's mine.

Source: Gestwicki, 1999, p. 148.

such as using wet paint to attach the glitter instead of glue. They also have the social skills to interact with each other, which includes turn-taking.

In summary, knowledge of child development helps the adult select appropriate techniques for different age groups. It leads to implementing developmentally appropriate guidance techniques for children in various age groups and at different developmental levels. "A basic understanding of how children grow and the predictable patterns and stages through which they develop is necessary if teachers are to guide effectively. Matched with a teacher's own observations and experience, knowledge of normal stages of development provides an understanding of what to expect, the variations in behaviour and capacities of young children, and the confidence to support their growth" (Gordon & Browne, 1996, p. 23).

2. Varying Guidance Strategies with Ages and Stages of Development

Guidance techniques vary with the different ages and stages of children. Table 4.2 summarizes general guidance techniques appropriate for different age groups.

In summary, guidance techniques are dependent on the adult's knowledge about child development of various ages. Techniques appropriate for one age are not necessarily appropriate for another age. As children gain greater self-control over their actions, guiding their behaviour needs to reflect the children's increased understanding and self-control. "There are fundamental principles on which an effective child guidance approach is based, beginning with an understanding of child development theory and emphasis on guiding and teaching appropriate behaviors and attitudes. These principles help us create developmentally appropriate guidance practices and techniques" (Gordon et al., 1996, p. 28).

3. Influence of Various Other Factors on Behaviour

How children behave and how they interact with each other, with adults, and with the materials and equipment in their environment are dependent on many factors. Accordingly, techniques that might be used to guide children's behaviour must also be sensitive to and responsive to these factors. Some of these factors are more **intrapersonal** (i.e., they are intrinsic and internal to the individual). "Guidance is influenced by many factors such as individual style and temperament, culture, race, nationality, family background and personal experiences" (Gordon et al., 1996, p. 25).

intrapersonal
Refers to factors that are intrinsic and internal to the individual.

Style and Temperament

All children are unique. Child development may give us general information about children, but within each age range there will be variations. The shy child, the outgoing child, the active child, the slow-to-warm-up child (i.e., the hesitant or cautious child), and the fussy child all need different approaches. By using different approaches, the caregiver is able to model a variety of behaviour strategies to the child. Common elements to all of the approaches include

- careful and sensitive observation;
- establishing a trusting relationship with the child and family; and
- compassionate, sensitive, and honest caregiver interactions.

Culture, Race, and Nationality

In most child-care facilities in Canada, there will be a cultural mosaic of children and families. Within this cultural mosaic will be a variety of expectations, belief systems, and values about how to most effectively guide children. Meeting all of these expectations

Guidance Techniques for Various Ages

Ages	Guidance Techniques
Infants	• Respond "to them promptly, consistently, and warmly, and interact with them, giving them language, face to face so they can begin to understand the process of human communication" (Gestwicki, 1999, p. 68). • Provide consistent, nurturing responses. as infants express need through crying, vocalization, and body language. • Provide opportunities to explore freely in indoor and outdoor environments free of hazards (e.g., small pieces, loose pieces, sharp objects that can be put in the mouth) and unobstructed safe places to lie, crawl, or cruise on. • Provide predictable patterns of interactions, such as talking about changing diapers, repeating experiences in predictable sequences, singing a song before putting child to sleep, or tucking in child before leaving the room.
Toddlers	• Recognize the evolving need for a toddler's independence—toddlers want to do things by themselves. • Nurture and provide opportunities and time for toddlers to do things by themselves. The toddler will want to dress himself or herself. Encourage toddlers to do what they can—they can put on a jacket, hat, and boots and the adult does up the zipper. Allow for enough time to encourage the toddler to dress. • Encourage and praise the toddler's efforts—"Good job. You put your coat on." • Redirect behaviour to other activities or actions (e.g., instead of saying no to the toddler throwing the sand on the floor, redirect the behaviour to throwing sand into a bucket). • Provide similar activities and materials to avoid conflicts. Sarah had another shape sorter to give to Hannah. • Listen and look at the toddler to gain understanding of what the communication is. Sarah watched and listened to Emily and Hannah before she interacted. • Provide a safe environment both indoors and outdoors to explore freely. Toddlers need to develop control over their muscles. They need free unobstructed space to safely run, walk, climb, push and pull things, fill and dump materials, and put things together and pull them apart. • Provide real choices, and allow toddlers to do as much as they can by themselves (e.g., set and clean the table at mealtime).
Preschoolers	• Support preschoolers' growing independence by providing a variety of materials and learning opportunities to make choices and by encouraging them to solve their own problems. Alicia, Christine, and Jessica (see photos 3.4, 3.5, and 3.6 on pages 63 and 64) decided what their activity would be, what materials they needed, where they would work, and how long their activity would last. They solved their own problems associated with these tasks. • Provide "many opportunities to develop social skills, such as cooperation, helping, negotiating, and talking with the person involved to solve interpersonal problems" (Gordon et al., 1996, p. 11) (photo 4.9). • Support preschoolers' needs to explore a variety of activities within the learning environment (indoors and outdoors) through active play by providing a variety of learning experiences (sand, water, music, manipulatives, drama, quiet, creative arts, carpentry, science, math, books, etc.). • Redirect behaviour by asking children to solve their own problems. Kailey, one of the preschoolers, had been playing in the sand with a group of three other children. They had decided to create a "sand castle" using different moulds. There were only three moulds available. The children started to argue about who could have a mould. Kailey finally grabbed a mould away. Kaya went over and indicated that she thought that the group had a problem. She asked the children to identify the problem. Kailey answered that there weren't enough moulds. Kaya asked them what they could do about it. The group thought that they could find something else to use. They looked for suitable containers and brought them back to use in the sand area. • Recognize and provide alternative calming activities—quiet area, books, puzzles, choice to be alone.
School-aged children	• School-aged children have increased abilities in all domains to understand and negotiate their own limits. Set realistic limits collaboratively between children and adults. • Encourage children to negotiate their own solutions to problems with each other and with adults. • Encourage activities that provide choices, problem solving, and cooperation. • Encourage children to collaborate in creating their own learning opportunities.

may seem like an overwhelming task. The following are a few guidelines on how to make this task easier:

- Involve families as partners. This gives both the early childhood educator and the families opportunities to discuss common issues, learn from each other, and collaborate to develop the best way to interact with the children in the program.
- Develop active listening skills.
- Involve family members in problem-solving situations. This might include topics such as practising appropriate positive guidance techniques, examining the values of positive guidance, and looking for alternative strategies to support children.
- Create and display documentation panels of children engaged in effective social interactions.

Photo 4.9

Family Backgrounds

All families have their own particular values and beliefs about how to raise their children. It is important to acknowledge and support the families. It is easy to form attitudes and opinions on child-rearing practices that come from our own particular perspectives. For example, Janine was working in a centre that encouraged mothers to come in and breast-feed their children. The centre had done an excellent job of setting up a nurturing environment where this could happen. After a new family had registered, Janine found to her surprise and shock that one of the mothers that came to breast-feed her child was the mother of a three-year-old. There were also a number of comments made by other nursing mothers that this was "disgusting." The situation was resolved in the following manner:

- Janine and the staff first had to reflect on their own feelings. They all shared the view that nursing a three-year-old was not appropriate.
- Janine suggested that perhaps they should do some research on this topic first before they made any comments to the mother. The staff members agreed. All members agreed to retrieve information from a variety of sources.
- After sharing and discussing the information, the attitudes of the staff changed. Not all individuals agreed that they would breast-feed their own child for this period of time, but none of the staff still thought of this as "disgusting."
- The staff decided to bring in a local expert on breast-feeding to present a workshop on this topic to the parents.
- The supervisor discussed the reason of the upcoming workshop with the mother of the three-year-old. She was most supportive of the idea.

The workshop was a resounding success. Most of the nursing parents and some of the non-nursing families of other children attended. After lively discussions, all individuals agreed that there were merits to nursing to a later age and that this was the right of an individual to decide.

Photo 4.10

Web
exercises

Photo 4.11

Personal Experiences

How we nurture and guide children has much to do with the way we were raised. If you were raised in an environment that used physical punishment, you may think that this is an appropriate way to raise children. In this type of behaviour management, the child's behaviour is controlled by an external factor—physical punishment. Someone else is controlling the behaviour. In order to grow and develop appropriately, children need to learn to control their own behaviour. When children's behaviour is guided appropriately, they increasingly become more responsible for what they do and how they do it:

> Strategies for child guidance should not rely on methods for external control, but rather must stimulate the development of internal mechanisms and motivations for self-control. In this way children can be encouraged to become independent and self-directed rather than dependent and directed by others. As they grow toward adulthood, they will begin making more and more critical choices about what to do and how to behave. (Miller, 2000, p. xiii)

Factors in the Environment

Factors in the environment include

- *Providing appropriate choices.* Christine, Jessica, and Alicia were able to create their own learning experiences, solve their own problems, and make decisions on how to do their task and how to implement it (see photos 3.4, 3.5, and 3.6 on pages 63 and 64).
- *Providing appropriate number of materials in the environment.* Emily and Hannah (see photo 4.1 on page 84) needed more than one set of the same materials in order to avoid a potential problem. These girls are toddlers and it is not yet developmentally appropriate for them to share materials. Through activities such as this one, toddlers start to learn about personal limits in a positive way: "It is all right to use my own materials, but I cannot take materials from someone else. I need to find my own."
- *Providing challenges.* Josh was often found at the water table or in the drama centre pouring liquids from one container to another. If the water spilled over the container he would say, "Oh no!" When additional experimental toys and containers easier to pour with were provided (photo 4.10), it not only made the task easier to control for him, but also maintained his attention over time.
- *Providing opportunities to relax.* Children can get overwhelmed in an environment that offers continual stimulation. They need opportunities for quiet activities to relax. This encourages them to regulate their own need. Providing quiet areas "encourages children to recognize their own feelings and react appropriately to those feelings" (Crowther, 2003, p. 143). Alicia had been running and climbing outside nonstop. Gradually, her run was reduced to a walk. She looked around and noticed the quiet area set up in a corner of the yard. She went over, sat down, and began to look at a book (photo 4.11). Alicia had recognized her own need to relax.
- *Providing appropriate limits.* Limits should be concerned mostly with children's safety, such as walking in the room or using a one-way system for riding outside. Other limits can be modelled and reinforced more effectively, such as positive interactions and appropriate language usage.

4. Fostering Individual Problem-Solving Skills

Emily and Jacob both wanted to use the cement truck in the sand area. Jacob indicated that it was "Mine!" Emily explained that she needed it for the construction site she was working on (photo 4.12). Kaya heard the children arguing. As she walked over to the sand area, Emily looked at her and said, "I only need it for a little while." Kaya told her, "Why don't you tell Jacob?" Emily looked at Jacob and said, "I just need it for a minute. I'll give it right back." Jacob nodded and followed Emily. He watched her use the cement truck. When Emily was finished, she gave the truck back to Jacob. This type of strategy helps children develop later skills in **conflict resolution** (solving interpersonal problems such as disputes or arguments).

Kaya helped Emily negotiate her own problem with Jacob. The result was satisfactory for both children. This leads to greater social competence. "Research tells us that socially competent children are happier than their less competent peers. They are more successful in their interactions with others, more popular, and more satisfied with life. In addition, children's social relations have been linked to academic achievement, with more positive social relationships being associated with greater success at school" (Kostelnik et al., 2002, p. 6).

Photo 4.12

conflict resolution
Solving interpersonal problems such as disputes or arguments independently.

5. Fostering Self-Esteem and Respect Toward Others

Rashawn had watched the other children ride the wooden horse. When the children were finished, he climbed on the horse to try to ride it. His first attempts were not successful (photo 4.13). Dwayne walked over and showed him how to rock the horse. Rashawn tried again. This time he was successful. He looked over to Dwayne and beamed (photo 4.14). Dwayne responded, "Terrific, you are riding the horse by yourself."

Rashawn gained self-confidence in his ability to do things by himself. As children gain self-confidence, they also begin to develop a respect for self and their abilities. Rashawn received positive feedback by learning to ride the wooden horse by himself and by the positive verbal feedback Dwayne gave him. When children feel good about themselves, they are more likely to try new tasks, and confident in their ability to be successful. "[T]he way children think and feel about themselves is important. Positive, accurate self-perception provides the confidence, energy, and optimism children need to master life's tasks" (Kostelnik et al., 2002, p. 88).

Michael, the early childhood educator, observed Connor trying to cut out a circle to make a puddle. He could not handle the large paper and scissors together. Michael could see that Connor needed help. He decided to watch to see what Connor would do.

Photo 4.13   Photo 4.14

Connor finally put his scissors and paper down and ran to Liesl and said, "Will you help me please?" Liesl went with him and said, "How about I hold the paper and you cut" (photo 4.15). Connor had learned to respect Liesl's ability. He knew that she not only could cut well but that she was more than willing to help. Michael was astute to realize that Connor could find a solution by himself.

Photo 4.15

6. Guidance as a Process

Guidance is a process. For the early childhood educator, it involves observing, interacting, and reinforcing behaviours. For example, Kaya observed the group of children in the sand area. She watched and listened to their play. She did not step in until she noticed that there was a problem. She involved the children in solving their own problem—finding more moulds to play with. When the children were again actively involved in the sand play, Kaya went back to the group and indicated that she thought that they had solved their problem. In this way she was able to provide feedback to the children that their behaviour was acceptable.

For children, guidance is also a process. Children need to learn what behaviours are appropriate, how to act toward different individuals, and how to act in different situations. As children grow and develop, they begin to understand more about how their actions influence other individuals. Kailey learned that it was not appropriate to take materials away from another individual. She and her peers learned that they could solve a problem together that led to a positive outcome for all the members of the group.

In summary, guiding children's behaviour effectively requires many skills of the adult:

Child guidance is a very challenging process of establishing and maintaining responsible, productive, and cooperative behavior in children. Adult caregivers must devote a great deal of time, effort, and persistence over many years to help children become considerate and self-disciplined members of society. Knowledge of the natural stages of child development is the most powerful tool adults have to guide youngsters successfully through this process of maturing. (Miller, 2000, p. xii)

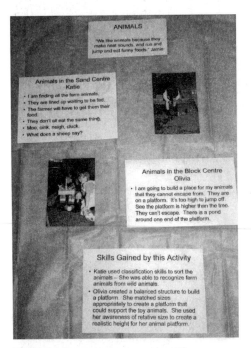

Photo 4.16

BUILDING SKILLS TO PLAN COLLABORATIVE LEARNING EXPERIENCES

The children in the preschool program had been very interested in animals. They had a collection of toy animals and expressed an interest in finding out where the animals lived. The information about the children's interest had been documented and placed on the parent board (photo 4.16). The families became quite interested in the project. They posted ideas about this interest on the collaborative sharing board. These included field trips (to a farm, to the zoo, to a pet store, to the butterfly pavilion, on nature walks) and collecting of appropriate videos and books. One of the family members was the coordinator of activities between families and the preschool program. He organized the families and their children to collect and bring in the resources and to arrange appropriate field trips. The children, families, and staff discussed the various opportunities and decided the following:

Photo 4.17

- All the children and some of the family members would go to the library to borrow books on various animals.
- All the children and families would collect materials that could be used to support animal play in the preschool room.
- A group of grandmothers would bake cookies and have a bake sale to raise money to buy some more animals. Their grandchildren would help with the task.
- The staff would gather additional resources to increase their own knowledge and to provide resources in the environment.
- Field trips would be arranged for the zoo, a dairy farm, the pet store, and several nature walks.

Photo 4.19

Photo 4.18

The result was that the children engaged in many activities that involved animals across the curriculum—reading, creating environments for animals, dramatic play, and sorting and matching animals (photos 4.17, 4.18, 4.19, and 4.20). These activities continued over six weeks for most of the children.

When children learn to collaborate with peers and adults, they gain valuable skills that lay the foundation for future participation within their social environments:

Thus, the disposition to participate, contribute, and share in the responsibility for the work of the group and one's larger community can—when the effort is not especially interesting—be developed and strengthened and can serve as a foundation for our children's effective participation in a democracy for their whole lives. (Harris Helm & Beneke, 2003, p. 15)

A collaborative process has numerous advantages to the adults caring for young children. These include

- *Sharing of expertise and resources.* One of the families of the children owned a dairy farm and could offer appropriate information and resources. Joint collection of materials can decrease the time of all participants and enriched the experience for the children.
- *Participating as a group.* This can empower all individuals to contribute and share in the responsibility of the children's learning.
- *Interacting continuously.* This empowers all partners to gain knowledge about the progress and interests of the children.

Photo 4.20

Chapter Four Critical Skills for Facilitators

Self-Reflective Questions about the Collaborative Process

1. Do I believe that a collaborative process is of value? Why?
2. Do I believe that the children and families can be empowered to partici-pate in creating learning experiences?
3. Why would this be a valuable process? What advantages to the program, the children, and myself can I anticipate as a result of this collaboration?
4. How will this help me develop a better-quality program? What expertise and information can families bring to the program?

- *Planning as a group.* Group planning serves to spread the workload around and enrich the experiences of adults and children through broadened ideas and resources.

Skills to Enhance the Collaborative Process

There are several steps involved in setting up a collaborative process. This process is ongoing. As new children enter the program, as new resource people are identified, and as new interests evolve, the process will continually need to be adjusted and revised (see Figure 4.8). Before attempting to set up a collaborative process, the facil-itator must reflect on some critical components. Some of these are discussed below.

Recognizing Personal Motivation

Melanie, a first year ECE student, was very shy. She was worried about interacting with the parents of the children in her first field practicum situation. She decided to ask her supervisor for some help. Her supervisor sympathized and gave her a list of questions that she had posed for herself to help her in this process. She offered to discuss the questions with Melanie after Melanie had reflected on these questions.

Recognizing Personal Strengths and Limitations

Melanie had always enjoyed younger children. She found it very easy to establish a rapport and interact with them. She could spontaneously set up activities for them that they seemed to enjoy. Melanie knew that she already had unique skills, experi-ences, and knowledge to work with children and families. She also had some idea of what skills and knowledge and experiences still needed to be developed. Each of us should similarly reflect upon what skills, experiences, and knowledge we already have and still need. Reflect upon how you can use a collaborative process to help you gain these skills, experiences, and knowledge. Who would be part of your collabo-rative process?

Listening and Focusing on the Message Rather Than Placing Blame

Melanie had worked very hard to set up a good creative activity for the children. She had collected many resources and felt that the children had really enjoyed her activity. Much to her dismay, however, her supervisor did not agree. She told her that the children had enjoyed the activity but that it would be a much better learning experience if she made a number of changes. Melanie's immediate reaction was that this was unfair. Wasn't the important thing that the children enjoyed themselves? She felt that the supervisor was being picky. Why wasn't her hard work appreciated?

It is much easier to blame someone else for our problems. This way we do not have to reflect upon how we might have done a better job. This type of focus is a block to learning. Melanie was looking for justification on how her actions were adequate, not looking for new ways of doing or learning. She decided that she really did not have much choice. She revised her activity and tried it again. To her amazement, she had more children participate, the children spent more time at the activity, and they talked much more to her about what they were doing. Her supervisor praised her new efforts.

Melanie talked to her supervisor and asked her why this learning activity had been so much better. Her supervisor responded by saying that she had spent more effort in setting up a learning experience that empowered children to solve their own problems, make their own choices, and work the way they wanted to. She asked Melanie to reflect upon her own activity and indicate how it was different. When Melanie thought about it, she realized that she had told the children what they had to do; she had picked out all the materials they had to use and so, in fact, the result was more her effort than the effort of the children. Through this process, Melanie became much more open in her attitude toward learning to work with children. After all, that was why she was enrolled in the early childhood education program.

The Collaboration Process

Collaboration is "working together at every level through collaboration among teachers, children and teachers, and parents and the larger community" (Fraser, 2000, p. 8). The collaboration process can be visualized in three steps—identification of partners, building a collaborative network, and maintaining the network (see Figure 4.9).

collaboration
Working together in a diverse group (children, families, staff, community members, and other professionals) toward the common goal of best practices within a child-care program.

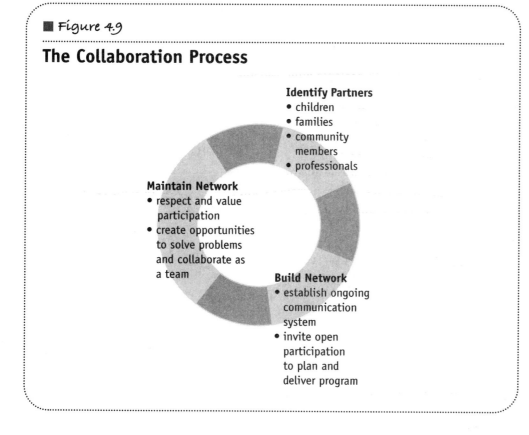

■ Figure 4.9

The Collaboration Process

Identify Partners
- children
- families
- community members
- professionals

Build Network
- establish ongoing communication system
- invite open participation to plan and deliver program

Maintain Network
- respect and value participation
- create opportunities to solve problems and collaborate as a team

1. *Identification of the partners for the collaborative process.*

- *Children.* "Children are active learners, drawing on direct physical and social experiences as well as culturally transmitted knowledge to construct their own understanding of the world around them" (Gestwicki, 1999, p. 10). Christine loved to read. She was fascinated by her facilitator's collection of different versions of common fairy tales. She checked the shelf daily to see if new additions had been made to the collection. One day she proudly brought in a new book. She had found it in a bookstore and brought it to the class to read. She was fascinated by the differences in the story. She showed

Photo 4.21

her book to her peers and to the adults in the room. She pointed out some of the changes that she had noticed in the story: "Little Red Riding Hood has a real name. It is Brigitta. See you can see her name on this page" (photo 4.21). The rest of the children in the group were as impressed as Christine that Little Red Riding Hood had a real name. Christine continued to relate the differences that she had found to her peers.

Christine took charge of her own learning. She not only expanded on her interest to read, but also helped to search for new materials and references. She took the lead in sharing what she had learned.

The role of the facilitator is to set the stage for learning to occur: "Teaching strategies support children's active learning and rely less on direct transmission of knowledge that young children have not created themselves" (Gestwicki, 1999, p. 10).

- *Families.* "Developing partnerships with families is an integral part of the role of an early childhood teacher. To work effectively with children, teachers must work effectively with their families" (Wilson, 2001, p. 72). The collaboration between the families and the preschool room was clearly seen at the beginning of this section. Families were collaborating at various levels:

    - helping plan learning experiences—field trips, gathering materials and resources;
    - helping implement learning experiences—adding suggestions to the planning board, participating by arranging fund-raising, participating on field trips;
    - sharing expertise—owners of the dairy farm encouraged the field trip to that setting; and
    - interacting with the staff and children on an ongoing basis—reading documentation of children's efforts, sharing, and bringing in new ideas/materials.

- *Community members.* Various community members help and support child-care at various levels. Many businesses within the community rely on the families for support (e.g., the purchase of clothing, books, food, and toys) and services (e.g., medical and recreational). Collaboration with community members not only leads to increased sharing of expertise, but may also lead to better understanding of the needs of the child and family. In the example at the beginning of this section, the pet store became a resource for children to visit and gain more insight into how animals live and what their needs are.

- *Other professionals.* It is vitally important that the facilitator becomes aware of other services in the community. Collaboration between health-care officials, early childhood specialists, dental services, licensing agencies, and other community services develops good healthy living habits and provides expertise and help when a child is ill, when families are in need of services, or when you suspect neglect or abuse.

2. *Building a network for the collaborative process.* To build a collaborative network with all the partners takes time, commitment, and enthusiasm. Your first step is always to get to know your families and your community. Establish a resource file that will give you information about the services in your community (see Figure 4.10). The information in Figure 4.10 can be gathered on individual sheets as shown, and filed in a binder or filing cabinet, kept on index cards, or kept on individual sheets by category. Gathering the information should be a team effort and should be ongoing, allowing for revisions and additions.

The next step in the process would be to build the communication network. Skills included in this area are:

■ Figure 4.10

WWW

Community Resource Collection

Category of Services	Name of Service	Type of Service Offered	Contact Name	Contact Information
Health Related				
Support Services for Special Needs				
Social Services				
Recreational Services				
Good Places to Visit				
Free Materials				
Resources				

Chapter Four Critical Skills for Facilitators

- *Active listening.* See the discussion on communicating effectively with adults on page 88.
- *Open door policy.* Encourage families to come into the child-care facility as their schedules permit. Create opportunities for families to participate—at lunch time, during activity time, on field trips, or for special projects.
- *Reciprocal respectful interactions with all partners.*
- *Focusing on people, not problems.* It is easy to focus on a problem as you can then work toward a solution. Often one forgets that real people may be involved. Involve the individuals to help solve the problems.
- *Frequent communication.* Set up a system of ongoing communication that will encourage participation. Ask the various partners to share their ideas on how this might work. Parent boards, daily sharing forms, newsletters, documentation panels, idea boxes, and planning meetings are all viable options. It may be necessary to use more than one option to meet everyone's needs.
- *Flexibility.* The system established needs to evolve and grow as the program expands and grows.
- *Genuine interest and enthusiasm.* It is always a pleasure to work with someone who expresses interest and enthusiasm. Within the child-care setting, children will often provide the link between the partners. Expressing the joy of caring for someone's child is a powerful motivator for continued interaction.

3. *Maintaining the network for the collaborative process.* Many of the points discussed in the previous section (building networks) also apply in this section. Maintaining a network involves the following skills:

- *Valued participation.* In order for any system to work, the contributions of the participants must be valued and acknowledged. Set up some systems that will provide feedback and positive reinforcement to all partners. Some suggestions include family outings, family meals, celebrating special days together, sending home newsletters, videos of special events, documentation panels, and photo albums of learning activities.
- *Group problem solving.* If problems arise, it is much easier to solve them with the support of others. Solutions become much easier to find and put in place when all partners collaborate.
- *Evaluation.* Joint evaluation of the process and program with concrete ideas on how to improve.
- *Forming working committees.* These may include board members, planning committees, fund-raising committees, and program committees.
- *Revising and adapting.* New families will join the program, others will leave, and new community opportunities will arise. The format of the network needs to constantly be revised and changed to keep track of any changes or new ideas.

In summary, collaboration with all partners—children, families, staff, community members, and other professionals—leads to a rich, rewarding experience for all. Through a collaborative process, all individuals gain skill in working together, solving problems together, and learning to appreciate each other's talents and skills. It leads to different individuals with varied skills that work together toward a common goal. "In short we need people who are competent problem solvers, creative, flexible, and personally responsible for their welfare and the welfare of those in their families and neighborhoods" (Abbott & Ryan, 1999, p. 9).

BUILDING EFFECTIVE ADVOCACY SKILLS

Traditional roles of early childhood educators have been based on the practices of early education and early child-care. These traditional images have been challenged by the many issues facing early childhood educators practising in the field. "[T]oday's practitioners are increasingly being faced with the need to become involved in public-interest issues that impinge directly on their primary role obligations to the children in their care" (Jensen & Hannibal, 2000, p. 4).

Early childhood educators need to learn to advocate for their individual self-interest and for the interest of the children and families they care for. Self-interest issues include

- Advocating for increased salaries. ECE salaries are very low across Canada.
- Advocating for employee benefits—health insurance, drug and dental plans, sick leave, retirement plans, and vacations.
- Advocating for improved working conditions—regulated hours, adult facilities, opportunities for advancement and additional training/education, and regulated break times.
- Advocating for enhanced quality programs.
- Advocating for all staff to be qualified in early childhood care.
- Advocating for professional recognition.

Early childhood educators also need to learn to advocate for the well-being of children and their families. Issues for children and families include

- Advocating for an adequate number of child-care spaces.
- Advocating for the family's right of choice of daycare setting.
- Advocating for subsidies for families to enroll children within child-care.
- Advocating for quality, affordable child-care.
- Advocating for services for children with special needs.
- Advocating for resources for families in need.

What Are Advocacy Activities?

Advocacy activities can be both formal and informal activities. Informal activities often support causes that are launched by other agencies or associations, such as the call for support to establish legislative recognition of early childhood educators in Ontario initiated by the Association of Early Childhood Educators (Ontario). Often these activities include

- signing petitions;
- sending form letters to the appropriate political officials;
- calling a member of parliament to express concern or identify a stance on an issue;
- agreeing to be interviewed on radio or in the newspaper about an issue;
- joining a demonstration in a particular locale to express opposition;
- raising awareness of quality issues for young children through displays during special weeks (e.g., Week of the Child, Week of the Family);
- organizing a child-related display during registration week for recreational activities; and
- informing families and community members of issues and asking for their support.

More formal activities are usually arranged and implemented by provincial child-care organizations, medical support groups (e.g., the Canadian Paediatric Society or the

Canadian Institute of Child Health), or coalitions (e.g., the Ontario Coalition for Better Child Care). The activities engaged in by these agencies may include

- mass mail-out of posters and brochures about an issue;
- sending personal letters to support an issue to the appropriate political officials;
- television and newspaper coverage about an issue;
- presentation of issues during parliamentary procedures;
- publications on quality care and information packages on quality care; and
- political action during election times to try to gain support on issues from political candidates.

Gaining skill in advocacy requires early childhood educators to take a proactive stand. "A critical step in this venture is clarifying and obtaining consensus on the beliefs and values of practitioners in order to establish a professional code of ethics" (Jensen & Hannibal, 2000, p. 4). This has already been done in many jurisdictions. The early childhood associations of both British Columbia and Ontario have published a code of ethics.

Characteristics of Effective Advocates

According to Jensen and Hannibal (2000, pp. 6–10), the characteristics of effective advocates are that individuals must

1. have the skill to find information about advocacy issues and use this information effectively;
2. reflect on and apply the values and ethics to advocacy issues in order to effectively engage in appropriate action;
3. be sensitive to interpersonal relations when communicating with peers, other professionals, families, and community members;
4. continue to build and reflect on personal professional values and commitment to become an advocate; and
5. develop learning skills to continually monitor, reflect, and act on changing information about issues in the field.

Strategies for Developing Advocacy Skills

According to Jensen and Hannibal (2000, p. 7), advocacy skills can be learned and mastered. It is a gradual process. This process should start in your student years and will continue to grow during your professional life. These skills can be gained through issue debates; issue interviews, advocacy speakers, and community discussion panels; role-play and simulation exercises; on-site program studies; awareness of advocacy literature; and getting involved.

Issue Debates

Jennifer, a student in early childhood education, became very concerned when she read in *The Globe and Mail* (March 15, 2003) about the child who had supposedly been repeatedly locked in a closet to control his behaviour. She remembered what it felt like, because her parents had used a similar method to control her behaviour. She decided to bring the article to her child guidance class. The class discussed and debated the issues about time outs. As a result, the class was able to understand the negative impact that this type of time out could foster and list appropriate alternative strategies.

What Can You Do?

- Clip out common issues you find in newspapers, magazines, on the Internet, or in journals and bring them to class for discussion.
- Become a member of your association (student memberships at reduced costs are available).
- Interview leaders in the field to find out what they believe and why.
- Talk to families to find out their issues and concerns.

Issue Interviews, Advocacy Speakers, and Community Discussion Panels

Moira had not been overly concerned about issues in early childhood education. She was more concerned about finishing her studies and finding work in the child-care field. During her studies, she became pregnant. She could only finish her first year of the program. She found it impossible to find affordable infant child-care to continue her studies. There was only one centre that offered infant care. Private home care was too expensive. Finally, her parents offered to care for their grandchild so that Moira could complete her studies.

Moira's attitude toward issues in early childhood had changed. She was able to talk to her classmates and relate her experiences and the importance of advocating for the children and families. Her class initiated several community discussion panels around issues in the community. One issue that was addressed was teen pregnancies. Moira and some of her classmates became part of an advocacy group to put pressure on the local school board to offer child-care in the high school for children of teens so that they could continue their studies. A pilot program was started the following year. Moira was very pleased to be hired as one of the early childhood educators in that program.

What Can You Do?

- Attend local community discussion groups.
- Attend conferences.
- Bring in speakers to the classroom as part of your assignments that talk about the issues.
- Interview advocates to identify what the current issues are and what suggested advocacy strategy is suggested.
- Attend community forums to remain current.

Role-Play or Simulation Exercises

Michael, Rachel, and Joanna had decided to collaborate on one of the assignments for their issues course. They decided to deal with the issue of time out as a role-play exercise. They assigned the roles of parents and early childhood educator. The role-play involved a face-to-face discussion of the parents with the early childhood educator to convince her that time out for their toddler was not appropriate.

The group was surprised at how real the situation became for them. They got very positive feedback and further discussion from the rest of the class. This type of exercise encourages the learner to look at the issue from a different perspective. It is valuable in preparing yourself for your need to deal with issues in the future.

What Can You Do?

- Look over your assignments and do them in alternative ways (e.g., role-play or discussion groups) or bring in a guest speaker followed by a panel discussion.
- Research to see what the current issues are and present information as a panel discussion.
- Create a display that describes an issue and offers some possible solution strategies.

On-Site Program Studies

Most early childhood programs deal with advocacy issues within some of their courses. Be sure to attend these sessions. Participate fully and clarify points that you do not understand. Try to gain some idea of what strategies you could implement as a student.

What Can You Do?

- Use active listening.
- Involve yourself in some advocacy component in your program and area.
- List some of the skills you already have that you can put to use immediately.

Becoming Aware of Advocacy Literature

Advocacy literature includes journals (e.g., *Child Welfare, Young Children, Interaction,* and *Canadian Children*), media material (e.g., newspaper articles, television programs, and videos), public information (posters, pamphlets, and displays), government publications (pamphlets, posters, booklets, news releases, documents, and briefing papers), and material from advocacy groups.

What Can You Do?

- Visit and/or read as much information as you can.
- Start a file to keep track of some of the issues.

Becoming Involved

To become more involved, consider the following:

- Join a professional organization.
- Start to create a network of people—identify key individuals in the community and attend public meetings or board meetings.
- Join or obtain information from a lobby group or coalition.
- Participate on a **task force**. This is a local group that is looking at a particular issue in the community (e.g., hunger, poverty, or increasing child-care spaces) in order to identify the need and develop recommendations to address the problem.

> **task force**
> A local group of individuals set up to look at a particular issue in the community (e.g., hunger, poverty, or increasing child-care spaces) in order to identify the need and develop recommendations to address the problem.

In summary, advocacy skills are extremely important in the field of early childhood education. Early childhood educators may need to advocate on behalf of themselves, the children under their care, or the families they work with. All of us are capable of advocating for issues that concern us. As early childhood educators, because of our training, interest in the well-being of children and their families, and the enjoyment of what we do, we are in a unique position to make an impact. It takes time, dedication, and a belief in ourselves that we can make a difference. The rewards are tremendous—working together on a common cause, empowering ourselves to know that we can make a difference, learning to increase our skills, working with diverse groups of people, and sometimes precipitating real change.

BUILDING SKILLS TO UNDERSTAND LEGISLATIVE REQUIREMENTS

All licensed child-care falls under legislative requirements. These requirements

- vary across Canada;
- mandate regulation to provide child-care services;
- regulate teacher–child ratios;
- state teacher training requirements;
- regulate centre size and group size; and
- list health and safety requirements.

Early childhood educators need to know the regulations and guidelines that are used by the jurisdictions that they work in. The regulations are usually available through the child-care services branch of that jurisdiction. "Each of the provinces and territories has a provincial program of regulated child care that usually encompasses nursery or preschool, centre-based full-day child care, regulated family child care and school-aged child care. The provincial child care programs provide legislated requirements for operation of services and a variety of funding arrangements, usually under a social community services ministry" (Friendly, Beach, & Turiano, 2002, p. 1).

It is important to know the regulations that you will be working under. This empowers you to work under conditions that are known to you, which, in turn, empowers you to understand

- which working conditions are justified and which ones should be changed;
- what you need to know about setting up safe and healthy environments for children;
- what types of activities should be engaged in regularly; and
- what conditions you need to advocate to change.

BUILDING A CONTEXT OF HOW EARLY CHILDHOOD FITS INTO THE SOCIETAL SYSTEM

The children that you will work with are all part of a societal structure. Within this structure you will find a variety of variations in the practices and ideas on how children should be raised. These ideas and practices depend on many factors:

- economic status of the family;
- belief systems (religious, political, philosophical, cultural);
- background experiences of the adults in the community;
- ethnic background;
- value placed on educational activities;
- family stability;
- type of family grouping;
- types of recreational activities available;
- health of family; and
- services available to family (e.g., medical, dental, psychological, speech and language, and support for special needs).

Children are sensitive to all of the influences within their community. Early childhood programs must support the community the child lives in. "Children learn best in the context of a community in which they are safe and valued, their physical needs are met, and they feel psychologically secure" (Gestwicki, 1999, p. 11). In order to create such a community for children, the adults need to value the experiences that the children bring to the daycare setting and be knowledgeable about the backgrounds the children come from. It is the interaction of all factors that leads to healthy growth and development (see Figure 4.11).

KEY POINTS

BUILDING EFFECTIVE COMMUNICATION SKILLS
- Interactive process—encode, send, decode, understand.

1. **Skills with children:**
   - Active listening.
   - Observing and interpreting.
   - Communicating—clarifying messages, responding verbally and physically to messages expressed, turn-taking.

The Interaction of Influences in the Early Years

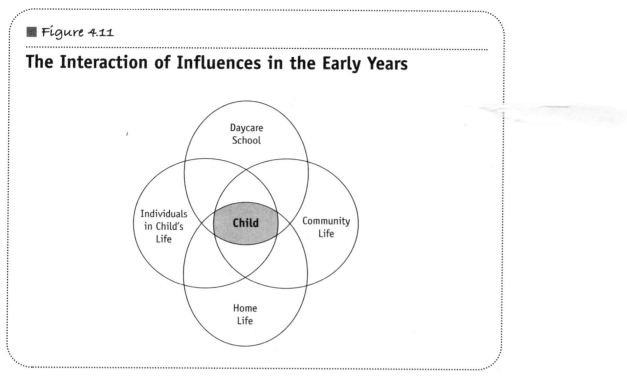

Note: The interaction point in the centre is the child.

2. **Skills with adults:**
   - Active listening.
   - Communicating effectively—paraphrasing, expressing, understanding, asking questions, taking cues from speaker.
   - Providing appropriate location for discussions.

BUILDING EFFECTIVE OBSERVATION SKILLS
- Criteria for good observation skills: reliability, validity, freedom from bias, objectivity, conciseness, observation over time, observation in more than one setting.
- Acquire participant observations.
- Use a variety of types of tools for different purposes.
- Interpret observations.

BUILDING DEVELOPMENTALLY APPROPRIATE GUIDANCE SKILLS
1. **Knowledge base:**
   - Child development and ages and stages of development.

2. **Guidance techniques for various ages:**
   - Infants—consistent, prompt, predictable patterns of interaction.
   - Toddlers—recognize need for independence; encourage and praise efforts; redirect behaviours; provide safe environments (indoor and outdoor) for free exploration.
   - Preschoolers—support growing independence; provide experiences to encourage cooperation, negotiation, and other social skills.
   - School-aged children—set realistic limits; encourage negotiation, problem solving, and collaboration skills.

3. **Influencing factors on children's behaviour:**
   - Style and temperament; individual backgrounds.

BUILDING SKILLS TO PLAN COLLABORATIVE LEARNING EXPERIENCES
- Set up collaborative learning situations.
- Build skills to enhance collaboration.
- Engage in a collaborative process.

BUILDING EFFECTIVE ADVOCACY SKILLS
- Knowledge of self-interest issues.
- Knowledge of well-being of families and children.
- Knowledge and participation in advocacy activities.
- Applying skills of effective advocates.
- Building advocacy strategies.

BUILDING SKILLS TO UNDERSTAND LEGISLATIVE REQUIREMENTS
- Knowledge of licensing requirements.
- Procurement of regional requirements.

BUILDING A CONTEXT OF HOW EARLY CHILDHOOD FITS INTO THE SOCIETAL SYSTEM
- Interaction of many variables.

EXERCISES

1. Observe an interaction between a child and an adult. Record what is happening as you observe the interactions. Using Figure 4.2 (page 86) as an example, describe the process that you observe.

2. Using the chart on page 117, observe a child-care professional interact with children. Record the types of interactions that you observe. Reflect upon the quality of one of the interactions you observed. Share your reflections with a small group of peers:

   a) Was the message understood? How do you know?
   b) How do you think the individuals felt during and after the interaction? How do you know?

3. Jason arrived with his three-year-old son Sam just as the daycare was opening. Sam was still in his pyjamas. He was crying and clinging to his father. Jason looked at Jetta, the early childhood educator, and said, "Here, he's your problem now." He pried Sam's fingers from his neck, handed him to Jetta, and quickly left.

   Reflect upon this situation and answer the following:

   a) What do you need to do immediately?
   b) What additional information do you need?
   c) What strategies could you use when Jason comes to pick up Sam in the evening?

4. Look at photo 4.22 on page 118. What factual information can you record about the children? What additional information do you need to gather? Compare your observations with another individual. Evaluate your efforts by answering the following questions:

   a) Is your information objective?
   b) Is your information complete?

Interaction Patterns

INTERACTIONS	DESCRIPTION OF BEHAVIOUR OBSERVED
Listening	
Observing	
Interpreting	
Clarifying	
Verbal Responses	
Physical Responses	
Turn-Taking	
Other	

c) Can you interpret any information from what you observe in this photo?

d) Did you both require the same additional information?

5. In a small group, look over the list of behaviours below. Decide which of these behaviours are subjective and which are objective, and indicate why for each of your answers. Compare your answers with the larger group.

- Jane did the dishes.
- Jason put on his shoes.
- Judy used a tripod grasp to write her name in the upper left-hand corner of a small white piece of paper.
- Arrive at 10 o'clock.
- Make a peanut butter sandwich.
- Sarah put her shoes on the right feet.
- Drawing of circle—thin red crayon line, covered the whole paper.
- Put 15 red circular beads of the same size on a red piece of gimp.

Photo 4.22

6. In a small group, create a list of positive guidance techniques for two age groups. How are your lists similar or different?

7. Jillian, the mother of a two-year-old, tells you that her son is really testing her. He won't do anything he is told. He is simply into everything. This morning he cleared out all of her kitchen cupboards. Everything was all over the floor. He gets really upset with his older (four-year-old) sister. He tries to take everything she is playing with away from her. Jillian indicated that none of her techniques work. She wants to know why he is so good at daycare and so bad at home.

   a) How would you respond to her initially?
   b) What additional information might you wish to get from Jillian before you try to advise her?
   c) What strategies might you use to help her?

8. Look over the advocacy skills listed. Which one of the issues listed could you become passionate about? What strategies that are listed could you use?

9. Look at some newspapers or magazines. Identify one issue related to child-care. What advocacy strategies could be used to help deal with this issue?

10. Obtain a copy of the legislation requirements in your area. In a small group, list and discuss the major categories of requirements. Which of the requirements affect you directly as you are entering into the field?

11. Using Figure 4.8 (page 104), develop a profile for yourself to show the influences that are prevalent in your life at this time. Compare your results with someone else's.

REFERENCES

Abbott, J., & Ryan, T. (1999). Learning to Go with the Grain of the Brain. *Education Canada, 39,* 8–11.

Crowther, I. (2003). *Creating Effective Learning Environments.* Scarborough, ON: Thomson Nelson.

DeVito, J., Shimoni, R., & Clark, D. (2001). *Messages: Building Interpersonal Communication Skills* (Canadian ed.). Toronto, ON: Addison Wesley Longman.

Doherty, G. (2003). *Occupational Standards for Child Care Practitioners.* Ottawa, ON: Canadian Childcare Federation.

Firlik, R. (2003). Early Years Summit Preschool–Kindergarten: Collaboration Makes a Difference. *Young Children, 58*(1), 73–78.

Fraser, S. (2000). *Authentic Childhood: Experiencing Reggio Emilia in the Classroom.* Scarborough, ON: Nelson Thomson Learning.

Friendly, M., Beach, J., & Turiano, M. (2002). *Early Childhood Education and Care in Canada.* Toronto, ON: University of Toronto, Childcare Resources and Research Unit.

Gestwicki, C. (1999). *Developmentally Appropriate Practice* (2nd ed.). Scarborough, ON: Nelson Canada.

Gordon, A., & Browne, K. (1996). *Guiding Young Children in a Diverse Society.* Needham Heights, MA: Allyn & Bacon.

Harris Helm, J., & Beneke, S. (2003). *The Power of Projects: Meeting Contemporary Challenges in Early Childhood Classrooms*. New York, NY: Teachers College Press.

Jensen, M., & Hannibal, M. (2000). *Issues, Advocacy and Leadership in Early Education*. Needham Heights, MA: Allyn & Bacon.

Kostelnik M., Whiren, A., Soderman, A., Stein, L., & Gregory, K. (2002). *Guiding Children's Social Development: Theory to Practice* (4th ed.). Albany, NY: Delmar Thomson Learning.

Miller, D. (2000). *Positive Child Guidance* (3rd ed.). Albany, NY: Delmar Thomson Learning.

Nilsen, B. (2001). *Week-by-Week Plans for Observing and Recording Young Children*. Albany, NY: Delmar Thomson Learning.

Wilson, L. (2001). *Partnerships: Families and Communities in Canadian Early Childhood Education*. Scarborough, ON: Nelson Thomson Learning.

BUILDING PARTNERSHIPS

My Friends

My friend Terry comes from India. He is very tall.

CHAPTER
5

My friend Troy is Canadian. He is short.

My friend Daniel comes from Africa.

My friend Sarah has only a mommy.

CHRIS

"Being sociologically mindful also means paying attention to the hardships and options other people face. If we understand how others' circumstances differ from ours, we are likely to show compassion for them and to grant them the respect they deserve as human beings. We are less likely to condemn them unfairly …"
(Mooney et al., 2001, p. 10)

Chapter Outcomes

After reading this chapter, the reader will

1. Describe the social structures and identify how each structure affects the child and his or her family.
2. Discuss how family health influences the lives of children.
3. Describe the characteristics of a well-functioning family.
4. Describe some of the reasons that might lead to families becoming dysfunctional.
5. Describe how parenting styles affect the developing child.
6. Explain the relationship between appropriate recreational activities and healthy growth and development.
7. Discuss how cultural diversity impacts on the care of young children.
8. Describe potential partners and the value each partner adds to the daycare setting.
9. Identify strategies for developing partnerships.
10. Identify potential resources that are gained through developing partnerships.
11. Discuss what partners need to maintain a partnership relationship.
12. Identify strategies for communicating, planning, and evaluating with partners.

COMMUNITY CONTEXT

"Society is a system of interconnected parts that work together in harmony to maintain a state of balance and social equilibrium for the whole" (Mooney et al., 2001, p. 11). The interconnecting parts of a social system include institutions (e.g., schools, daycares, and families), social groups (e.g., circle of friends or the staff of a daycare centre), **culture** (customs, beliefs, and language), and social status (e.g., child, doctor, or parent) (see Figures 5.1, 5.2, and 5.3). Understanding of the various social structures helps to put into perspective how

culture
"[T]he values, beliefs, and material objects that constitute a people's way of life" (Macionis et al., 1997, p. 637).

- children and families interact with each other and with others;
- the various roles in families (father, accountant, husband, son, brother) affect the relationships and well-being of individuals;
- the organization of social structures may influence individuals both positively and negatively, depending on the experiences that they may have in a social group; and
- children's development (social, emotional, cognitive, and physical) is influenced by all of these factors.

Children function within the social institutions in either primary or secondary groups (see Figure 5.2). Understanding of the interactions that occur in various social groupings leads to better understanding about how children

- form relationships with primary caregivers and other individuals;
- learn about themselves and about others;
- learn to interact within different social groups;
- form and maintain friendships; and
- learn to work by themselves or with others to accomplish tasks.

Figure 5.1

Elements of Social Structure: Social Institutions

TRADITIONAL INSTITUTIONS

- Family
- Religion
- Politics
- Economics
- Education

ADDITIONAL INSTITUTIONS

- Science
- Technology
- Mass media
- Medicine
- Sports
- Military

Figure 5.2

Social Groups

PRIMARY GROUP

- Small numbers of individuals
- Interact intimately (e.g., mother, father, and newborn interacting to establish attachment)
- Interact informally (e.g., friendships)

SECONDARY GROUP

- Small or large numbers of individuals
- Interactions based on accomplishment of tasks (e.g., working together to complete a painting)
- Interactions impersonal and formal (e.g., playing as one team member on a baseball team to win the game)

Figure 5.3

Social Status

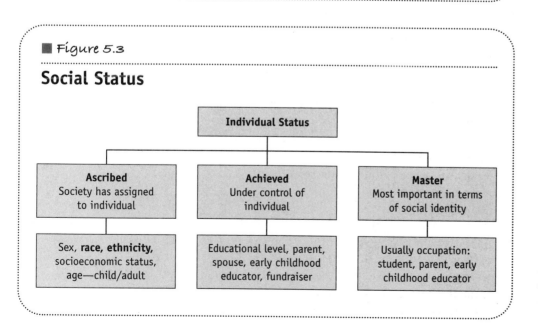

ascribed social status
Status society has ascribed to the individual (e.g., sex, race, ethnicity, or socioeconomic status).

achieved social status
Status under the control of the individual (e.g., educational level, volunteer, or parent).

master social status
Social identity—usually based on occupation.

race
A group of people sharing inherited physical characteristics such as skin colour, facial features, hair texture, and body shape.

ethnicity
A "shared cultural heritage. Members of an ethnic category may have common ancestors, language, and religion which, together, confer a distinctive social identity" (Macionis et al., 1997, p. 311).

■ Figure 5.4

Elements of Culture

BELIEFS

- What is perceived or defined to be true (e.g., Does spanking a child lead to future aggressive behaviour?).

VALUES

- What is perceived to be good or bad.
- The quality of interactions in the early childhood years lay the foundations for healthy development in all domains.

SYMBOLS

- A representation of something.
- Used to communicate with each other.
- Include language, gestures, facial expressions (e.g., raised eyebrows to express lack of understanding), body language (e.g., leaning away to express invasion of private space or shaking of the head to mean no), and objects (e.g., books or signs, or a shamrock identified as good luck).

norms
Rules or guidelines for social behaviour.

sanctions
Consequences associated with the breaking of social norms.

It is also important to understand the role that culture plays within the community context. "Culture refers to the meanings and ways of life that characterize a society. The elements of culture include beliefs, values, **norms**, **sanctions**, and symbols" (Mooney et al., 2001, p. 11) (see Figure 5.4). The interaction between the cultural and social elements and structures leads to better understanding about

- why individuals behave the way they do;
- what values are placed on behaviours, actions, and aspirations; and
- how actions and behaviours influence child-rearing practices.

All of these factors—social institutions, groups, status, and culture—are interconnected and play a role in the development of a child (see Figure 5.5):

- The economic situation of a family will dictate the number and quality of experiences that a family can afford when raising a child.
- The political climate will dictate the quality of care and education that the child will receive. "Children ensure that a society goes on and determine the quality of that society. Societies and governments have an obligation to the future to devise systems that ensure effective parenting, support good child development, and take into account socioeconomic factors associated with a changing economy and the increasing participation of women in the labor force" (McCain & Mustard, 1999, p. 11).
- Religious beliefs will influence some of the values and norms that a child is raised with. "Religion unites people through shared symbols, values, and norms. Religious doctrine and ritual establish rules of 'fair play' that makes organized social life possible" (Macionis, Clarke, & Gerber, 1997, p. 485).
- The status of the family will influence the interactions the child will have with others. "We praise university professors, film directors, or dance choreographers as 'cultured,' because they presumably appreciate the 'finer things in life'…. By contrast, we speak less generously of ordinary people, assuming that everyday cultural patterns are somehow less worthy" (Macionis et al., 1997, p. 75).

Interplay of Social Structures

ECONOMICS—DICTATE CHOICES THAT CAN BE MADE

- child-care—live-in-nanny
- meals—variety and nutrition as recommended by Canada's Food Guide
- enriched experiential background—frequent trips to visit extended family or vacation nationally and internationally
- environment rich in learning materials—books, toys, equipment, musical instruments, CDs

SOCIAL STATUS

- Lara—female, toddler, dependant
- Mother—dentist, parent, daughter, spouse
- Father—doctor, parent, son, spouse

RELIGION

- family follows own religious beliefs, not tied to formal religion
- Lara does not attend programs through a church organization

POLITICS

- province of Alberta sets guidelines for child-care services
- one adult in four with full two-year training

EDUCATION

- high educational level of parents
- provide early educational experiences for Lara—reading, musical activities, educational toys, swimming
- daycare inconvenient and a desire of higher quality led to hiring of in-home nanny

TECHNOLOGY

- environment rich in experiences: video, camera, computer, television, CD player, keyboard

FAMILY

- Lara first Canadian born
- both parents born in Iran
- mother completed high school in Germany, father in England; both parents completed university education in Canada
- extended family abroad

BELIEFS

- children need to be exposed to unconditional love
- all aspects of development need to be nurtured to raise a healthy child
- positive behaviour is important

VALUES

- strong sense of family
- growing up with a strong sense of heritage
- growing up confident and polite
- successful in her personal choices

MEDICINE

- knowledgeable dental and medical care

CULTURE

- different cultural celebrations, such as New Year (March 21)
- encourage use of Farsi and English at home
- greetings—kiss on first right then left cheek
- music and dance encouraged at family gatherings
- Persian food often eaten

- The culture that a child is raised in will influence the values and beliefs that the child grows up with. "Culture affects every aspect of our lives. Children's games, for example, may seem like light-hearted fun, but through them we teach young people what our culture deems important" (Macionis et al., 1997, p. 70).

FAMILY DYNAMICS

In addition to the factors identified above, children are also influenced by the way their family is structured and functions. "The structure of the family and the character of relationships within it makes up the primary setting for child development" (Hanvey, 2002, p. 8). According to the Canadian Council on Social Development (Hanvey, 2002), families develop healthy living styles for all members when the following factors are in balance: family health, family function, family support mechanisms, parenting styles, and family recreation. These factors are key to the healthy development of young children. When families are free from worry, are healthy and fit, have knowledge about how to raise children, and are able to play as a family, children gain by building many positive experiences that lead to growth and development in all domains—physical, emotional, social, and cognitive.

1. Family Health

Consider the following:

- Almost 75 percent of children in Canada live with families whose parents are in good health.
- "Ten percent of children under 12 live in families where a parent is restricted in their activity at home because of a health condition—a figure which has remained virtually unchanged since 1994" (Hanvey, 2002, p. 10).
- One common health-related problem is depression. Parental depression is often linked to income. The lower the income, the greater the chance of depression. Twenty percent of children live in homes with a depressed parent (Hanvey, 2003).

Good parental health is one of the critical factors that leads to healthy development of children. Parents who are suffering from illness or depression often lack the energy to care for their children appropriately or to provide the stimulation needed. Celina and Yannis have a newborn, Carlos, who is nine weeks old. They also have two other preschool children, a boy and a girl, who attend a daycare in the area. Yannis is a long-distance truck driver. He had been given short-distance runs so that he could be closer to home, but has now left for a long-distance run.

Carlos has been a difficult baby. He cries all the time. It is hard to settle him. He cries when he is being cuddled, held, or played with. Celina is exhausted. She misses her work, and she would rather be anywhere than at home with a screaming infant. She is very unhappy with her life at this time. In the evening, after she has picked up her other two children, she puts Carlos in his playpen and tells her children that they can watch their brother and watch TV while Celina has a nap.

Celina has no idea what the children are watching or doing. Contrary to her routines before Carlos was born, she does not talk to her children about their day nor does she check to see if they might be hungry. When her husband returns, he realizes that Celina needs help. The doctor diagnoses that Celina is depressed. With medication and help, Celina manages to overcome her depression and revert back to her normal self.

Children in circumstances similar to the children of Celina and Yannis are often also left to care for and entertain themselves. Often this leads to inappropriate activities such as

- lack of personal attention and care;
- too much watching of inappropriate TV;
- playing too many video games (photo 5.1);
- lack of supervised play outside; and
- lack of knowledge about where children are or what they are doing.

The health of children is another cause of stress for families. When a child is ill, the family members may not always be able to take the time off work to cope with a sick child. Leaving a sick child in someone else's care often causes stress in the workplace. Family members will worry about the health of their child and may not function as efficiently as usual. Family members who cannot afford alternative care, or who may lose a day's pay for every day they are not at work, face the additional burden of worrying about how to make up that income to meet their bills. This again could lead to a less effective functioning family unit.

Photo 5.1

What Can You Do?

- Avoid making judgments or jumping to conclusions.
- Gain as much information about the child and family so that you can offer a more informed program for the child.
- Have a variety of parent resources available (e.g., listing of local services and information pamphlets of services provided).
- Be open-minded and flexible.
- Work with the family members as partners to plan an appropriate program for the child.

2. Family Functioning

Children's first teachers are the family members that they are in touch with. The quality of the interactions during these first years lays the foundations of all future abilities. "The quality of early sensory stimulation influences the brain's ability to think and regulate bodily function" (McCain et al., 1999, p. 25). In fact, early deprivation, abuse, and/or neglect can have long-lasting negative consequences. "Negative experiences in the early years have long-lasting effects that can be difficult to overcome later" (McCain & Mustard, 1999, p. 26).

The majority of Canadian children grow up in families that function well. In these households emphasis is placed on

- positive ongoing communication;
- encouraging equality in interactions (all view points are listened to and appreciated, without bias);
- joint problem solving (families make decisions together, involving all family members in the decision making process);
- sensitivity to emotional growth and development (feelings are acknowledged and respected of all family members equally); and
- role differentiation (roles are not assigned according to gender).

The number of children living in dysfunctional households is directly proportional to levels of income. In households earning less than $20 000, 23 percent of the children live with dysfunctional families. In comparison, in households earning less than $40 000, only 9 percent of children live with dysfunctional families (Hanvey, 2002).

dysfunctional families
Families that do not function well together (e.g., they fail to solve problems together, fail to communicate adequately with each other, are emotionally neglectful, and may not function appropriately in their family roles).

Some of the reasons for **dysfunctional families** (i.e., families that do not function well together, fail to solve problems together, fail to communicate adequately with each other, are emotionally neglectful, and may not function appropriately in their family roles) include

- poverty;
- divorce;
- ill health;
- depression;
- alcohol or substance abuse;
- crime and violence; and
- abuse and neglect.

It is important to consider all factors when dealing with children that are from dysfunctional families. These children tend to be high-needs children, requiring more attention, more empathy, and more loving care. Caregivers must be sensitive to the circumstances surrounding the child and try not to lay blame for these circumstances.

What Can You Do?

self-fulfilling prophecy
Situation in which "we behave according to the expectations of others" (Mooney et al., 2001, p. 140).

- Avoid labelling the child and the family to avoid the **self-fulfilling prophecy**: "The self-fulfilling prophecy implies that we behave according to the expectations of others" (Mooney et al., 2001, p. 140). When someone is continually labelled as stupid, the individual may form a negative self-concept and start to believe that he or she is stupid and thus behave in a "stupid manner."
- Establish a respectful relationship with all families. Strive for an open manner, active listening, clear communication, and equal treatment of all families.
- Provide support as needed. Use active listening, make available or post listings of support services, refer families to other support services, and provide early and late snacks to children.

3. Family Support Networks

How well families function is also dependent upon the support structure that the family can access. These support structures include a network of friends, relatives, neighbours, and sometimes professionals such as nurses. Within a support network, individuals are able to talk about their problems, exchange services such as child-care, and receive suggestions and advice. "Networks within and outside the family often provide much-needed support for children and their parents. If a child does not receive adequate care within the family, support networks can provide them with positive and nurturing experiences" (Hanvey, 2002, p. 10). Support networks include

- family members, friends, and neighbours;
- support groups (e.g., play and learn groups, support groups for children with special needs);
- medical support groups (for breastfeeding or failure to thrive); and
- informal groups—groups formed through identified need by individuals or agencies such as child-care settings or resource centres.

Low-income families (families with incomes less than $20 000 per year) and their children often do not receive the level of social support needed. Many families in lower-income areas do not have the needed support structures. They may be isolated from their family, lack the self-confidence to socialize, or lack the resources to entertain others.

What Can You Do?

- Identify needs within the community.
- Identify existing resources within the community.
- Advocate for resources not within the community.
- Empower all families to help in the planning and implementing of strategies to maximize support services for all within their community.

4. Family Parenting Styles

Key to the healthy development of children are the positive interactions and stimulation in the first three years of life. It is during this time that brain development is most rapid, and that billions of brain neurons are formed. This development leads to an integrated network of connections within a child's brain that last a lifetime. "A child who misses positive stimulation or is subject to chronic stress in the first years of life may have difficulty overcoming a bad start" (McCain & Mustard, 1999, p. 52). Parenting style is constant across all income levels. However, many parents often request information on appropriate childrearing practices.

What Can You Do?

- Provide resources to families on positive parenting strategies (e.g., newsletters, workshops, bulletin boards, guest speakers at meetings).
- Become aware of parenting training programs in the community so that these can be posted and recommended.
- Form informal community discussion groups about positive guidance techniques and encourage diverse participation (e.g., invite extended family members, community members, politicians).
- Conduct periodic parenting workshops within the daycare community on positive parenting.
- Post strategies to encourage discussion about alternatives.

5. Family Recreation

Children need recreational activities—both physical and social—for healthy growth and development in all areas (social, emotional, cognitive, and physical) to occur. Recreational activities have been identified as leading to greater success at school, higher self-confidence, and better social skills (Hanvey, 2002). In Canada, 89 percent of children between birth and three years of age are at or above age norms for motor and social development (Government of Canada, 2002). Children in lower-income families tend to spend less time in social and motor activities, as these families have fewer resources to spend on recreational activities. As a result, these children often have

- delays in normal motor activities such as crawling, walking, and riding;
- delays in social competence;
- delays in language competence;
- poor self-confidence; and
- subsequent decreased success in school years.

For children four to nine years old, there has been a steady decline in participating in recreational activities since 1994. Children are increasingly less physically active, leading to increased obesity and less time in active play. "Over half of children and youth aged 5 to 17 are not active enough for optimal health benefits" (Hanvey, 2002, p. 42). The rate of decline is greatest among the children in lower-income families. Young children learn best through active play. Since many children spend up to eight hours of their day in a daycare setting, it is critical that caregivers provide opportunities for

- participation in outdoor activities daily, at least one hour in the morning and one hour in the afternoon;
- practising physical skills—such as climbing, riding, sliding, swinging, running, and balancing—daily;
- engaging in physical activity that builds strength, endurance, balance, and coordination; and
- engaging in outdoor activities with peers in noncompetitive social settings.

In summary,

Families are shaped by the physical and community environments in which they live. Communities provide both basic infrastructure for family life, including housing, education, and employment. Physical surroundings can greatly affect children's health and well-being, and research is beginning to provide evidence that growing up in a community that is perceived to have higher levels of cohesion, stability and social support will lead to healthier child development. (Government of Canada, 2002, p. 3)

CULTURAL DIVERSITY

Canada is undergoing considerable demographic change that is marked by the growing strength of non-European cultures and languages. On the basis of ethnic origins there has been a significant increase in recent years of the non-European mother tongues while those of Canadian, British, French and other European backgrounds have had little overall growth. (Jedwab, 2003, p. 1)

There has been an increase in the number of individuals declaring themselves as Canadian only, and this accounts for the perceived drop in the number of individuals declaring themselves from English or French backgrounds. Statistical diversity varies

Ethnic Diversity in Canada

Identification of Ethnic Origin	Countries of Origin	Percentage
English	England, Ireland, Scotland	24%
Canadian	Canada (individuals identifying themselves only as Canadian)	29%
French	France	11.5%
Native	Canada (all provinces and territories)	4%
European	Germany, Holland, Italy, Poland, Ukraine, Spain, Portugal, Greece, Russia, Belgium, other European nations	21 %
Non-European	See "Visible minorities" below	10.5%
Visible minorities	Total	9.7%
	China	2.5%
	Southern Asia (India and Pakistan)	2.2%
	Africa	1.6%
	Philippines, Latin America, Southeast Asia, Arab nations, Korea, and Japan	3.4 %

Sources: Macionis et al., 1997; Jedwab, 2003.

across Canada and is usually more pronounced within larger urban centres. Table 5.1 presents an outline of ethnic diversity in Canada.

The impact of this change in diversity affects the general population in the following ways:

- The percentage of those whose mother tongue is neither English nor French has increased to nearly 30 percent.
- There is an underrepresentation of cultural activities in the performing arts and mass media.
- There is a lack of understanding about different belief/value systems held by various cultures.
- Prejudice toward some cultures has increased due to current world events. For example, after the terrorist attacks of September 11, 2001, many families of Arab background and of the Muslim faith faced discrimination. One four-year-old came to daycare in tears. When asked why she was upset, she said, "My mommy and daddy are not bad. Why do people think they are bad?" Someone had sworn at her parents on the way to daycare.
- Greater demands are made on daycare and educational systems to deliver quality programs.
- Greater knowledge is required by early childhood educators and teachers in order to understand the complexity of a multicultural environment and develop sensitivity to issues within a multicultural context.

What Can You Do?

- Provide materials and resources that represent individuals from various ethnic groups—pictures, stories, books, eating utensils, dress-up clothes, food, and so on.
- Avoid focusing too heavily on main-culture religious holidays such as Christmas and Easter.
- Depict special cultural events accurately—festivals, special occasions, and various religious events.
- Invite visitors of various ethnic groups to come and interact with the children.
- Depict cultural events by providing materials and resources in various languages. Include books, music, alphabets, writing utensils, and prints of paintings from different cultures.
- Visit local museums that depict aspects of Canadian cultural heritage.
- Research what the ethnic diversity is in your area and learn more about that culture.

WORKING WITH PARTNERS

Working with partners helps to decrease some of the work for early childhood educators and provide a higher-quality program for the children. It serves to cement relationships between the home and the school. In order to develop effective partnerships a number of criteria need to be considered.

Identification of Partners

Kaya, an early childhood educator, often feels a sense of isolation and frustration. She leaves the house at 6:00 A.M. and is usually not back home until after 6:00 P.M. Over the past two years, she has worked with 24 different co-workers. Most of these co-workers had very little training or no training in early childhood education. This situation, coupled with minimum wage salaries, seems to guarantee a high turnover of staff.

Each time a new staff member is hired, Kaya is involved in training that person. The quality underpinnings of her program suffer as often the new staff member either does not understand the quality issues or brings a more adult-focused approach to dealing with young children.

Kaya is learning to cope with these problems by actively finding and encouraging partners to help her. Sharing the load and frustrations helps her to put things into perspective, gives her some valuable help to cope with problems, and helps her maintain a positive outlook toward her chosen profession. Some of the partners she has worked with include family members, community members, mentors, and other professionals.

Family Members

Web exercises 🖑

In most cases, family members are working. Balancing a work schedule and home life is busy enough without adding more work. Kaya has tried a variety of strategies that help her to find and involve families in meaningful ways (see Table 5.2). This helps families form closer relationships with centre staff and gain greater insights into

Strategies to Find and Include Family Members

Web exercises

Strategy	Description	Result
Posting periodic letters that identify interesting interactions within the program	Information about exciting events that are about to occur—field trips, visitors, special events. Sign-up list of activities that families could do to help (see Figure 5.6).	Two families went to the library with their children and picked out series of books. Five families took their children to a nature area and took photographs of animal tracks to bring back. One father offered to come in to show the children how to make plaster moulds of the tracks.
Posting schedule of activities per week	Listing major interests of children along with planned activities. Comment section for input from families. List of materials to enhance activities.	Books—some families accessed library and some brought personal books. All families collected materials. Listing of where to purchase puzzles, beads. Listing of additional ideas—fossils, using disinfected chicken or turkey bones, creating dinosaur silhouettes, famous paintings of dinosaurs, a dinosaur song
Listing of current issues	Not enough shade in the playground.	One family member formed a working group of interested family members to look into the problem. Group approached local Kinsmen Club, which funded building of a deck.
Documentation book of children's activities that could be signed out to take home overnight	Photo albums with written descriptions about the various learning activities. One album per activity or interest, such as sand play or dinosaur interest.	Albums signed out frequently. Families started to bring in photos or work done at home to add to the albums.

their child's day, and it offers real suggestions and help to improve the program for their child. It helps also to reduce some of the everyday stress and frustration for Kaya and cuts down some of her preparation time.

These activities helped strengthen the bond between the families and the staff. A sense of joint responsibility toward the care of the children started to emerge. Over time, Kaya was able to identify and request help from

- key individuals who had time, interest, and energy to help organize pertinent activities;
- individuals who could participate in meaningful alternative ways (e.g., preparing a monthly newsletter, collecting materials, identifying resources, and preparing materials by making puzzles out of pictures, creating box blocks, or cutting down clothes to fit children);

Discoveries in the Snow

WE DISCOVERED THAT:

- You collect snow on your boots by shuffling your feet.
- Different boots made different tracks.
- We found different tracks that animals and birds made in the snow.
- We could copy tracks we found in the snow.

WE WANT TO CONTINUE TO WORK ON WHAT WE LEARNED. PLEASE HELP US WITH:

- Taking us out around our neighbourhood to find tracks.
- Taking photographs or drawing pictures of tracks that we see.
- Bringing in books on tracks that you have.
- Making models of tracks.

- individuals who could come during program time to help with special activities; and
- individuals who would participate in board activities and short-term small projects or committees.

Here's another example of the value family members can bring to a daycare setting. The Sunshine Kinderschool lacked appropriate outdoor gross motor equipment. A group of family members decided to raise money for the materials to build a wooden play structure. Another group worked on getting community partnerships. Each partner would provide the cost of one piece of equipment, such as a slide or clatter bridge. One of the fathers worked on a construction site. He was able to borrow the grader to prepare the ground. When all the equipment arrived, one group of parents and grandparents helped to put the equipment in place. Another group brought a picnic lunch and snacks. Together the families, the community, and the staff helped to build an appropriate play ground for their children.

Community Members

Gaining partnerships in the community takes much longer. Kaya decided that the first step for her would be to try to identify those community members that had materials or equipment that could be donated. The steps in this process included the following:

1. Brainstorming with staff and family identified potential free resources that could be used in the daycare.
2. Staff and family members identified who in the community might have these resources—retailers (for camera supplies, wallpaper, and fabric), builders, restaurants, hotels, telephone companies, moving companies, shoe stores, printers, gardening firms, professionals (e.g., doctors, nurses, and dentists), hospitals, and newspaper offices.
3. A support letter was developed (see Figure 5.7).
4. Staff identified which resources they wanted to gather. Telephone contact was made with the different agencies, and then a letter was mailed. This activity was organized and implemented by family volunteers.

This process served a number of significant purposes:

- Contact was established with potential community members.
- Community members collected and donated materials. This not only saved the centre money, but also expanded the partnership list.
- Awareness was created in the community about the care and needs of young children.
- These community partners could be approached in the future to display advocacy information and post information about conferences or workshops.
- The partnership expanded to include staff, families, and community members. All these individuals were working toward a common goal—improved quality care for young children.

Mentors

Kaya realized that it was important to maintain a positive attitude toward her work—children, families, and staff. She had maintained contact with one of the faculty members at the community college where she had taken her early childhood education program. This faculty member agreed to become a mentor for her, and eventually to the program as a whole. This gave Kaya opportunities to contact another expert to discuss relevant issues and brainstorm solutions. Kaya found it a stress reliever just to be able to talk to someone else about the problems she encountered. Additionally, Kaya was able to put the issues and concerns into perspective because she was able to articulate what they were.

Mentoring may also occur on a formal level. An experienced early childhood educator (mentor) is paired with an inexperienced individual (protégé). This could be a student in training, an early childhood educator who is in need of professional development, or an individual that works in child-care and needs training. Usually, the mentor is assigned an individual and is paid for this endeavour. Mentoring serves the following purposes (Gestwicki & Bertrand, 2003):

- providing specialized training—working with children with special needs, developing advocacy strategies, and working with families;
- increasing skills needed to work with young children—observation, planning, environment, and outdoor play; and
- providing experiential training—support and feedback.

In three mentorship studies conducted in Canada with early childhood education students (Gestwicki & Bertrand, 2003, p. 137), the effectiveness of mentorship programs was evaluated. The following benefits were identified for both mentors and protégés:

Sample Letter Requesting Materials

Name of Daycare: ....

Address of Daycare: ....

....

Enterprise Name: ....

Address: ....

....

Date: ....

Dear [contact name]:

Thank you for your support. The materials that you have agreed to collect and supply for our program will be of great benefit to the children in our program. We use these materials [drop in correct choice]:

- For the creative efforts of children. Children use the paper for cutting and pasting, decorating, colouring, and painting on.
- For building. The boxes provide excellent opportunities to decorate and use as building blocks or dramatic play spaces. Cardboard boxes are also ideal for young children to use as they can be more safely built to greater heights. If they fall, children are less likely to get hurt.
- To teach children various means of attachment and a different perspective in creating with a different media. The wires are used to attach items together such as paper, cardboard, hinged items (windows on box sculptures, booklets, doors) and connecting vehicles. The wires are also used in weaving and creating wire sculptures. Wires are a great alternative for beading. The wire is always stiff and therefore lends itself to greater success with beading.
- To make the dramatic play of the children much more realistic and meaningful. Children will be able to gain a better understanding of the roles and responsibilities of the people in their community.
- To create storage for small items that children can easily organize themselves and use in various other aspects of the program such as sand and water play and in painting and gluing activities.

In appreciation [use collage of children for children to sign and send with letter],

[Signatures of staff]

Sample Letter Requesting Materials

- increased reflective practices;
- improvement for child-care practices; and
- valuable personal insights and learning about childhood practices.

Other Professionals

Kaya accessed other resources in her community to make her job and the job of her co-workers easier. These resources include public health services, associations, libraries, other child-care centres, and parent organizations. As before, she first had to create a listing of all the relevant organizations within her community. The second task was to identify what kinds of resources or services could be accessed by these various types of organizations (see Table 5.3).

Needs of Partners

The partners discussed previously have varying degrees of expectations. Families have the highest stake in establishing a partnership with a child-care centre staff. All families want to be assured that the health, safety, and well-being of their child are met at all times. Differences in expectations arise based on the cultural diversity of the children and families within each daycare setting.

Partnerships will flourish as long as all the needs of all the partners are met—staff, families, community members, and other professionals. Some common needs that may be identified for all partners are discussed below.

Web
exercises

Motivation

In order to establish and maintain an ongoing involvement with partners, all individuals involved must be motivated to want to participate. Some of the partners have a natural motivation to want to form a partnership. Family members are greatly interested in participating with the child-care staff to offer the best opportunities for their children. Lara's parents are very motivated to find the best care for her. They decided that it was not in her best interest to continue to attend the daycare that she had been enrolled in. They did not like to wake her up in the morning to meet their personal work schedule. They also did not like the regulated ratio of children to staff within the child-care setting. Thus, they opted for a live-in nanny.

Health-related services are also interested in maintaining healthy and safe environments for children. This is part of their mandate. Lara's father (a medical doctor) was also concerned that within daycare settings the spread of common ailments such as the cold and other childhood diseases was high. When Lara was ill, there were few opportunities to find viable alternatives for her care. A live-in nanny also solved this problem.

Since motivation is already in place, a logical next step is to ensure that the partnership is developed and will flourish over time.

Web
exercises

Partnership Climate

Care must be taken to establish a climate that is built on mutual trust. All individuals must feel that they are free to express ideas and opinions and that these ideas and opinions are accepted and valued. There needs to be recognition that disagreements are a natural part of all human relationships. It is how these disagreements are handled that is important. Individuals must feel that disagreements can be discussed openly and used as learning situations. Consensus can be built after commonalities in viewpoints are discovered and as individuals mutually agree to compromise.

Lara's parents discussed their concern with the child-care staff and indicated why they were removing Lara from their care. The child-care staff could understand that there was nothing that they could do to improve the ratio of adults to children. They

Professional Contacts and Resources

Professional Contacts	Resources
Public Health 1. Public health nurses 2. Public health inspectors 3. Pediatricians	• Consultation on illness, immunization, or other health concerns. • Resource materials—pamphlets, posters. • Regional/provincial health and safety requirements. • Information about sanitization procedures and products. • Information about inspection requirements—lighting, ventilation, kitchen facilities, garbage disposal. • Discussions—health-related concerns/issues.
Associations Early childhood professional association (usually provincial or territorial)	• Periodic newsletters or publications containing information about current issues, updates on political actions, advocacy issues, upcoming events, and research. • Opportunities to network with other professionals—committee work, board work, presenting at conferences, and workshops. • Professional development—conferences and workshops and, in some areas, accreditation possibilities.
Libraries	• Children's books, videos, music, pictures, and artwork on term loan. • Adult resources—journals and books on specific topics of interest.
Art galleries	• Consultation about art techniques and materials. • Field trips and specialized visitors. • Workshops to increase awareness about art.
Museums	• Consultation about history of local area. • Field trips and specialized visitors. • Workshops about historical events in the region.
Other child-care centres	• Area meetings—support meetings for individuals working in similar areas (e.g., infants, toddlers, preschool, school-aged, supervisors, special needs). • Sharing resources and ideas—jointly purchase specialized equipment and rotate use.
Parent groups (Most areas have groups that form to support each other, such as breastfeeding, special needs, and play groups.)	• Access valuable information and specific resources about specialized topics (e.g., health related or disability related). • Valuable source for guest speakers at staff meetings.
Board for child-care centre	• Help with advocacy issues, fundraising, and day-to-day concerns.
Fire Department	• Information about fire-retardant materials. • Resources to meet fire department inspection requirements.

could sympathize with the family frustration of waking up Lara in the morning to take her to daycare and her needs to be cared for when she was ill. Again, there was nothing the child-care centre could do about these concerns. Although they indicated that they would miss Lara, they could accept the family decision and an amicable end to the partnership occurred.

Feelings

It is especially important to recognize and respect the feelings of all partners. This is not always easy to do. The child-care provider may get a clue about the feelings of family members and children by listening to and observing interactions carefully. They should pay close attention to

- the body language of family members and children;
- the content of messages that are communicated;
- the manner in which messages are communicated; and
- the interaction patterns between the children and the family.

It is appreciated when feelings that are expressed are acknowledged. It is equally important to clarify personal impressions of feelings that have not been expressed. When Lara's mother picked up Lara from her daycare experience in the afternoon, Lara was busily playing with the blocks. Lara did not run to her mother as she usually did. The caregiver noticed Lara's mother's expression. She quickly went over to Lara and said, "Lara, your mother is here. Why don't you show her what you are doing?" Lara immediately looked up at her mother and smiled. As Lara's mother walked over to join Lara, the caregiver explained that the blocks were new and that all the children had been fascinated with the blocks all day. The caregiver had noticed that Lara's mother was a little hurt that Lara ignored her. She quickly redirected Lara's attention to her mother and explained why Lara's unusual behaviour was occurring. She also indicated that all the children were behaving similarly. Lara was not the only one to react this way.

Mutual Support

Individuals will get involved in partnership relationships when they feel that the relationship is a supportive one. Each partner needs to feel that all are sharing in the accomplishment of tasks. Some strategies that could be put in place to offer support include

- forming small groups to work on projects together;
- appointing leaders to take on specific projects to ensure project completion and offer encouragement;
- posting or publishing successes in newsletters;
- referring individuals with similar concerns or problems to each other; and
- ensuring that one staff member per group of children is always available during drop-off and pick-up times.

Kaya's group of children included a number of children from Jewish backgrounds. At Christmas, she posted a notice to indicate she needed some help in celebrating some of the Jewish customs. A number of parents signed up that they were interested in helping. When the parents came to pick up the children, Kaya asked each one if they could take this on as a project. One of the parents volunteered. She contacted the other parents to find out what kinds of help they could offer. This group of parents organized a number of resources—props, books, special snacks, decorations, and relevant procedures.

Unique Skills and Knowledge

All individuals have talents, knowledge, and skills that are unique to them. When partnerships make use of the talents, knowledge, and skills, everyone gains. The children and staff gain

- from the specialized expertise of the individuals;
- by learning new skills;
- by becoming more aware of the skills and talents of others;
- by receiving more individual attention; and
- by being exposed to more diverse ideas and viewpoints.

The partners gain

- satisfaction from being able to share special skills, knowledge, and talents;
- greater awareness of what the children are capable of achieving; and
- greater awareness of the complexities of the early childhood years and appropriate care.

Photo 5.2

Caregivers are not always aware of the skills and talents that families or community members bring to the table. In order to find out what skills and talents might exist, a caregiver could

- ask parents in the intake interview what skills they might have;
- post a list inviting families to indicate their special skills or talents;
- create a bulletin board display that highlights specialized skills and knowledge of families;
- talk to family members at drop-off or pick-up times about special interests; and
- listen to the children talk about what special things they have done with their families that the caregiver could tap into.

Kaya had noticed that Jenna's mother, Mary, often wore stylish hats when she dropped off her daughter. Kaya complimented Mary on her hats. Mary responded that this was her business. She was concerned that many individuals were not wearing the sun protection needed and decided to develop a line of cheap, stylish hats. She said she often wore her own hats to advertise her business. Kaya asked if Mary could share her skills with the children. Mary was very flattered. She said she would use some of her old hats that could not be sold and bring them for the children. She designed individual hats for each child. Children could pick a hat that they liked and add their own design to it. The design of the hat could be easily changed by attaching different Velcro pieces as decorations (photo 5.2).

Developing a Sense of Ownership

Individuals will continue to support and nurture a partnership relationship if they feel that they are contributing something worthwhile. There needs to be a sense of ownership and pride in what has been accomplished. When other family members saw the hats that had been created for the children, they became very interested in the concept of hat design. One of the fathers worked for a local newspaper. He asked one of the reporters to come in and do a human-interest story on hats and the importance of head protection. The centre soon came to be known affectionately as the "Great Hat Place." Staff, children, and family members were proud to be part of this venture. This served to

- raise awareness about the need for head protection;
- raise awareness of child-care in the community;
- provide some free advertisement for Mary's hat business and the daycare itself; and
- develop a sense of pride in all individuals associated with the centre.

Value of Time Spent

This is an age in which time is becoming a critical commodity. Families are working full-time and raising children simultaneously. With governmental cutbacks, many of the functions that used to be embedded in "jobs" have now fallen away or have been delegated to volunteers. As a result, many families and professionals are already overextended. It is critical, therefore, to give a clear picture of what the time involvement might be before asking individuals to commit to a task or project. Individuals are much more likely to participate if they know that this task requires three hours, or three meetings of one hour each.

Web exercises

Building Success

The greatest motivator to keeping partnerships in place is the success of the partnership. Everyone likes to be involved in successful operations. There are strategies that can be employed to lead to greater chances of success. These strategies include

- Starting with a small project—for example, collecting shoeboxes and covering these to make them appear more like real bricks. This type of project involves no cost. Individuals can take a few boxes home at a time to cover and return. Therefore, many individuals can be involved with a small time commitment from each.
- Setting a realistic budget. When costs are involved, carefully consider whether the project is financially feasible. If funding is required, make sure that the funding source will support the project.
- Avoiding projects that require ongoing funding sources. These require new proposals every year. Funding sources are not stable, and program components may be dropped if funding dries up. Instead, aim to attract a one-time funding source such as getting funding to put in a new piece of equipment in the playground.
- Carefully setting up working groups. Ensure that each group has a leader that can be relied upon to move the group from ideas to action.
- Avoiding working on too many projects at the same time. This has a tendency to spread the resources too thinly and would require someone to coordinate the activities.
- Setting realistic timelines to accomplish each activity or project.
- Involving all partners in the planning process.
- Expressing appreciation for the work that has been accomplished.

Communication with Partners

Communication with partners is usually high during the planning phases of a project. During the implementation stage, however, communications tend to drop off. Since these partners may be involved in other projects in the future, it would be prudent to continue to build links. Communication is one of these links that can keep relationships alive. Some of the techniques that might be used include

- sending out a thank-you letter to all participants upon the completion of a project;
- including individuals in the mailing of periodic newsletters about the program and the children;
- providing online access to information;
- sending pictures of the children engaged in activities related to the project; and
- sending out information that tells the partners how their donations were used by the children.

Planning with Partners

It is important to involve all partners in the planning process. Since it is difficult to work in large groups, planning might be done by small working groups. These groups can each work with a staff member. Groups could come together based on a common interest (e.g., building a garden with the children in the outside play area). Small groups that could come together to plan and implement this idea could include

- a group to design and ready the garden beds;
- a group of individuals to gather resources (e.g., books, pictures);
- a group of individuals to gather and share information with the larger partner group—families, staff, and community members;
- a group of individuals to research appropriate plant choices, prices, and locations prior to involving the children;
- a group of individuals to go on a field trip with children to pick out appropriate plants;
- a group of individuals interested in building the garden with the children; and
- a group of individuals interested in helping the children maintain their gardens.

In the above scenario, there is limited time involvement for anyone. Individuals can get involved at different levels. Some of the interactions are hands-on; others can be completed without actually spending time within the child-care centre. Individuals can choose the desired level of participation and involvement.

In some instances, individuals may well be interested but cannot find the time to meet. Alternative ways to involve these individuals could be to use telephone conferencing. This way the individual can participate from home with the rest of the groups. Additionally, computer technology is a great help to bridge gaps. Keeping individuals in touch via e-mail provides an additional mechanism for including partners.

Evaluating as Partners

Any process needs to be evaluated. All partners should share this evaluation. Evaluations can be formal or informal. Informal evaluations include simply talking about the project informally, or jotting ideas on how the process might have been improved. Formal strategies usually require individuals to fill in an evaluation form. This type of evaluation should be reserved for larger, more complicated projects. All evaluations should include the following:

- Identification of the strength and needs of the process, completed activity, or project.
- The feelings of individuals. Did they understand the significance of what they were doing as it related to the children? Was the activity valued by the individuals? Did the process proceed smoothly? Did they enjoy working on this activity/project? Would they consider another project in the future?
- Time. Was the amount of time adequate for the work accomplished? In the future, would more or less time be appropriate? Did they feel that the time was well spent?

- Were the various approaches to sharing information adequate? Could other methods have been used?
- Suggestions or comments. Any additional concerns or suggestions should be addressed.

In summary, working with partners is a valuable experience for all individuals involved. Partnerships provide an excellent opportunity to

- learn from each other;
- expand the horizons and approaches to teaching and learning;
- learn about new ways to approach and solve problems;
- embrace a community spirit to work together for the well-being of children; and
- work together toward a common goal—better-quality child-care for children and families.

KEY POINTS

COMMUNITY CONTEXT
- Social systems are interconnected units with all units interconnected and dependent on each other.

FAMILY DYNAMICS
- Family health—health-related problems may lead to stress and less effective management behaviours.
- Family functioning:
  - Families that function well use positive communication, joint problem solving, sensitivity, and role differentiation.
  - Causes of dysfunctional family life include poverty, divorce, ill health, depression, alcohol and substance abuse, crime and violence, and abuse and neglect.
- Family support networks include family members, friends, neighbours, community support groups, medical support groups, and informal groups.
- Family parenting styles: positive styles lead to healthy development and positive early interactions.
- Family recreation:
  - Recreational activities linked to greater success of children overall.
  - Lack of recreational activities linked to a variety of delays in behaviour.

CULTURAL DIVERSITY
- Varied statistics per province and within urban or rural areas.
- Impact of diversity seen in languages spoken in homes, underrepresentation and lack of understanding of some cultures, and increased prejudice toward some cultural groups.

WORKING WITH PARTNERS
- Strategies to involve families need to be set.
- Partnerships need to be valued.
- Partners can become mentors.
- Other community partners can be used as resource people.

- Needs of partners: to feel valued, respected, and recognized for their skills and knowledge.
- Communication with partners: types of communication—newsletters, online access, and documentation of children's work.
- Planning with partners: utilize all partners equally and appoint leaders.
- Evaluation can be a formal or informal process, and it should include all aspects of the program.

EXERCISES

1. Utilize the chart below to identify how your personal beliefs and values are influenced by each of the listed categories.

www

SOCIETAL INSTITUTIONS	PERSONAL BELIEFS	PERSONAL VALUES
Family		
Religion		
Politics		
Economics		
Education		
Science		
Technology		
Mass Media		
Medicine		
Sports		
Military		

2. Robert is a family man who is 35 years old. He has two preschool children. He and his wife are lawyers. They have a job-share arrangement with the firm they work for. Each individual works half time to be able to stay home and raise their children. Robert has just discovered that he has the West Nile virus. This will lead to time off work, chronic fatigue, and possible severe future consequences to his health.

   Reflect upon the status of this family. What will be the immediate effects of Robert's health problems? What will be the long-term effects? How will this affect the children?

3. In a small group, discuss how your family functioned, using the characteristics outlined below.

   a) Positive ongoing communication.
   b) Encouraging equality in interactions.
   c) Joint problem solving.
   d) Sensitivity to emotional growth and development.
   e) Role differentiation.

4. In a small group discuss why each of these reasons—poverty, divorce, ill health, depression, alcohol or substance abuse, crime and violence, and abuse and neglect—might lead to dysfunctional family life. In your discussion, reflect upon how this will impact on the children in the family.

5. Janine believes that children need to learn to do as they are told. She has two children, one three years old and one nine months old. After her infant is put in her crib, Janine will let her cry, as she believes that her infant will become spoiled if picked up too often. Her three-year-old will be punished if he is noncompliant. Punishment usually involves time-out (he is placed in the bathroom for 10 minutes) or a removal of a privilege (e.g., he may not watch a program on TV).

   Reflect upon how these practices might influence her children. What types of behaviour might you expect these children to exhibit at home, and at daycare? What might be the long-term effects of these behaviour guidance techniques? If this parent came to you for help, what might you advise?

6. Explain why children who are engaged in appropriate recreational activities might

   a) be more successful in school,
   b) have higher self-confidence, and
   c) have better social skills.

7. You have been hired to work in a daycare setting that has the following cultural diversity: two Native families; one French family (child does not speak English); three Chinese families; one black family; two Filipino families; and the rest are Canadian families. What are some of the strategies you might use to ensure that you are meeting all of the cultural diversities within your setting?

8. In a small group, develop a resource list of potential partners in your area. Contact each of the potential partners to fill in the types of resources that are available from that agency.

AGENCY	CONTACT INFORMATION	POSSIBLE RESOURCES	WWW

9. Discuss how the formation of partnerships is of benefit to

   a) the staff of a daycare centre;
   b) the children in the program;
   c) the families served; and
   d) the larger community.

10. If you were approached to become a member of a board of directors for a child-care centre, what aspects would you consider in order for you

    a) to accept the position?
    b) to continue to remain in that position over time?

11. You are working within a child-care centre. You have been given the job of trying to increase the concept of partnerships. Using the chart below, identify the strategies you might employ.

COMPONENT	STRATEGIES	WWW
Communication		
Planning		
Evaluation		

REFERENCES

Gestwicki, C., & Bertrand, J. (2003). *Essentials of Early Childhood Education* (2nd Canadian ed.). Scarborough, ON: Nelson.

Government of Canada. (2002). *Early Childhood Development Agreement.* Ottawa, ON: Government of Canada.

Hanvey, L. (2002). *The Progress of Canada's Children 2002* (Rep. No. 2002). Ottawa, ON: Canadian Council on Social Development.

Hanvey, L. (2003). *The Progress of Canada's Children*. Ottawa, ON: Canadian Council on Social Development.

Jedwab, J. (2003). Demography, Diversity and the Arts in Canada. Canadian Heritage [Online]. Available: http://www.pch.gc.ca (December 6, 2003).

Macionis, J., Clarke, J., & Gerber, L. (1997). *Sociology* (2nd Canadian ed.). Scarborough, ON: Prentice-Hall Canada Inc.

McCain, M., & Mustard, F. (1999). *Early Years Study, Final Report*. Toronto, ON: Publications Ontario.

Mooney, L., Knox, D., Caroline, S., & Nelson, A. (2001). *Understanding Social Problems* (1st Canadian ed.). Scarborough, ON: Nelson Thomson Learning.

QUALITY IN EARLY CHILDHOOD EDUCATION

"Quality child care is care provided by knowledgeable, committed and sensitive caregivers in a milieu that supports their efforts to provide an optimal environment designed to foster children's well-being, development and competence. Care provided in this manner explicitly recognizes the needs of parents for caregiving that supports and strengthens their child-rearing efforts through effective and informative communication and mutual respect." (Cooke, 1986, p. 129)

Chapter Outcomes

After reading this chapter, the reader will

1. Define quality in child-care with respect to family, children, early childhood educators, directors of programs, and other professionals.

2. Discuss the evolving character of quality in Canada.

3. Explain why quality is linked to
    a) training of early childhood educators;
    b) children's learning environments;
    c) family values and needs;
    d) early childhood characteristics;
    e) group size and adult-to-child ratios;
    f) culturally appropriate programs;
    g) sound nutritional practices;
    h) sound health practices;
    i) sound safety practices; and
    j) planning with families as partners.

4. Explain quality differences in various age groups—infants, toddlers, preschoolers, and school-aged children.

QUALITY DEFINED

The concept of quality is not easy to define. The individuals who use the services—families, children, early childhood educators, and other professionals—may each have a different set of criteria of what is meant by quality. Each of these perspectives may seem different, but when a combination of criteria is considered, a much broader and more inclusive definition of quality evolves. "Definitions of quality differ considerably among stakeholder groups and across countries. Although national quality guidelines are necessary, they need to be broad enough to allow individual settings to respond to the developmental needs and learning capacities of children" (Organization for Economic Co-operation and Development, 2001, p. 2).

1. Family Considerations

John and Melanie were new parents. Melanie had been at home for six months, but decided to go back to work because they both felt that they needed the extra income to support their new family. The couple did not have a car and had to rely on the public transit system. Both parents already spent two extra hours a day commuting to work. John and Melanie created a "shopping list" of what they wanted in a child-care setting by developing a series of questions and points to consider when looking at different daycares (see Figure 6.1).

John and Melanie found that most of the settings that they looked at seemed to have mechanisms in place to look after the health and safety of children (**custodial care**). They also found that many of the centres had hours of operation that did not match their work schedules. Often they found centres that they liked but could not afford. Finally, they found a daycare close to Melanie's work. The centre offered extended hours, and John and Melanie were able to receive a subsidy to help with the cost.

custodial care
Care for the physical health and safety of children.

Family Considerations for Choice of Child-Care

1. Is this a healthy and safe environment for our child?
2. Is the centre open during the hours that we need?
3. Can we afford the fees?
4. Will the centre treat our child appropriately (no spanking, handling her with love, calling us when she is sick, picking her up when she cries, taking her outside every day, keeping her clean)?
5. Will the centre be flexible to feed her when she is hungry, and let her sleep when she is tired?

Thus, from a family's perspective, quality is defined in terms of the family need and concern for the child. Quality programs for families are generally concerned with

- the health and safety of their child;
- affordability;
- accessibility;
- flexibility of schedule to meet the child's and family's needs; and
- supportiveness of the values the family holds (personal, cultural, and religious).

2. Considerations for Children

Josh trusted that the child-care program he was enrolled in provided him with safe opportunities to fully engage in a wide range of developmentally appropriate activities that engage all his senses. Through play, Josh meets his needs to optimize his growth and development in all areas: social, emotional, cognitive, and physical:

Web exercises

Photo 6.1

- *Active play with real materials.* Josh is provided with opportunities to learn through play (photo 6.1). Play is the natural way that all young children learn. "Play is pleasurable, spontaneous, integrative activity that provides a medium for learning and development in all domains" (Gestwicki, 1999, p. 45). Josh had learned to control the levers on the digger in order to scoop up sand and drop it in a designated spot. Through this activity, Josh gained control over his fine and gross muscles to manipulate the levers, learned to coordinate his actions (moving the levers, picking up the sand, and turning to dump the sand in a designated spot), and was able to see the result of his actions (scooping up the sand and creating a pile of sand). He was actively engaged in an activity that he picked and enjoyed.
- *Social interactions with other children.* Josh enhances his abilities to communicate and interact effectively. Josh and Gabrielle had been in the dramatic area, washing and changing their "babies." The powder puff had fallen into the water. Gabrielle showed the powder puff to Josh and said, "Wet." Josh responded by saying that the powder puff was "dripping" and "no good" (photo 6.2). He then ran to get Gabrielle a new powder puff to use.
- *Making appropriate choices.* Josh establishes self-confidence in his abilities and pride in his accomplishments. Josh had been painting. He was able to pick the size of brushes to use. He had started with

Photo 6.2

Photo 6.3

Photo 6.4

one of the smaller brushes. He went to the shelf and picked out a larger brush, and continued to paint until his whole page was covered (photo 6.3). When he was finished, he ran to get one of the early childhood educators, Pritti.

- *Interactions with adults.* Josh receives help and nurturance to guide his learning. When Pritti joined Josh at the easel, she said, "I see that you have covered the whole page with your favourite colour—blue." Josh beamed and said, "Too wet, help please." Pritti correctly interpreted his statement to mean that he needed help to transfer his painting to the drying rack. Several times during the morning, Josh went over to the drying rack to check if the painting was dry yet. When it was dry, he brought it to Pritti and asked for help to hang it in the art gallery. Josh chose a frame for his painting and it was hung in a place that he chose. When his mother came to pick him up, he took her over to the "art gallery" to show her his painting.

- *Gross motor activities.* Josh gains control over his body. This leads to greater skill development and greater confidence in his ability to engage in tasks within his environment. Josh had helped build an obstacle course within the classroom. He had been hesitant at first to climb over the hobbyhorse, but after he watched other children climb over, eventually he decided to try to climb over. He quickly gained confidence in his ability and was successful with this task (photo 6.4).

- *Solving his own problems.* Josh becomes more independent. He had been sliding down the slide that was covered in snow (photo 6.5). He found that the snow built up at the bottom of the slide and stopped him from moving. He was stuck at the bottom of the slide. Pritti walked over to see if any help was needed. She watched as Josh figured out how to get off the slide in his heavy snowsuit. When he was off, he said, "I did it!" He looked at the pile of snow at the bottom of the slide, and then ran to get a snow shovel. "Come help," he called as he ran to clear the snow from the bottom of the slide. Some of his peers helped him to remove the snow from the bottom of the slide, and he and others continued to enjoy sliding down the slide.

Thus, from the child's perspective, quality means that he or she can

- be involved in active play;
- interact in a positive, nurturing atmosphere with children and adults;
- make personal decisions and have those decisions accepted and valued;
- be given opportunities to solve problems; and
- be given opportunities to make choices by exploring the indoor and outdoor environments.

3. Early Childhood Educators

Jenny, an early childhood educator, has been working in a daycare centre with infants for the past three years. Previously she had experiences in a toddler program and a preschool program. She has just transferred to a new centre that used multi-age groupings as the basis for its program. She is concerned about how she can

- gain more knowledge about the new approach to interact with the children and their families effectively;
- work effectively within a new staff;
- provide developmentally appropriate experiences for the children of diverse ages in safe nurturing environments;
- identify materials and equipment that will be safe and challenging for the diverse ages; and
- adapt to the new philosophy and program.

Thus, from the perspective of the early childhood educator, quality is concerned with

- personal growth and development;
- personal performance and knowledge;
- how to fit in; and
- pride in doing a good job.

4. Directors of Programs

Debbie is the director of a program that provides services to families with toddlers, preschoolers, and five- to six-year-old children. She is directly concerned about

Photo 6.5

- *Staffing.* Debbie wants to ensure that she has qualified and professional staff to work with the various age groups in the centre. She is also concerned that there is a good fit of staff to staff, staff to children, and families and staff to the philosophy of the centre. She checks to ensure that the lunches and snacks are appropriately nutritional and that the environment is kept clean and safe.
- *Ratios.* Debbie has to ensure that there are two adults working with 10 toddlers, three adults working with 24 preschoolers, and two adults working with 20 school-aged children. This means that she has to hire additional staff to cover morning and afternoon shifts.
- *Programs.* The philosophy of this centre is to encourage children to learn through play. Parents are considered vital partners in the program for their children. Debbie is concerned with her role. She wants to continually evolve as director and leader to ensure the programs meet the philosophy of the centre. She continually monitors and helps to adapt the programs to meet the changing needs of the children and families.
- *Families.* Families are considered crucial partners. Debbie is continually striving to build a collaborative environment between children, their families, staff, and other professionals.
- *Funding.* Additional funding is required to continue to enhance the educational opportunities for the children. Funding is needed for new equipment and toys, and for field trip experiences. Debbie is involved in identifying and implementing fund-raising activities and identifying and applying for money through various grant opportunities.
- *Advocacy.* Debbie spends much of her time in raising community awareness about the importance of the early years and the importance of providing subsidies for families who cannot afford appropriate daycare for their children. She attends and speaks at many public functions and is a member of a variety of committees in human services fields related to child-care.
- *Evaluation.* Debbie is concerned with the quality of the interactions within the program and the growth and development of the children. She monitors these aspects through informal discussions and yearly formal evaluations of the staff. Formal evaluation of the program is done by using the Early Environment Rating Scale (ECERS) and the Infant/Toddler Environment Rating Scale (ITERS).

Thus, from the perspective of program directors, quality relates to

- the day-to-day administration of the program as a whole;
- appropriate staffing;
- appropriate communication strategies with all partners—families, children, staff, and other professionals;
- monitoring centre quality;

- ensuring congruence with licensing requirements;
- raising the quality of the program through fund-raising to purchase additional supplies or participate in extracurricular activities; and
- raising community awareness of the benefits of quality child-care.

5. Other Professionals

A number of other professionals are also concerned about aspects of quality. Some of these individuals work with staffs more at an arm's length to set guidelines that influence aspects of quality. These include

- *The board of directors.* The board is concerned that the centre continues to meet the **mission statement** (statement of intent and philosophy of the program), that the appropriate bylaws and policies are in place for operation of the centre, and that adequate funding is available to support staffing and program needs.
- *Health departments.* Health departments are more concerned about the physical health and safety of children. Typically, health departments set and monitor guidelines for the handling of ill children, for immunization schedules, for appropriate sanitary practices, and for nutritional requirements.
- *Fire departments.* Fire departments are concerned with the physical safety of children. Typically, fire departments set and monitor guidelines to prevent emergencies and to react to emergencies.
- *Governments.* Governments are concerned with financial and structural mechanisms. Some of these mechanisms are funding guidelines for staffing and subsidies to parents, requirements for adult-to-child ratios, and maximum group sizes.

Other professionals work much more closely with centre staff to provide support and help to the families and staff of child-care programs. These include

- *Consultants.* Specialized consultants offer support to children in a variety of capacities. They are interested in the quality of the specialized area that they are dealing with, such as special needs, speech and language, and counselling services.
- *Licensing professionals.* Licensing professionals are concerned with monitoring the quality of implementation as directed by the legislative requirements set by governments.
- *Advocacy groups.* Groups such as the Coalition for Better Daycare in Ontario equate quality of the early years with long-term benefits. Benefits are often identified globally (ready to learn, establishing lifelong learning patterns) in order to promote quality practices.
- *Policy makers.* "Policy makers have recognized that equitable access to quality early childhood education provides the foundations of lifelong learning for all children and supports the broad educational and social needs of families." (Organization for Economic Co-operation and Development, 2001, p. 1). This recognition should translate into the writing of policies such as income support, expanding access, parental leave, raising quality, developing coherent and coordinated policies, improving staff training and working conditions, and development of an appropriate philosophical framework for teaching young children (Organization for Economic Co-operation and Development, 2001).

In summary, quality definitions of child-care depend on the perspective of the participants involved with child-care. These perspectives are not mutually exclusive but are complementary. It is therefore necessary to combine all perspectives to develop an interactive, comprehensive definition of quality child-care (see Figure 6.2):

mission statement
Statement of intent and philosophy of a program.

Interaction of Quality Perspectives

Considering the emphasis that has been placed on concepts like "the readiness to learn," "lifelong learning" and promoting "early childhood development" in Canada over the past few years, it would appear that a well-designed, common, understandable and valid ECEC [early childhood education and care] quality indicator is a basic requirement for improving service delivery, for accountability and for policy making. (Cleveland et al., 2003, p. 9)

QUALITY IN CANADA

The statement of quality care at the beginning of this chapter was the result of a federal task force study in Canada in 1986. The report identifies issues across Canada that need to be addressed to move all child-care into a better-quality system. Today, in 2004, we are still struggling with many of these issues (see Chapter 9). However, there is a much greater awareness of the need to provide quality education to young children based on a number of factors:

- *Federal initiatives such as the second federal/provincial/territorial (except Quebec) agreement in March 2003.* "The purpose of this agreement, termed 'the first step to a national child care program,' is explicitly to 'improve access to affordable, quality, provincially and territorially regulated early learning and childcare programs and services.' Governments recognize the importance of being accountable to Canadians and have committed to transparent public reporting that will give a clear idea of the progress being made in improving access to affordable, quality early learning and child care programs and services" (Cleveland et al., 2003, p. 2).

- *Commissioned reports such as the Early Years Study, April 1999, Government of Ontario.* "New understanding of brain development in the early years and its effects on subsequent learning, behaviour and health for individuals has led a number of governments and other organizations to take steps to provide better circumstances in and outside the home for early childhood development.... In addition, the Early Years Study was asked to consider collaborative and partnership models that would actively engage federal, provincial and municipal governments, school boards, communities and the private sector" (McCain & Mustard, 1999, p. 1).

- *National studies such as You Bet I Care!* "This report documents the findings of the largest, most systematic and most multi-jurisdictional study ever conducted in Canada to explore the relationship between centre quality and centre characteristics; teaching staff wages and working conditions; and teaching staff characteristics and attitudes" (Goelman et al., 2000, p. ix).

- *Research such as studies on brain development.* "A baby is born with a head on her shoulders and a mind primed for learning. But it takes years of experience looking, listening, playing, interacting with parents—to wire the billions of complex neural circuits that govern language, math, music, logic and emotions" (Begly, 1997, p. 28).

- *Publications such as* Newsweek's *special edition on Your Child.* In this full-length bonus publication, *Newsweek* provides critical information about language, physical, social, and emotional development in the first three years of life. Additionally, the issue supplies current research on brain development and on how primary caregivers can provide necessary quality experiences to young children to ensure a strong and healthy start to development.

- *Increased education.* "Most children are living with parents who have post-secondary education" (Hanvey, 2003, p. 9). This means that family awareness of the needs for their children has also increased. "There were very few differences related to family type or income—indicating that both low-income parents and single parents, despite their hardships, are positively parenting their young children" (Hanvey, 2003, p. 12). Families who positively parent their own children are more likely to demand care that also provides a positive environment.

A number of quality statements have been developed, based on solid research, from a variety of different sources (Doherty-Derkowski, 1994; Association for Early Childhood Education, 1988; Canadian Child Day Care Federation, 1994; Goelman et al., 2000). All of these statements link quality to the issues discussed below.

1. Appropriate Training

Quality childcare responds to children's needs by offering continuous opportunities for learning and nurturance. The goals of the services are determined by the needs of the children and the shared philosophies of parents and care providers. A reliable framework of routines which support the physical, social, intellectual and emotional needs of the children facilitates their learning. All practices that take place are based on sound child development theories and current research. (Fanjoy, 1994, p. 4)

Dillon loved to look at books. He often took a break from his activities to look at books. Beth noticed Dillon's love for books, and she carefully observed what his interests were. She noticed that he tended to pick out books about animals and vehicles. Beth made sure that a variety of books on these topics were available to him in various areas of the room. She also noticed that Dillon was starting to sign as he looked at a book. Beth used this "**teachable moment**" to encourage dialogue with Dillon (photo 6.6).

teachable moment
Observing children and using the information gained by observing to spontaneously enhance or build on that skill (e.g., observing a child sign while reading or sitting with the child and signing what the child points to in the book).

Beth is a trained early childhood educator. She knew that she needed to carefully observe children in order to provide learning opportunities of interest to the children (e.g., interest in books) and identify existing and emergent skills (e.g., signing). Beth took sign language training in order to work more effectively with children with special needs. In this way she was able to follow Dillon's lead to start to interact with him through active communication (through teachable moments).

Training in early childhood education gives the adult skills to ensure that the children's experiences, the materials they use, and their interaction patterns are developmentally appropriate. One important skill is knowledge of child development.

Beth noticed that Isabel was shyly looking at her from behind the doll chair. She was holding the hair dryer in front of her face (photo 6.7). Beth knew that peek-a-boo was a stage of development for this age. She hid her face behind a book. When she looked up, Isabel had lowered her hair dryer and was beaming back at her (photo 6.8). As this game continued, Beth and Isabel would sometimes copy each other and at other times would invent new ways of playing peek-a-boo. Beth realized the importance of this activity. She knew that this activity would:

- *Encourage and reinforce Isabel's self-concept.* "I am being noticed. What I do is of importance."
- *Reinforce patterns of turn-taking.* "I hide my face, I wait to see what Beth will do, then I hide my face again."
- *Build on Isabel's imitative skills.* Older infants and toddlers spend much of their time in imitative play. It is the best way to learn about the world around them. Isabel hid her face totally behind the doll and chair, sometimes she hid only her eyes, and sometimes she hid her eyes behind her hands.

Photo 6.6

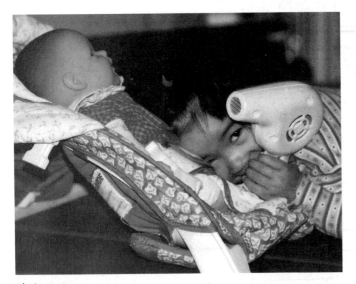

Photo 6.7

Photo 6.8

Photo 6.9

Web
exercises

Beth based much of what she did and the types of learning activities she set up on sound child development theories and current research. She knew that toddlers draw using their whole hand and by using a whole arm movement. Beth provided large paper (taped down to prevent it from sliding) to encourage whole arm movement and sturdy crayons that did not break easily and were also easy to hold (photo 6.9). Beth anticipated that other toddlers would also want to draw and would want their own materials, so she made sure that she had duplicate items ready for others. In this way she prevented possible conflict between toddlers who have not yet grasped the concept of sharing.

2. Children's Learning Environments

Children's learning environments support the physical, social, intellectual, and emotional needs of all the children. Consider the following statement from the Village Daycare Society:

> The Village Daycare Society is a child-oriented centre where all children learn through play in a safe and nurturing environment. We are aware that children have individual needs and we will recognize these needs during the children's time span in our centre, whether it is social, emotional, physical, or intellectual support that is required. (Village Daycare Society, 2001)

The needs of the children are supported through an environment (see Figure 6.3) that encourages active exploration. Learning areas are set up (see photos B to K in Figure 6.3) to encourage choice, and materials are provided to support various aspects of the children's learning:

- *Physical.* Play flows from inside to outside freely. Activities that can be utilized inside are also utilized outside. Children can participate in a variety of gross motor activities outside (see Figure 6.3, photos H to K)—running, climbing, jumping, riding, and balancing—individually or in groups.
- *Social.* Social activities are encouraged throughout the day. Children can choose to work by themselves (solitary play, as shown in photo 6.10) or in group play. Grace and Tianstians (see Figure 6.3, photo I) are engaged in associative play. They are playing together to try to twirl the hoops around their waists. They are talking to each other about what they are doing, but each child is doing his or her own

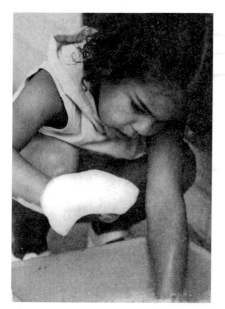

Photo 6.10

Photo 6.11

Photo 6.12

thing. Edwina is listening to the children. She comments on their activities and refers the children to one another. "Look, Grace has managed to twirl her hoop."

- *Intellectual*. Intellectual growth is challenged by the various activities children can engage in, both indoors and outdoors (see Figure 6.3, photos B to K). The children had planted a garden outside. Alex is talking to Wanda. They are trying to identify what the various plants are. Alex correctly identified the growing beans. He is estimating how tall the beans will grow (photo 6.11).
- *Emotional.* Emotional well-being and growth are fostered in a number of ways. Children have opportunities to find quiet corners to relax in or to find some privacy (see Figure 6.3, photo D). Children are encouraged to interact positively with each other and with adults within the program. Caregivers are sensitive to the children's needs and know when to step in or when to step out. Grace had been playing by herself away from the children. She finally had found a place to hide—behind a large tree (photo 6.12). Nayoung noticed that Grace was watching her and smiling at her. She asked Grace if she would like to do something with her. Grace skipped over to Nayoung and said, "Let's sing and dance." Nayoung and Grace sang and danced together (photo 6.13), and soon other children joined in. Nayoung slowly withdrew from the group. The children continued to sing and dance.

3. Support to Families

Early childhood educators are supportive of families, their values, and their needs. The Cedar Road Aboriginal Head Start (AHS) Program, for example, is a program that demonstrates strong collaboration with all potential partners. The philosophy of the centre states: "We recognize that our aboriginal children are our community's most valuable resource. We are dedicated to improving cultural awareness and respect for traditional beliefs. Families are a critical part of our program's continuance and success. Cedar Road AHS Program is determined to enhance the lives of children, their families, and the community by providing a caring, supportive, and vital community service" (Cedar Road AHS Program, 2003, p. 4). The centre employs a number of strategies that lead to family involvement:

Photo 6.13

Chapter Six   Quality in Early Childhood Education

Figure 6.3

Village Daycare Society 2-1/2 to 5-year-olds

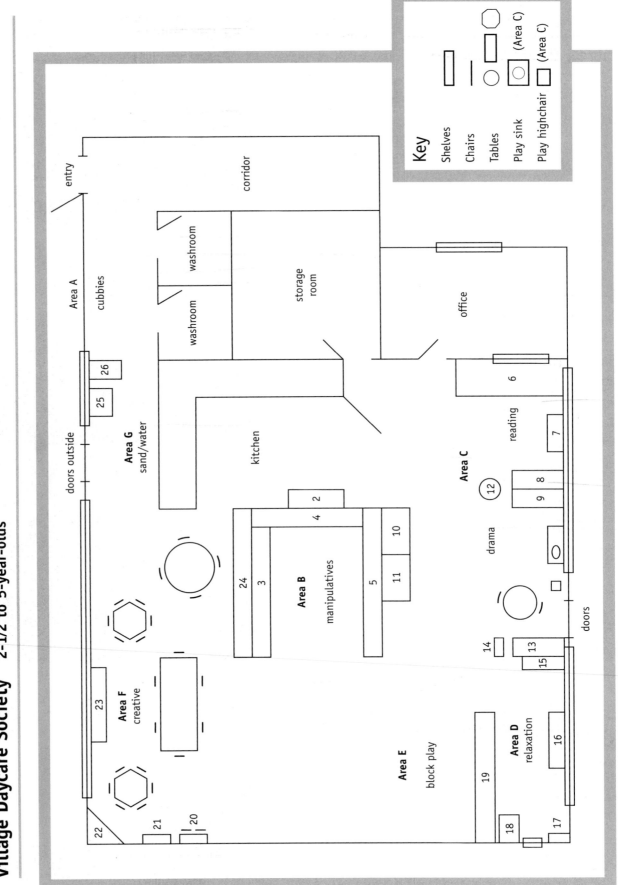

■ Figure 6.3 (continued)

Village Daycare Society

2-1/2 to 5-year-olds

Area C - Photo C

6. Adult files
7. Books
8. Pillows
9, 10. Dramatic play props
11. Playfridge
12. Playstove
13. Dramatic play props
14. Block accessories

Area A - Cubbies- Photo A

Areas D and E - Photo D

15, 16. Couches
17, 18. Adult storage
19. Block shelf

Area E - Photo E

Block play
Large group area

Area F - Photo F

20. Cut and paste
21. Drying rack
22. Computer area
23, 24. Creative supply

Area B/Area G - Photo B

1. Kitchen counters
2. Trays for dishes
3. Manipulative shelves
4. Sand/water table
5. Sand/water toy storage

Figure 6.3 (continued)

Village Daycare Society

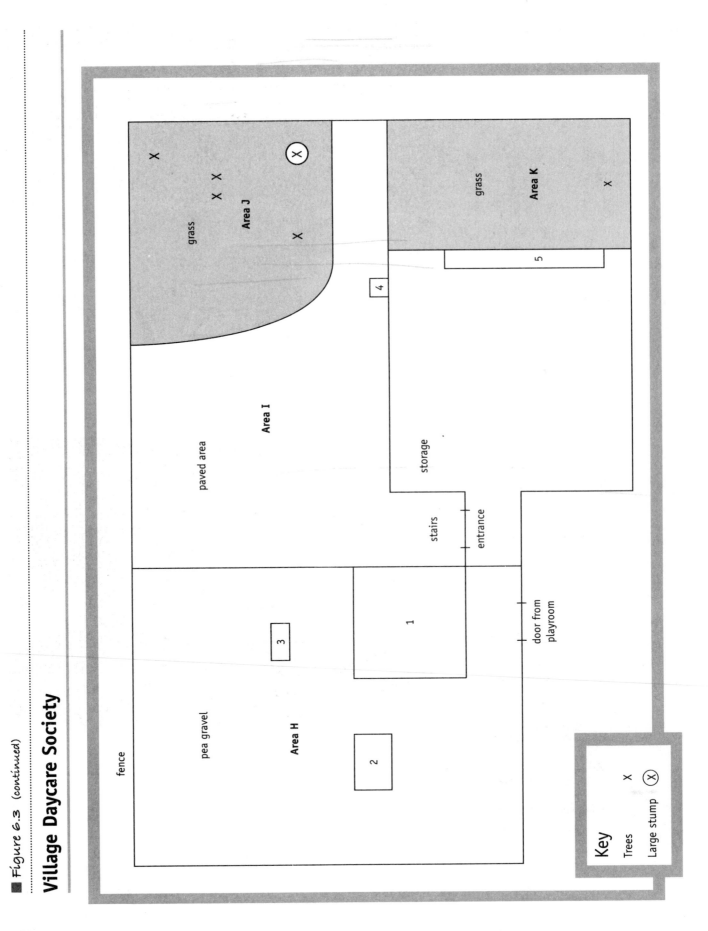

Key

Trees   X

Large stump   (X)

Village Daycare Society

Area I - Photo I
4. Playhouse

Area H - Photo H
1. covered sand
2. climber
3. teeter-totter

Area J - Photo J
Grassy, shaded area

Area K - Photo K
5. Garden

Web
exercises

- *Working with families as partners.* The board of directors of the AHS is made up of family volunteers. Family members who have not had experiences in certain board job requirements receive training to become more effective. All family members volunteer six days a month within the child-care program. The elders participate by teaching the young children about the language and specific customs particular to their region.

Photo 6.14

- *Interacting with children and families in a manner that reflects mutual respect, trust, and cooperation.* Family members are valued for the skills they have and can bring to the program. One of the elders makes the traditional, highly valued button blankets (photo 6.14). Under her guidance, the children have learned to make miniature button blankets out of paper. Workshops have been organized for interested family members to learn to make button blankets. The button blankets created will be worn by the children to celebrate the children's move from the preschool headstart program into the elementary school program. In this way, one important part of the culture is maintained and passed on through the different generations.

Web
exercises

- *Providing an environment that reflects cultural values.* Great care has been given to include cultural items of significance within the children's environment and the adult environment. This has been accomplished by

  - the use of paintings and murals (photo 6.15);
  - displaying items of cultural significance (pictorial and real; see the discussion of the environment in Chapter 11);
  - including labels in the Aboriginal language (photo 6.16); and
  - displays about cultural events.

Photo 6.15

1	Küül
2	Gup'l
3	Kwilii
4	txaapx
5	Kaduuns

Photo 6.16

The Collaborative Process—Cedar Road Aboriginal Head Start Program

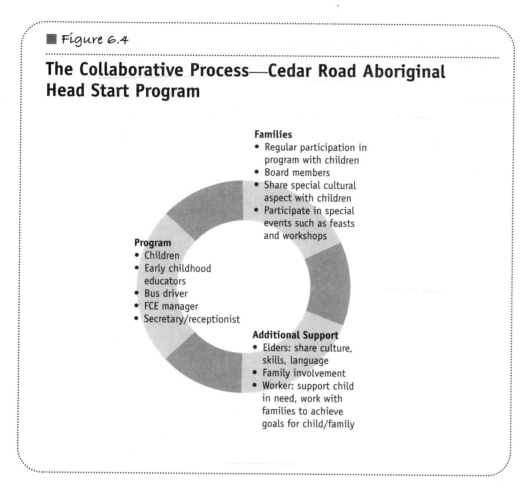

Families
- Regular participation in program with children
- Board members
- Share special cultural aspect with children
- Participate in special events such as feasts and workshops

Program
- Children
- Early childhood educators
- Bus driver
- FCE manager
- Secretary/receptionist

Additional Support
- Elders: share culture, skills, language
- Family involvement
- Worker: support child in need, work with families to achieve goals for child/family

- *Engaging in special celebrations.* Children, families, and staff participate in a number of special celebrations by holding traditional feasts. One such occasion is in December, the feasting month (Ha'liluulgit).
- *Designing a program that reflects cultural beliefs and customs.* Monthly plans identify cultural events such as seaweed month (Ha'lixla'ask). Children actively engage in Aboriginal language activities—simple stories, songs, and labelling activities. Cultural events are embraced and incorporated through activities such as field trips, elders telling stories, participating in celebrations, eating Aboriginal foods, and learning to make items of cultural value (such as button blankets). Family members are encouraged to share their knowledge and skill within the program.
- *Keeping families informed.* Newsletters are sent home monthly to keep families informed of upcoming events.

The collaborative process employed by the Cedar Road AHS Program (see Figure 6.4) provides the basis of a strong and enduring partnership. All individuals involved in the education and care of young children are actively involved in the planning and implementation of quality learning experiences. This collaborative process continues while children are enrolled within the program and is adapted with each new intake of children and their families.

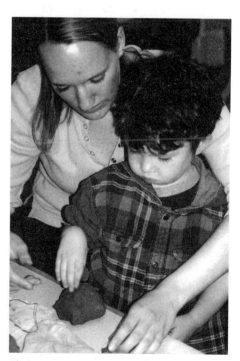

Photo 6.17

4. Early Childhood Educator Characteristics

Early childhood educators should be responsive, engage in positive interactions, engage in high verbal exchanges with children, and use developmentally appropriate practices (Doherty-Derkowski, 1994):

Web
exercises

- *Responsiveness.* Keegan had been watching the children and Nicola mould the clay. He moved closer to Nicola. Nicola asked him if he wanted to join in. Nicola moved her chair back. Keegan promptly came and sat on her lap. He started to poke the clay gently (photo 6.17). Nicola also started to poke the clay, modelling different techniques. Keegan started to manipulate his clay in different ways. Nicola realized that Keegan wanted to participate, but was not sure he wanted to manipulate the clay. He needed some reassurance and some modelling to start to manipulate the clay himself. Without Nicola's timely interaction, Keegan might not have engaged in this activity at all. Nicola observed Keegan, was sensitive to Keegan's mood, and initiated an interaction to help Keegan's desire to participate.

- *Positive interactions.* Nicola interacted positively with Keegan. She noticed Keegan's interest in the activity. She knew that Keegan might be reluctant to try as the clay looked messy. She provided Keegan with a safe way to try this new activity, manipulating the clay. Keegan needed the body contact and modelling to encourage him to try.

    - *High verbal interactions.* As Nicola started to manipulate her clay, she talked to Keegan about what she was doing. She described her activity—rolling, pounding, and forming the clay. As Keegan started to manipulate the clay, she also described his actions—squeezing, poking, and making holes in the clay.

    - *Use of developmentally appropriate practices.* Justin had been playing with the dinosaurs. When Timmy came over and touched one of the dinosaurs, Justin quickly pulled all the dinosaurs toward him and said, "My dinosaurs!" (photo 6.18). Nicola noticed what had happened. She quickly brought over another set of dinosaurs and gave them to Timmy. The two boys each played with his personal set of dinosaurs (parallel play). Nicola used developmentally appropriate practices to guide the two toddlers. Developmentally, toddlers see the world from their own particular perspective: "I am using the dinosaurs, so they are mine," or "I see the dinosaurs so they are mine to use." Sharing is not a developmentally appropriate activity for toddlers, so Nicola did the following:

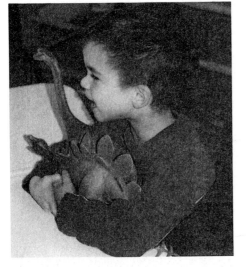

Photo 6.18

- She recognized the appropriate stage of development of the toddlers.
- She ensured that there were duplicate materials available. Toddlers are attracted by what other children are doing. They want to use exactly the same thing, not something that is somewhat the same. The dinosaurs were the same size, type, colour, and number.
- She ensured that appropriate materials were available. The dinosaurs were the appropriate size and realistic replications of dinosaurs the toddlers saw in their books.

Web
exercises

5. Group Size and Ratios

Group sizes and adult-to-child ratios should encourage positive interactions. "Quality childcare recognizes that small group size contributes to the quality of interaction among children and care providers, which determines the frequency of interaction among the children and care providers, which determines the frequency of individualized attention children receive. Small groups (either multi-age or same age) foster the development of independence, cooperation and mutual respect in children" (Canadian Child Day Care Federation, 1994, p. 8).

Lindsay and Naomi are each working with three infants. Each is primarily responsible for three of the children, but they also work as a team to support all six infants to better meet individual needs. Lindsay was feeding one of her infants a bottle. As she was feeding her infant, she was talking to Jerimia, who was sitting at her feet looking at a book. Her other infant had just woken up from a nap and was crying to be picked up. Naomi quickly scanned the environment. Two of her infants were playing quietly and her third infant was napping. Naomi quietly told Lindsay that she would get the crying child. Lindsay scanned the room to ensure that all infants continued to play appropriately. See Chapter 10 for adult-to-child ratios in Canada.

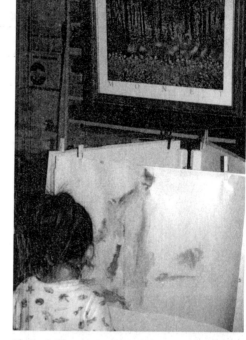

Photo 6.19

6. Culture and Programs

Culture is the most powerful social influence on human life. As we become more culturally diverse as societies, we experience unique social phenomena that can affect how we define ourselves as national social orders. (Schultz, 2003, p. 1)

Culture is not easy to define for Canada as a whole. Each region in Canada is different in many ways:

Regionalism is an important diversity in Canada, so important, in fact, that examining the nature of regionalism is critical if we are to have a complete understanding of social life in Canada. Canadians from different regions are diverse in many ways. From a regional perspective, for example, Canadians find themselves different in the areas of geography, climate, income, ethnicity, social class, and attitudes toward each other. (Angelini, 2003, p. 29)

Across Canada, each daycare setting reflects the unique cultural mix of that community. For example, 86 percent of the visible minority population lives in Canada's cities, with the highest percentage (41 percent) in Toronto. A breakdown of ethnic origins reported (excluding British, French, and Canadian) is as follows (Pendakur & Hennebry, 1998):

Photo 6.20

- Italian—most frequently reported in Toronto, Montreal, and Edmonton.
- Chinese—most frequently reported in Vancouver.
- German—most frequently reported in Calgary, Ottawa-Hull, and Halifax; second highest reported in Vancouver.
- South Asian—second highest reported in Toronto.
- Caribbean—second highest reported in Montreal.
- Aboriginal—second highest reported in Edmonton.

It is important to gain an understanding of the types of ethnic origins within the children's community to more accurately represent diversity. Often less visible minorities are underrepresented in favour of visible minorities. It is important to represent all ethnic diversity within the child-care setting. In order to create culturally appropriate programs, child-care professionals should "foster a knowledge and appreciation of a variety of cultures through respectful introduction of art, music, foods, clothing, literature and customs" (Canadian Child Day Care Federation, 1994, p. 5):

Photo 6.21

- *Art* (photos 6.19 and 6.20; also see photos 6.15, 6.16, and 6.17 on pages 164 and 165).
- *Music.* Include songs and music from various cultures and in the original languages (see the Resources section at the end of this chapter for some examples), and multi-ethnic props to encourage movement (photo 6.21).
- *Foods.* Provide meals and snacks that respect various cultures, and utilize a variety of eating utensils, such as chopsticks, various types of spoons, and various types of serving dishes and bowls.
- *Clothing.* Provide realistic clothing that represents various cultures, such as moccasins, embroidered belts, button blankets, aprons, or special-occasion national costumes (photo 6.22).
- *Literature.* Provide books, pictures, stories, and poetry that are representative of various cultures (see the Resources section at the end of the chapter for some examples).
- *Customs.* Invite families to share cultural events, customs, special celebrations, feasts, dances, and games. Some examples are Ha'liluulgit (feasting month in December), Chinese New Year, El Dia de los Muertos (the Day of the Dead, which honours the ancestors), and Hanukkah (Copple, 2003).

7. Nutrition

Photo 6.22

Good nutrition is an essential ingredient of quality child-care. Tasty, colourful, nutritious foods and a pleasant, relaxed eating environment contribute to a child's sense of well-being. A child develops lifelong eating habits as a result of early eating experiences. As a child-care provider, you need to know the nutritional requirements of children and how to provide a nutritious diet. Equally important is the atmosphere you create at meals and snacktime. (Shapiro Kendrick, Kaufman, & Messenger, 1995, p. 133)

Sound nutrition practices involve the following:

- Providing nutritious meals and snacks. Utilize *Canada's Food Guide to Healthy Eating.*
- Using mealtime as a social time to interact with children. Talk about what they are eating and encourage self-help skills (photo 6.23).
- Providing opportunities for tasting different types of food. Use this opportunity as a learning experience—describe similarities and differences in taste, texture, smell, and appearance.
- Providing flexible, individualized schedules for feeding infants and toddlers.
- Providing snacks when children are hungry—when children arrive, before they leave, mid-morning, and mid-afternoon.
- Never using food as a punishment or reward for inappropriate behaviour or appropriate behaviour.
- Never forcing a child to eat something he or she does not wish to eat.

8. Health Practices

Photo 6.23

For sound health practices, you should do the following:

- Model healthy practices. Wash your hands after eating or toileting, clean the environment as needed, eat nutritious snacks and meals, and eat with children.

- "Establish and adhere to procedures with regard to
  - regular hand washing
  - personal hygiene
  - toileting and diapering
  - isolation of children who become ill during the day and exclusion if needed
  - food preparation and storage
  - laundering, storage of use of personal items
  - general cleaning and housekeeping" (Canadian Child Day Care Federation, 1994, p. 11).

- Encourage children to participate in healthy routines according to their ability. Clean-up can become a fun activity. Jordan helped to clean up the mural that he and others had made on a clear divider. He had a choice of tools that he could use—sponges, squirt bottles filled with water, a bucket of water, and paper towels (photo 6.24).

- Communicate regularly with parents about children's health formally (see Figures 6.5 and 6.6) and informally by talking to families at drop-off and pick-up times.

- Maintain regular ill health records (Figures 6.5 and 6.6), immunization records, and allergy records (see Figure 6.7).

Photo 6.24

9. Safety Practices

For sound safety practices, you should do the following:

- Regularly check the indoor and outdoor environments, materials, and equipment to ensure that they are developmentally appropriate and safe to use. Check for broken parts, sharp corners, and dangerous objects (e.g., too small or sharp).

- Observe and supervise children carefully indoors and outdoors to avoid potentially dangerous situations. Yvonne noticed that Sarah had taken off her sandals before riding the tricycle (photo 6.25). She immediately explained to Sarah the dangers of riding without shoes. Sarah put on her shoes and continued to ride.

- Ensure that staff has first-aid and CPR training for the age groups they are working with.

- Ensure the emotional security of all children. Angela noticed that Calla was upset—she was crying. She immediately went over to her to find out what was bothering her (photo 6.26). Calla said that the older children wouldn't let her play in the sand area. Angela said, "Let's go and tell the children how you feel." Calla and Angela went over to the sand area. Angela encouraged Calla to tell the children how she felt. Calla said, "Sad, I want to play too." One of the children said, "We don't need anyone any more, we have a baker, a seller, and a customer." Angela responded, "We seem to have a problem. Calla is sad because she wants to play with you. You have told her that you do not need her help. What could we do about this problem?" One of the other children responded, "We could have more than one customer." The other children nodded in agreement.

- Share safety information with children and families such as sun safety, outdoor safety, and West Nile virus information.

- Develop and post policies for behaviour management, safety/emergency procedures, and reporting suspected child abuse (Canadian Child Day Care Federation, 1994, p. 14).

Photo 6.25

Photo 6.26

■ *Figure 6.5*

Record of Ill Health

Name: .... Date: ....

When started: .... Length of time continued: ....

Symptoms observed: ....

....

....

....

Temperature: .... How taken: ....

Additional problems observed

1. Change in behaviour: ....

2. Change in habits:

– eating: ....

– drinking: ....

– toileting: ....

Additional information [List exposure to new food, situations, animals, medication, insects, experiences, other illnesses]: ....

....

....

Steps taken to help child: ....

....

Signature of caregiver: ....

Child-care facility: ....

Telephone number: ....

10. Planning and Evaluating

Plan and evaluate a developmentally appropriate curriculum based on partnerships with children, families, and daily observations of children:

- Encourage input of family members formally and informally to ongoing curriculum development and evaluation of learning activities—talk about children's interest and progress, share resources and observations, prepare individual child portfolios to send home, and conduct a yearly formal evaluation of the program.

■ Figure 6.6

Record of Ill Health

Child's Name: ....

Health Problem	Date	Action Taken
....	....	....
....	....	....
....	....	....
....	....	....
....	....	....
....	....	....

■ Figure 6.7

Record of Allergies

Child's Name: ....

Allergy	Symptoms	Action Needed
....	....	....
....	....	....
....	....	....
....	....	....
....	....	....
....	....	....
....	....	....

- Involve children in planning. Children created a web of their planning about sea life (see Figure 6.8), and engaged in group discussions (see Figure 6.9). (The children's work represents children in Vancouver who have experience with and access to the ocean.)
- Use formal tools to help plan the layout of the environment such as the Infant and Toddler Environmental Rating Scale, Early Childhood Environmental Rating Scale, School Age Environmental Rating Scale, and the Family Day Environmental Rating Scale (Harms, Clifford, & Cryer, 1998; Harms, Cryer, & Clifford, 1990; Harms, Vineberg Jacobs, & White, 1996; Harms & Clifford, 1989).

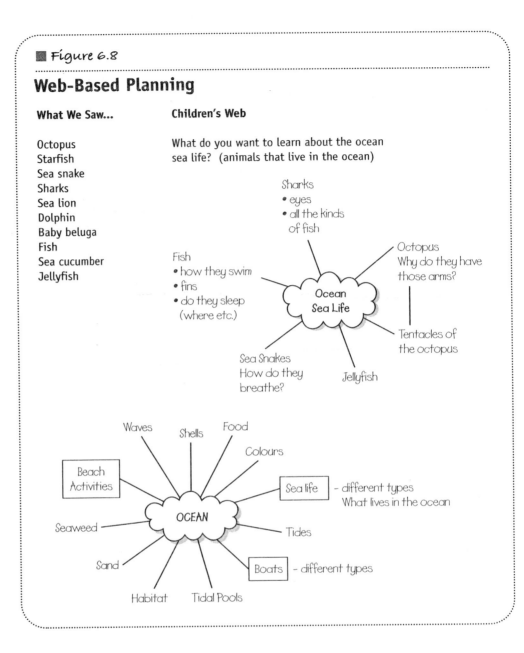

■ Figure 6.8

Web-Based Planning

What We Saw...

Octopus
Starfish
Sea snake
Sharks
Sea lion
Dolphin
Baby beluga
Fish
Sea cucumber
Jellyfish

Children's Web

What do you want to learn about the ocean sea life? (animals that live in the ocean)

Sharks
• eyes
• all the kinds of fish

Fish
• how they swim
• fins
• do they sleep (where etc.)

Ocean Sea Life

Octopus
Why do they have those arms?

Tentacles of the octopus

Sea Snakes
How do they breathe?

Jellyfish

Waves   Shells   Food
Colours
Beach Activities
Sea life — different types
What lives in the ocean
OCEAN
Seaweed
Tides
Sand
Boats — different types
Habitat   Tidal Pools

QUALITY DIFFERENCES ACCORDING TO AGE GROUP

Most quality practices are similar for different age groups. However, there are some differences that relate to interaction patterns, safety concerns, and materials and equipment. Information is compared in Tables 6.1 and 6.2 on pages 174 and 175.

SUMMARY

Quality in early childhood programs involves a coordinated effort of families, professionals, and governments. It is based on and reinforces the values that a society holds toward the raising of children. It impacts on every aspect of the young child's life. These early years are the critical years for appropriate brain development and growth in order to

Small Group Discussion (Two Small Groups)

- What is the ocean?
  The sea

- What lives in the ocean?
  Clams, lots of stuff, crabs, lobsters,
  sea urchins, bay whales, jellyfish

- What kinds of things do you find
  at the ocean?
  Bathing suits, buckets, shovels, seashells

- What can you do when you go to the ocean?
  Swim, when it's summer, look for shells,
  build a sandcastle, bring a beach ball

- What would you like to learn about
  the ocean?
  Where starfishes are in the ocean; what do
  shovels help you with; what fishes are in the
  ocean; what jellyfish do; where jellyfish live

- What is the ocean?
  Is blue and has big waves.
  Has animals and seashells and rocks.
  Water

- What can you find in the ocean?
  Animals, seaweed, sea crabs,
  starfish, whales, goldfish, belugas,
  lobsters

- What kinds of things do you find
  when you go to the ocean?
  Seashells, starfish

- What can you do when you go to
  the ocean?
  Play with shovels and buckets,
  make a sandcastle, play and go in
  the ocean and go swimming, make
  a house of sticks, float in the water
  with a boat, eat at the ocean

- What would you like to learn about
  the ocean?
  Learn about the sea, sea stars

- grow and develop appropriately—social, emotional, physical, and cognitive development;
- engage fully in learning experiences;
- develop skills and abilities;
- develop life-long learning attitudes; and
- develop appropriate attitudes toward self and others.

KEY POINTS

QUALITY DEFINED
- Varying perspectives of quality are linked to
  - services needed by the family;
  - daily requirements of the children;
  - working conditions and job requirements of the early childhood educator and directors; and
  - services provided by other professionals.

Comparison of Nonmobile Infants, Mobile Infants, and Toddlers

Category	Nonmobile Infants	Mobile Infants	Toddlers
Interaction patterns	Sensitive and reactive to infant's signals Verbalizing routines, and actions to infants Respond to vocalizations of infants	Observe infant's signals and actions to interact Listen to first words Respond to signals, first words, and actions appropriately Redirect positively as needed	Listen to toddler's verbalizations and respond appropriately Observe toddler's interactions and respond or redirect positively Clarify verbalizations and actions to other toddlers Help toddlers solve own problems
Safety concerns	Watch for small items (to prevent mouthing, choking) Keep away from dangling cords Protect from mobile infants Protect from sharp corners to bang against	Watch for small items (to prevent mouthing, choking), strings, scarves, plastic bags Hide dangling cords and handles to prevent pulling down Guard gates in dangerous areas (stairs, doors) Watch for plastic bags, dangling cords on dress-up clothing, small toys that encourage mouthing and choking	Hide dangling cords and handles to prevent pulling down Ensure that there are open areas to provide opportunities to run safely Ensure furniture is stable to pull up on, cruise along Watch for sharp corners that can injure cruising toddlers Establish simple safety rules (e.g., safety harness in car) Provide increased opportunities to solve problems for themselves Establish and talk about simple safety rules (e.g., look both ways before crossing the road)
Materials	Soft items, easy to observe, grasp, and manipulate Within reach of hands and feet Materials that include texture, sound, and movement	Choices on low sturdy shelves Large enough to grasp and manipulate Small pieces with supervision to encourage pincer grasp	Increased number of choices Some smaller pieces to encourage different types of grasping and manipulation (*Note:* close supervision must be provided for this activity to prevent children from mouthing these objects) Objects that encourage increased cause-and-effect observation
Equipment	Soft pillows to protect from fall and support sitting Sturdy furniture to pull up on	Toys to take apart, put together, pull and push Sturdy toys to use to push to walk Sturdy furniture toys to pull up on and cruise along Stairs and climbers to crawl up and down, pull up, and balance	Puzzles, noise makers, toys that can be stacked, moved, pulled apart or put together Push, pull, and riding toys Stairs and climbers to climb, jump from, balance on, and hang from

Comparison of Preschoolers and School-Aged Children

Category	Preschoolers	School-Aged Children
Interaction patterns	Listen and respond to verbalizations and actions Redirect positively Encourage preschoolers to solve own problems Know when to interact and when to leave play alone	Listen and respond to verbalizations and actions Redirect positively Know when to step in to help solve problems and when to leave children to solve own problems
Safety rules	Establish safety rules together Provide learning experiences to practise to reinforce safety rules	Post safety rules Provide written information about safety rules Involve children in practice of safety rules such as becoming crossing guards
Materials	Increased number of choices in environment Increased challenges in manipulation and gross motor activity Increased materials that encourage problem solving—sorting, sequencing, patterning, matching, counting, writing, reading	Increased emphasis on materials that encourage writing, reading, computation Increased need to engage in tasks to follow rules
Equipment	Equipment to offer greater challenges in climbing, jumping, balancing, developing endurance, strength, and coordination (e.g., more complex climbers and two-wheel bikes)	Equipment to offer greater challenges in climbing, jumping, balancing, developing endurance, strength, and coordination (e.g., skates and more complicated climbers) Specialized equipment for team sports (e.g., goal nets and basketball hoops)

QUALITY IN CANADA

- Quality indicators include
  - education of staff;
  - adult and program support of the needs of all children;
  - involving and supporting the needs of families;
  - appropriate group sizes;
  - appropriate adult-to-child ratios;
  - cultural appropriateness; and
  - sound health and safety practices.

QUALITY DIFFERENCES ACCORDING TO AGE GROUP

- Differences in assessing quality according to age group include

  - the educational training needs of staff;
  - group sizes;
  - adult-to-child ratios;
  - types of health and safety practices; and
  - variation in programming needs.

EXERCISES

1. In a small group, develop a chart (using the format below) that compares the quality expectations of each group linked to child-care. Discuss the information. How are they similar, the same, or different? Reflect on which of these aspects you consider critical at this stage of your career. Repeat this exercise again after one year in the program, shortly before graduating. Reflect upon the information gained. How have you changed? Do you anticipate changing again? How and why?

LINKED GROUP	QUALITY INDICATORS
Families	
Children	
Early childhood educators	
Directors	
Other professionals	
Self-reflection I	
Self-reflection II	
Self-reflection III	

2. Recent research, especially on brain development, has made an impact on our society's concept of early childhood education. In a small group discuss how the information presented in this chapter has influenced

   a) policy makers,
   b) families, and
   c) early childhood educators.

3. Reflect on the education you have had to date. In a small group discuss

   a) What knowledge you have gained that directly applies to your work with young children, and why this knowledge is pertinent.
   b) What knowledge you still need to become more effective in your work with children. Explain how this new knowledge will help you.

4. Visit a toy store or toy department. Using the chart below, list some toys or materials that would support the learning of children. Discuss your results in a small group. Toys and materials available to children reflect the value on learning that our society promotes. What types of learning did you find most often supported? Least often supported? Why do you think these values are promoted?

TOYS/MATERIALS	LEARNING PROMOTED BY TOYS/MATERIALS	WWW
Social		
Emotional		
Language		
Cognitive		
Fine Motor		
Gross Motor		

5. Reflect upon your personal values. How do you feel young children should be treated? How do you think they learn best? How do you feel cultural issues such as religious holidays, different home languages, and different eating habits should be handled in a daycare situation? Compare your viewpoints to the ones listed in this chapter. How are they the same? Different? How might you need to adjust your thinking to reflect individual cultures in a daycare setting?

6. In a small group, discuss strategies that will help you to interact in a developmentally appropriate manner with young children. Focus on

    a) developmentally appropriate interactions with infants, toddlers, preschoolers, and school-aged children, and

    b) positive behaviour guidance techniques that should be common to all children.

Web exercises

7. You are an early childhood educator in a preschool program in Nova Scotia. You offer a half-day program, and you are the only individual in the room. You have two different groups (morning and afternoon). The age range of the children is 17 months to 5 years, and you have 12 children in each group. In a small group discussion, identify potential problems that you think you might arise.

8. Form a small group with individuals from different cultures. Be careful that you do not identify culture simply by visible characteristics. Canada has many other ethnic groups such as German, Italian, French, and Aboriginal. Discuss what types of cultural aspects influenced each of you directly. How would you incorporate these cultural aspects within a preschool setting? In your discussion, include ideas as listed in this chapter.

9. Discuss the importance of setting up and modelling sound health practices.

10. In small groups, visit local playgrounds when children are playing there. List some of the potentially dangerous conditions you see. Compare your results, and prepare a set of recommendations to rectify the problems you observed.

11. What are some strategies you might use to include family members in planning, implementing, and evaluating an early childhood program?

RESOURCES

Multicultural Literature for Children

Aardema, V., & Vidal, B. (1981). *Bringing the Rain to Kapiti*. Toronto, ON: Penguin Books Canada.

Base, Graeme. (2001). *The Watering Hole*. Toronto, ON: Random House.

Bateman, R. (1998). *Safari*. Toronto, ON: Madison Press Ltd.

Brett, J. (1996). *Goldilocks and the Three Bears*. New York, NY: PaperStar Book.

Brueder Grimm & Eniskat, K. (1995). *Die Bremer Stadtmusikanten*. Berlin, Germany: Proost International.

Cleaver, E., & Toye, W. (1977). *The Loon's Necklace*. Toronto, ON: Oxford University Press.

Dabcovich, L. (2003). *The Polar Bear Son and Inuit Tale*. New York, NY: Clarion Books.

De Coteau Orie, S., & Canyon, C. (1995). *Did You Hear Wind Sing Your Name? An Oneida Song of Spring*. Markham, ON: Thomas Allen and Son Canada.

Dwyer. M. (2002). *Aurora: A Tale of the Northern Lights*. Anchorage, AK: Alaska Northwest Books.

Forkum, S. (2002). *The Three Little PUA'A*. Waipahu, HI: Little Rainbow Books.

Haslam, A., & Parsons, A. (1995). *Arctic People*. Toronto, ON: Stoddart Publishing Company Ltd.

Holling, H. (1942). *Paddle-to-the-Sea*. New York, NY: Houghton Mifflin Company.

Ingalls Wilder, L. (2003). *Winter on the Farm*. New York, NY: Harper Trophy.

Joose, B., & Lavallee, B. (1991) *Mama Do You Love Me?* San Francisco, CA: Chronicle Books.

Kiss, A., & Ruurs, M. (1996). *A Mountain Alphabet*. New York, NY: Tundra Books.

Krebs, L., & Cairns, J. (2003). *We All Went on Safari: A Counting Journey through Tanzania*. Cambridge, MA: Barefoot Books.

Kusugak, M. (2001). *My Arctic 1,2,3.* Willowdale, ON: Firefly Books Ltd.

Moxeley, S. (1995). *Skip Across the Ocean: Nursery Rhymes from Around the World.* London, UK: Frances Lincoln Ltd.

Palazzo-Craig, S., & Nagano, M. (2001). *The Magic Peach: A Story from Japan.* New York, NY: Troll.

Rattigan, J., & Hsu Flanders, L. (1993). *Dumpling Soup.* Boston, MA: Little Brown and Company.

Schuch, S., & Sylvada, P. (1999). *A Symphony of Whales.* New York, NY: Harcourt Brace & Company.

Wallace, M. (1999). *Inuksuk.* Toronto, ON: Owl Books.

Wallace, M. (2001). *Make Your Own Inuksuk.* Toronto, ON: Owl Books.

Waters, K., & Slovenz-Low, M. (2003). *Dancer Ernie Wan's Chinese New Year.* New York, NY: Scholastic.

Winch, J. (2003). *The Old Man Who Loved to Sing.* Toronto, ON: Scholastic.

Multicultural Resources

Hammersmith, B., & Sawatsky, L. (1995). *The Beat of a Different Drum: An Aboriginal Cross-Cultural Handguide for Child-Care Workers.* Saanichton, BC: BC Association of Aboriginal Friendship Centres.

Hill, L. (2000). *Connecting Kids: Exploring Diversity Together.* Gabriola Island, BC: New Society Publishers.

Jones, G., & Moomaw, S. (2002). *Lessons from Turtle Island: Native Curriculum in Early Childhood Classrooms.* St. Paul, MN: Redleaf Press.

Kirchner, G. (2000). *Children's Games from Around the World.* Toronto, ON: Allyn & Bacon.

Multicultural Music

Baby's First Songs from Around the World. (2000). St. Laurent, QC: St. Clair Entertainment Group, Inc.

Brooks, M. (1995). *Snowflake Town.* Whitehorse, YT: SOCAN.

Charno, N., Shapiro, M., Charno, J., & Faro, R. (1998). *Latin Lullaby.* Roslyn, NY: Ellipsis Arts.

Daquioag, W. (2002). *Hawaiian Lullabies Volume II.* Waipahu, HI: Entertainment Music Enterprise & Tami Records.

Dressler, S., Charno, J., & Charno, R. (1999). *African Lullaby.* Roslyn, NY: Ellipsis Arts.

Mozart, L., Mozart, W., & Suessmayr, F. (1998). *Merry Music for Children.* Budapest Chamber Orchestra, Hungarian Radio and Television Children's Chorus, and Budapest Symphony Orchestra. Hungary: Hungaroton Records Ltd.

Vienna Boys' Choir. (1981). *Folk Songs for Children.* Germany: PolyGram.

REFERENCES

Angelini, P.U. (2003). Regionalism in Canada: The Forgotten Diversity. In P.U. Angelini (Ed)., *Our Society: Human Diversity in Canada* (2nd ed., pp. 3–32). Scarborough, ON: Nelson.

Association for Early Childhood Education. (1988). *High Quality Care.* Toronto, ON: Association for Early Childhood Education, Ontario.

Begly, S. (1997). How to Build a Baby's Brain. *Newsweek, 28,* 28–32.

Canadian Child Day Care Federation. (1994). *National Statement On Quality Child Care.* Ottawa, ON: Canadian Child Day Care Federation.

Cedar Road Aboriginal Head Start Program. (2001). *Parents' Handbook.* Prince Rupert, BC: Cedar Road Aboriginal Head Start Program.

Cleveland, G., Colley, S., Friendly, M., & Lero, D. (2003). *The State of Data on Early Childhood Education and Care in Canada: National Data Project Final Report.* Toronto, ON: Childcare Resource and Research Unit.

Cooke, K. (1986). *Report of the Task Force on Child Care*. Ottawa, ON: Canada Government
Publishing Centre.

Copple, C. E. (2003). *A World of Difference: Readings on Teaching Young Children in a Diverse
Society*. Washington, DC: National Association for the Education of Young Children.

Doherty-Derkowski, G. (1994). *Quality Matters: Excellence in Early Childhood Programs*.
Toronto, ON: Addison-Wesley.

Fanjoy, S. E. (1994). *National Statement on Quality Childcare*. Ottawa, ON: Canadian Child
Care Federation.

Gestwicki, C. (1999). *Developmentally Appropriate Practice* (2nd ed.). Scarborough, ON:
Nelson Canada.

Goelman, H., Doherty, G., Lero, D., LaGrange, A., & Tougas, J. (2000). *You Bet I Care!
Caring and Learning Environments: Quality in Child Care Centres Across Canada*. Guelph,
ON: Centre for Families, Work and Well-Being, University of Guelph.

Hanvey, L. (2003). *The Progress of Canada's Children*. Ottawa, ON: Canadian Council on
Social Development.

Harms, T., Clifford, R., & Cryer, D. (1998). *Early Childhood Environment Rating Scale*
(revised ed.). New York, NY: Teachers College Press.

Harms, T., & Clifford, R. (1989). *Family Day Care Rating Scale*. New York, NY: Teachers
College Press.

Harms, T., Cryer, D., & Clifford, R. (1990). *Infant/Toddler Environment Rating Scale*. New
York, NY: Teachers College Press.

Harms, T., Vineberg Jacobs, E., & White, D. (1996). *School-Age Care Environment Rating
Scale*. New York, NY: Teachers College Press.

McCain, M., & Mustard, F. (1999). *Early Years Study Final Report*. Toronto, ON: Publications
Ontario.

Organization for Economic Co-operation and Development. (2001). *Executive Summary:
Starting Strong—Early Education and Care Report on an OCRD Thematic Review*. Toronto,
ON: Childcare Resource and Research Unit.

Pendakur, R., & Hennebry, J. (1998). *Multicultural Canada: A Demographic Overview*.
Ottawa, ON: Strategic Research and Business Planning Multiculturalism, Department of
Canadian Heritage.

Schultz, F. E. (2003). *The Social Concepts of Multicultural Education* (9th ed). Annual Editions
Multicultural Education [02/03], 1–223.

Shapiro Kendrick, A., Kaufman R., & Messenger, K. (1995). *Healthy Young Children: A
Manual for Programs*. Washington, DC: National Association for the Education of Young
Children.

Smith, M. (ed.). (1997). Special Edition, Your Child. *Newsweek, 28*, 1–96.

Village Daycare Society (2001). Program Brochure. Burnaby, BC: Village Daycare Society.

THE LEARNING ENVIRONMENT

"We value space because of its power to organize, promote pleasant relationships between people of different ages, create a handsome environment, provide changes, promote choices and activity, and its potential for sparking all kinds of social, affective, and cognitive learning. All of this contributes to a sense of well-being and security in children. We also think that the space has to be a sort of aquarium which mirrors the ideas, values, attitudes, and cultures of the people who live within it." (Gandini, 1991, p. 6)

Chapter Outcomes

After reading this chapter, the reader will

1. Identify how children learn best.
2. Discuss the principles of effective organization of the environment.
3. Discuss how learning environments can be varied to increase children's interest and imagination.
4. Identify the core learning activities within effective environments.
5. Describe how to organize the environment into various interest groups.
6. Describe what types of materials are needed for diversity and inclusive care.
7. Compare the similarities and differences in schedules for the various age groups.
8. Identify and compare the similarities and differences for the following routines: greeting, personal care, mealtimes, napping and resting, health practices, and safety.
9. Identify and discuss the importance of adult personal space.

INTRODUCTION

> Young children learn through play. Play is enjoyable, may be social, is controlled by the children involved, provides learning without pressure, is intrinsically motivating, is free from rules set by adults, and provides opportunities for children to express themselves in a multitude of ways. (Crowther, 2003, p. 24)

"Many of today's young children are spending a large number of hours in a 'new' environment—childcare. Children who enter childcare as infants can spend as many as 12 000 hours there before they enter school" (Isbell & Exelby, 2003, p. 11). Therefore, learning environments need to be carefully set up to consider children's ages, individuality, and modes of learning to be effective. The learning environment should do the following:

- *Reflect that this is a children's learning space.* "[M]irrors of the ideas, values, attitudes, and cultures" (Gandini, 1991, p. 49) of the children and adults within that space.
- *Be an aesthetically pleasing space that is warm and welcoming for everyone.* "Why should you be concerned with beauty in an environment for young children? Because beautiful spaces, like beautiful things, inspire us, make us feel happy, and nurture our creativity. When happy and content, we are apt to become engaged in interesting projects. We come to value and appreciate the beauty in the world around us" (Isbell & Exelby, 2003, p. 63).
- *Promote many choices and challenges and spark interest in active learning.* "Young children need space to use materials, explore, create, and solve problems; space to spread out, move around in, talk freely about what they are doing; space to work alone and play with others; space to store their belongings and display their inventions; and space for adults to join them in support of their intentions and interests" (Hohmann & Weikart, 1995, p. 111).

PRINCIPLES OF EFFECTIVE ORGANIZATION FOR CHILDREN'S LEARNING

There are some underlying principles of effective organization of children's environments that are based on

- how children learn;
- how children are affected by their learning environments (e.g., what developmental materials and experiences the children need); and
- how best to attract and maintain children's joy in learning.

Effective organization of the learning environment contributes to active exploration by children. There are a number of core elements that should be considered critical in any learning environment (see Table 7.1 and Figure 7.1).

Web exercises

Children are affected and intrigued by the visual images of their learning environment. They pay attention to what they see (photo 7.1). It is important to provide opportunities for children to pay attention to the environment to capture their interest and entice them to more closely examine their learning spaces. Here are some ideas for adding variety to the environment (Crowther, 2003):

Photo 7.1

- If designing a new centre, consider differential ceiling heights. Research has shown that the combination of height and colour of walls influences cooperative behaviour (Read, Sugawara, & Brant, 1999).
- Changing or varying the heights of walls and ceilings can be accomplished by draping material that has been fire-proofed, hanging items such as pots and pans in the housekeeping area, and hanging framed pictures, plants, and mobiles.
- Provide various levels of play—platforms, lofts, and climbers. These should be anchored securely into walls or into the floor.
- "Configuration of wall space—walls can be changed by adding texture and dimension with curved dividers or partitions. These structures can be covered with material (burlap, felt, satin, netting) to add a softer space to the room or to provide interesting ways to display materials" (Crowther, 2003, p. 26) (photo 7.2).
- Maximize the environment and challenge children's creativity by placing related centres together—sand and water, carpentry and creative arts, reading and writing, dramatic play and block play.

Photo 7.2

"A number of studies have addressed the importance of appropriate lighting within learning environments. Poor lighting and/or fluorescent lighting have been linked to hyperactivity, decreased productivity, and poorer health (Harmon, 1951; Ott, 1976; Liberman, 1991)" (Crowther, 2003, pp. 32–33). The most appropriate lighting is natural light. Windows should take up at least 20 percent of the wall space (Hawkins & Lilley, 1992).

Principles of Effective Organization for Children's Learning

Principle	Explanation	Strategies
Display space	Area used to display children's creative efforts at children's height with children's input Nurtures children's pride in accomplishment and shows respect for their efforts	All creative efforts should be mounted in appropriate frames—(see Figure 7.2 on page 188) Hang creative efforts on walls, bulletin boards, back of shelves Display three-dimensional objects attractively on flat surfaces—shelves, tables (photo 7.3)
Traffic flow	Children's ability to move from one learning area to another Makes it possible for children to find areas of choice	Block off areas that need more privacy (reading, quiet, writing areas) or need closer supervision (carpentry) with low shelves or low dividers Secure exits from visitors and to prevent children wanting to leave Provide spill-out areas for play that may extend boundaries (blocks, drama, music) Provide large open areas for gathering large groups (story time, gross motor activity, music activities) Infants and toddlers need area free from clutter—prevent tripping or falling on toys Easily visible to children (encourages making choices) and adults (appropriate supervision and observation) Clear path to emergency exits Clear flow of traffic from one area to another—drama to blocks to washroom
Separation of areas (noisy vs. quiet and messy vs. nonmessy)	Noisy areas (blocks, carpentry, music, drama) Quiet areas (reading, writing, activities such as puzzles) provide opportunities to relax, rest, or concentrate Messy areas (water, sand, carpentry, creative arts) encourage creativity—children concentrate on tasks instead of cleanliness (photo 7.4) Nonmessy areas (books, writing, manipulatives)	Distance—place blocks on one side and reading at the other side of the room Sound absorption—blocks on rug surface, rug Messy and easy-to-clean surfaces—tile, tarp tapped down with slip-proof materials attached to tarp, near water source, smocks to protect clothing Encourage children to clean up as part of routine; child-sized materials on hand—brooms, dustpans, pails, squirt bottles, sponges, and garbage cans in each area
Specialization areas	Space for large group activities—gross motor activity activities (photo 7.5) and project work that can remain over longer periods of time (photo 7.6) Place to be alone	Large clear, carpeted area Protected quiet area—playhouse (photo 7.7), decorated large box with windows and doors, hanging see-through fabric over an area (photo 7.8), tents, protection from intrusion sign (e.g., stop sign, traffic light)
Storage (see Figure 7.3 on page 189) Web exercises ☝	Where and how materials and equipment are displayed to maximize independent use by children System so children know where materials are and where to return them to Collect containers to gather materials	Clear storage containers—easy to see items in containers Mobile units for items that can be used in more than one area—storage cabinets on wheels and caddies that can be moved from place to place Centralized unit—accessible from more than one location Labelling system—picture and word or recognizable symbol (see Figure 7.4 on page 191) Storage by type to prevent dumping and make it easy to find specific item (e.g., all round beads in one container) Baskets to collect things inside or outside to take to a specific work area (photo 7.9) All storage accessible to all children *(cont'd)*

Principles of Effective Organization for Children's Learning

Principle	Explanation	Strategies
Spaces to encourage individual and group interactions	Environments structured to provide opportunities to be alone or in group activity	Soft areas throughout room to encourage relaxation Areas planned for small group interactions Open space to encourage large group play
Visibility	Ease with which adults and children can see various areas	Low shelves and dividers Pictures, photos, and written descriptions to help attract children to the area
Adaptability	Modify as needed to accommodate changing interests and development of children	Keep large, heavy, hard-to-move objects in places that are more permanent Utilize wheeled units, with lockable wheels to maximize adaptability
Balance	Balance between quiet and active play, group and individual play, safety and risk taking	Arrange so that in all learning spaces there is opportunity for individual reflection—add soft areas with pillows, and add books to encourage children to look for ideas
Inclusion	Children from various ethnic backgrounds, children with special needs, children with varying abilities	Adapt the schedule, routines, materials, and activities to provide equal access Modify environment for physical handicaps—wider doors, ramps, hand bars near sinks and toilets All children should be able to access all areas—indoors or outdoors
Developmental appropriateness Web exercises	Materials and activities, set up that are appropriate for children of various ages and abilities	Materials and equipment suitable for a variety of ages and abilities Activities and experiences that take into account the various ages and abilities
Use of colour	Appropriate uses of colour schemes have been shown to reduce systolic pressure, aggression, stress levels, moodiness, illness, and overall noise levels, and have shown increases in academic achievement and IQ scores (Crowther, 2003, p. 33)	Utilize overall colour scheme to calm, relax, quiet behaviour (e.g., green, turquoise, blue) Children's artwork should predominate—avoid bright intense colours that will clash or minimize the artwork Avoid high primary colours as an overall colour scheme as they tend to excite, or stimulate behaviour (e.g., red, orange)
Decreasing noise	Much of the noise in environments is not damaging to the ears, but can adversely affect attention span, concentration, and social interactions.	Use absorbent materials—carpets in block and gross motor areas, firm foam on carpentry bench, acoustic tiles in ceiling Create sound barriers with upholstered furniture or dividers Provide music to calm (Campbell, 1997)

Source: Crowther, 2003, pp. 25–26.

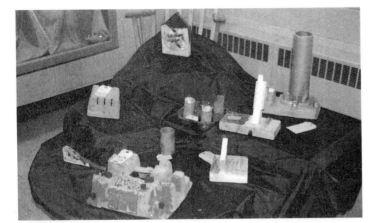
Photo 7.3

Photo 7.8

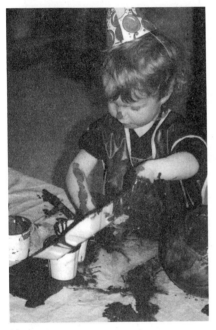
Photo 7.4

Photo 7.7

Photo 7.5

Photo 7.9

Photo 7.6

■ Figure 7.1

Sample Floor Plan of Effective Organization

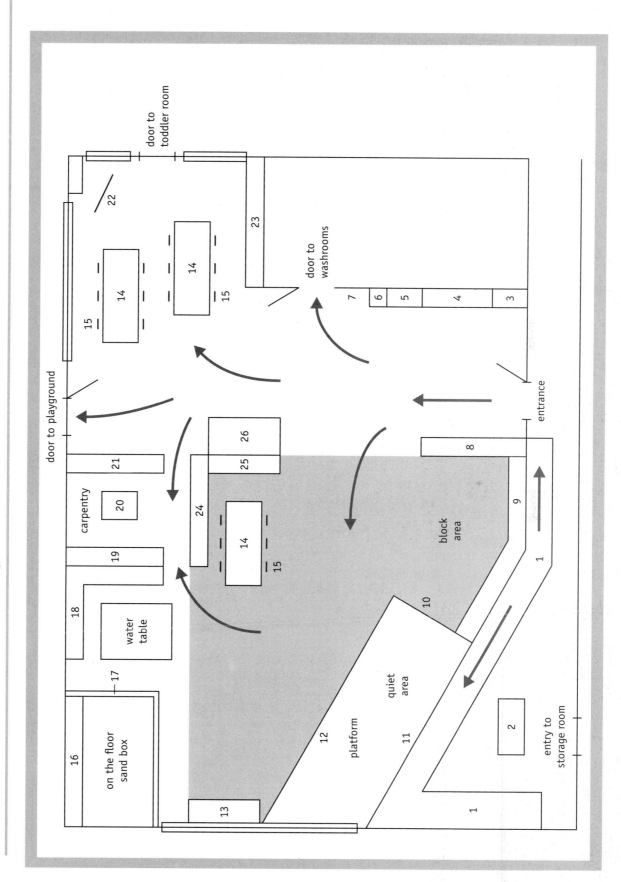

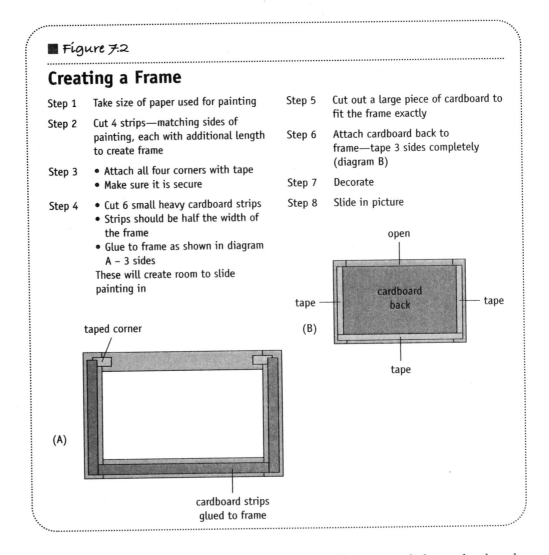

■ Figure 7.2

Creating a Frame

Step 1   Take size of paper used for painting

Step 2   Cut 4 strips—matching sides of painting, each with additional length to create frame

Step 3   • Attach all four corners with tape
          • Make sure it is secure

Step 4   • Cut 6 small heavy cardboard strips
          • Strips should be half the width of the frame
          • Glue to frame as shown in diagram A – 3 sides
          These will create room to slide painting in

Step 5   Cut out a large piece of cardboard to fit the frame exactly

Step 6   Attach cardboard back to frame—tape 3 sides completely (diagram B)

Step 7   Decorate

Step 8   Slide in picture

open

tape — cardboard back — tape

(B)

tape

taped corner

(A)

cardboard strips glued to frame

---

full-spectrum fluorescent lighting

Fluorescent lighting that has the full spectrum of wavelengths of light; the closest match to sunlight.

Photo 7.10

The use of **full-spectrum fluorescent lighting** (fluorescent lighting that has the full spectrum of wavelengths of light, the closest match to sunlight) provides many of the benefits found with natural light (Hathaway, 1994). The following are some strategies that can be implemented to help minimize the effect of poor lighting:

- having at least one hour of outdoor play each day;
- setting up some learning areas, such as reading and writing, near unshielded closed or open windows;
- adding individual light sources to some learning spaces (incandescent lights are better than fluorescent lights);
- creating reflection of natural light by the use of strategically placed mirrors; and
- using full-spectrum fluorescent lighting (Crowther, 2003).

Children feel comfortable in spaces that reflect their home lives. "Young children find it difficult to adjust to a school environment that involves schedules, spaces, materials, language, expectations, behaviours, and situations that are different from their home" (White & Coleman, 2000, p. 225). A home-like atmosphere can be created by

- adding comfortable adult furniture, curtains, pillows;
- providing a doll area depicting a realistic home setting (photo 7.10);

Storage Ideas

1. BOTTLES

Description:
- Cut off the bottom of a clear white bottle.
- Punch two holes at each side of bottle at end that has been cut off.
- Hang with fishing line or yarn on hook in desired area.
- Place materials in bottle with end hanging out of hole in the bottom.

Ideal for:
- yarn
- ribbon
- string

Keeps materials tangle-free

Larger clear water bottles:
- Cut off top of bottle to desired height.
- Sandpaper the top to make sure edge is not sharp.

Ideal for:
- beads
- small manipulative toys
- creative supplies
- pencil crayons and other writing utensils

2. CLEAR CONTAINERS WITH LIDS

Many items such as rice, drink crystals, candies, and nuts may come in clear containers with lids.
Take off the label. May require soaking in soapy water.

Ideal for:
- creative supplies
- things that roll when spilled, like beads
- materials for rotation

3. TREASURE BOXES

Shiny metal containers are ideal for creating surprises or storing children's treasures.

(cont'd)

Storage Ideas

4. HOLDERS

Description:
- Use small boxes of appropriate sizes.
- Fill box with paper scraps or sand to make it less likely to tip.
- Decorate box—paint, colour, or cover with paper, clear plastic, packing tape, or clear MacTac
- Cut slots of appropriate size.

Ideal for:
- scissors
- knives
- paint brushes (keeps brush tips in good condition)

5. SMALL STACKABLE CONTAINERS

Ideal for:
- small manipulative toys
- sewing materials
- creative supplies
- nails, screws, nuts and bolts

- including books and magazines in various areas (these should depict various races, ethnicities, and cultures, and include modern lifestyles and appropriate gender roles—see the Resources at the end of this chapter);
- including pictures and photographs of family members (appropriately framed); and
- adding play figures and dolls that portray the realities of the community—special needs, ethnicity, culture, and gender.

CHILDREN'S LEARNING SPACES

All children need to have defined learning spaces that optimize independence and choice. Learning spaces should cover all the domains of development—physical, cognitive, language, creative, social, and emotional (Harms, Clifford, & Cryer, 1998; Isbell et al., 2003; Hohmann et al., 1995; Crowther, 2003). These learning spaces should be provided indoors and outdoors. Outdoor play spaces should reflect a smooth flow from indoor to outdoor play. What can be done indoors should also be able to be accomplished outdoors. Materials in all areas should be enough to support children's choices, various developmental levels, and interests.

Learning spaces to encourage physical development can be used for the following:

- Small building toys, creative art materials, sewing, beading, puzzles, pegs and pegboards, and writing materials.
- Gross motor activities. Provide gross motor equipment such as slides, swings, ladders, steps, ramps, bars, rings, mats, balls, riding toys, push/pull equipment, and balance beams.
- Music and movement. Props include scarves, ribbons, material, capes, instruments, and dance props. Provide various kinds of music—folk, pop, and classical.

Learning spaces to encourage emotional development can be used for the following:

- Music activities—songs, soothing music to relax by, music about feelings (see the Resources at the end of the chapter).
- Sand area. This is a soothing sensory activity. Provide both wet and dry sand with materials to allow for pouring, sifting, scooping, and digging.
- Water area. Water play is also a soothing sensory activity. Provide materials for pouring and filling.
- Books (see the Resources section at the end of the chapter for suggestions).
- Place to be alone—a soft, comfortable area, protected from intrusions. Activities for relaxation in this area include games for concentration, puzzles, and books.

Learning spaces to encourage creative development can be used for the following:

- Creative art activities. Provide materials available for drawing, painting, sculpting, collage, and sewing. Display children's creative efforts in the environment.

■ **Figure 7.4**

Labelling Systems

All containers should be labelled by picture and by word. The advantage of this system is that children can easily find what they need and can find the appropriate container to return items to when the container is empty.

This system not only provides opportunities to keep the environment organized, but also serves to transfer and apply skills of:

1. matching items—real item to picture or symbol
2. sorting items—put like items together
3. one-to-one correspondence
4. counting

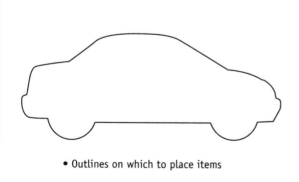

- Outlines on which to place items

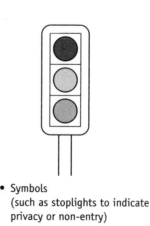

- Symbols (such as stoplights to indicate privacy or non-entry)

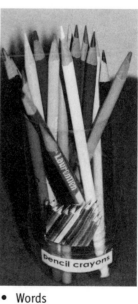

- Words

- Block play. Hang framed photographs of local buildings, construction sites, and imaginary buildings. Provide a variety of blocks—hollow, unit blocks, cardboard bricks, and foam blocks—to encourage creativity. Other accessories for the area include miniature people, vehicles, animals, tracks, and train sets.
- Carpentry area. Provide soft wood and tools such as hammers, nails, saws, clamps, screwdrivers, screws, and sand paper.
- Sand area. Provide moulds, digging utensils, containers of various sizes, sieves, fences, animals, and vehicles. Post photographs of current interest in the sand area such as construction sites, sandcastles, and farms.
- Writing. Provide writing utensils, paper (lined and unlined), booklets, tape, stapler, dictionaries, story books, pictures of current interest to children, and alphabet letters (lowercase and uppercase) to create words.
- Music. Provide musical instruments reflective of cultures represented in the room. Write down the words and music of songs children make up and post them. This will encourage others to learn or play the songs, and it increases children's awareness of another way to write (see Figure 7.5). Provide magnetized notes and a magnet board.

Learning spaces to encourage language development can be used for the following:

- Book areas. Provide books on a variety of topics—picture books, easy reading books, poetry books, nursery rhymes, and storybooks to read aloud. Books should reflect current interests of children. Books should be in a variety of areas—for example, books about construction can be placed in the block play area.
- Scribe centre. A place where children can dictate stories while an adult records what they say. Provide the same materials as in the writing area.
- Music area. A place for singing, listening to songs, and looking at books (see the Resources at the end of the chapter).
- Language games and activities in other areas such as math, science, and writing. Language activities occur in every learning area.

Learning spaces to encourage cognitive development can be used for the following:

- Sand area. Children can make comparisons such as small and large, heavy and light. Provide various sized containers, measuring cups, and accessories.

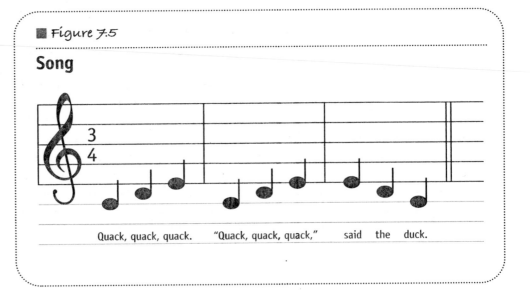

■ Figure 7.5

Song

- Water area. Can be used for comparisons such as heavy vs. light, and to show whether an object sinks or floats. Provide various sized containers, measuring cups, and accessories.
- Book area. This helps create awareness of an alternate form of communication—learning to read.
- Writing area. Children learn about matching, sorting letters, sequencing letters into words, and writing words such as their own names.
- Math area. Children learn about sequencing, patterning, counting, and one-to-one correspondence. Provide materials such as beads, nesting cups, small blocks, small vehicles, and geometric shapes and animals of different sizes and colours.
- Block play area. Children learn about problem solving, creating stable structures, patterning, sequencing, counting, comparisons, matching, and sorting.

Learning spaces to encourage social development can be used for the following:

- Dramatic play area. This area provides opportunities for role-play and imaginative play. Provide materials that reflect children's interests—housekeeping, community helpers, and so on.
- Welcome space. A place to talk to the welcoming early childhood educator, hang personal belongings, share information about home or the daycare, and say good-bye to family members. Give an identity to the space—put up information about the program, upcoming events, schedules, and children's creative efforts. Ensure that the entrance is highly visible so staff can see families and children arrive to greet them.

ORGANIZATION OF LEARNING AREAS

The easiest way to organize the learning environment is by setting up interest centres. Interest centres/learning centres should be arranged to support children's growth and development in all areas. Harms, Clifford, and Cryer (1998) have developed tools to help practitioners set up and evaluate the children's environment. Relevant interest areas for different age groups are listed in Table 7.2.

Interest centres (core learning areas such as sand or blocks that are defined by children's current interests such as building structures in sand or with blocks and by common materials and learning experiences) should be established as well-defined areas: "Define the edges of areas clearly and physically. Use a change in flooring (where carpet ends) dividers, bookshelves, or a hanging canopy to indicate the edges of an area" (Vergeront, 1996, p. 4). Two areas can be adjacent to each other but should not overlap as this may lead to confusion about how materials are to be used and where, and overall poor usage of the area. Each area needs to have an adequate amount of materials and space to support the number of children who may decide to play there. "Establishing well-defined interest areas is one concrete way to foster children's capacity for initiation, autonomy, and social relationships. Because the areas are accessible on a daily basis, children know what materials are available and where to find them. The consistent and therefore dependable organization of space gives children the opportunity to anticipate where they would like to work and what they would like to do with the materials there" (Hohmann et al., 1995, p. 115).

Web
exercises

interest centres
Core learning areas such as sand or blocks that are defined by children's current interests (e.g., building structures in sand or with blocks) and by common materials and learning experiences.

TABLE 7.2

Interest Centres for Different Age Groups

Infants and Toddlers	Preschool Children	School-Aged Children
Books and pictures	Space for gross motor play	Arts and crafts
Activities for eye–hand coordination	Books and pictures	Music and movement
Active physical play	Activities for fine motor activities	Blocks and construction
Art	Art	Drama/theatre
Music and movement	Music and movement	Language/reading activities
Blocks	Blocks	Science and nature activities
Pretend play	Sand and water play	
Sand and water play	Dramatic play	
	Nature/science	
	Math/numbers	
	Activities for computers	

Sources: Harms, Cryer, & Clifford, 1990; Harms et al., 1998; Harms, Vineberg Jacobs, & White, 1996.

Photo 7.11

OUTDOOR SPACES

The outdoor environment should reflect and extend the play that occurs indoors. Children should be able to continue their activity outdoors—continue to work on a project or extend play activities outdoors. Jacob did not want to go outdoors. He wanted to finish reading his books. Nancy asked him if he would like to finish looking at the books outside. Jacob was quite happy to do this (photo 7.11).

In order for activity to continue outside, there needs to be some similarities between the outdoor and indoor environments. Consider the following:

- Quiet, soft areas should be sheltered from the wind and the sun and provide comfortable places in which to sit. Quiet activities such as drawing, reading, and puzzles can be easily set up outside by asking the children to bring out some of the things they might like to use outdoors (photo 7.11).
- Most learning areas can be experienced equally well outdoors and indoors—sand, water, dramatic play, music and movement, writing, creative art, and block play.
- Physical activity lends itself to outdoor play. Children have more opportunity to engage in gross motor skills outdoors if that space is set up to encourage the development of such skills as

  - endurance and strength (photo 7.12);
  - coordination and balance (photo 7.13);
  - climbing and sliding (photo 7.14);
  - taking safe risks (photo 7.15); and
  - exploring the environment through walking, running, and jumping (photo 7.16).

Photo 7.12

Photo 7.13

Photo 7.14

Effective use of the outdoor environment includes some critical factors. Paying close attention to these factors not only will make the outdoors more enjoyable for children, but also will provide for greater safety:

- protection from the elements—shaded areas, trees, vines, covered areas, and walls to protect from the sun and wind (photo 7.17);
- a variety of surfaces for different types of play—paved, grassy, and protected areas under climbing equipment (photos 7.17 and 7.18); and
- areas for active play and relaxation (photos 7.17 and 7.18).

Photo 7.15

DIVERSITY AND INCLUSION

Children growing up during the beginning of this brand new millennium are living in the first generation in the history of the world when exploring our differences has become part of everyday life. Children of all ages, and from all sorts of cultures, countries, languages, heritages, religions, abilities, economic circumstances, lifestyles and other backgrounds are meeting each other in the place we live, learn, work, play and worship. (Hill, 2000, p. 3)

Children need help and guidance to learn to accept and value individuals who are different. Some strategies for promoting inclusion include the use of

- books and pictures that show people of different cultures, races, ages, and abilities, particularly representative of the diversity in their community (see the Resources at the end of the chapter for some examples);
- books and pictures that represent a variety of nonstereotypical roles such as female construction workers and male nurses;
- books in mother languages;
- props that represent various cultures—dolls of different races, dolls that are anatomically correct, ethnic clothing, various cultural eating and cooking utensils, writing utensils form various cultures, and signs from different cultures;
- different ethnic foods at snack time and mealtimes; and
- music and musical instruments from various cultures (see the Resources section at the end of the chapter).

Photo 7.16

Photo 7.17

Photo 7.18

Photo 7.19

Photo 7.20

Photo 7.21

ROUTINES

1. Schedules

The daily schedule should provide a balance between structure and flexibility. Structured activities include arrival, dismissal, outdoor time, mealtime, and rest or sleep time. These activities occur regularly each day and generally will have structured times. There are, however, some exceptions, which include the following:

- *Mealtimes for infants.* Infants are on individual schedules. Infants will also have individualized food requirements.
- *Snack times.* Snack times should be flexible in when they are served, how often, and when needed. Young children may need a snack when they first come in the morning. Many children have already had a long morning prior to coming to the daycare centre. They may be hungry when they arrive.
- *Sleep time.* Infants will have an individualized schedule. They may sleep more than once a day. By the time a child reaches the toddler years, their sleep patterns start to regulate, and they may only need a scheduled nap in the afternoon. Preschoolers may no longer need a sleep time. The nonsleepers should be separated from the sleepers and be provided with relaxing activities such as books, puzzles, drawing, and games for concentration.

Daily schedules should reflect a substantial part of the day to be in active play both indoors and outdoors. Ideally, play should flow from the indoor environment to the outdoor environment. However, there should be at least one outdoor play period a day. Samples of schedules for various age groups are presented in Figure 7.6.

2. Greeting and Dismissal Routines

Greeting children and family members when they first arrive is most important. It sets the tone for the day. Both in the morning and at the end of the day a smoother transition from one setting to another is provided. One staff member should be assigned to this role, while another cares for the children in the playroom. A friendly smile and greeting reassure the child and family member that they are welcome, valued, and respected. The staff, child, and family members have an opportunity to

- greet each other and discuss aspects of the child's experiences at home; create a space that encourages interactions—in the hall, in an alcove, in a corner of the classroom (photo 7.19);

Sample Schedules for Various Age Groups

SAMPLE INFANT SCHEDULE

7:30–9:00	Greeting/arrival
A.M. time	Individualized routines of diapering, personal hygiene routines, feeding, snack for older infants, sleep time Free play time
10:00–11:00	Outdoor play or walk
Noon	Lunchtime for older infants
P.M. schedule	Individualized schedules of diapering, personal hygiene routines, feeding, snack for older infants, sleep time Free play
2:30–3:30	Outdoor play or walk
4:00–6:00	Dismissal

SAMPLE TODDLER SCHEDULE

7:30–9:00	Greeting/arrival Diaper changes as needed (ongoing over day) Snack times as per individual schedule (ongoing over day)
7:30–8:00	Join children in the preschool playroom
8:00–9:00	Toddler room Free play
9:00–9:15	Snack
9:15–9:30	Dress for outside play
9:30–10:30	Free play
10:30–10:45	Inside/undressing
10:45–11:45	Free play (outside) Washroom/diapers
11:45–12:00	Large group music and movement
12:00–12:30	Lunchtime
12:30–12:45	Personal hygiene routines
12:45–2:45	Sleep time
2:45–3:00	Washroom/diapers
3:15–3:30	Dressing and outdoor play
3:30–4:30	Inside/undressing
4:30–4:45	Snack
4:45–6:00	Free play Dismissal

SAMPLE PRESCHOOL SCHEDULE

7:30–9:00	Greeting/arrival
7:30–8:00	Combined age-group free play
8:00	Free flow snack/free play
8:30	Washroom (independent use as needed over day)
8:45	Coatroom/washroom/outside
9:00	Outdoor free play
10:10	Coatroom/washroom
10:15	Free play—block area, sand and water area, art area, puzzles and book area, science/animal life/plants, house area, computer area, toy shelf, easel
11:10	Tidy up
11:20	Recall/small group
11:30	Large group—music
11:45	Lunch
12:15	Washroom/personal hygiene/sleep
2:00	Sleep/quiet play in cubby area for early risers
2:15	Wake up/coatroom washroom
2:45	Outdoor free play
3:50	Coatroom/washroom
4:00	Story/snack/activities/ dismissal
6:00	Centre closed

- fill in any family information forms both at the start and the end of the day; appropriate space needs to be provided to encourage family members to fill in routine forms (see Figure 7.7); and
- engage in personal greeting or farewell routines; set up an area near a window to soften the separation from the family member (photos 7.20 and 7.21).

Sample Family/Staff Information Forms

1. CHECK-IN/CHECK-OUT FORM

Name	Date	Time in	Signature	Time out	Signature
Tom	Oct.2	7:45	Jane Oliver	5:45	Tom Oliver
....	....	....	....	....	....
....	....	....	....	....	....
....	....	....	....	....	....
....	....	....	....	....	....

Importance of Form: By using a separate form, the caregiver has an immediate overview of how many children are present at any given time. Long term information patterns about the time the child spends at the centre and who is likely to bring or pick up the child emerge. In an emergency situation there is clear information about who picked up the child and when. This form can be doubled up to use in case of emergencies, such as taking attendance following a fire drill or to indicate when ratios are low enough at the end of the day to allow a staff member to go home.

2. DAILY INFORMATION—INFANT

Name of Child: Amanda

Information to Share

What kind of morning did the child have? .... Normal .... Fussy .... Other?

Woke up several times during the night crying, rubbing her gums—teething.

Did the child have breakfast? .... Milk .... Other foods

Hungry but does not want to eat—gave her cold fluids, milk and water—brought from home some mashed fruit she likes, as cold seems to soothe her

Any special needs/requests:

Brought several teething rings that can be cooled—please keep cool and give to her as needed

Daily Observations

Meals	Sleeping	Diaper changes	Other	Time
....	....	....	....	....
....	....	....	....	....
....	....	....	....	....

Milestones observed: ....
....
....

Emerging interests: ....
....
....

Other comments: ....
....
....

■ Figure 7.7 *(continued)*

Sample Family/Staff Information Forms

3. DAILY INFORMATION—TODDLER

Name of Child: ....

Information to Share

What kind of morning did the child have? .... Normal .... Fussy .... Other?

....

Did the child have breakfast? .... Yes .... No

Daily Observations

Meals	Sleeping	Diaper changes	Other	Time
....	....	....	....	....
....	....	....	....	....
....	....	....	....	....

Any special needs/requests? ....

....

....

Milestones observed: ....

....

....

Emerging interests: ....

....

....

Other comments: ....

....

....

4. DAILY INFORMATION—PRESCHOOL/SCHOOL–AGE CHILD

Name of Child: ....

Information to Share

Did the child have breakfast? .... Yes .... No

Milestones observed: ....

....

....

Emerging interests: ....

....

....

Type of day/night: ....

....

....

Other comments: ....

....

....

Importance of Daily Observation Forms: These forms provide a crucial information exchange to help the child make the transition from home to daycare and vice versa. They help caregivers and family members to understand the child's behaviour and provide clues on how the caregiver or family members should react to the child (e.g., feed the child who has not had a chance to have breakfast, or provide some quiet time to the child who has not had enough sleep during the night or day).

Diapering Area—Infants or Toddlers

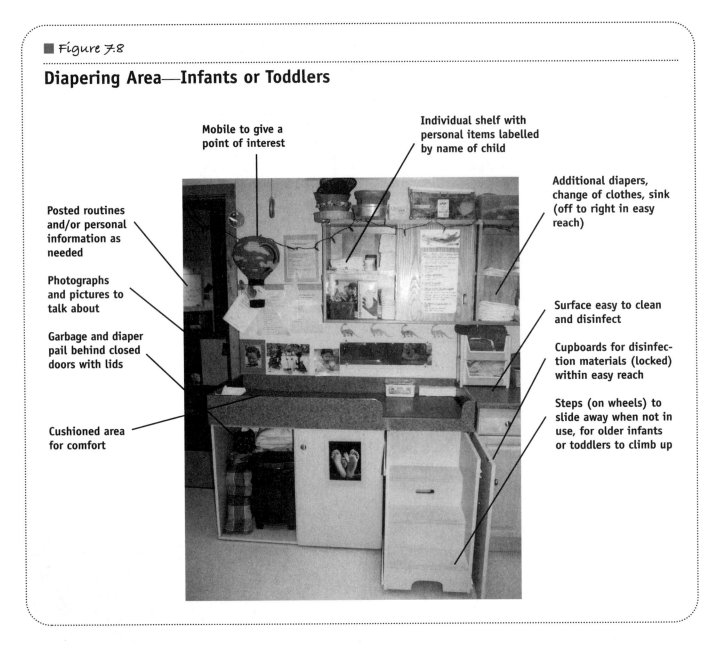

Mobile to give a point of interest

Individual shelf with personal items labelled by name of child

Additional diapers, change of clothes, sink (off to right in easy reach)

Posted routines and/or personal information as needed

Photographs and pictures to talk about

Garbage and diaper pail behind closed doors with lids

Cushioned area for comfort

Surface easy to clean and disinfect

Cupboards for disinfection materials (locked) within easy reach

Steps (on wheels) to slide away when not in use, for older infants or toddlers to climb up

3. Personal Care Routines

Infants and Toddlers

The diapering area should be well organized with everything in reach of the caregiver (see Figure 7.8). The diapering area should be well away from food preparation areas and should be easy to be sanitized and kept clean. The diapering surface must be disinfected after every use. Materials such as disinfectants should be kept out of reach or locked away. Garbage and dirty diapers should be kept in separate containers with tight-fitting lids. Descriptions of diapering routines should be posted along with any pertinent individual information about the children.

Older infants and toddlers can get very heavy. Provide steps to encourage infants and toddlers to get up to the diapering surface by themselves. The area should be enhanced with attractive materials for the child to look at and talk about while on the diapering surface.

Photo 7.22

Toddlers who are starting toilet training may need a potty chair, or may start to use a regular child-sized toilet. There are removable toilet seats that will aid the toddler's efforts. Toilet paper should be within easy reach of the toilet.

Older Toddlers and Preschoolers

Children should become independent in personal caring for themselves. Personal-care routines include

- *Dressing oneself appropriately.* Cubbies need to be set up so that children have a place for personal belongings, shoes, jackets or coats, a place to sit, and personal identification for their space (could be photographs, names, or symbols) (photo 7.22).
- *Hand washing.* To be independent, children need to be able to reach all parts of the sink, and have all needed materials available (soap, towels, garbage can). Instructions should be posted to encourage appropriate hand-washing routines. The area should be kept clean at all times (photo 7.23). Check the temperature of water—it should be no hotter than 48°C.
- *Personal grooming.* Personal grooming items (toothbrushes, face-cloths, combs and brushes) should be kept in personal spaces—individual hooks or holders for toothbrushes and facecloths and individual bags for brushes and combs. All personal items should be clearly labelled by photo or symbols and name.
- *Using the toilet.* Have child-sized toilets with toilet paper nearby. School-aged children will need separate toileting spaces for boys and girls.

4. Mealtime Routines

Snack Times

Snack time in many centres is an open time. Children may have a drink or a snack whenever they are hungry. This means that an area needs to be kept open at all times. There should be a refrigerator in the

Photo 7.23

Chapter Seven   The Learning Environment

room that will keep the food from spoiling. Advantages of this type of system include the following:

- Children can monitor themselves. They can eat when they are hungry and learn to monitor appropriate quantities of food.
- It is less disruptive to children's activities. They can decide when to stop an activity to have snack.
- Children become more independent. They can wash their hands, get their own snack, and clean up after themselves (dishes, table, floor).
- Children engage in small group socialization with peers of choice.

Disadvantages are that

- Closer supervision is needed to monitor children's behaviour—hand-washing, getting the snack, and cleaning up. You must also be aware of what, how often, and how much the child has eaten.
- Maintaining a sanitary environment to eat in is more difficult.

In some centres, snack time is a large group's activity—everyone has snack together, including the adults. Advantages of this type of system include the following:

- The appropriate number of tables can be cleared and set up immediately, so there is no need to save a space for the snack. This is often a consideration in centres that do not have a lot of space.
- Adults can keep track of children's food intake.
- Adults can ensure that all children have washed their hands and cleaned up after themselves.
- There is the opportunity to engage in large-group social activity with peers and adults (e.g., you can talk about the food or the children's interests).

The disadvantages to this type of routine are that

- Adults control the behaviour of children. Children are directed to do things— stop their activity, clean up, wash their hands, come to the table, and so forth.
- Children may not be hungry at this time or they may have been hungry earlier.
- The children cannot interact in smaller, more intimate groupings.

Photo 7.24

Some centres offer a combined approach. Children have some snacks and drinks available to them as they wish. There is also a set snack time provided. Children may join the larger-group time if they wish. The staff of these centres feel that they are meeting the best of both worlds—independence and group activity.

Lunch

Since hot prepared lunches are a requirement in most daycare settings, this is usually a large-group activity. Care should be taken to ensure that the children are in smaller groups around more than one table. Mealtime should be an aesthetically and socially pleasurable time for everyone. Some strategies that could be used include

- using individual placemats or table cloths to make the area more inviting (photo 7.24);

- adding to the table flowers or attractive centrepieces that children have created;
- setting the table to represent different cultures—finger bowls and finger foods, chopsticks, soup plates, different types of forks (dessert, fish, regular);
- providing serving dishes so that children can serve themselves (photo 7.25); and
- encouraging children to clean up by themselves by providing a place to return dirty dishes to and bowls for scraping off excess food or emptying liquids (photo 7.26).

Feeding Infants

Usually family members bring in the food for the infant. There should be a fridge and microwave within the infant room. Infants will be on independent feeding schedules, as discussed with family members. Establish a cozy, quiet corner with a comfortable adult-sized chair. This provides an opportunity for relaxed, pleasant interactions between adult and child while feeding the infant his or her bottle. The infant should always be held, never left to drink with a bottle propped up. Infants are very quick to reach and grab. No hot liquids should be anywhere within grabbing range.

Sometimes mothers may be able to take the time to nurse their infants. The same quiet corner could be used for this purpose. Alternatively, the cozy corner used to rock a tired infant to sleep could also be used.

Photo 7.25

5. Napping and Resting Routines

Infants

Infants should be on individual sleep schedules similar to the ones established at home. In most jurisdictions in Canada, it is required that infants have a regulation crib in which to sleep. (According to the Hazardous Products Act, the height should be 66 cm from the lowest position of the mattress, there should be no more than 3 cm between crib side and mattress, and the mattress must be at least 15 cm thick. Watson et al., 2000). Many jurisdictions require a separate sleep room. Most licensing requirements in Canada require that cribs be placed at least 0.9 m apart. The crib sides should always be in a locked position. Crib sides should be protected by bumper pads (remove them when the child starts to pull himself or herself up to sitting or standing position). The mattress should be moved to the lowest setting as soon as the infant is able to sit up.

Since there will be varying sleep schedules for the infants, it might be wise to create visual barriers between the cribs (e.g., curtains or blinds hung from the ceiling). These at least serve to protect the child who is still resting from visual intrusion. Some infants may need to be rocked prior to falling asleep. A cozy corner should be developed in the playroom that is protected from intrusion. An adult-sized rocking chair is ideal to rock infants to sleep.

Soft music provides a soothing stimulus for infants to fall asleep (see the Resources section for some music suggestions). The electronic equipment should be kept out of reach, and electrical cords should be safely tucked away.

Photo 7.26

Toddlers and Preschoolers

Within this age group there will be children who will sleep a long time (up to two hours), part of that time, or not at all. An area needs to be set up for the sleepers. Usually cots or mats that are used only for sleeping and stored at other times are provided. These should be placed at least 91.4 cm apart. Each child should have personal items such as sheets, blankets, pillows, and cuddly toys to help them sleep. All items should be washable and changed regularly. Lights should be dimmed, and soft music played. If possible, opening windows for proper ventilation would be advisable. Children may wish to have their backs rubbed to go to sleep. Caregivers may need cushions or blankets to make this procedure more comfortable.

For the early risers or nonsleepers, a quiet restful area should be set up. These children should be in a separate area from the sleeping children and should have a choice of quiet activities, such as books, concentration games, puzzles, or other manipulative toys. If space is a problem, separate areas can be set up in a cloakroom, or in a corner of the room by a window protected by shelves.

6. Health Practices

The centre must keep a record of a variety health-related practices—immunization, ill health, and emergency information forms. As a result, there is a need to ensure that confidentiality is adhered to. This requires the child-care setting to provide a system of locking away these records. A locked filing cabinet is a good idea.

If a child should become ill during the day, there needs to be a space that can be used to isolate the child until he or she is picked up. An office space could be used for this purpose, as long as the child can still be supervised in this setting. A quiet area can also be created in the corner of the room. The child's cot can be set up, shelves or dividers can be placed around the cot for privacy, and a no-intrusion sign can be hung to remind other children that this child is not to be disturbed.

Many childhood diseases can be transmitted by contact with infected surfaces. This requires regular cleaning and disinfection of toys, furniture, and the general environment. It becomes much easier to maintain a healthy environment if

- walls and furniture are painted with a washable paint for easy cleaning;
- a sink is accessible for cleaning purposes (close to the rooms and used for cleaning purposes only);
- child-sized sinks and adult-sized sinks are within the room for easy handwashing;
- any poisonous substances are kept out of reach of children or locked away;
- any medication is kept in a locked space;
- there is a telephone within each room;
- common safety procedures (e.g., fire drills), emergency numbers, and contact information are posted in an accessible location;
- food preparation areas are removed from children's play areas and from washroom areas;
- all exits (indoors and outdoors) have protective barriers;
- access to children by strangers is prevented (locked entry to daycare with a buzzer system);
- garbage cans are frequently emptied in a larger bin with a tight lid; and
- both child-sized and adult-sized cleaning items are provided—children love to help, and this is an opportunity to model appropriate cleaning practices and get children involved in the routine.

w(w)w

Emergency Plan

Fire Department number: .... [Posted by telephone].

Exit to leave by: .... Alternate exit: ....

Emergency meeting place: ....

Emergency shelter location: ....

Responsibility

Name of Individual or Alternate	Tasks
	Telephone fire department
	Gather children and take outside
	Bring emergency items—flashlight, emergency cards, files, list of names of children present
	Ensure that no one is left in rooms
	Turn off lights and close doors
	Take attendance at designated meeting place

7. Safety Routines

One of the primary considerations for caregivers is the safety of the children. Young children are naturally curious. Their behaviour is often impulsive. They do not yet understand the consequences of their actions. They do not realize that a situation could be potentially dangerous. "Teachers and administrators have a major responsibility to protect the safety of the children in their care. This can be a particularly challenging task, especially when young children are involved. Their developmental characteristics and limited experience require adults to establish and practice high standards of safety" (Marotz, Cross, & Rush, 2001, p. 190).

General Routines for All Age Groups

There are some general safety routines that are consistent for all children. These include

- protecting children from leaving the room or playground—place latches or door knobs out of reach on all doors and gateways or cover with child-proof openers (no longer necessary for school-aged children);
- using seatbelts or car seats when transporting children and ensuring that children always sit on a back seat, as air-bag inflation is potentially lethal to young children;
- cleaning up spills and scattered toys to prevent slipping;
- covering each electrical outlet or installing childproof receptacles (best method);
- posting an emergency evacuation plan in every room—identify exits, meeting points, and procedures (see Figure 7.9);
- keeping an emergency route to the emergency exit clear;

Chapter Seven The Learning Environment **205**

- practising fire drills—be aware of fire drill procedures (fire drill report, attendance, turning off lights and closing doors, emergency information, contacts, children's emergency files);
- using fire-retardant materials for draperies and floor covering;
- keeping room temperature between 20°C and 25°C year round; and
- wearing wide-brimmed hats and sunscreen (SPF 30) for outdoor activities.

Safety Considerations for Infants

To protect infants from physical harm,

- place infant on a mat or large pillow when on the floor, away from sharp objects and any furniture; and
- ensure they are securely fastened in strollers and highchairs.

To protect infants from choking,

- ensure there are no drawstrings, buttons that can be reached, or decorative items such as pompoms on clothes;
- make sure that no dangling cords (electrical, curtain, or blind cords) are near enough to grab;
- ensure that no small items that could be put in the mouth and cause choking are within reach.

Web exercises

Safety Considerations for Mobile Infants and Toddlers

To protect mobile infants and toddlers from physical harm,

- close doors or prop open with a wedge to avoid pinching fingers;
- place rocking chairs in a protected corner of room to avoid pinching fingers;
- place safety locks on cupboard doors and drawers with dangerous products or move products to high shelves;
- install safety gates in dangerous areas such as stairs, bathrooms, between rooms, and at entry to room;
- check all furniture for tipping when children use furniture as support to pull themselves up;
- have sturdy toys that don't tip to push along as child walks;
- pad sharp edges of furniture or cupboards;
- ensure that open spaces are free from obstruction (furniture, toys, books);
- check toys and equipment for broken parts, slivers, and possibility of pinching;
- have cushioned floors such as rugs in playrooms and absorbent surfaces under climbers and slides;
- provide toys that are easy to grasp and large enough to be mouthed (smaller toys that could cause choking should only be available when there is direct supervision of a caregiver); and
- avoid substances that stain such as dyes or inks, as these may be absorbed through the skin.

To protect them from choking,

- check toys and equipment for small or broken parts;
- check to see that materials provided are nontoxic, such as markers and play dough;
- supervise drawing activities (children may bite off the tops of wax crayons and markers and swallow them);
- provide opportunities to learn to use tools and utensils (such as scissors and plastic knives) safely;

- cut grapes and other small fruit and vegetables into bite-sized pieces; and
- tie a knot in plastic bags before they are discarded to prevent children from placing them over their heads.

Safety Considerations for Preschoolers

Here are some safety considerations for preschoolers when they are working with various tools:

- *Carpentry area.* Clamp down items before children start hammering because holding an object and hammering could cause a painful bruise. Always return tools to labelled storage containers because the impact of hammering will cause tools and nails to bounce and fall, and they may land on someone's hand or foot or be stepped on. Use safety equipment such as child-sized gloves and child-sized safety glasses. Locate the carpentry area away from high-traffic areas or have this area protected by shelves or in a corner.
- *Creative area.* Scissors should have blunt ends. Check to ensure they can cut; if scissors are not sharp enough they can be dangerous, as they may be used inappropriately. Needles should be sturdy and have blunt ends and large eyes. Check to ensure that the needle will go easily through the material provided. Knives and cutters should be sturdy plastic. Check their edges to make sure they are not sharp enough to cut fingers or hands. Paintbrushes should have blunt ends to prevent accidental poking. Sharp objects such as toothpicks should be made blunt.
- *Safe storage.* Scissors and knives should be stored with points down to model correct handling. Place cylindrical items in a container to prevent falling off the table—rolling pins, markers, crayons, and pencils.
- *Safe products.* Use water-based paints, markers, and glues; food colouring or natural vegetable colouring; and chalk on wet surfaces (to prevent chalk dust from flying around).

Playground Safety

For playground safety, note the following:

- Weather protection:
  - have children avoid metal on hot days (e.g., metal slides can become very hot and may cause burns); and
  - have shaded areas (trees, arbour of vines, awnings, free-standing roof) and windbreaks (evergreen hedges, walls).

- Protection from falls:
  - provide cushioned surfaces under slides, swings, climbers;
  - check height of climbing equipment (should be a maximum of 1.8 m) and platforms (a maximum of 1.2 m; for school-aged children, a maximum of 1.8 m);
  - check railings on platforms, stairs, and ramps;
  - ensure that children wear CPSI-approved helmets when using riding toys; and
  - check for curled mats and for any protruding parts, and ensure that treads on stairs are securely fastened.

- Protection from injury:
  - swings are no longer permitted in some jurisdictions due to the high risk of injury; if used, provide a clear boundary around swings to prevent children from being hit by swing;

Poisonous Plants*

Amaryllis	Caladium	Gladiola	Oak (acorns)
Arrowhead	**Castor bean**	Golden chain tree (acorns and	Peony
Azalea	Cherry tree (leaves and twigs)	leaves)	Philodendron family
Barberry	Chinaberry	Holly	Poison oak/ivy/sumac
Berries of bittersweet,	Chinese evergreen	Hydrangea	**Poinsettia (leaves)**
mistletoe	Chrysanthemum	Iris (underground roots)	Pokeweed
Black lotus tree (bark leaves,	Crown of thorns	Jerusalem cherry	Rhododendron
pods and seeds)	Dieffenbachia	Jimsonweed	**Rhubarb (raw leaves)**
Boxwood	English ivy	Lily-of-the-valley (leaves and	Water hemlock
Bulbs of daffodil, hyacinths,	Euonymus privet	flowers)	Wisteria (seed pods)
narcissus, and jonquil	Four o'clock	Mountain laurel	**Yew (berries and foliage)**
Buttercup	Fruit pits or seeds	Nightshade family	

* Note: highlighted plants may cause fatality if ingested. Source: Crowther, 2003.

- keep ball area away from high-traffic areas, especially riding paths; and
- ensure stability of equipment by checking ladders, ramps, poles, platforms, moving parts, rot in wood, and rust in metal.

- Protection from entrapment:

  - ensure that all openings are safe—rungs and spaces between railings should be 8.9 cm wide and spaces for rungs should be more than 22.9 cm apart; and
  - check for hooks or protruding parts (bolts, nuts, and other small parts can catch fingers or clothing).

- Accessibility and protection:

  - ensure there are paved pathways for wheelchairs; and
  - provide ramps to other play areas, such as climbers and playhouse.

- Protection from poisonous materials:

  - use sand to cover animal excrement;
  - avoid poisonous plants (see Figure 7.10);
  - use organic pesticides on lawn, shrubs, trees, and flowers; and
  - ensure that playground area is away from pollution of traffic and loud noise.

- Protection from glare:

  - avoid bright primary colours or silver material on equipment; and
  - wear UV-protected sunglasses.

ADULT SPACE

Adults need to have a separate space. The caregiver's job is demanding. Much of their day is spent at the child's level, using child-sized furniture. Adults need the opportunity to gain some respite from the "hustle and bustle" of the activities within the child-care setting. Adult areas should:

- be furnished with comfortable adult-sized furniture;
- have a place where adults can safely store personal belongings;

- provide opportunities for adults to have a quiet snack, meal, or drink; and
- have a work area where adults can reflect and create pertinent resources, materials, and reports.

Adults also need a place to interact with families, other professionals, and peers. Ideally, another room can be set aside for this purpose. If the adult personal space is used for these purposes, the area should be used after hours. Office space can be used to meet with individuals during program hours.

KEY POINTS

PRINCIPLES OF EFFECTIVE ORGANIZATION FOR CHILDREN'S LEARNING
- Effective organization is based on children's learning and developmentally appropriate materials and experiences.
- Effective environments

  - display children's activities;
  - allow for traffic flow;
  - separate learning areas;
  - provide storage of children's learning materials;
  - provide inclusive care;
  - have a good use of colour; and
  - limit noise.

- You can create variety in the learning environment through

  - differential ceiling heights;
  - different levels of play; and
  - adding texture and dimension to walls.

- Lighting is important because poor light is linked to a number of adverse effects. Use strategies to minimize the effects of poor lighting.

CHILDREN'S LEARNING SPACES
- Create a home-like atmosphere.
- Respect all domains of development—physical, emotional, creative, language, cognitive, and social.

ORGANIZATION OF LEARNING AREAS
- Learning spaces for different age groups (infants, toddlers, preschoolers, and school-aged children) focus on developmental needs of that age.

OUTDOOR SPACES
- Outdoor spaces provide an extension of indoor play.
- They should help develop increased gross-motor competence, offer protection from elements, and provide opportunity for active play and relaxation.

DIVERSITY AND INCLUSION
- Include diverse representations of culture and ethnicity and nonstereotypic role representation in materials and resources.

ROUTINES

- Schedules and routines are different for various age groups, especially with respect to mealtimes, nap and rest times, and personal hygiene.
- Have interaction routines at greeting time and dismissal.
- Provide space for nursing mothers.
- Provide opportunities for naps and or quiet activities.
- Follow appropriate health practices for health-care information, ill children, and routines to decrease spread of disease.
- Safety considerations vary for the different age groups.
- Ensure playground safety by protecting against weather and physical harm, providing cushioned ground cover and safe equipment, and setting safety boundaries.

ADULT SPACE

- A separate space for adults should include a relaxation area and space for storage of personal materials.

EXERCISES

1. In a small group, discuss how children learn best. Using the basic principles as outlined in Table 7.1 (pages 184–85), reflect on how each of these principles relates to how children learn.
2. Observe at least three centres for children in your area. Fill in the criteria as listed in the chart below.
3. Compare how the same learning centres are set up to encourage the development of different domains—cognitive, language, creative, physical, social, and emotional. Choose three areas to compare (e.g., sand, water, manipulatives, blocks, music and movement, books, gross motor, art, carpentry).

CRITERIA TO OBSERVE	DESCRIPTION OF HOW CRITERIA WERE USED IN CENTRE 1	DESCRIPTION OF HOW CRITERIA WERE USED IN CENTRE 2	DESCRIPTION OF HOW CRITERIA WERE USED IN CENTRE 3
Differential Ceiling Height			
Strategies Used to Vary Height of Walls			
Various Levels of Play			
Adding Texture and Dimension to Walls			

4. Discuss why there are differences in the types of learning areas that are appropriate for different age groups. Use the information in Table 7.2 (page 194) to help your discussion.

5. All 15 children are dressed and ready to go outside. It is a cold winter day with snow on the ground. One child is not ready to go out. She wants to take her books out with her to read. How might you facilitate her request? What additional materials would you need?

6. Your play area is devoid of shade or shelter. It gets too hot or cold to play outside. The board of directors has offered to do some fund-raising to correct this situation. They have asked your staff to make some recommendations. Prepare three different scenarios for this situation. Right now, the playground is fenced. It has a small grass-covered hill in the centre. In front of the door is a large asphalt area. A riding path curls from the asphalt surface around the hill and back again. A large wooden climber sits at the far end of the playground in one corner, about 4 m in from the fence. A sandbox is on the other side bounded by the fence and the side of the building.

7. Go to the public library and find resources for diversity. Your resources should focus on inclusion, nonstereotypic roles, and the cultural aspects of your community.

8. Compare the schedules of the infants, toddlers, and preschoolers. How are they the same? How are they different? Account for the similarities and differences.

9. Develop a checklist to observe routine care facilities for a group of infants, toddlers, and preschoolers. What suggestions would you make for adaptations or improvements?

10. Reflect on the advantages and disadvantages for the different snack time systems described on pages 201–202. Which system would you use? Explain your choice.

11. Explain why it is important to encourage nursing mothers to come into the centre to nurse their infants.

12. Jimmy's mother asked that he no longer sleep in the afternoon. He is four years old. His mother indicates that she cannot get him settled at night if he sleeps in the day. Jimmy is the only nonsleeper in your group. What might you do to facilitate Jimmy's mother's request?

13. Look over the health practices listed in this chapter. What strategies might you use to encourage children to become more independent in implementing health practices?

14. Develop a checklist that could serve to identify safety checks that should be conducted indoors and outdoors. Try your checklist in a child-care environment. Reflect on how well your tool worked. Do you need to make some additions? Is the information collected clear? Can you make recommendations from the information you collected?

15. Discuss why it is important for adults working with young children to have a separate space.

RESOURCES

Books to Enhance Emotional Development

Bradman, T., & Cockcroft, J. (2001). *Daddy's Lullaby*. London, UK: Bloomsbury Publishing Plc.

Dale, P. (2000). *Big Brother, Little Brother*. Cambridge, MA: Candlewick Press.

Dijs, C. (1996). *Daddy, Would You Love Me If?* New York, NY: Simon & Schuster Children's Publishing Division.

Eastman, P. (1960). *Are You My Mother?* New York, NY: Random House.

Eastman, P. (1977). *Flap Your Wings.* New York, NY: Random House.

Gilmore, R., & Sauvé, G. (1999). *A Screaming Kind of Day.* Markham, ON: Fitzhenry & Whiteside.

Harris, P. (1995). *Looking at Opposites: Hot, Cold, Shy, Bold.* Toronto, ON: Kids Can Press.

Hutchins, H., & Ohi, R. (2002). *I'd Know You Anywhere.* Willowdale, ON: Firefly Books Ltd.

Joose, B., & Lavallee, B. (1991). *Mama Do You Love Me?* San Francisco, CA: Chronicle Books.

Kopper, L. (1996). *I'm a Baby, You're a Baby.* Toronto, ON: Puffin Books.

MacDonald, A. (1998). *The Memory Stone.* Charlottetown, PEI: Ragweed Press.

Magnus, E. (1992). *Around Me.* New York, NY: Lothrop, Lee & Sheppard Books.

Books to Listen to and Sing Along With

Adams, P. (1973). *There Is an Old Lady Who Swallowed a Fly.* Singapore: Child's Play International Ltd.

Frazee, M. (1999). *Hush Little Baby.* New York, NY: Harcourt Brace & Company.

Hammerstein II, R., Rodgers, R., & Warhola, J. (1959). *My Favorite Things.* New York, NY: Simon and Schuster Books for Young Readers.

Raffi & Allender, D. (1987). *Shake My Sillies Out.* New York, NY: Crown Publishers, Inc.

Siomades, L. (1999). *The Itsy Bitsy Spider.* Honesdale, PA: Bell Books.

Warlow, A., & Chesterman, J. (1984). *Rain.* Aylesbury, UK: Ginn and Company Ltd.

Books to Enhance Diversity

Base, G. (2001). *The Watering Hole.* Toronto, ON: Random House.

Bateman, R. (1998). *Safari.* Toronto, ON: Madison Press Ltd.

Brett, J. (1996). *Goldilocks and the Three Bears.* New York, NY: PaperStar Books.

Cleaver, E., & Toye, W. (1977). *The Loon's Necklace.* Toronto, ON: Oxford University Press.

Dabcovich, L. (2003). *The Polar Bear Son: An Inuit Tale.* New York, NY: Clarion Books.

De Coteau Orie, S. & Canyon, C. (1995). *Did You Hear Wind Sing Your Name? An Oneida Song of Spring.* Markham, ON: Thomas Allen and Son Canada.

Dwyer, M. (2002). *Aurora: A Tale of the Northern Lights.* Anchorage, AK: Alaska Northwest Books.

Forkum, S. (2002). *The Three Little PUA'A.* Waipahu, HI: Little Rainbow Books.

Grimm, B., & Eniskat, K. (1995). *Die Bremer Stadtmusikanten.* Berlin, Germany: Proost International.

Hall, N. (1999). *Creative Resources for the Anti-Bias Classroom.* Scarborough, ON: Delmar Publishers.

Haslam, A., & Parsons, P. (1995). *Arctic People.* Toronto, ON: Stoddart Publishing Company Ltd.

Holling, H. (1941). *Paddle-to-the-Sea.* New York, NY: Houghton Mifflin Company.

Ingalls Wilder, L. (2003). *Winter on the Farm.* New York, NY: Harper Trophy.

Kiss, A., & Ruurs, M. (1996). *A Mountain Alphabet.* New York, NY: Tundra Books.

Krebs, L., & Cairns, J. (2003). *We All Went on Safari: A Counting Journey through Tanzania.* Cambridge, MA: Barefoot Books.

Kusugak, M. (2001). *My Arctic 1,2,3.* Willowdale, ON: Firefly Books Ltd.

Moxeley, S. (1995). *Skip Across the Ocean: Nursery Rhymes from Around the World.* London, UK: Frances Lincoln Ltd.

Palazzo-Craig, J., & Nagano, M. (2001). *The Magic Peach: A Story from Japan.* New York, NY: Troll.

Rattigan, J., & Hsu Flanders, L. (1993). *Dumpling Soup.* Boston, MA: Little, Brown and Company.

Schuch, S., & Sylvada, P. (1999). *A Symphony of Whales.* New York, NY: Harcourt Brace & Company.

Wallace, M. (1999). *Inuksuk*. Toronto, ON: Owl Books.

Wallace, M. (2001). *Make Your Own Inuksuk*. Toronto, ON: Owl Books.

Waters, K., & Slovenz-Low, M. (2003). *Dancer Ernie Wan's Chinese New Year*. New York, NY: Scholastic.

Winch, J. (2003). *The Old Man Who Loved to Sing*. Toronto, ON: Scholastic.

Music to Enhance Emotional Development

Baby Reflections. (2000). *Nature's Lullabies*. Don Mills, ON: Baby Reflections.

Campbell, D. (1992). *The Mozart Effect Music for Children: Relax, Daydream & Draw*. Pickering, ON: The Children's Group Inc.

Murray, A. (1997). *There's a Hippo in My Tub*. Mississauga, ON: Capitol Records, Inc.

Musical Reflections. (1999). *Lullabies: Cherished Bedtime Classics*. Don Mills, ON: Musical Reflections.

Raffi & Creber, M. (2002). *Let's Play*. Toronto, ON: Troubadour Records Ltd.

Raffi & Shine Band. (1989). *Raffi in Concert*. Willowdale, ON: Troubadour Records Ltd.

Stone, J. (1998). *Baby Needs Mozart*. Hollywood, CA: Delos International, Inc.

Walker, W. (2000). *Heartbeat Pacifier*. Don Mills, ON: Baby Reflections.

Music for Diversity

Brooks, M. (1995). *Snowflake Town*. Whitehorse, YT: SOCAN.

Charno, J., Shapiro, M., Cahrno, R., & Faro, R. (1998). *Latin Lullaby*. Roslyn, NY: Ellipsis Arts.

Daquioag, W. (2002). *Hawaiian Lullabies Volume II*. Waipahu, HI: Entertainment Music Enterprise & Tami Records.

Dressler, S., Charno, J., & Charno, R. (1999). *African Lullaby*. Roslyn, NY: Ellipsis Arts.

Mozart, L., Mozart, W., & Suessmayr, F. (1998). *Merry Music for Children*. Budapest Chamber Orchestra, Hungarian Radio and Television Children's Chorus, and Budapest Symphony Orchestra. Hungary: Hungaroton Records Ltd.

Vienna Boys' Choir. (1981). *Folk Songs for Children*. Germany: PolyGram.

REFERENCES

Campbell, D. (1997). *The Mozart Effect*. New York, NY: Avon Books.

Crowther, I. (2003). *Creating Effective Learning Environments*. Scarborough, ON: Nelson Thomson Learning.

Gandini, L. (1991). Not Just Anywhere: Making Child Care Centres into "Particular" Places. *Childcare Information Exchange*, March/April, 5–9.

Harmon, D. (1951). *The Coordinated Classroom*. Grand Rapids, MI: American Seating Company.

Harms, T., Clifford, R., & Cryer, D. (1998). *Early Childhood Environment Rating Scale* (revised ed.). New York, NY: Teachers College Press.

Harms, T., Cryer, D., & Clifford, R. (1990). *Infant/Toddler Environment Rating Scale*. New York, NY: Teachers College Press.

Harms, T., Vineberg Jacobs, E., & White, D. (1996). *School-Age Care Environment Rating Scale*. New York, NY: Teachers College Press.

Hathaway, W. (1994). Non-visual Effects of Classroom Lighting on Children. *Educational Facility Planner, 23*, 12–16.

Hawkins, W., & Lilley, H. (1992). *CEFPI's Guide for School Facility Appraisal*. Columbus, OH: The Council of Educational Facility Planners International.

Hill, L. (2000). *Connecting Kids: Exploring Diversity Together*. Gabriola Island, BC: New Society Publishers.

Hohmann, M., & Weikart, D. (1995). *Educating Young Children*. Ypsilanti, MI: High/Scope Press.

Isbell, R., & Exelby, B. (2003). *Early Learning Environments That Work*. Beltsville, MD: Gryphon House, Inc.

Liberman, J. (1991). *Light Medicine of the Future*. Santa Fe, NM: Bear & Company Publishing.

Marotz, L., Cross, M., & Rush, J. (2001). *Health, Safety and Nutrition for the Young Child*. Albany, NY: Delmar.

Ott, J. (1976). *Health & Light*. New York, NY: Pocket Books.

Read, M., Sugawara, A., & Brant, J. (1999). Impact of Space and Color in the Physical Environment of Preschool Children Cooperative Behavior. *Environment and Behavior, 31,* 413–428.

Vergeront, J. (1996). *Places and Spaces for Preschool and Primary*. Washington, DC: The National Association for the Education of Young Children.

Watson, L., Watson, M., Cam Wilson, L., & Crowther, I. (2000). *Infants and Toddlers* (1st Canadian ed.). Scarborough, ON: Nelson Thomson Learning.

White, C., & Coleman, M. (2000). *Early Childhood Education Building a Philosophy for Teaching*. Upper Saddle River, NJ: Merrill.

PROGRAM VARIETY ACROSS CANADA

"Curriculum development is a complex process requiring a commitment to a broad-based educational philosophy; extensive knowledge of human growth and development; practical experiences with children and an understanding of their interests; and an ability to consolidate and interpret an ever-expanding body of research about teaching and learning." (Hohmann & Weikart, 1995, p. 3)

Chapter Outcomes

After reading this chapter, the reader will

1. For the High/Scope approach in early childhood education, describe
   a) the High/Scope concept of an active learning environment;
   b) the meaning of key experiences and how they are integrated into the curriculum; and
   c) the role of the adult.

2. For the Reggio Emilia approach in early childhood education, describe
   a) why the environment is a key component;
   b) how collaboration is used as a central component in curriculum development;
   c) how a project approach is used in teaching young children; and
   d) the importance of documentation.

3. For the Montessori approach in early childhood education, describe
   a) why the environment is a key component;
   b) how children are viewed;
   c) the sensitive periods; and
   d) the role of the teacher.

4. Describe how each of the following Aboriginal Head Start program components relates to the care of young children:
   a) culture and language
   b) education
   c) health promotion
   d) nutrition
   e) social support
   f) parental and family involvement

5. Define the role of resource centres.

6. Describe the role of the Hastings/Prince Edward County Early Years Centre.

7. Describe the role of the Westcoast Child Care Resource Centre.

INTRODUCTION

Across Canada a variety of philosophical approaches to teaching young children are used. Most approaches are based on the right of the child to learn through play in an inclusive setting. Since the quality of a program is dependent on the interactions with the child, the family, and the community, most program philosophies tend to be adapted to reflect regional characteristics. As a result, few programs follow a "pure" theoretical approach (as prescribed by the philosophical underpinnings of that particular approach). However, some approaches, such as Montessori and High/Scope, require specialized training. Most programs have adapted approaches to the Canadian settings. The order of philosophical programs discussed does not reflect a particular order, but does, to some degree, follow a pattern of where the programs are located in Canada, from east to west.

Philosophical approaches that are used to service children and families directly can be categorized into two major types:

1. Programs that have been developed based on a philosophy adopted from an external source—e.g., High/Scope, Reggio Emilia, Montessori, and Head Start.
2. Programs developed by the centre staff, families, and board members, which are often based on a variety of philosophical approaches.

Additionally, there are a number of support programs available to support child-care centres and/or families. These include resource centres and child-care societies. Support programs may offer services directly to children or may offer resource help to families and child-care providers.

THE HIGH/SCOPE COGNITIVELY ORIENTED CURRICULUM APPROACH

The Sheridan Child Care Centre at the Trafalgar Road Campus follows the High/Scope Curriculum. The philosophy of the centre embraces the optimal development of each child and recognizes the uniqueness of each family:

> Our program provides a total curriculum which allows for the optimal growth of children in all areas of development, including social, emotional, physical, and cognitive development. The children are supported in a safe, nurturing, and stimulating environment that promotes self-esteem and emphasizes child-selected and child-directed activities. Each child and family is recognized as being unique. Family styles, values, and traditions are respected and reflected in the curriculum. (Sheridan College Child Care Centre [program brochure], 2003)

Web exercises

Children in the Active Learning Environment

The cornerstones of this approach involve active learning through key experiences: "The key experiences are a series of statements describing the social, cognitive, and physical development of children ages $2^{1}/_{2}$ to 5.... Key experiences are organized around these topics: creative representations, language and literacy, initiative and social relations, movement, music, classification, seriation, number, space, and time" (Hohmann & Weikart, 1995, p. 23).

According to Hohmann and Weikart (1995, pp. 24–29), early childhood educators using this approach set up an environment that encourages children to do the following:

Photo 8.1

- *Initiate individual learning activities that are based on current interests.* Matthew had built towers with the alphabet blocks. He indicated that he was a "big bad wolf" and would blow down the tower. He tried to blow down the tower. He discovered that he had to move his face close to the tower to blow down the blocks. He also discovered that he could not blow over the whole tower, "just the part I'm blowing on" (photo 8.1). Through this process he learned about balance, about the dynamics between wind force and resistance, and how to solve problems—moving his head to the appropriate position and monitoring the force of air needed to blow over the tower.

  Matthew's activity represents one of the key experiences—**creative representations.** He was relating one experience, the story of the "Three Little Pigs," to his experiences in building with blocks. He created his own unique model with blocks and he imitated the actions of the "wolf."

creative representation
Representing personal experiences from one situation to another.

Photo 8.2   Photo 8.3   Photo 8.4

trial and error
Trying a task by manipulating objects such as puzzle pieces into various positions until the piece fits into the correct spot.

seriation
Arranging things in order (e.g., large to small) or pattern (e.g., red, blue, red, blue).

Photo 8.5

one-to-one-correspondence
Forming sets of objects where one object is paired with another (e.g., one fork beside a plate).

- *Make decisions about which materials to use and how to use them.* Teryll watched several children crawl through the wooden tunnel. When the children were finished, he went over and turned the tunnel over. He stepped inside the tunnel and held on to the two sides. He discovered that he could rock the tunnel while standing within it (photo 8.2). Through this activity he learned to use materials in different ways and learned to control his body movement to create a new action. Teryll's activity represents another of the key experiences—learning about *space*. He observed other children using the tunnel. He changed his perspective to use the tunnel in a different way. While he was using the tunnel, he experienced a different body position, as he needed to adapt his body to balance and rock the shape. This demonstrated an additional key experience—learning through *movement.*

- *Involve all of their senses in active play.* Samia mixed earth and water. Periodically she would touch her mixture and smell her mixture. She created thick and thin mixtures, some of which she poured from container to container (photo 8.3). She learned about texture and viscosity and developed coordination and control over her fine motor skills. As she emptied and filled her containers, she learned about the key experience—*space and time.* She was able to stop pouring before the container overflowed, and she was able to control the rate of movement in how fast she poured the liquid.

- *Actively explore the environment and the materials within the environment to discover relationships, such as similarities, differences, and cause and effect.* Julie had been trying to put the nesting barrels in order of size. She would pick up one piece, and compare it to the next piece before she could put them in order. When she thought she was finished, she noticed that she had missed one piece (photo 8.4). She tried to fit this piece into various spots, until she discovered where it fit (**trial and error**). Julie learned about sizes, big and small, and the sequence of size, large to small (**seriation**). Seriation is another key experience. Julie also talked about what she was doing. She was able to verbalize which pieces were bigger or smaller and if they fit into the sequence she was creating. This activity relates to the language and literacy key experience—describing objects and talking about experiences.

- *Use materials in innovative ways, such as combining materials to build with or moulding clay to change its shape (transforming materials).* Julie noticed a collection of bears in a basket as she was sequencing the barrels in order of size. She opened each barrel and placed one bear in the barrel (**one-to-one-correspondence**) (photo 8.5). She talked about a large bear in a large barrel. She started to add more than one bear to the containers. She counted the number of bears she had put into the containers. Julie was demonstrating another key learning experience—she was learning to use numbers through one-to-one-correspondence, and counting.

- *Be involved with developmentally and age-appropriate materials and equipment.* Matthew was using a small measuring cup with a lip to pour his own milk at lunchtime: "I am doing a good job. I didn't spill any" (photo 8.6). When he had finished, he offered to pour some milk for other individuals. Some of the children wanted to pour their own and others let him pour the milk. Matthew was encouraged to take care of his own needs (key experience—*initiative social relations*) by using materials that will increase the likelihood of success. He was provided with a small measuring cup that was not too heavy for him to handle, which had a lip that made it easier to pour into another container. Matthew demonstrated other components of the key experience—initiative and social relations. He initiated social contact by offering to pour milk for others and indicated pride in his ability to pour his own milk.

Photo 8.6

- *Engage in gross motor activity.* The playground at the Sheridan Child Care Centre offered many opportunities to explore using gross muscles (see Figure 8.1). Additional opportunities existed to explore in alternative ways. Cameron had the opportunity to climb a tree with branches that were low enough and sturdy enough to be safe to climb (photo 8.7). This activity encouraged Cameron to use both **anchored movements** and **nonanchored movements** (key experience—*movement*).

- *Interact with peers and adults to talk about their experiences.* Ashley was sorting the dinosaurs. She told Nancy that she was going to put all the big dinosaurs together (photo 8.8). As she continued to sort, she indicated to Nancy that she was now sorting them into families—fathers, mothers, and babies. She handed Nancy a dinosaur saying that this one didn't belong—it was different. Nancy asked her how this one was different. Ashley replied that it was only a skeleton. Ashley was involved in demonstrating another of the key experiences—**classification**. She was learning to distinguish different sizes, explore how the dinosaurs were the same or different, eliminate any dinosaur that did not belong in the set, and explain similarities and differences—sizes and attributes such as skeletal form.

anchored movements
Movements through bending, twisting, rocking, or swinging arms or legs.

nonanchored movements
Movements through running, jumping, hopping, skipping, marching, or climbing.

classification
Arrangement of items into groups or subgroups using more than one attribute.

Photo 8.7

Photo 8.8

Figure 8.1

Sheridan Floor Plan

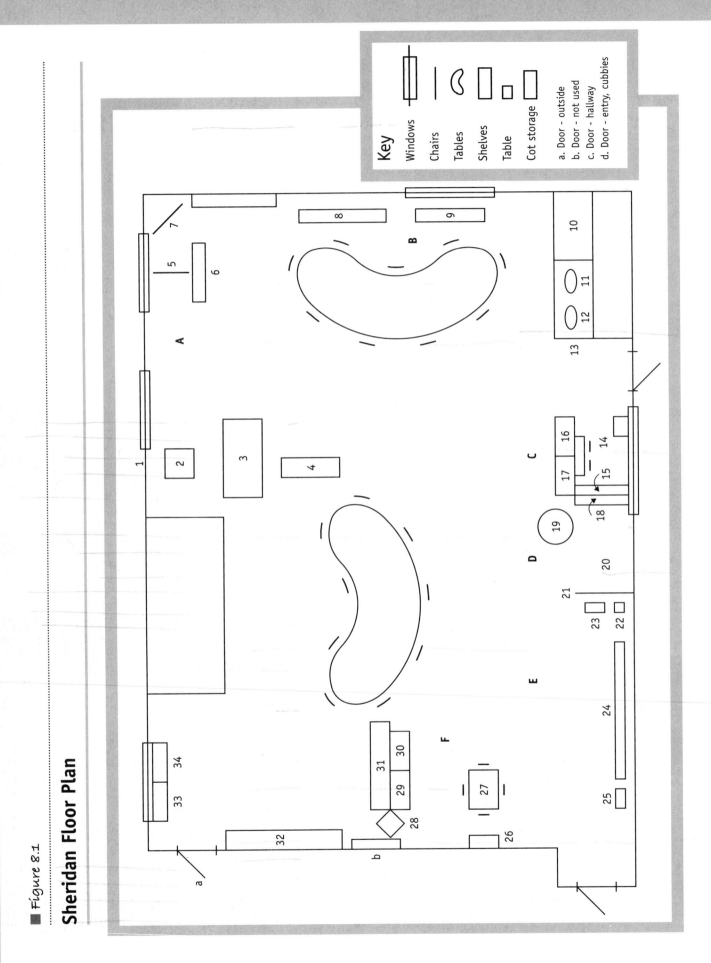

Key

Windows

Chairs

Tables

Shelves

Table

Cot storage

a. Door – outside
b. Door – not used
c. Door – hallway
d. Door – entry, cubbies

Figure 8.1 (continued)

Sheridan Floor Plan

Area A - Photo A (Sand/Water/Art)

1. Wall display
2. Water
3. Sand
4. Sand toys
5. Easel
6. Creative supplies
7. Drying rack

Area B - Photo B

8. Table toys
9. Carpentry bench
10. Adult storage
11. Adult sink
12. Child sink
13. Child fountain

Area C - Photo C

14. Printing/puzzles
15. Puzzles, writing materials
16. Table toys
17. Table toys

Area D - Photo D

18. Books
19. Soft chair
20. Soft area - pillows, mattress
21. Fence

Area E - Photo E

22. High chair
23. Washer/dryer
24. Kitchen utensils
25. Stuffed toys

Area F - Photo F

26. Dress-up props
27. Kitchen table
28. Fridge
29. Stove
30. Sink

Area G - Photo G (Blockset Gathering Area)

31. Small blocks and block accessories
32. Large blocks
33. Vehicles
34. Vehicles

Sheridan Outdoors

Area A
climber

shredded tire surface

gate

Area B
picnic

fenced-in
riding hill

Area C

Area D
balance beam

paved riding area

entrance to
daycare

Daycare

garden

Area E

Area G

covered
toddler deck

Area F

flower garden

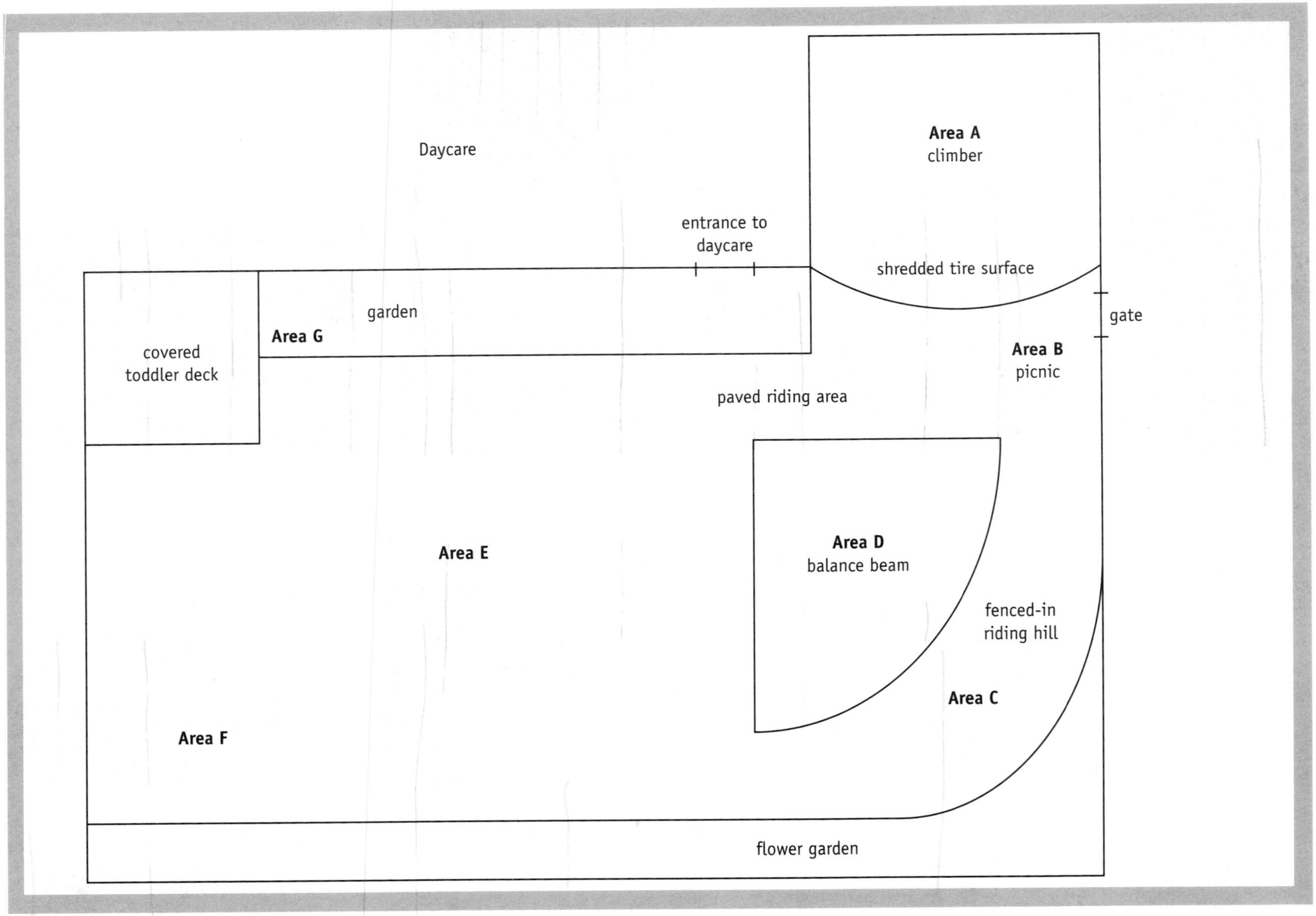

Sheridan Outdoors

Area A - Photo A

Area E - Photo E
Sandbox garden

Area F - Photo F
Club house garden

Area B - Photo B
Picnic Area

Area G - Photo G

Area C - Photo C

Area D - Photo D

Photo 8.9

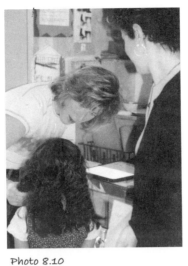

Photo 8.10

Photo 8.11

- *Describe their experiences by using their own words*. During a music circle, children were asked pass a bag around as they listened to the music. When the music stopped, the child who had the bag was asked to pick a card out of the bag, and then indicate to the other children what action was indicated on the card. When Ashley picked a card out of the bag, she told the children, "This card tells you to clap. Everyone is to clap." The children clapped in time to the steady beat of the music that was playing (photo 8.9). Ashley demonstrated several of the key experiences. Ashley was able to read and interpret the symbol on her card and explain it to her peers (key experience—*language and literacy*). She was also able to clap to a steady beat (key experience—*music*).

Adults in the Active Learning Environment

The primary role of the early childhood educator within the learning environment is to set the stage for learning. Adults observe the children's interactions in order to provide active learning experiences. Through observation, the adults gain insight into the children's interests and abilities. Thus the role of the early childhood educator includes

1. *Providing appropriate arrangements of the learning space* (see Figure 8.1).
2. *Providing a variety of developmentally appropriate learning materials and the time to use these materials* (see Figure 8.1).
3. *Listening to and interacting with the children to encourage their thinking*. When Ashley arrived at the daycare, she was excited to show her new hairstyle to Nancy, her teacher. Nancy listened carefully and responded by talking about how Ashley's hair looked different. She encouraged Ashley to talk about the changes in her hair and what she thought about the new hairstyle (photo 8.10).
4. *Encouraging children's independence*. When the children went outside to play, Ashley noticed that the slide was still wet. She told Nancy that she could dry the bottom of the slide by herself so that no one would get wet (photo 8.11).
5. *Encouraging active exploration with adults, peers, and the learning experiences in the environment*. Jacob decided that he wanted to read all the children's names. Nancy noticed his activity. She sat down next to him and the two took turns reading the names and symbols on the card (photo 8.12).

Solving Problems Together

Problem?

Not tidying up at clean-up time

Solutions?

Tidy up when we finish using something

Listen to the song ♪♫♪

Tidy up the classroom when we hear the song

Stop, look around, and tidy up what we see.

Photo 8.14

6. *Working together with children to form partnerships in learning*. The adults had identified a problem during clean-up time. The problem was posted on the bulletin board (Figure 8.2). The children discussed various solutions. When agreed upon, these were posted.

7. *Discovering and inventing new learning opportunities with the children*. The children had been interested in using large pieces of material in various ways. While they were outside, they asked Melanie to help them drape the blue netting over various items—riding toys, wagons, and climbing equipment (photo 8.13). Eventually, John volunteered that they could build a tree house. John climbed into the tree and Melanie handed him the netting (photo 8.14). The netting was eventually attached to various branches and provided a safe shelter both for the climbers and nonclimbers.

8. *Observing children to plan on-the-spot interactions or long-term plans*. When the staff observed children's interest in using large pieces of material for various activities, they decided to provide materials for these opportunities outside—blue netting, appropriate riding toys that could be covered, boxes large enough to climb in and cover, clothes pegs, and string to attach the material.

Photo 8.12

Photo 8.13

9. *Encouraging and welcoming family involvement.* This can be done through

- providing materials from home—chopsticks to eat with and dress-up clothes reflecting family occupations;
- providing expertise to create choices of materials and experiences—children can use the materials in ways that reflect their background experiences such as eating with chopsticks;
- providing opportunities to utilize home language—books, staff members who speak home languages represented in the environment, involving family members in the program, and learning essential phrases and words of home languages; and
- involving families as partners—visitations to the program and having families as members of the board or members on committees.

10. *Helping to create "respectful support from adults"* (Hohmann & Weikart, 1995, p. 71). Identify what type of body language to use, how much space to leave between children and adults when interacting, and how children signal various emotions—such as excitement, sadness, and confusion.

THE CAPILANO COLLEGE CHILD-CARE ADAPTATION TO THE REGGIO EMILIA APPROACH

Web exercises

This particular approach to early childhood education started in the municipality of Reggio Emilia in Italy in 1963:

Photo 8.15

> The municipal early childhood educational system of Reggio Emilia has always been characterized by progressive thinking and a firmly rooted commitment to research experimentation, sustained by ongoing and permanent staff training. Other distinctive features of the system include the organization of work strongly based on collegiality and interrelations, the importance given to the environment as an educational interlocutor, the presence of the atelier, the essential and intensive co-participation of the families and community members and the synergistic relationships with the outside community. (Malaguzzi, 1997, p. 19)

The Reggio Emilia approach is to use a project approach to teach young children. The project approach "is based on the image of the child who has enormous potential and who is the *subject of rights.* The aim of the project is to promote children's education through the development of all their languages: expressive, communicative, symbolic, cognitive, ethical, metaphorical, logical, imaginative, and relational" (Malaguzzi, 1997, p. 19). Malaguzzi refers to these languages as "The Hundred Languages of Children."

Photo 8.16

The Capilano College Child Care Centre in Vancouver, BC, has adopted a Reggio Emilia approach. The cornerstone of the approach in this child-care setting is based on collaboration—with children, families, and the college community. "We respect and value the uniqueness and contribution of all children and families. Through collaboration with parents our centre is able to develop a quality child care community" (Capilano College Child Care Centre [mission statement]). Another cornerstone involves the right of the children to take charge of their learning. Adults are seen to guide and nurture children's learning. "We nurture and guide young children as they explore and investigate their interests. We provide a balance of activities that help children to progress in their social, emotional, physical and cognitive development" (Capilano College Child Care Centre [mission statement]).

Photo 8.17

1. The Environment

"When you enter a school for young children, you get an instant feeling about the children and the teachers. Their voices, their clothes, their motions all carry messages about who they are. But all too seldom does the physical environment carry the same kinds of messages" (Gandini, 1991, p. 5). Gandini identifies the key aspects that would make the environment a more personal space:

- a sense of personal space;
- a sense for the life of the particular community;
- a particular school with its own history; and
- an awareness of surrounding space.

"A Sense of Personal Space"

A feeling of warmth and welcome is immediately evident on entering the centre. Softness has been added by a subdued warm colour scheme, the addition of table-cloths, strategically placed plants, and points of interest for children (photo 8.15). Children's artwork predominates—in the halls and in the rooms, tastefully displayed and in appropriate frames (photo 8.16). All the rooms in the centre—infant, toddler, and preschool spaces—exude light, spaciousness, and a home-like atmosphere. Large floor-to-ceiling windows frame the rooms with a panoramic view of a naturally wooded hillside (photo 8.17). Children and adults are encouraged to bring personal items of value to display and discuss (photo 8.18).

Photo 8.18

"A Sense for the Life of the Particular Community"

Care has been taken to ensure that the children feel a sense of connectedness with each other (see Figure 8.3 on page 229). Large doorways, two kitchens placed between two rooms, a joint deck, and windows between areas (photo 8.19) offer children opportunities to

Photo 8.19

- observe the activities of other children and adults, such as normal daily cooking routines;
- interact with other adults and peers; and
- share exciting experiences and discoveries.

Photo 8.20

Photo 8.22

Photo 8.21

Photo 8.23

"A Particular School with Its Own History"

The daycare centre has been in operation for over 30 years. A history wall depicts children from the past along with pictures of what they look like today. Another part of the wall depicts the evolution of the centre to the new facility—tearing down and rebuilding the new structure that stands today. The children were involved in some of the planning of the new centre. They decided what aspects they wanted to retain. The children decided to keep their outdoor playhouse (photo 8.20) and the tree that had been struck by lightning (photo 8.21).

"An Awareness of Surrounding Space"

The daycare centre nestles humbly in a natural environment of hills and majestic trees. The playground depicts the natural setting of British Columbia. Great effort has been used to maintain the natural beauty—driving paths around the "old tree" (photo 8.21), natural ground coverage and wooden play structures to blend in with the environment (photo 8.22), and staff and children's efforts to add natural beauty to their environments (photo 8.23).

Throughout the centre there are also reminders of the other important part of Vancouver's environment—the ocean. A small wooden boat rests in the playground, beside the playhouse that the children wanted to keep as part of the outdoor dramatic play activities (photo 8.21). Indoors, children's artwork and projects depict ocean life (see photo 8.18 on page 227). Collections of precious items—such as shells, stones, and driftwood—are displayed.

2. Collaboration

In an interview with Lela Gandini, Loris Malaguzzi (the founder of this approach) identified collaboration in the following way:

It must embody ways of getting along together, of intensifying relationships among three central protagonists, of assuring complete attention to the problems of education, and of activating participation and research. These are the most effective tools for all those concerned—children, teachers, and parents—to become more united and aware of each other's contributions. They are the most effective tools to use in order to feel good about cooperating and to produce, in harmony, a higher level of results. (Edwards et al., 1998, p. 65)

Figure 8.3

Floor Plan of Capilano College Child Care Centre

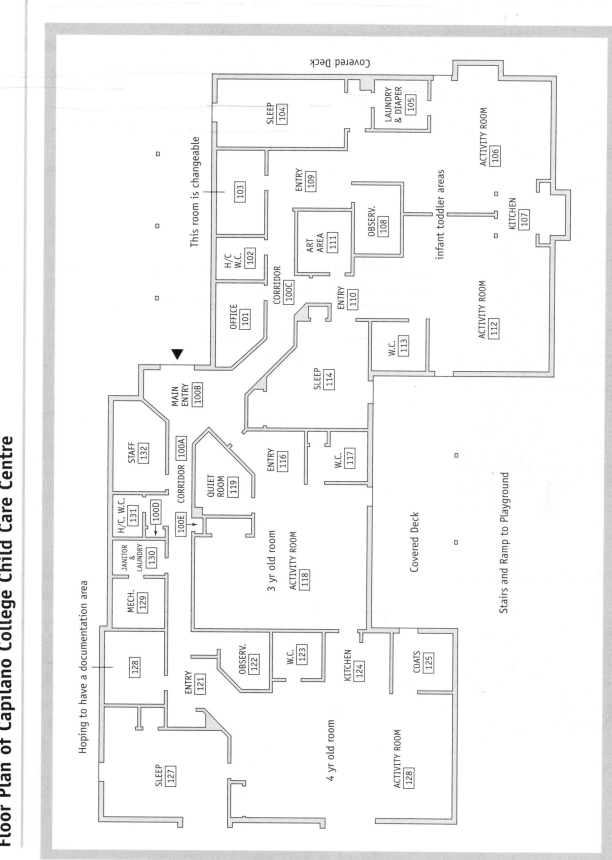

Hoping to have a documentation area

SLEEP 127

128

ENTRY 121

OBSERV. 122

W.C. 123

MECH. 129

JANITOR & LAUNDRY 130

H/C W.C. 131

100D

STAFF 132

CORRIDOR 100A

100E

QUIET ROOM 119

4 yr old room

ACTIVITY ROOM 128

KITCHEN 124

COATS 125

3 yr old room

ACTIVITY ROOM 118

ENTRY 116

W.C. 117

MAIN ENTRY 100B

OFFICE 101

H/C W.C. 102

103

This room is changeable

SLEEP 104

CORRIDOR 100C

ART AREA 111

ENTRY 110

SLEEP 114

W.C. 113

ENTRY 109

OBSERV. 108

LAUNDRY & DIAPER 105

ACTIVITY ROOM 106

KITCHEN 107

infant toddler areas

ACTIVITY ROOM 112

Covered Deck

Covered Deck

Stairs and Ramp to Playground

Photo 8.24

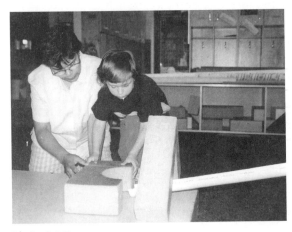

Photo 8.25

Photo 8.26

Central to a collaborative process is "that children have an inherent desire to grow, to know, and to understand things around them" (Edwards et al., 1998, p. 44). The children at the Capilano College Child Care Centre actively engaged in constructing their own learning through collaboration with each other and the adults in the program. Collaboration occurs when they do the following:

- *Interact with adults to make meaningful decisions.* Mackenzie is helping to reorganize the art area. Her suggestions and comments are listened to as she works with her facilitator to create an appropriate creative area (photo 8.24).

- *Interact with adults to accomplish tasks.* Madison wanted to create a track to drive her cars down. When she rolled down one of her cars, it flew off the table and crashed into a bookcase. Pritti heard the noise and asked what had happened. Madison replied that the cars were going too fast and "flew off the table." Pritti and Madison worked together to solve the problem. Madison suggested a foam block. Pritti got the block and placed it at the end of the track. Madison felt it was "too close" (photo 8.25). Madison was delighted that the strategy worked. She asked Pritti to move the foam block to various positions on the table. Madison and Pritti talked about the speed of the car, the distance it travelled, and how to effectively stop the car.

- *Interact with peers to share ideas, materials, and experiences.* Delilah, Lucas, Jake, and Celine decided that they would like to do some finger-painting. The children used shaving cream and eyedroppers to add food colouring to the shaving cream. As the children explored the shaving cream to create different designs and change the colour of their mixtures, they talked about the following (photo 8.26):

  - Smell. "Smells like soap."
  - Texture. "It feels cool." "I think it is slippery." "Feels like soap."
  - Changing colours. "Look, it turned blue." "Mine too." "Mine has light blue dots."
  - Process. "How did you get purple?" "You just keep putting more colour in, especially red." "I want to try that too." "Here, you can have the red." "It's changing, it's getting purple."

- *Interact with adults who carefully observe their interests and actions in order to provide appropriate learning experiences.* Pritti, the early childhood educator, had provided the clay activity as a result of discussion with the children. She observed and interacted with the children as they formed the clay into various shapes. Later, she recorded her observations and displayed them in the hall (see Figure 8.4).

Another level of collaboration occurs among the staff of the facility. The staff collaborate to provide appropriate learning experiences for the children. Collaboration at this level means that staff must

Clay Experience

We revisited the maps that the children drew a few days ago while walking around the College Campus. After some discussion the children moulded some things they had seen using clay.

- "Bus, you can make rectangles and circles for the wheels."

- "Clay is really hard and you can't roll it up!"

- "Flattened, see?!"

- "Look what I'm doing, first I'm doing stuff, then I keep doing the same thing, and I keep doing it!"

- "I got the bridge, and the arrows, and birds, and the buildings, and students, and another bird!"

- "I have rocks and arrows."

- "I did a tree and the bus!"

- "...the theatre!"

- "I would like to make my ladder."

- "I rolled it and um, that stick thing and a spoon."

- "...a theatre is where you make puppets and..."

- "No, it's where you watch a movie."

- "This is just the truck that the ladder rests on."

- "The ladder was on a *car* not a *cart!*"

- "Look what I did!"

- "That's hanging on a cart there and the truck's driving it along."

- "It has to be scrapes going like this..."

- "I'm making the rocks, and um, the rocks transform into a square."

- "Pritti, the face is on there 'cuz one time a little boy was making that and his neck was a fork and his feet and body was a potato head."

- "No, this is the head and that's the legs, and then you squeeze it!"

- "That's my map!"

- "We're making stuff from the maps, the rocks that transform into a square."

- "I think that's glue."

- "I had to cut it, too."

- "We should watch the video after lunch."

- *Coordinate their efforts.* The staff meets regularly to share their observations about the children. Documentation panels are created (see Figure 8.4) to show a record of what has occurred. These records serve as a reference point to children and staff to reflect upon and create ever-evolving new experiences.
- *Make decisions on what new materials or experiences are needed to continue to engage children's interests and learning.* Examples include field trips, resources (books, photographs, pictures), and actual tools and materials such as clay.

- *Discuss who will take the lead to facilitate specific learning activities.* Adults often must research the topic to further expand children's learning—associated vocabulary, what additional experiences can be offered, what resources are available within the centre or elsewhere, and what specific knowledge is needed about the topic. Preparation includes collecting, displaying, and organizing the materials appropriately.
- *Make decisions on new directions the children may be interested in.* As children are involved in an activity, the learning can often lead in new directions. The clay experience (see Figure 8.4) reflected the children's experiences on the field trip. The interests expressed in their clay experiences include the process of forming clay, the various representations (vehicles, objects, and people), and transformations. Any one of these could lead to new interests. Only by communicating with each other about what each staff member has observed can a decision be made about what new directions might evolve.

The families of the children also play an active part in the collaborative process. Families are naturally interested in what their children accomplish during the day. The documentation panels (see Figures 8.4 and 8.5) are clear indications about the activities, interests, and accomplishments of their children. They provide a natural link between families and the daycare experiences. This leads to dialogue between the children and families and between staff and family members to

- further explore the topic;
- provide additional resources and ideas;
- become part of the process (on field trips, within the centre, collecting resources, or sharing information about ongoing interests about the child); and
- provide a closer connection between home and school by actively engaging children in reflections about their learning experiences and extending the learning experiences in a different environment—observing and talking about the campus from the car.

Additionally, family members have opportunities to visit their children during any part of the day, and involve themselves through collaboration with staff to optimize children's interactions and learning experiences.

Collaboration also occurs among the college administration, daycare, and families. When the British Columbia government cut subsidies to families to continue their education, educational opportunities to families shrank drastically. Many already had young children. They could not afford to pay for tuition and child-care. The Capilano College administration created a program of bridge funding. The bridge funding encouraged families to continue their education, and offered daycare support to their children. This bridge funding continued until the families were eligible for student loans to continue their studies.

3. Project Approach

Teachers facilitate children's exploration of themes and work on short- and long-term projects. Project ideas originate in the continuum of experience of children and teachers and in their practice of constructing knowledge together. Projects may start either from a chance event, an idea or a problem posed by one or more children, or an experience initiated directly by teachers; for example, a study of crowds originated when a child told the class about a summer vacation experience, while a project on fountains developed when children decided to build an amusement park for birds. (Gandini, 1993, p. 7–8)

Documentation of a Project Initiated by the Children

Figure 8.5 A

It all started when the children
Showed an interest in cutting paper.
Some learned how to hold scissors:
"Thumbs up, fingers down." They started
by snipping strips into bits. Then some
went on to cutting straight strips with
and without guidelines and curves with
guidelines. We called it
"Snipping bits and cutting Strips."

Figure 8.5 B

As a result we amassed a pile of
colourful snippings that were just perfect
for a sorting session. Once again the
children dove in, this time to separate
our bag of mixed bits into the various hues.
Some of the children were keen to count
them, so we set up a counting session with
a colour coded chart. With encouragement
and support from an adult some children
learned how to go from 20's to 30's. Andrew
counted up to 173!

Figure 8.5 C

After seeing a book of mosaics the
Children were inspired to create one of
their own. Mitchell drew a shark on a
Transparency and the image was projected
And magnified on the wall. A small group
Of children worked co-operatively to trace
this figure onto a large sheet of paper. They
learned to shift positions to keep their
shadows out of the way.

Figure 8.5 D

The next part was to apply glue to the
Guidelines provided by an adult and the
children took to this like a shark to water!
The glue sticks were a source of mechanical
Fascination: "Look how far down it goes . . .
Oh, look how long it gets!" Working together
the children layed row upon row of coloured
snippings while learning to abide by the
instructions: "Keep it close to the one above
it; don't let too much white show. Press it
down a little so it will stick."

Figure 8.5 E

As the guiding adult I saw the children apply
themselves fervently to this sequence of
tasks, and I was amazed at the persistence
I saw demonstrated by the children! Petra
helped everyday and it was a proud moment
for her to ceremoniously place the last piece
on the paper!

Photo 8.27

Evidence of the various projects children have been involved with is visible throughout the centre—on the walls, on the windows, and on shelves—both in the rooms and in the halls. Many of their projects have been documented in writing, through photographs, and through children's artwork. A project might follow the following process:

1. This particular project started with an activity initiated by the children (see Figure 8.5a).
2. The initial experience evolved to several new activities—including sorting by colour and counting (Figure 8.5b).
3. The learning experience was adapted to reflect new interests and experiences (Figures 8.5c and 8.5d).
4. After much persistence, the project was finished (Figure 8.5e). A record of this project remains on the walls of the centre.

The process of any project involves a number of underlying principles:

- "The curriculum is not established in advance. Teachers express general goals and make hypotheses about what direction the activities and projects might take; consequently they make appropriate preparations. Curriculum emerges in the process of each activity or project and is flexibly adjusted accordingly" (Gandini, 1993, p. 7). As they worked on the mosaic, the children went through several transitions before the end project evolved (see Figure 8.5). Each of the activities was a valuable learning activity—from learning to cut to using materials in creative ways (e.g., sorting, matching, counting, and creating a picture cooperatively).
- Time to complete activities is another important principle. Children may be involved in short- or long-term projects. The formal daycare schedule becomes much more flexible as the children's own sense of time is considered. Children are encouraged to set their own pace to complete activities.
- In order to continue to work on projects, children need to have appropriate learning spaces. There needs to be accessible, well-organized storage of materials so that they can find what is needed (photo 8.27). They need adequate places to keep work in progress so that work can continue over time.
- Finally, documenting children's efforts becomes critical. The documentation is a way of sharing information with everyone, to refresh memories, to plan for new strategies and materials, and to acknowledge the effort of everyone involved.

4. The Importance of Documentation

"[T]ranscriptions of children's remarks, and discussions, photographs of their activity, and representations of their thinking and learning using many media are carefully arranged" (Gandini, 1993, p. 8). The purpose of documentation is as follows:

- to share the learning experiences with other children, families, and other staff;
- to learn more about the children's ideas, interests, and learning;
- to maintain involvement of all individuals;
- to provide an opportunity to exchange ideas;
- to show children that their work is valued; and
- to provide a record of what has happened over time.

THE MONTESSORI APPROACH

Montessori was a physician, anthropologist, and educator who believed that early education should be guided by a scientific approach. The Children's House in Italy was a progressive approach for the early 20th century. In addition to such innovative methods as individual choice, mixed-aged grouping, and didactic materials, Montessori's original intent to serve the families and the community was a precursor to what we currently call a family resource centre. (White & Coleman, 2000, p. 261)

Web
exercises

1. The Environment

The environment, one of the key components of a Montessori approach, is highly organized (photo 8.28). The purpose of this organization is to nurture children's independence. The environment, in effect, becomes the teacher of the children. "In the prepared environment, teachers arrange materials for instruction and demonstrate the procedures for using the materials. Children can decide what materials they want to work with and how they want to work with them. This process leads children to organize their experiences and thinking through certain activities and, consequently, educate themselves" (Harms, Vineberg Jacobs, & White, 1996, p. 263).

Photo 8.28

Materials within this environment are **didactic** (i.e., they instruct certain concepts). The cylinder sets (photo 8.29) provide a good example of didactic materials. Once the cylinders have been removed from their nesting place, the materials must be placed into one specific spot. If one cylinder is in the incorrect spot, it is impossible to return all cylinders to the container.

didactic
Refers to something that instructs or teaches.

The learning environment has four basic areas:

- *Daily living centre.* This area deals with home-based experiences (e.g., cleaning, sewing, and gardening). Materials in this area are more open-ended, and are usually created by the teachers of the program.
- *Sensorial centre.* "In the third year of life, according to Montessori, the child can begin to order and classify impressions through hands-on examination of specifically prepared materials. Sensorial materials were designed with this purpose in mind; they originated from Montessori's own designs" (Roopnarine & Johnson, 2000, p. 203) (see photos 8.30, 8.31, and 8.32).
- *Language centre.* "Language development in a Montessori classroom is fostered throughout all the environment: the social environment of community and free exchange between children; the exact terminology offered by the teacher through specific lessons; the songs, rhythms, and conversation shared during whole-group gatherings; the selection of quality books found in the library corner; and the specific didactic materials developed to promote language and literacy development" (Roopnarine & Johnson, 2000, p. 204) (see Figure 8.6 and photo 8.33).

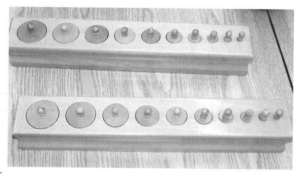

Photo 8.29

Photo 8.30

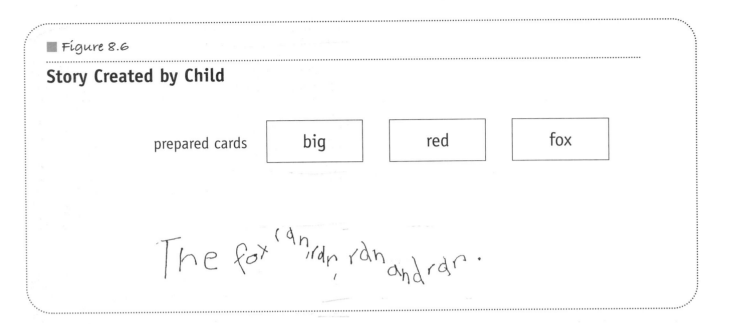

Figure 8.6

Story Created by Child

prepared cards | big | | red | | fox |

The fox ran ran, ran andran.

- *Mathematics centre.* "Mathematical thinking originates in many other seemingly unrelated activities that happen before experiences in the math area proper. Montessori felt that the order, precision, attention to detail, and sense of sequence fostered through use of the practical life and sensorial materials lay the foundation for what she termed the 'mathematical mind'" (Roopnarine & Johnson, 2000, p. 205).

In addition to these four areas, music, art, drama, and movement are also part of the program.

2. The Children

Unique Individuals

Children are seen as unique individuals, each with a set of personal characteristics and needs:

> [W]e shall notice that the child has a personality which he is seeking to expand; he has initiative, he chooses his own work, persists in it, changes it according to his inner needs; he does not shirk effort, he rather goes in search of it and with great joy overcomes obstacles within his capacity. He is sociable to the extent of wanting to share with everyone his successes, his discoveries, and his little triumphs. (Montessori, 1965, pp. 131–132)

Alicia and Hannah both enjoyed completing a puzzle. Each girl had her own approach. Hannah usually worked on several puzzles and would work with one spot on the puzzle at a time. She would try different pieces in that spot, turning the pieces around to see if they would fit, until she found the correct piece (photo 8.30). Alicia usually worked on one puzzle at a time and would work with one piece at a time. She would try one piece in each spot until she found the spot it would fit in (photo 8.31). When Hannah completed her puzzles, she immediately informed everyone around her that she had done it: "See, I did it." She frequently needed to be reminded to put her puzzles away. When Alicia completed a puzzle, she quietly put the puzzle back and continued with another puzzle or went to a new area.

Photo 8.31

Absorbent Mind

"The concept of the absorbent mind pertains to the belief that mental growth, similar to physical growth, is the result of a natural, internally regulated force. Each child must educate herself rather than be educated by others" (White & Coleman, 2000, p. 362). There are two stages of development—the unconscious stage and the conscious stage.

During the unconscious stage (birth to three years), children learn about their world by active exploration. Child-care providers must continually talk about what the child is doing in order for that child to make relevant connections between dialogue, materials, actions, and reactions. Michael and Levi had been pouring dried peas from one container to another. They had been quietly playing side by side, each concentrating on his activity. Yonit quietly described their activity—half-full, full, over-flowing, and empty. At certain times during her description, Levi would look up at her and smile. As Michael emptied his peas, he inadvertently poured some peas over Levi's arm. Levi immediately pulled back and said, "Ouch" (photo 8.32). Play stopped for a few moments as the two children looked at each other. Yonit quietly explained what happened to Michael: "When you dumped out your peas, some of them landed on Levi's arm. The peas hurt Levi." Both children listened, and then quietly returned to their play.

Photo 8.32

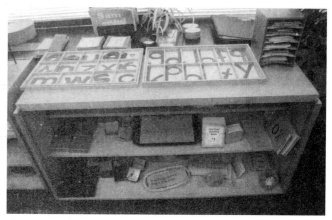

Photo 8.33

Neither child was consciously trying to fill or empty the containers. They were involved in **functional play**. Each child had no obvious purpose in mind. They simply enjoyed the sensory experience of the texture, sound, and actions of the peas. Yonit's dialogue provided a link to what they were doing and the materials in their environment. Her explanation to the children about Levi's accident gave both children information to help them to understand the link between the peas landing on Levi's arm, his pain from the contact, and why it had hurt.

As children's skills increase, they gradually start to explore their environment with purpose. One of the children's favourite stories was the *Gingerbread Boy*. Children asked to have a number of the words from the story added to the writing centre (photo 8.33). Many language activities occurred as a result of this experience:

functional play

"Repeated practice of skills through interactions with objects, people, and communication without a specific product or purpose" (Crowther, 2003, p. 263).

- the children matched the words to the words in the story;
- they matched the letters to the words;
- they created their own words using the templates provided; and
- they created their own stories (see Figure 8.6).

Sensitive Periods

"The term *sensitive periods* refers to phases when children are more susceptible to certain behaviours and can learn specific skills more easily" (Hainstock, 1986). Sensitive periods occur until a child is almost 5 years old during rapid physical, language, and cognitive growth (Morrison, 1997). During a sensitive period, the child does the following (White & Coleman, 2000, pp. 262–263):

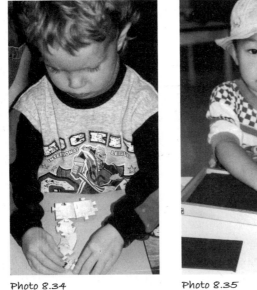

Photo 8.34

Photo 8.35

Photo 8.37

- *Reacts to a stimulus in certain ways.* Benjamin put the puzzle together by looking at only one aspect of the puzzle—fitting one of the knobs into a hole. He ignored the picture while doing this task (photo 8.34).
- *Learns to adjust behaviours and gain knowledge.* Benjamin had not looked at the puzzle he was putting together carefully (photo 8.34). He had not realized that there was a picture on the puzzle. When he saw another child complete the puzzle, he learned that the completed puzzle was a hologram image of dolphins. He was fascinated that he could "Make the dolphins move in the picture." His next attempts focused on trying to put the puzzle together by looking at the pieces in relationship to the picture.
- *Makes choices that reflect individual development.* Lee enjoys working with geometric shapes. He picked the blue triangles because they are "big" and he liked blue. He was able to put the triangles together to form a rectangle (photo 8.35). He proceeded to use all the triangles to complete rectangles.
- *Becomes so absorbed in one characteristic of the environment that all other characteristics are ignored.* Katherine had learned to walk across the balance beam (photo 8.36). She walked across the beam ten times. She ignored all the other activities going on around her. When it was time to go inside, her caregiver had to go over to her and stand in front of her to get her attention. She had been so absorbed in her task that she had not heard the signal to go inside for lunch.

The characteristics of sensitive periods include exploration through manipulation (hands and tongue), movement, a fascination with small and detailed objects, and an interest in the social aspects of life:

- *Manipulation.* Aislyn manipulated the colour tablets in several ways. First she picked up a red colour tablet and looked at it carefully, turning it over and over, running her fingers along the edges. She put it down and picked up a blue one, then a yellow one, and repeated the process. Next she lined them up in front of her, the matching colours together. Lastly, she stacked them up (photo 8.37).

Photo 8.36

- *Movement.* "The child, if left without guidance, is disorderly in his movements, and these disorderly movements are *the special characteristics* of the *little child*. In fact, he 'never keeps still,' and touches everything" (Montessori, 1965, p. 52). During early spring, the children went on a field trip to a conservation area. They were delighted to explore the environment—running, touching, and smelling. Jordan found it fascinating to throw rocks into the water. At first, he tried to throw his rock underhand. It tended to land anywhere but in the water. Michael, his teacher, noticed Jordan's efforts. He suggested that Jordan might try to throw the rock overhand. Jordan tried this new technique and was delighted that his rock now hit the water (photo 8.38).

Photo 8.38

- *Detailed objects.* Giancarlo was fascinated with the *Where's Waldo?* series of books. He often searched out these particular books. He would sit, look at a page, and then point to small details that fascinated him. Often he would softly verbalize what he was looking at (photo 8.39).
- *Social aspects.* Children are very interested in the social aspects of their home life and often engage in similar role-play at the daycare setting. J.J. had become very interested in all aspects concerning "babies." His mother was expecting a second baby. J.J. helped to set up the "bathing area." He insisted that it should be just like the one at home. After the area was set up, he bathed the "baby" (photo 8.40). He completed all of the routines—bathing, drying, dressing, and putting the baby to bed.

3. The Role of the Teacher

Montessori referred to the teacher as a "nonteacher." The following are the primary roles of the nonteacher (Montessori, 1965):

Photo 8.39

- Observe. Observation is the cornerstone of teaching. It gives the teacher the tools to appropriately plan the learning environment, provide appropriate learning materials, understand children, respond to children based on small differences in behaviours, and provide appropriate guidance.
- "Free the child to learn" (Montessori, 1965, p. 15). In order for children to be empowered to be free to learn, time blocks need to be flexible to the children's needs, appropriate choices need to be provided, and the environment needs to be structured and organized so that children can find what they need.
- Provide appropriate guidance. Instruct children on how to use materials, set limits on behaviour, establish initial connections between the child and materials, invite the child to participate, and provide appropriate encouragement.
- Provide lessons that serve to be a "blueprint" for future learning activities, such as specific lessons on how to use materials.
- Redirect behaviour in the case of roughness, rudeness, and disruptive or inappropriate behaviour.
- Be an observer when children are gainfully engaged in activities.

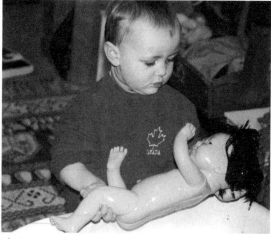

Photo 8.40

Chapter Eight   Program Variety Across Canada

Head Start programs started originally in the United States as a response to poverty and to the growing awareness "that intelligence, rather than being a fixed characteristic, depended to a greater extent on stimulation in early childhood" (Roopnarine & Johnson, 2000, p. 23). Several models were implemented over the years with varying degrees of success (Roopnarine & Johnson, 2000):

- *Behaviourist model.* An emphasis was placed on the acquisition of skills that were thought to be lacking in the home environment. Teaching children was a process of didactic methodologies (teacher-directed instruction) and a system of rewards.
- *Play-based program.* Play activities and related experiences such as field trips were the focus of the curriculum.
- *Cognitive interactionist model.* This model emphasized play and a child-centred environment, along with a focus on strategies to foster children's thinking especially with logical, mathematical concepts.
- *High/Scope program* (see description starting on page 217).
- *Montessori program* (see description starting on page 235).

The best-known longitudinal study of the results of a Head Start program was the Perry Preschool Project. Children who had attended the Perry Preschool were compared to children who had not had this experience. Children who had attended the Head Start program

- were much more likely to graduate from high school;
- were much more likely to continue their education after high school;
- were less likely to attend special education classes;
- were less likely to be arrested as juveniles;
- had fewer teen pregnancies;
- showed higher rates of employment; and
- were less dependent on receiving welfare assistance.

Additionally, "When costs were compared between programs and a control group, the high quality preschool program yielded both long-term benefits to society and saved $7 in benefits such as remedial education for every dollar invested" (Schweinhart & Weikart, 1986, as cited in Roopnarine & Johnson, 2000, pp. 25–26).

With the positive results of this study, it is not surprising that a great number of Head Start programs proliferated. In Canada, the best-known Head Start program is the Aboriginal Head Start (AHS), funded by Health Canada and found in 144 urban and northern communities throughout Canada. "The primary goal of the initiative is to demonstrate that locally controlled and designed early intervention strategies can provide Aboriginal children with a positive sense of themselves, a desire for learning, and opportunities to develop fully as successful young people" (Division of Childhood and Adolescence, 2003, p. 1). The AHS has adopted the High/Scope curriculum philosophy as an optional training approach.

Aboriginal Head Start Beliefs and Values About Children

Web
exercises

While First Nations people, Métis, and Inuit have distinct cultures and languages, they also share common beliefs, values, and histories. It is with this in mind that the "Statement of Beliefs and Values About Children" was written:

We believe:

- That children are a gift from the Creator.
- That our children have a right to live proudly as Aboriginal people in the lands of their ancestors.
- That children have a right to learn their respective Aboriginal language(s) and histories, and adults have a responsibility to pass on the instructions that the Creator gave them in the beginning of time as are reflected in our languages, cultural beliefs, and cultural practices.
- That each child is part of what makes a community whole.
- That it is essential for children to develop meaningful relationships with Elders, the carriers of knowledge and history.
- That adults are community role models who are to teach children how to live a good life.
- That children deserve opportunities to gain knowledge and experience of how to live a good life.
- That children acquire knowledge by watching, listening, and doing, and adults are responsible for encouraging and guiding them in all those activities.
- That children, through being loved, valued, and encouraged, will gain the courage, the strength, and the wisdom to use the power of a good mind and spirit in all that they do.
- That children have a right to enjoy the opportunities that education offers.
- That children have a right to live in healthy, self-determining communities that are free from violence. (Cedar Road Aboriginal Head Start Program [brochure])

AHS Program Components

The Cedar Road Aboriginal Head Start is a program in Prince Rupert, BC that follows the six AHS program components—culture and language, education and school readiness, health promotion, nutrition, social support, and parental and family involvement.

1. Culture and Language

Culture and language provide children "with the positive sense of themselves as aboriginal children and build on their aboriginal Language and experience of Culture in their community" (Cedar Road Aboriginal Head Start [brochure]).

Photo 8.41

Children in the Cedar Road program experience culture in a variety of ways. Culture is not something that is displayed or talked about. It is something that has been integrated into the daily lives of children as they attend the preschool program:

- The environment has numerous displays, photographs, and other items of interest throughout the environment (photo 8.41). Many of these displays include labelling in both English and Misoo.
- The children's calendar follows many of the traditional activities. July was the month of the sockeye (Ha'lilaxsimisoo). This is the month that fishermen were actively fishing. Children participated by visiting the local fish hatchery during the time that Coho salmon fingerlings were released.

■ *Figure 8.7*

Preschool Schedule

8:45–9:00/12:45–1:00	**Attendance taken and time is recorded**
9:00–9:15/1:00–1:15	**Roll call/circle time show & tell for child's special day**
9:15–9:25/1:15–1:25	**Wash hands/sit down for breakfast/lunch**
9:25–9:45/1:25–1:45	**Breakfast/lunch**
9:45–9:55/1:45–1:55	**Children brush their teeth**
9:55–10:45/1:55–2:45	**Free play**
10:45–11:00/2:45–3:00	**Story time**
11:00–11:15/3:00–3:15	**Clean up and home preparations**

- The experiences of the children are further enhanced by providing opportunities to eat traditional meals—salmon and rice. Families are involved by bringing in donations of fish that they have caught. Salmon is served with rice and may be smoked in a smoke house, fried, boiled, salted, jarred, or canned, and sometimes opportunities occur to eat dried fish strips (Kyiwoxs).
- Language learning is a shared responsibility. As children gradually learn the language at school, they pass on the new knowledge to their families. When newsletters are sent home, common events and names of things are written in both languages. This represents a continual cycle of learning, with all individuals learning from each other.

2. Education and School Readiness

Education should "[s]upport and encourage each aboriginal child to enjoy life-long learning" (Cedar Road Aboriginal Head Start [brochure]).

The children are encouraged to actively explore their environment through active play both indoors and outdoors (see the schedule in Figure 8.7). The children's play includes choices of materials to use in a variety of interest centres—dramatic play, sensory activities, art, song and movement, gross motor, fine motor, cooking, sand and water, manipulatives, and blocks. Children are encouraged to

Photo 8.42

- make choices of the type of activities they would like to become involved in (photo 8.42);
- make choices about what materials to use and how to use them (photo 8.43);
- engage in activity with other children and adults (photo 8.44);
- solve problems (photo 8.45); and
- become increasingly more independent (photo 8.46).

3. Health Promotion

The program aims to "[e]mpower parents, guardians, caregivers, and those involved with the AHS to increase control over and improve their health" (Cedar Road Aboriginal Head Start [brochure]).

Photo 8.43

Health promotion is a central part of the program for the children. The schedule identifies a number of good health-care practices (see Figure 8.7). Staff members continually model and reinforce sound health-care practices such as hand washing, cleanliness in the environment, and wearing appropriate clothes inside and outside.

Information is shared with parents and families through periodic workshops and monthly newsletters. The parent handbook identifies sound health practices. Since

Photo 8.44   Photo 8.45

families are involved at all levels of the program (e.g., they volunteer in the children's rooms, participate in special events such as feasts, and become board members), there is ample opportunity to model and reinforce good health practices.

4. Nutrition

The program aims to "[e]nsure that children are provided with food which will help meet their nutritional needs, and to educate the staff and parents about the relationship of nutrition to children's ability to learn, physical development and mental development" (Cedar Road Aboriginal Head Start [brochure]).

Children start the program each day with a healthy breakfast or lunch (see Figure 8.7). Information about good nutrition is shared

- in newsletters (e.g., recipes such as different ways of cooking fish);
- through publications such as the *Interior B.C. Native Food Guide* (adapted from the *Canada Food Guide*);
- through cooking experiences with the children (e.g., elders sometimes participate to teach children and staff about more traditional foods); and
- in community celebrations (e.g., feasts that bring everyone together to celebrate special occasions such as children moving on to public school).

5. Social Support

The program endeavours to "[e]nsure that the families are made aware of resources and community services available to impact their quality of life" (Cedar Road Aboriginal Head Start [brochure]). The centre hires a family involvement worker who helps families find and obtain the resources that they may need.

Photo 8.46

6. Parental and Family Involvement

The program aims to "[s]upport the parents and family's role as the children's primary teachers" (Cedar Road Aboriginal Head Start [brochure]).

Families are an integral part of the program:

- family members participate by volunteering in the program for six hours every month;
- elders offer expertise—cooking and sewing (e.g., traditional button blankets);
- families plan and cooperate special events such as feasts; and
- families participate on the board.

RESOURCE CENTRES

Resource centres are just what their name implies: agencies that provide "resources" to a group of individuals, such as early childhood educators, families, and individuals working with children with special needs. These resources could include

- books, articles, and pamphlets on specific topics;
- workshops and conferences on topics such as child-rearing, developmentally appropriate practices, and the curriculum;
- referral information (e.g., to medical, speech and language, and child-care professionals, or to specialized programs such as music and art);
- direct services to families and children (e.g., toy-lending library, playroom drop-in centre, workshops, breastfeeding clinics, home child-care services, applications for subsidies for child-care); and
- direct services to child-care programs (e.g., resource consultant services, workshops, and conferences).

In many areas, resource centres started to provide support and much-needed resources to the early childhood community. Many of the programs and services existed as small mini-hubs of service with very little interaction between them. Many individuals within child-care programs felt very isolated. Resource centres were a way to decrease the isolation. Additionally, many centres and families could not afford to purchase materials or equipment that could enhance their children's development. Toy-lending libraries offered one way to bridge this gap. Another gap in services was the lack of opportunity to receive pertinent training in areas such as positive child guidance techniques and developmentally appropriate curriculum ideas. Resource centres again bridged this gap by providing workshops and resources.

Today, many of these aspects remain within the resource centre models, but there has been greater diversification and increased specialization and not all resource services fall under the umbrella of resource centre services. Resource centres may still operate locally within a specific community, may operate to service the county or regional municipality, or may service the entire province or territory. The four examples below—BC Aboriginal Child Care Society, Ontario Early Years Centre, Hastings/Prince Edward County Early Years Centre, and Westcoast Child Care Resource Centre—cover most of the types of services found across Canada.

BC Aboriginal Child Care Society

The BC Aboriginal Child Care Society (ACCS) was started in 1995 to provide child care resources to BC Aboriginal communities. Since 1995 ACCS has helped to establish 58 licensed child care programs, nine family daycare homes, 800 child care spaces for Aboriginal children, and more than 100 permanent jobs in First Nations communities in BC. Services provided by ACCS are funded by contributions from private and public foundations, corporations, and provincial grants. The Society also relies on donations from local business and individuals. (ACCS [brochure])

The services offered by ACCS include

- Print resources

    - funding opportunities inventory
    - culturally focused ECE program handbook
    - resource training kit for Aboriginal child-care programs
    - best practices for Aboriginal ECE programs

- Curriculum boxes

    - hands-on play materials reflecting west-coast Aboriginal traditions
    - theme-based subjects such as animals and the environment, family and community, food and nutrition, school readiness, music and movement, and speech and language
    - courier services provided by Greyhound Courier Express

- Advisory and support services

    - existing Aboriginal ECE programs
    - new Aboriginal ECE programs
    - child-care resource and referral programs
    - post-secondary ECE programs
    - community services that serve Aboriginal children
    - funded by BC Ministry of Community and Aboriginal and Women's Services

- Resource library

    - books, videos, and newsletters
    - topics including Aboriginal folklore and legends, children's stories, health programs, and administration

- Host Agency for the Office of the Provincial Advisor for Aboriginal Infant Development Programs

    - support for infants who are at risk for developmental delays
    - funded by BC Ministry of Children and Family Development

- Workshops and training

    - topics include enhancing community participation, fund-raising, evaluation, curriculum, challenging behaviours, and music and movement

- Annual conferences
- Membership services

    - ACCS bimonthly newsletter
    - electronic mailing list
    - access to resource library and curriculum boxes
    - discount on print resources

Ontario Early Years Centre

An Ontario Early Years Centre is a place for parents and caregivers of children up to the age of six to go to get information they need about their children's development and about services to support that development. Every Ontario Early Years Centre offers the services listed below, which are free to all parents and caregivers of young children.

- Early years learning and literacy for parents and children
- Programs to support parents and caregivers in all aspects of early child development
- Programs on pregnancy and literacy
- Links to other early years programs in the community
- Outreach activities to ensure all parents can become involved with their local Ontario Early Years Centre. (Ontario Early Years, 2003)

Photo 8.47

Photo 8.48

Funding for the Early Years Centres comes from Health Canada, and the federal government transfers money to the provinces to improve the quality of early years programs and services.

Hastings/Prince Edward County Early Years Centre Services

Early Years Centre

This centre offers playrooms and a resource lending library. When children and caregivers or family members arrive at the centre, they are greeted and registered by one of the staff and they proceed to a play area of choice. Early learning activities, organized by a variety of curriculum themes, are set up in a number of rooms. Each room encourages interactive play among infants, toddlers, preschoolers, and adults. Each area has comfortable seating for adults and children and a full range of developmentally appropriate materials and equipment to meet the various age and skill requirements of the participating children (photos 8.47 and 8.48).

The playrooms provide opportunities to

- interact socially—children and adults (photo 8.49);
- model innovative ideas, experiences, and equipment (photo 8.50);
- encourage active exploration of the environment (photo 8.51);
- discuss areas of common interest; and
- involve community professionals and playroom participants in interactive sessions.

Resource Lending Library

"The resource library offers a variety of books, toys, puzzles, videos, CD's cassette players, curriculum kits, back packs, and computer software. There is also information available to assist parents and caregivers with topics such as child development, health and safety, discipline, parenting skills, nutrition, etc." (Hastings/Prince Edward County Early Years Centre [brochure]):

- *Parent/caregiver courses, conferences, workshops, and informational discussion groups.* The topics covered by these educational events cover areas related to children, families, and parenting. Qualified early childhood educators lead discussion groups and also interact informally to answer questions that may be posed by caregivers.
- *Newsletters.* Newsletters are issued four times a year and contain information about upcoming events, creative play activities, and information to help caregivers move toward more quality child-care.
- *Outreach playgroups.* There are seven drop-in playgroups in operation within various locations in Hastings County.

Early Literacy Program

The early literacy program provides language and literacy resources, including books, resources to help with school entry, and language learning activities and brochures (see the Resources section at the end of the chapter). Education about literacy is provided through conferences, workshops, courses, and presentations. Linkages have been established with other agencies in the community, and consultation is provided by the creation of resources to support a program's specific needs.

Photo 8.49

Photo 8.50

Photo 8.51

Resource Consultant Program

This program supports families and children from birth to 12 years with special needs. The services provided to families include

- collaborating with families in response to family priorities, needs, and choices;
- assisting families in choosing appropriate child-care;
- helping families to complete funding applications;
- connecting families with other community resources;
- providing training related to inclusive care; and
- providing consulting services on-site (making suggestions, answering questions, discussing progress, and offering resources to help the child with special needs).

Licensed Home Child-Care

The Hastings/Prince Edward County Early Years Centre accepts home child-care programs that want to become licensed facilities. An early childhood educator monitors home child-care programs to ensure that licensing criteria are met.

Breastfeeding Clinic

A drop-in breastfeeding clinic is offered within the Hastings/Prince Edward County Early Years Centre. A public health nurse provides support to mothers who are concerned about their infant's health, their infant's feeding patterns, their own personal health, and/or problems related to breastfeeding.

Westcoast Child Care Resource Centre

The Westcoast Child Care Resource Centre was started by a group of individuals who recognized that there was a need to

Web exercises

- bring together the child-care community in Vancouver;
- strengthen child-care in the community; and
- establish a space that would provide a meeting place, resources, and supports to existing services.

"Westcoast Child Care Resource Centre was incorporated in 1987. We are a registered charitable society governed by a volunteer Board of Directors and staffed by experienced individuals with expertise in child care, child development, family support, community development and related areas" (Westcoast Child Care Resource Centre [brochure]). The organization is funded in a variety of ways, including

- subscribers;
- fees for service;
- grants from the province of British Columbia and the City of Vancouver;
- funding by Human Resources Development Canada, and a variety of fund-raisers and special projects; and
- tax-deductible donations from the public and private sectors.

"Our mission at Westcoast Child Care Resource Centre is to enhance the lives of children and families in BC and beyond. We do that by providing affordable child development and child care information, referrals, training and resources for families, caregivers and others who provide services to children and families" (Westcoast Child Care Resource Centre [brochure]). The services offered include the following:

- *Resource and information services, including an information line.* An average of 20 000 questions are posed by parents and child-care providers and answered by this service yearly.
- *A resource library.* This library covers broad-based information about early childhood programs, child development and behaviour, programming, public policy, nonprofit management, centre-based administration, financial management, and other issues related to children and families; the collection includes more than 11 000 books, reports, videos, and other documents in a variety of languages.
- *Multilingual child-care resources.* The centre responds to requests for translations and interpretation in 17 languages.
- *Professional development.* The centre offers workshops, conferences, and early childhood student support. Workshops in family child-care are provided in several languages.
- *A Web site.* The centre's site (at http://www.wstcoast.org/) provides, a listing of all resources, job postings, and upcoming events.
- *Training.* Courses and workshops in several languages are offered to parents, child-care providers, and others working with children and families.
- *Consulting services.* These services involve program quality, diversity, child development, family support, program administration, not-for-profit management, and others.

KEY POINTS

THE HIGH/SCOPE COGNITIVELY ORIENTED CURRICULUM APPROACH

- Active learning environment. Children initiate activities, make choices, actively explore using all their senses, discover relationships through direct experiences, transform and combine materials, use age-appropriate tools and equipment, use their large muscles, and talk about their experiences using their own words.
- The key experiences are creative representations, language and literacy, initiative and social relations, movement, music, classification, seriation, numbers, and space and time.

- Adults provide developmentally appropriate materials and space and time. They encourage children to use materials, to think, and to be independent. Children and adults are active and interactive, are partners, and learn together.
- Family involvement. Families bring materials from home. The approach utilizes the expertise of families (e.g., customs and language) and treats families as partners.

THE CAPILANO COLLEGE CHILD-CARE ADAPTATION TO THE REGGIO EMILIA APPROACH

- The environment emphasizes a sense of personal space, the life of the community, the history, and an awareness of surrounding space.
- Collaboration:
  - Children and adults interact to make meaningful decisions and accomplish tasks.
  - They interact with peers to share ideas, materials, and experiences.
  - The staff coordinates efforts, makes joint decisions, takes on leadership roles;
  - Families and staff explore topics, provide additional ideas and resources, become partners in the process, and provide a closer connection between home and centre.

- Project approach:
  - Start with chance event, idea, or problem.
  - Evolve and change over time.
  - Principles include flexibility, time, appropriate learning spaces, and documentation.

- Documentation is important to learn about children, maintain involvement, exchange ideas, value children's efforts, and provide a record.

MONTESSORI APPROACH

- Environment includes didactic materials and several basic areas (daily living centre, sensorial area, language centre, and mathematics centre).
- Children are viewed as unique individuals with absorbent minds (unconscious stage and conscious stage).
- At sensitive periods children are more susceptible and learn more easily. Characteristics include being manipulative, having continual movement, looking at detailed objects, and becoming interested in social aspects.
- The role of the teacher is to observe, free the children to learn, prepare the environment, provide guidance and lessons, and redirect inappropriate behaviour.

HEAD START PROGRAMS

- Aboriginal Head Start program components include culture and language, education, health promotion, nutrition, social support, and parental and family involvement.

RESOURCE CENTRES

- The BC Aboriginal Society offers print resources, curriculum boxes, advisory and support services, a resource library, workshops and training, conferences, and memberships.
- The Hastings/Price Edward County Early Years Centre offers drop-in playgroups, a resource lending library, courses, conferences, workshops, discussion groups, newsletters, and outreach playgroups.

- The resource consultant program collaborates with families by helping them choose child-care, helping with funding applications, connecting them with other resources, helping with transitions, and providing support services. The program also provides training for child-care programs.
- The Westcoast Child Care Resource Centre has a multi-level funding structure. It provides an information line, a resource library, multilingual child-care resources, professional development, a Web site, training, and consulting services.

EXERCISES

1. In a small group discuss five key elements of an active learning environment. How is this approach the same as or different from what you have been used to?
2. Using the key experiences as identified on pages 217–19, and page 224, observe a group of preschoolers at three different times for 15 minutes each time. How many of the key experiences did you identify? Which ones were missing? Why do you think you did not observe these?
3. Compare the role of the adult among the High/Scope, Reggio Emilia, Montessori, and Head Start approaches. How are the roles different? How are they similar?
4. Reflect upon the key elements—personal space, life of the community, own history, and awareness of surrounding space. How many environments have you seen that reflect all these principles? Visit a child-care centre. Which of the elements did you observe? Which ones were missing? What recommendations would you make for change?
5. In a small group discuss the collaborative process. What are the elements of the process? Who are the partners? What strategies would you need to use to set up a collaborative process?
6. Compare the environment of Montessori and Reggio Emilia. How are they the same? How are they different?
7. Compare the values and beliefs of the Aboriginal Head Start program to the values and beliefs Maria Montessori had about children. Reflect on how our values influence how we treat children.
8. Describe the role of the teacher in the Montessori approach. How is it different from other approaches?
9. Read the information on the Cedar Road Aboriginal Head Start program. What features of this program make it unique? What features do you find particularly interesting?
10. Look at each of the three resource type programs on the book's Web site at http://www.ece.nelson.com. What are some distinctive features of each? Which of the services do you find most helpful to you? Why?

RESOURCES

Grey, L. (2003). *Creating a Kid Literate Home*. Belleville, ON: Hastings/Prince Edward County Early Years Centre.

Grey, L. (2003). *Learning and Growing with Friends*. Belleville, ON: Hastings/Prince Edward County Early Years Centre.

Grey, L. (2003). *Music for the Whole Child*. Belleville, ON: Hastings/Prince Edward County Early Years Centre.

Grey, L. (2003). *Building Baby's Intelligence*. Belleville, ON: Hastings/Prince Edward County Early Years Centre.

REFERENCES

Crowther, I. (2003). *Creating Effective Learning Environments*. Scarborough, ON: Nelson Thomson Learning.

Division of Childhood and Adolescence. (2003). Program Overview of Aboriginal Head Start. Health Canada [On-line]. Available: http://www.hc-sc.gc.ca/fnihb-dgspni/fnihb/cp/index.htm.

Edwards, C., Gandini, L., Forman, G. (eds.) (1998). *The Hundred Languages of Children: The Reggio Emilia Approach—Advanced Reflections* (2nd ed.). Greenwich, CT: Ablex Publishing Corporation.

Gandini, L. (1991). Not Just Anywhere: Making Child Care Centres into "Particular" Places. *Childcare Information Exchange*, March/April, 5–9.

Gandini, L. (1993). Fundamentals of the Reggio Emilia Approach to Early Childhood Education. *Young Children 49*(11), 4–8.

Hainstock, E. (1986). *The Essential Montessori*. New York, NY: Plume.

Harms, T., Vineberg Jacobs, E., & White, D. (1996). *School-Age Care Environment Rating Scale*. New York, NY: Teachers College Press.

Hohmann, M., & Weikart, D. (1995). *Educating Young Children*. Ypsilanti, MI: High/Scope Press.

Malaguzzi, L. (1997). *The Hundred Languages of Children* (2nd ed.). Reggio Emilia, Italy: Reggio Children.

Montessori, M. (1965). *Dr. Montessori's Own Handbook: A Short Guide to Her Ideas and Materials*. New York, NY: Schocken Books Inc.

Morrison, G. (1997). *Fundamentals of Early Childhood Education*. Upper Saddle River: NY: Prentice-Hall.

Ontario Early Years. (2003). What Is an Ontario Early Years Centre. http://www.ontario earlyyears.ca [On-line].

Roopnarine, J., & Johnson, J. (2000). *Approaches to Early Childhood Education*. Toronto, ON: Prentice Hall Canada Inc.

Schweinhart, L., & Weikart, J. (1986). Lasting Differences: The High/Scope Preschool Curriculum Comparison Study Through Age 23. *Early Childhood Education Research Quarterly 1*, 15–45.

White, C., & Coleman, M. (2000). *Early Childhood Education: Building a Philosophy for Teaching*. Upper Saddle River, NY: Merrill.

ISSUES IN EARLY CHILDHOOD

"This year's report on The Progress of Canada's Children *shows mounting and clear evidence that there are groups of children who are increasingly being excluded from fully participating in Canadian society. What does this mean? Social exclusion occurs whenever the 'environments where people grow up, live and work, and the institutions that govern them, arbitrarily limit their opportunity to participate in society' (Hertzman, 2002, p. 1). The consequences of social exclusion can be devastating for children: they suffer a lack of recognition and acceptance; they feel powerless and voiceless; they are economically vulnerable; and ultimately, they have diminished life experiences and face limited life prospects." (Hanvey, 2003, p. 2)*

Chapter Outcomes

After reading this chapter, the reader will

1. Explain why poverty has such a powerful effect over all aspects of children's development.
2. Define social exclusion.
3. Explain how children are denied access to a variety of social services.
4. Explain why a child with special needs is often excluded from developmentally appropriate services.
5. Discuss how accessibility limits children's right to participate fully in a variety of services.
6. Define the five dimensions of quality—structural, contextual, adult work environment, safety and basic care, and process quality.
7. Explain how each of the five dimensions of quality impacts on the well-being of young children.
8. Explain how stress impacts the quality of life for children, families, and child-care providers.
9. Discuss how the concept of school readiness may conflict with healthy child development.

INTRODUCTION

> Children have risen to the top of government agendas at various times over the past decade, only to fall again whenever there is an economic downturn, a budget deficit, a federal-provincial relations crisis or, more recently, a concern over terrorism and national security. (Hertzman, 2002, p. vii)

In fact, many of the same issues have been addressed over and over again in government-sponsored studies and reports (Cooke, 1986; Hanvey, 2003; McCain & Mustard, 1999; Hanvey, 2003). Although some strides have been made, many of the same issues are as prevalent today as they were in the comprehensive study on child-care in 1986 (Cooke, 1986). The Canadian Council on Social Development issues a report on the progress of children every year. Every year the same issues surface, every year it is evident that as a society we are losing ground in our efforts to protect our children, and every year more children are put at risk. This chapter will identify the major issues facing children and families in this century.

POVERTY

Web exercises

> Children are dependent on their families for income, care, food, shelter, health and safety and relationships. Consequently, while children's well-being and future prospects can be affected directly by developmental, enriching environments, they are also enhanced if their families are sustained economically and socially through employment, income security and community support. (Friendly & Lero, 2002, p. 2)

In 1998, the Canadian government passed a *unanimous* resolution to eliminate child poverty by the year 2000. Since that resolution was passed, child poverty has increased by 21 percent and one in six children still lives in poverty (Elder & Robertson, 2003).

There is a direct correlation between poverty and the well-being of children. Brain development research has shown that optimal brain development in infants occurs when infants are raised in environments that foster high levels of attachment. There are critical periods in a young child's development during which stimulation becomes extremely important. It is during these critical periods that the brain becomes "wired." This "wiring" ensures that the child will develop normally in cognition, language, sensory, physical, emotional, and social domains. Healthy brain development is optimal when children receive

- stimulation through all their senses (visual, verbal, emotional, touch, smell, and taste);
- appropriate nutrition;
- appropriate, sensitive, and warm interactions; and
- appropriate health and safety care (Hertzman, 2002; McCain & Mustard, 1999; Begly, 1997; Shore, 1997).

Families who live in poverty have less time to spend with their children. They work longer hours; are more likely to suffer from ill health, stress, and depression; are more likely to have established patterns of dysfunctional family life; and are less likely to have appropriate social support (Hanvey, 2003). It is not surprising that children raised in these types of environments are less likely to establish strong attachment patterns.

Living in poverty also means that families will be less likely to afford nutritious foods, to have time or money to spend on leisure activities, and to have stimulating resources available to their children.

In a research study conducted in Vancouver, children in all kindergarten classes were assessed (Hertzman, 2002, pp. 5–6). The assessment included five areas of development—physical health and well-being, social competence, emotional maturity, language and cognitive development, and English communication skills. The results were compared between high-risk neighbourhoods and low-risk neighbourhoods (based on socioeconomic status). In order to be classified vulnerable, children had to score in the bottom 10 percent of the test (see Table 9.1).

■ TABLE 9.1

Comparison of Test Results

Areas of Development	% Vulnerable in High-Risk Neighbourhoods	% Vulnerable in Low-Risk Neighbourhoods
Physical health and well-being	22%	0%
Social competence	17%	0%
Emotional maturity	16%	2%
Language and cognitive development	21%	0%
Communication skills	16%	0%

Source: Hertzman, 2002.

In conclusion, there is a clear connection between socioeconomic status and the health and well-being of young children: "As one looks across the socioeconomic spectrum from the children of the wealthiest and most educated families, to those from the middle, to those from families with the least income and education, an increasing proportion of children are vulnerable in terms of readiness for school: intellectually, socially, and physically" (Hertzman, 2002, p. 1).

Personal Reflections

As a child, I grew up in post-war Germany. My family and I were refugees from East Germany. We were given accommodation in a small village in the attic of a three-story house. We had a large attic room and two smaller rooms at our disposal. There was no running water. The only washroom was two floors down, or in the courtyard outside. Our heating consisted of a pot-bellied stove heated by coal or wood in one of the rooms. Coal and wood were rationed, as was food. I can often remember going to bed hungry and cold. Washing day consisted of getting up early in the morning to light a fire under a large boiling tub outside in the courtyard, filling it with water from the pump, boiling the laundry, wringing it out and hanging it up to dry on the clothes line, or in the colder weather carrying the wet laundry up to the back attic room.

When I was about three years old, my parents created a room in the larger attic room. It was a huge room and I had a nook in one corner. In the middle of the attic there was a ladder that went up to a loft. Before I moved into my new room, my parents warned me never to climb up to the loft because it was dangerous. They asked the chimney sweep to also talk to me. The chimney sweep said that I had to promise never to go up to the loft. He told me that a monster lived in the loft and that the monster loved to eat little girls especially. He said his job was to clean the chimney, and if he did this regularly, the monster could not come down the stairs. I lived in fear of falling asleep. I remember watching the top of the ladder to see if the monster would appear. (I now understand that the chimney had a large opening that I could have fallen into. This was meant to protect me.)

We soon immigrated to Canada. My father had immigrated earlier. I remember when we arrived that he had a quart of milk waiting for me, a set of small bottles filled with various types of jam, a large chocolate bar, and butter. He said that from now on I could drink as much milk as I wanted. I had my own room. We had a kitchen and another room, and our own bathroom. The apartment was heated and we had a washing machine in the basement. I remember feeling so lucky to live in this wonderful new place.

To this day, I still have a fear of open ladders, or open stairways. I know that there is nothing there to harm me, but I still tend to rush up or down holding my breath. I have developed a greater empathy for individuals less fortunate than I and have involved myself in many efforts in the community, especially related to hunger and appropriate living conditions.

—Petra, early childhood educator

What Can You Do?

- Look at the Web site Campaign 2000 (http://www.campaign2000.ca/). It is regularly updated and gives information on how individuals and groups can become involved.
- Find out who your member of parliament is and write a letter to him or her to ask what your community is doing to help children.
- Learn more about the issues of poverty in your neighbourhood. You can get this information from your municipal council. Learn about the real issues in your neighbourhood to become informed. You can, therefore, be more empathetic to the children and families that you will be working with. What is the average salary for your area? What are the average rent and food costs? What are the average daycare costs? Reflect on how well you would live on the bottom salary ranges without family support.
- Support local initiatives such as task forces on poverty, huger, and breakfast clubs.

SOCIAL EXCLUSION

Social exclusion is a seemingly socially acceptable mechanism for denying certain individuals the right to participate in the same activities in which others participate. Exclusion is usually justified by rules, regulations, mores, or some other arbitrary reason. Children are most vulnerable to be excluded because they are totally dependent on their caregivers. There are many reasons for social exclusion, including poverty, special needs, and accessibility concerns.

social exclusion
A seemingly socially acceptable mechanism for denying certain individuals the right to participate in the same activities that others participate in.

Poverty

The number one cause of social exclusion is poverty. Families who live in poverty cannot afford to include their children in the types of activities that more affluent members of society can afford. Subsequently children are often denied access to

- *Daycare programs.* "Even though more than 70% of young children have mothers in the paid labor force, only 12% of children 0–12 years have access to a regulated care space" (Elder & Robertson, 2003, p. 3).
- *Enough subsidy to afford daycare.* "Another factor that illustrates that cost prevents many families from using regulated ECEC [early childhood education and care] services for their children is the difference between the maximum subsidy and the fees that parents must pay for ECEC. In most provinces the maximum subsidy is less than the average cost of full daycare and parents must pay the difference" (Elder & Robertson, 2002, p. 3).
- *Quality care.* "The extreme variations in both child policies and child care quality across jurisdictions must be addressed. The variation in areas such as adult–child ratios, group size, and required levels of ECEC-specific education for staff contributes to the variations in quality observed in this study" (Goelman et al., 2000,

p. xiv). Moderate- to low-income families cannot afford the price of quality daycare. Their choices are limited to what is available at a cost that they can afford. Often this means unregulated care—27 percent of children are cared for by relatives, 16 percent by siblings, and 30 percent by nonrelatives in someone's home (Hanvey, 2003).

- *Affordable housing.* "As rents rise and become increasingly out of reach for families, vacancy rates have plummeted in recent years. As a result, more than 40% of renter households are paying more than 30% of their monthly income on rent, which leaves them little money for food, transportation, or other basics" (Hanvey, 2003, p. 19). The impact on children is often most detrimental. Lack of affordable housing often forces families to live in less-than-desirable circumstances, often at the mercy of slum landlords.
- *Recreational activities.* "Approximately three quarters (72%) of all children participated in recreation at least once a week in 1998—but not if the child was consistently poor" (Hanvey, 2003, p. 20).

Personal Reflections

I remember how scared I was when I knew I was knocked-up
again. I was scared to tell my husband. I had just managed to get a job, and the two kids were with a neighbour down the street. We thought with the two of us working, we could afford a better place for us and the kids. I got a little money stashed away, but it didn't last when the baby came. The landlord put the rent up, so we had to move again. We couldn't afford the rent. The new place was a real dump—dark and always smelled. The kids were all in one room. The baby never stopped crying. My husband and I were always at each other. Finally, he left us. The jerk just up and left one day and never came back. I had no one to turn to, no money, no friends. We never left the dump—the kids watched TV all day. When I wasn't crying, I slept. I got food from the food bank, but they said I couldn't come back again, I'd been there too much. So I went to the soup kitchen at the church. I was behind in my rent and the landlord said if I didn't pay up he'd throw us on the street. I was really down. My three-year-old broke his arm when he fell outside. When I took him to the hospital, they thought that I'd smacked him. They called the Children's Aid Society. They took one look at the place we lived in and said the kids couldn't stay in a dump like that. They took the kids away, but helped me get on mother's allowance and into a low rental. I got the kids back. Once the kids got into school, they were always in trouble. I think they spent more time in the hall than learning anything. I just can't help thinking I should have done better by them.

—Jenna, a newly pregnant mother with two other children

Many children grow up in similar circumstances. They face endless depressing circumstances. Many of these children continue to live in these circumstances throughout their whole childhood. They rarely attend daycare, do not participate in recreational programs, have few resources to stimulate their intellect, and often reach school already significantly behind their age peers in their ability to learn. They are truly excluded from most of the stimulation and healthy living conditions that are the right of every child. "What is particularly troublesome about these indicators of social exclusion and their relationship to poor children in Canada is that, throughout the 1990's, the poor became poorer while the rich got richer—forcing these children away from full participation in society" (Hanvey, 2003, p. 20).

What Can You Do?

- Provide an aesthetically pleasing environment for children that nurtures their needs to actively explore their environment using all their senses.
- Ensure that children are outside each day. Outdoor spaces should have many opportunities to engage in active gross motor play to build strength, endurance, coordination, balance, and skill.
- Provide a variety of experiences for children that build on their background experiences. These could include going on field trips to local points of interest such as parks, beaches, conservation areas, zoos, and museums.

Special Needs

Between 5 and 20% of children have special needs. The disabilities may range from a physical disability through a specific medical condition or illness, to developmental delays or a mental disorder. The disability may be visible or invisible (e.g., epilepsy). It may be apparent at birth or emerge as the child grows older. Or it may come later as a result of an injury or illness. Its causes may be known (e.g., genetic) or as is the case with many children with developmental problems, its cause may be more speculative (e.g., environmental) or unknown. (Child & Family, 2003, p. 1)

Web exercises

Children with special needs are particularly vulnerable to be excluded from a variety of services. Barriers to inclusive care are

- *Poverty.* Poor families have insufficient resources to sustain services for their children. Often families are forced to drive children great distances to obtain help. Individuals without cars find it prohibitive even to try to use a public transit system. Children require more appointments with doctors and other specialists. Many individuals may find themselves in a job situation that does not allow for time off for appointments for their child.
- *Inadequate funding.* Families may not have access to the funds to provide the required services and equipment, to make structural adaptations to meet the needs of the child with special needs, or to provide for the additional staffing.
- *Lack of space.* Many centres already have the maximum number of children with special needs that they are licensed for.
- *Limited professional help.* Families may not be able to access professional help, such as resource consultants and therapists.
- *Community attitudes.* There may be community-wide negative attitudes toward including children with special needs.
- *Limited access for staff to obtain additional training* (Child & Family, 2003; Friendly & Lero, 2002).

Personal Reflections

When our executive director told us that we were going to accept a child with special needs, I was horrified. I can still remember the kid next door. He looked and acted differently. He was big, didn't speak very well, and always tried to follow me around. I can remember being scared whenever he was outside. I also am finding it difficult to work with the children I have now—how am I going to cope with a new child with problems coming into the centre? This is not what I signed up for. If I wanted to work with children with special needs, I'd work in a centre that had them. I finally got up my nerve to say something. I said that it wasn't fair to the other children. We didn't have extra help and the time we took with this new child would take time away from the other children. Some of the staff agreed with me. Others started to argue that we needed to be more open-minded and flexible. Well, finally we took a vote. The vote was against accepting the child to the centre. When we told the supervisor of our decision, she indicated that this was not an option. However, she said that she would ensure that we would be able to access specialized training. I reluctantly decided to participate in the training offered. This training did not change my mind completely—I still felt very insecure around children with special needs, but it did increase my confidence in my own abilities and it did make me see that children with special needs had a right to be in a daycare.

—Sarah, early childhood educator

Families with children with special needs face many challenges. Their challenges last well beyond the preschool years. Their children's problems will follow them into the school system and sometimes beyond the school years. They are continually faced with the challenges of finding appropriate help, placement, and understanding of their unique problems in trying to raise with a child with special needs.

What Can You Do?

- Show sensitivity to the feelings and challenges that families face. Practise active listening to hear what their concerns might be.
- Make information about other services (e.g., financial support and respite care) available.
- Try to be nonjudgmental. Remember, only the families know what it's like to live with that child.
- Be flexible and understanding if families are not always on time or the child is not always in the program for the whole day. Families often have to coordinate many appointments with their work schedules.
- Try not to add to parents' workload. They may already be overloaded with requirements from other professionals.
- Don't overwhelm parents with bad news. Emphasize the strengths of the child.
- Acknowledge efforts and give parents credit for successes (Child & Family, 2003, p. 3).

Accessibility

To be universally accessible, ECEC services must be available, affordable, and appropriate, requiring an adequate supply of services, while costs to parents must be affordable (either free, very low cost, or geared to income). In addition, services must fit needs and characteristics of the family and child; that is, they must be age and culturally appropriate and responsive to parents' work schedules. (Friendly & Lero, 2002, p. 13)

There are many barriers that prevent families from finding appropriate child-care:

- *Poverty*. Some families cannot afford the cost even when subsidized.
- *Lack of child-care space*. In some areas, not enough daycare spaces are available to handle the need.
- *Lack of quality daycare*. A number of studies across Canada have found that many child-care centres are not of sufficient high quality: "We have also noted that Canadian childcare is more likely to be of mediocre than high quality" (Cleveland et al., 2003, p. 17). Families may be forced to choose a child-care setting for their child that they know is not of the quality that they would wish. The greater the financial need, the higher the likelihood that families pick the child-care centre that is accessible. Quality care may not be a choice that these families can afford.

Personal Reflections

I was expecting my first child and I was a single parent. Although I knew I should get at least a year's maternity leave, my employer told me that he could not afford to keep my position open for me. I could get a job, but would probably not get the same job again. I liked my job, so I thought I'd start looking for daycare immediately. I started asking around to see where the best daycare was. After calling every daycare in our community—all six of them—I was stunned to find that only two offered care for infants and they had a long waiting list. I went to look at both. I really liked the first one, but could not possibly afford it on my salary. The other daycare was very nice and I put my child on the waiting list. In the meantime, I still needed to find someone to look after my baby. Someone suggested I try the family-home daycares. There were ten listed in the phone book. I called them all and found only four of them had room for infants. When I went to look at the four, I didn't really like any of them. I was running out of time, so I finally picked the one closest to work. At least it would not be as long a day for both of us.

—Kerri, single parent

What Can You Do?

- Provide information to families about alternate care (e.g., listings of licensed family home providers), and keep in touch with other daycare centres to see if they have openings.
- Advocate for increased daycare spaces in your community.

QUALITY

The study entitled *You Bet I Care!* (Goelman et al., 2000) examined quality in child-care settings throughout Canada. Quality was studied by looking at process quality and by looking at the following additional four dimensions—structure, context, the adult work environment, and safety.

Structural Dimensions of Quality

The structural dimension looks at information about group size, adult–child ratios, and the size and accessibility of indoor and outdoor space. In all structural dimensions, there is variability across Canada (see specific information on group size, adult–child ratios, and size of indoor/outdoor space in Chapter 10). These characteristics alone do not lead to quality; however, they do aid individuals in moving toward quality.

When group sizes and child-to-adult ratios are too high, quality is jeopardized because it becomes more difficult to

- engage in first-hand interactions between children and adults;
- individualize children's learning experiences;
- provide physical and emotional safety for each child; and
- provide personal feedback to children about their learning experiences.

The *You Bet I Care!* study did find that the majority of centres in their sample across Canada were providing a level of care that met the basic needs of physical and emotional safety of children (Goelman et al., 2000, p. 74). However, meeting basic needs is a mediocre requirement at best.

The size and accessibility of outdoor and indoor spaces have more direct impact on quality education for children. The sizes of indoor and outdoor spaces vary greatly across Canada. Some jurisdictions have no requirements for outdoor play. Consider the example shown in Figure 9.1. The daycare is licensed for 16 preschoolers. It is in the basement of a building. The centre has a large variety of materials and interest centres for children to make appropriate choices. Once the children and two adults are in the program, there is an overwhelming feeling of crowdedness. It is hard to get away from other children to find a quiet area in which to work. The noise level is high and escalates toward the end of the morning. The outdoor space is too small to hold all 16 children. Children usually play in the outdoor space until nine children have arrived, and go back outside in the afternoon when eight children are left.

Web
exercises

It is easy to see how limited space might limit the ability to create a higher-quality environment. The staff of this centre have worked very hard to achieve an appropriate quality program for the children, but there are several problems:

- It is hard for them to provide quiet spaces—the room is too small to separate spaces more appropriately.
- Some of the permanent structures in the room take up child-care space. The kitchen, many doors, and entryways create a need to keep a large number of spaces clear.
- There is only one permanent rug. This limits the space in which block play and large group time can be held.
- The small outdoor area can not accommodate all the children at the same time. In addition, full exposure to sun and wind all day and a lack of shade limit appropriate outdoor play.

Contextual Dimensions of Quality

> Contextual dimensions of quality are factors outside the individual classroom that influence what goes on inside the room. These include, for example, the centre's auspice, its administrative structure, annual teaching staff turnover rate, and the centre's policies and practices. (Goelman et al., 2000, p. 4)

Jennifer worked in a centre in Alberta. She was one of two qualified staff (level 3) in the centre. The centre had a full range of programs—for infants, toddlers, preschoolers, and school-aged children. Each room had two staff members. Two staff members had level 2 qualifications (one year of ECE training) and the rest of the staff had (or were in process of obtaining) their Level 1 qualifications.

The centre had a full-time director and the appropriate policies and practices in place to pass licensing requirements. The annual staff turnover in the centre was extremely high—17 new staff members over one year. Every time a new staff member came, routines had to be put in place that took time away from other quality considerations. These included

- training new staff;
- introducing and preparing children and families;
- adjusting routines and daily activities to include the new staff member;
- holding additional team planning meetings with new staff; and
- reassuring families that their children would receive appropriate care.

Jennifer quit her job after one year. She found the continual changes too disruptive to the children's program and too exhausting for her to adapt to.

Child-care across Canada is plagued with similar problems. In most centres, policies and practices are set to meet licensing requirements. These requirements usually concern themselves with minimum standards only. As a result of poor salaries, limited possibility of advancement, and overall poor educational standards, it is not surprising that the daycare system across the country suffers from

- high staff turnover;
- difficulty in finding and keeping qualified staff;
- disruption of programs with so many staff changes; and
- burnout in child-care staff and administration.

Adult Work Environment Dimensions of Quality

> The adult work environment dimensions of quality include factors such as wage level, benefits, collegial support, recognition of staff needs. (Goelman et al., 2000, p. 4)

Web
exercises

Remuneration for ECE workers in Canada ranges from a low of $6.76 to a high of $13.48 per hour (mean gross hourly wage salaries) for centre-based staff, and from $12.07 to $22.00 per hour for an administrative director. The average salary of a centre-based staff member in Canada is $11.62 per hour, and that of an administrative director is $18.45 per hour. Many centre staff across Canada do not receive any benefits such as health care, pension plans, and sick leave plans. Many centre staff will never receive more than two weeks of holidays per year.

What does this mean? It means that if you are earning $6.75 an hour, your earnings have not kept pace with inflation. In fact, had your earnings kept up with the cost of inflation, you should be earning more than $9.50 today. This means that you have to either work longer hours or obtain another job to earn enough to reach the poverty line:

Figure 9.1

Observations of One Daycare

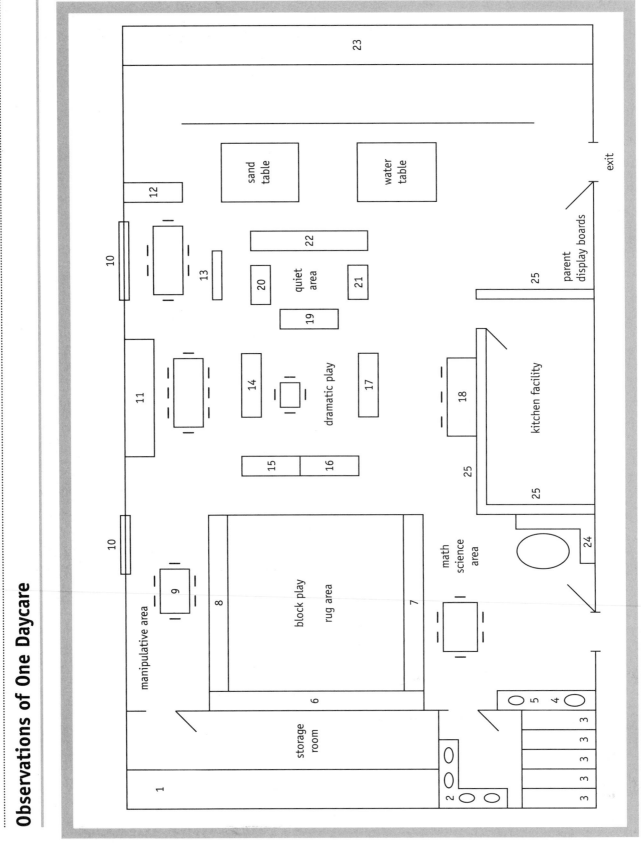

Observations of One Daycare

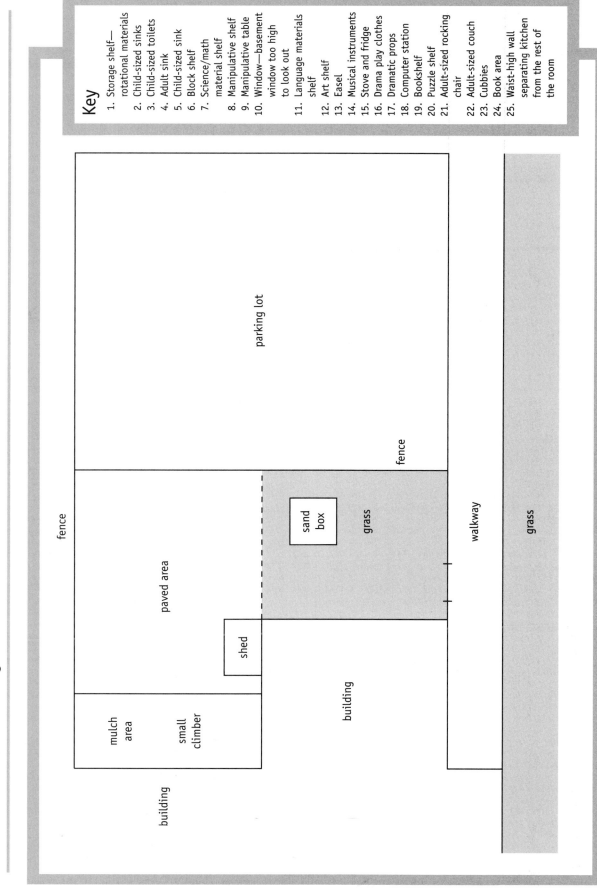

Key

1. Storage shelf—rotational materials
2. Child-sized sinks
3. Child-sized toilets
4. Adult sink
5. Child-sized sink
6. Block shelf
7. Science/math material shelf
8. Manipulative shelf
9. Manipulative table
10. Window—basement window too high to look out
11. Language materials shelf
12. Art shelf
13. Easel
14. Musical instruments
15. Stove and fridge
16. Drama play clothes
17. Dramatic props
18. Computer station
19. Bookshelf
20. Puzzle shelf
21. Adult-sized rocking chair
22. Adult-sized couch
23. Cubbies
24. Book area
25. Waist-high wall separating kitchen from the rest of the room

Manitoba's minimum wage is comparable to other provinces, but it still does not allow a Manitoban to live above the poverty line. In fact, a single person would have to work 56 hours per week at minimum wage just to reach the poverty line, and a single parent with two children would have to work 85.31 hours per week. As a result, many families with at least one adult in full-time employment often find themselves living in poverty. Having a job is simply no longer a guarantee that one can escape poverty. (Just Income Coalition, 2004)

Most of the gratification of working in the early childhood field comes from the children and the families. Few environments consider adult needs. Few environments have separate adult space. When asked why individuals continue to stay in the field and work with young children, some responses were as follows:

- Kaya (assistant director): "When the child makes their first attempt at a different skill set and they succeed, it's like a ray of hope that they will succeed; the joy that children express when they do succeed; the gratification a child shows that tells you they appreciate what you do—the child runs to give you a hug; and the gratification family members show—'You really make a difference.'"
- Naomi (early childhood educator): "I get such a thrill when a child just beams at what he or she has done. That's my greatest reward."
- Jodi (infant teacher): "I just love it when a child takes that first step, tastes a new food, or puts out his or her arms to me. It makes me feel so special."

What Can You Do?

- Use the information presented on salaries to bring the issue to the attention of the political system in your area.
- Increase public awareness of the valuable job you do. You are not a baby sitter. You are a professional. Refer to yourself as such.
- Whenever you get a chance, publicize the value of what you are doing—such as mall displays, newspaper articles, display of children's work, or an open house—and invite key local people to these events.
- Believe in yourself and show that you do. A person who is genuinely passionate about what he or she does tends to get others enthused. Show your enthusiasm!

Safety and Basic Care Dimensions of Quality

Safety and basic care dimensions are fundamental for—but not identical to—quality child care. Quality child care programs must be built upon a foundation that ensures the physical, emotional, and nutritional health and well-being of every child. Adults providing this care must be sensitive and responsive to children's needs. (Goelman et al., 2000, p. 4)

This is what is often referred to as custodial care. If this is all that is provided in a child-care centre, the centre again will reach only a mediocre level of quality.

In fact, all of the dimensions discussed to this point are those things that are easy to look at, very tangible, and easy to evaluate. Much of what is has been discussed is clearly outlined in regulations and guidelines. However, this alone does not lead to quality. Regulations and guidelines need to be expanded to include other dimensions, including process quality:

> Regulations may be a buffer that can move the quality of centre care from inadequate to minimal, but without the contribution of the other critical factors—adequate wages, financial stability, staff with ECE training-specific education—the centre cannot move beyond the level of minimal/mediocre to the provisions of a high quality sensitive, stimulating, and developmentally appropriate childcare environment. (Goelman et al., 2000, p. 74)

What Can You Do?

- Get involved. Join your provincial association. These associations provide key information about the issues and how to deal with them.
- Become knowledgeable about the issues and what some of the solutions are. For example, when you are negotiating for a salary or a raise, it helps to know what the average salaries are in your area, your province, or in the country. It gives you a much stronger position from which to negotiate.
- Follow the news. It will keep you in touch with what others are doing and what the current issues are.
- Join local groups such as infant teachers or preschool teachers. It will help to overcome some of the isolation you might feel. It gives you an opportunity to talk about and look for solutions together.

Process Quality

> The interplay of the above four dimensions provides a basic scaffolding upon which a quality child care program can be implemented. None of these dimensions, however, reflects what is frequently referred to as a process quality, a nature of the child's experience, especially the daily interactions between the child and the teacher and among children themselves. (Goelman et al., 2000, p. 4)

Across Canada, there have been a variety of approaches that vie for the limelight as the best approach to educating young children. The Reggio Emilia program has been quoted as the best early childhood program in the world (Hinckle, 1991). The High/Scope Curriculum model has gained international fame through its longitudinal Perry Street Study (Schweinhart & Weikart, 1986). The Montessori program has gained international acclaim—there are Montessori preschool programs in most parts of the world. The early childhood programs in Canada have been neatly divided between the educational system—junior kindergartens and senior kindergartens—and early childhood programs for children from infancy to age five (and after-school programs for 5- to 12-year-olds). The school system and the early childhood education system each has its own training and guidelines. Early childhood programs have mandatory maximum child-to-teacher ratios, but when you move into the educational system, you suddenly can teach up to four or five times the number of children with at least three times the salary. No wonder there is confusion about what should be taught and how it should be taught.

What we are all forgetting are the undeniable truths that research has expounded in the last ten years—what children need to "wire" their brains effectively:

> The infant brain, which is the master organ of the early development, is highly sensitive to the environment around it. Just as the infant's lungs grow and develop more fully in an environment of high air quality than in one of pollution, the infant brain develops best in an environment characterized by high levels of attachment, stimulation, and support. Access to such environments is a precondition for "healthy child development" and a prime determinant for school success. (Hertzman, 2002, p. 1–2)

Irrespective of the philosophical underpinnings of a program, the basic tenets of quality, as outlined in Chapter 6, must be present.

What Can You Do?

- Become knowledgeable about how to provide process quality to the age group of children with whom you are involved. This is something under your control. You can provide higher quality through the interactions that you have with the children.
- Continue to educate yourself. As a teacher, you will always be learning alongside the children. Subscribe to a good early childhood magazine such as *Canadian Children* or *Young Children*. If you are a member of a provincial or territorial association, you will also automatically be a member of the Canadian Child Care Federation. You will receive not only the newsletters or publications from your own association, but also the magazine *Interaction* from the Canadian Child Care Federation.

STRESS

Web exercises

Stress is a condition that is related to a feeling of not being able to cope with the demands made upon an individual. Not all stress is harmful. Moderate levels of stress can be positive to encourage an individual to complete a job or solve a problem. However, high levels of stress are linked to a number of physical and mental health problems, including high blood pressure, cancer, chronic fatigue, violence, and substance abuse (Brym et al., 2003).

Stress is also related to poverty. "People [i]n lower classes experience relatively high stress levels because of their deprived and difficult living conditions" (Kessler et al., 1994, as cited in Brym et al., 2003, p. 455). In addition, it is more difficult for poorer individuals to find appropriate relief from stress. "Moreover, people higher up in the class structure are often able to turn stress off. They can, for instance, more easily take a few days off work or go on vacation. People in lower classes have fewer resources that allow them to cope with stress by turning it off (Cockerham, 1998; Epstein, 1998; Evans, 1999). Finally, because they lack other resources for coping with stress, people in lower classes are more likely to turn to other more dangerous coping mechanisms, such as tobacco, alcohol, and illegal drugs" (Brym et al., 2003, p. 455).

Childhood Stress

Childhood stress "involves any unusual demand—something new or different—that forces children to draw on energy reserves that exceed what they would normally require for dealing with ordinary events in their lives" (Hart et al., 1998, as cited in Kostelnik et al., 2002, p. 147). When children are exposed to stress that they consistently do not or cannot deal with, behavioural disorders or psychological vulnerability may be triggered. Children learn to cope with stress based on how they observe others dealing with stress. If they learn negative coping habits, these habits in turn serve to increase the child's stress level (Kostelnik et al., 2002). Here are some causes for children's stress:

- *Personality.* Some individuals find situations more stressful than others. Often these tend to be children with low self-esteem.
- *Family life.* Stressful situations within the family (e.g., family arguments, the death of a pet or family member) can cause resulting stress in children.
- *Divorce.* Young children particularly are susceptible to stress when parents separate. They do not understand the process of the separation/divorce and react only to the circumstances—varying stress levels of family members and adjusting to living with one parent rather than two. Additionally, there is stress involved in how often the child sees the other parent—regularly, sporadically, or never.
- *Death.* Personal death is again hard for young children to understand. As with separation or divorce, they will react to the stress levels around them.
- *Working family members.* In today's world, most family members work, and stress may be caused by families striving to juggle many things at the same time and not finding enough time to spend with children to meet their needs.
- *Abusive or neglectful situations.* Many children are exposed to family violence, drug abuse, and alcohol abuse: "They see adults in their lives who have lost control—adults involved in verbal abuse, insults, threats, rejection, humiliation, and degradation of one another. Most frightening is the physical aggression they see, but even less severe aggression such as psychological and behavioral problems can result in children developing psychological and behavioral problems" (Kostelnik et al., 2002, p. 156).
- *Poor quality child-care.* Crowded environments, punitive care, constant stimulation, and long hours watching TV are all potentially stressful situations.
- *Natural disasters, war, terrorism, and violence.* "Because children are thrown most out of balance when predictability and stability in their world is threatened, high levels of stress and anxiety caused by fear and ambiguity can result" (Kostelnik et al., 2002, p. 163).

childhood stress
"[I]nvolves any unusual demand—something new or different—that forces children to draw on energy reserves that exceed what they would normally require for dealing with ordinary events in their lives" (Hart et al., 1998, as cited in Kostelnik et al., 2002, p. 147).

Personal Reflections

I was shocked when one of my three-year-olds burst into tears when we said it was time to go outside to play. I sat down with her to try to calm her down. Finally, it emerged that she was afraid of being shot. I reassured that no one would be outside to shoot her. We looked out of the windows at the children playing; we looked for a person with a "big gun" but could not find one. Finally, we went outside to play. She stayed within my visual range the whole time she was outside. Occasionally, she would look anxiously around her. When her mother picked her up that evening, I told her about what had happened. She informed me that there was a good reason that her daughter was frightened. Her cousin attended the school in Springfield, Oregon, where the school shootings had taken place. They did not know for a long time whether her nephew had been shot. The family had watched TV and tried to get in touch with a family member in Oregon. Later that night, they finally found out that he was not hurt. The mother expressed shock to hear how much it had affected her daughter.

—Justin, early childhood educator

What Can You Do?

- Make sure that all activities and experiences are developmentally appropriate for all of the children.
- Set up the environment to provide for areas that are relaxing and that provide opportunities for children to be alone if they wish.
- Learn to recognize signs of stress in children, such as behaviour changes, withdrawal, moodiness, fear, or aggression.
- Offer support and comfort to the child as needed.
- Share concerns with family members and collaborate to find appropriate strategies together.

Family Stress

Work is the leading cause of stress throughout the world. In one study of office workers in 16 countries, including Canada, 54% of the respondents cited work as a current cause of stress in their lives and 29% cited money problems—which are also work-related, since one's job is the main source of income for most people. (Brym et al., 2003, p. 307)

Other causes of stress include
- *The hectic pace of work.* Individuals have less time to spend on leisure activities, and "the pace of work is becoming more frantic for those who are employed in the paid labour force" (Brym et al., 2003, p. 307).

- *The increased number of hours on the job in nonunionized workplaces.* "[M]ost corporate executives apparently think it is more profitable to push employees to work more hours rather than hire more workers and pay benefits for new employees" (Brym et al., 2003, p. 307). Consider the case of Tom and Mary. Juggling job, family, and home, Tom and Mary both leave the house at 7:00 A.M. They take turns in dropping off or picking up their two children (ages two and four) at daycare. They do not pick up their kids until 6:00 P.M. Tom has to leave the house two evenings a week because he is enrolled in an upgrading course. Mary works every other weekend, but gets two days off during the week.
- *Less protection against job-loss.* Because people work in nonunionized workplaces, "they are not in a position to demand reduced working hours and more vacation time" (Brym et al., 2003, p. 307).
- *Fewer mechanisms for coping with stress-related problems.* Options such as taking time off from work to stay home with a sick child are not always available.

Personal Reflections

I can remember how frantic I was when the child-care centre called me to say that my child was running a temperature. I knew I would be docked a day's pay if I left to pick her up. What if she was ill for longer? Each day I was not working was a day without pay. I was already struggling to make ends meet. I thought, "Couldn't they just keep her on a couch in the office? They can give her the Tylenol that I would give her. I really can't do anything different than what they would do." When I got to the daycare and saw her, I felt just awful. How could I have thought that I could leave my sick baby with anyone else? She had the chicken pox. I missed a week of work. I don't know what I will do without the money for that week.

—June, mother of a sick child

What Can You Do?

- There is little anyone in child-care can do to alleviate poverty-related problems except to be a sympathetic listener. Often knowing that someone is there to listen to your problems gives at least some relief. Someone cares.
- Be flexible. During stressful times, families might not arrive or pick up their children exactly on time. Try to work out a schedule that maximizes the centre's staff so that families' and staff members' times are appropriately set.
- Post some resources to help families access relevant help.

Early Childhood Educators

The job of an early childhood educator can be very stressful. Individuals cope with children and their problems and their family problems all day long. Learn to turn off these problems when you close the centre door. Look forward to your evening with family and friends.

Lack of adequate funding is always a stressful situation. Learn to use other resources in the community. There are many ways that you can improve quality even without the materials and equipment that you feel are needed. Involve families as partners. They often will help to raise funds and collect materials to help out.

Staff friction is another cause of stress. Try to talk through your problems with a staff member rather than letting them fester. Open communication can often be the key to a less stressful environment.

DIVERSITY

In many areas in Canada, early childhood settings include children from many different cultures. Each geographical area is unique in cultural representation (see Chapter 4). One of the child-care centres in Vancouver had children from ten different ethnic groups. Some of the children were recent immigrants and could not yet speak English. There were six different languages represented in this group. In another area, all the children were Native and all spoke the same language. Each of these environments should reflect the cultural backgrounds of the children. It is much easier to do this if you have a unified group. Providing sensitivity to diverse groups is challenging.

 ## Personal Reflections

Josée and her family moved from a large urban centre to a small town. She telephoned the local daycares to enroll her three children. She decided to visit two of the daycares. When she arrived at the first one, the caregiver seemed surprised to see her. When she told her that she was Dr. Brown, the caregiver responded by inviting her to come in. Josée was surprised by the lack of diversity expressed in the environment. When she brought up this matter, the caregiver quickly responded that since none of the children were from a visible minority until now, she didn't think that this was a needed priority. She quickly assured Josée that if her children were enrolled, things would change. When Josée visited the second centre, she was pleasantly surprised to see a variety of culturally sensitive materials available for the children to use. None of the children, however, were from a cultural minority.

SCHOOL READINESS

There is a lot of pressure on children, families, and early childhood educators to "get their children ready for school." This often means that children are expected to be engaged in some highly inappropriate tasks. These might include

- spending a lot of time on paper tasks such as colouring pictures, circling words, and tracing letters;
- listening to the teacher for large time blocks;
- being exposed to a prestructured curriculum or prestructured learning activities based on perceived general interests and needs; and
- being taught skills in a structured teacher-directed manner.

Research clearly shows that children who are motivated to learn, who enjoy learning, who have positive attitudes to learning, who are empowered to make choices, and who are engaged in active play in a developmentally appropriate environment are far more ready for school than we can ever teach them to be (Gestwicki, 2003; McCain & Mustard, 1999; Crowther, 2003).

 Personal Reflections

I can still remember when I was in preschool. I am in grade two now, and I like it lots more. In preschool we had to do a lot of boring stuff. I remember I really liked to read. But I always had to do other stuff like sorting letters and tracing letters.

—Christopher, school-aged child

What Can You Do?

- Post or send newsletters home that talk about the importance of play in young children's lives and how it helps them to learn.
- Document children's work and hang it in the hallway where families can see it.
- Provide families with resources that talk about the importance of developmentally appropriate practices.
- Arrange for and invite families and staff to attend some workshops on developmentally appropriate practices for young children.

SUMMARY

This chapter has presented a number of issues that may make the field of early childhood education seem very bleak and uninviting. However, as an early childhood educator you are in a prime position to make a real difference in a child's life. The research clearly shows that quality programs for young children make a lasting difference. Reflect upon the great strides that Schweinhart and Weikart (1986) were able to document. You will be in a position to positively influence the most critical years in a child's life.

Personal Reflections

Take a moment and reflect with me on one of my most favourite memories. Jordan was nonverbal and very shy when he first came to the program. His grandmother stayed for a while with him the first few times he came. Each time she left we would go to the window and wave good-bye. Jordan would silently stand at the window while big tears overflowed and slowly cruised down his cheek. He would allow me to take his hand and he would silently walk around the room with me. I carefully observed all his interests and made sure that these were available to him when he first came in. It broke my heart to see him so sad. I never thought that things would change. About four weeks later, he walked in and gave me a very tentative smile. I was so excited, I thought that finally we had won the battle. He went straight over to the window to wave good-bye. Then he put his head down. My heart sinking, I walked over to him, and this is what I saw (photo 9.1). These are the memories I cherish and tuck away to bring back when things get tough.

—Ingrid Crowther

KEY POINTS

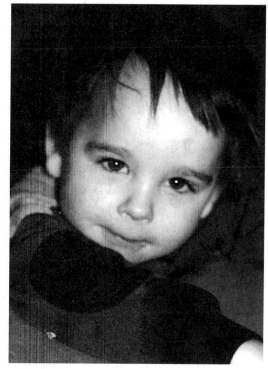

Photo 9.1

POVERTY

- There is a correlation between poverty and children's well-being.
- The federal government has a commitment to decrease child poverty.
- Poverty is linked to illness, depression, and dysfunctional family life.
- It's a major reason for social exclusion.

SOCIAL EXCLUSION

- Financial reasons—lack of quality daycare, affordable housing, and recreational activities.
- Special needs—lack of resources to sustain services, inadequate funding for inclusive daycare, limited access to resources and staff training, and negative attitudes.
- Accessibility of daycare—affected by poverty and lack of quality spaces.

QUALITY

- Structural quality involves group size, adult-to-child ratios, size of space, accessibility of indoor/outdoor spaces, and meeting minimum requirements.
- Contextual quality involves daycare centre's administrative structure, stability, policies and practices, lack of qualified staff, burnout, and high staff turnover.
- Adult work environment quality is affected by poor salaries, lack of benefits, and lack of adult space.
- Safety and basic care deals with the physical, social, emotional, cognitive, and health needs of every child.
- Process quality involves interactions between children and staff, and a variety of approaches.

STRESS

- Childhood stress can be caused by personality factors, death of a family member or pet, difficult family circumstances, abusive or neglectful situations, poor quality child-care, natural disasters, war, terrorism, and violence.
- Family stress is related to hectic work pace, increased hours of work, juggling various responsibilities, and limited mechanisms to cope with stress-related problems.

DIVERSITY

- Cultural diversity is area-specific.
- It can be uniform in some areas, but there is often a multi-ethnic representation in large urban centres. It can be hard to find resources for multi-ethnic settings.

SCHOOL READINESS

- Arbitrary expectations are sometimes placed on young children in order to promote school readiness. Children may be exposed to inappropriate tasks, prestructured activities and curriculum, and too many teacher-directed activities.
- We need to refocus on developmentally appropriate activities.

EXERCISES

1. Reflect upon your own life. Have there been any times when you have been in situations that might fall under poverty-like settings, or do you know of someone who was in such a situation? What have you learned from these experiences? How might you use this learning to help children and families who are living in poverty?

2. In a small group, discuss why poverty has such a profound effect on a child's overall well-being.

3. Define what is meant by social exclusion. Using the chart below, list the various aspects of social exclusion. Can you think of any others?

Social Exclusion Factors	
OVERALL FACTOR	SOCIAL EXCLUSION
Poverty	
Special Needs	
Accessibility	

4. In a small group, discuss and list which aspects of quality are usually included in the licensing of a daycare. Explain why these aspects are generally used.

5. You are working in a daycare situation. You start at 7:00 or 8:00 A.M. and end your day at 5:00 or 6:00 P.M. You have no scheduled breaks in the morning or in the afternoon. You are given an hour for lunch, but are expected to take that hour after the children have had their lunch. You feel that you should be able to take a break. How might you rearrange the day to be able to work in breaks for everyone? You do have a cook and a program supervisor as additional staff. There are three rooms of children, each requiring two staff members per room.

6. Quality in child-care is an interaction of all factors. Describe how quality might be affected by each of the following dimensions of quality:

   a) structural
   b) contextual
   c) adult work environment
   d) safety and basic care
   e) process

7. Define what is meant by process quality. List at least ten aspects of quality interactions that you might implement with one age group of choice in a daycare setting.

8. Define stress. Reflect upon your personal experiences. What types of situations cause you stress? Compare your reflections with those of other individuals. How similar are you? How closely do they compare to stress for children, for families, or for early childhood educators? How are they different?

9. You noticed that the behaviour of one of the preschool children has drastically changed. The child is more withdrawn and seems to be reluctant to participate in activities. You notice that the child seems very tired. You know that the family is going through a financial crisis. You do not want to add to their stress, but feel you must discuss what is happening to their child. What strategies might you use to talk to the family about this situation?

10. Why is the concept of getting children ready for school an inappropriate concept for young children?

REFERENCES

Begly, S. (1997). How to Build a Baby's Brain. *Newsweek, 28,* 28–32.

Brym, R., Lie, J., Nelson, A., Guppy, N., & McCormick, C. (2003). *Sociology: Your Compass for a New World.* Scarborough, ON: Thomson Nelson.

Child & Family. (2003). Children With Special Needs. Child and Family Canada [On-line]. Available: http://www.cfc-efc.ca/menu/specneed_en.htm.

Cleveland, G., Colley, S., Friendly, M., & Lero, D. (2003). *The State of Data on Early Childhood Education and Care in Canada: National Data Project Final Report.* Toronto, ON: Childcare Resource and Research Unit.

Cockerham, W. (1998). *Medical Sociology* (7th ed.). Upper Saddle River, NJ: Prentice-Hall.

Cooke, K. (1986). *Report of the Task Force on Child Care.* Ottawa, ON: Canada Government Publishing Centre.

Crowther, I. (2003). *Creating Effective Learning Environments.* Scarborough, ON: Nelson Thomson Learning.

Elder, E., & Robertson, P. (2002). Diversity or Disparity? Early Childhood Education and Care in Canada (ECEC). Campaign 2000 [On-line]. Available: http://www.campaign2000.ca/.

Elder, E., & Robertson, P. (2003). Poverty Amidst Prosperity: Building a Canada for All Children. Campaign 2000 [On-line]. Available: http://www.campaign2000.ca/.

Epstein, H. (1998). Life and Death on the Social Ladder. *New York Review of Books, 45,* 26–30.

Evans, R. (1999). Social Inequalities in Health. *Horizons* (Policy Research Secretariat, Government of Canada), *2,* 6–7.

Friendly, M., & Lero, D. (2002). *Social Inclusion Through Early Childhood Education and Care.* Toronto, ON: Laidlaw Foundation.

Gestwicki, C. (2003). *Developmentally Appropriate Practices* (2nd ed.). Scarborough, ON: Nelson Canada.

Goelman, H., Doherty, G., Lero, D., LaGrange, A., & Tougas, J. (2000). *You Bet I Care! Caring and Learning Environments: Quality in Child Care Centres Across Canada.* Guelph, ON: Centre for Families, Work and Well-Being, University of Guelph.

Hanvey, L. (2003). *The Progress of Canada's Children.* Ottawa, ON: Canadian Council on Social Development.

Hart, C., Burts, D., Durland, M., Charlesworth, R., DeWolf, M., & Fleege, P. (1998). Stress Behaviors and Activity Type Participation of Preschoolers in More or Less Developmentally Appropriate Classrooms: SES and Sex Differences. *Journal of Research in Childhood Education, 12,* 176–196.

Hertzman, C. (2002). *Leave No Child Behind! Social Exclusion and Child Development.* Toronto, ON: Laidlaw Foundation.

Hinckle, P. (1991). The Best Schools in the World. *Newsweek,* 50–64.

Just Income Coalition. (2004). Low Income Facts. Available: http://www.justincome.ca/facts/ (accessed May 17, 2004).

Kessler, R., McGonagle, K., Zhao, C., Nelson, C., Hughes, M., Eshleman, S., et al. (1994). Lifetime and 12-Month Prevalence of DSM-III-R Psychiatric Disorders in the United States. *Archives of General Psychiatry, 51,* 8–19.

Kostelnik, M., Soderman, A., Stein, L., & Gregory, K. (2002). *Guiding Children's Social Development: Theory to Practice* (4th ed.). Albany, NY: Delmar.

McCain, M., & Mustard, F. (1999). *Early Years Study: Final Report.* Toronto, ON: Publications Ontario.

Schweinhart, L., & Weikart, J. (1986). Lasting Differences: The High/Scope Preschool Curriculum Comparison Study Through Age 23. *Early Childhood Education Research Quarterly, 1,* 15–45.

Shore, R. (1997). *Rethinking the Brain.* New York, NY: Families and Work Institute.

REGULATION FOR CHILD-CARE IN CANADA

CHAPTER 10

CHAPTER OUTLINE

*"Each of Canada's 14 jurisdictions—
10 provinces, three territories and the
federal government—has its own
approach to early childhood education
and care. Each has a number of programs
for 'care,' 'education' and for meeting
other objectives such as ameliorating the
effects of poverty and supporting parents.
Overall, Canada does not have a national
strategy for early childhood education
and care." (Friendly, Beach, & Turiano,
2002a, p. 1)*

Chapter Outcomes

After reading this chapter, the reader will

1. Identify various child-care options in Canada.

2. Discuss why the qualifications of early childhood educators influence the overall quality of the program for young children.

3. Describe and explain the importance of licensing criteria in Canada.

4. Compare and contrast the differences in child-care and legislative requirements for infants, toddlers, preschoolers, and school-aged children.

5. Identify strategies to meet requirements for the various age groups (infants, toddlers, preschoolers, and school-aged children).

6. Define multi-age groupings.

7. Identify advantages of multi-age groupings.

INTRODUCTION

Photo 10.1

The care of young children in Canada is regulated according to the ages of the children—infants, toddlers, preschoolers, and school-aged children. There are a number of regulated program options:

- *Nursery school or preschool.* Care is provided for children for less than three hours per day.
- *Centre-based full-day child-care.* Care and supervision of children for more than three hours per day, but less than 13–24 consecutive hours—usually eight or nine hours per day.
- *Regulated family child-care.* Family child-care homes or family day homes have three to eight children (may or may not include caregiver's own children) in care within a home environment that is supervised by a licensed agency.
- *Nonregulated family child-care.* Family child-care homes and family day homes have three to eight children (may or may not include caregiver's own children) in care within a home environment that is not supervised by a licensed agency.
- *Group family care.* Care is provided in a home by two caregivers with maximum group size of 12 children, with no more than three children under the age of two. This kind of facility may be regulated or nonregulated.
- *School-aged care.* Provides services outside school hours, including before- and after-school hours and sometimes lunch hours.
- *Family resource centres.* Services provided for families include drop-in programs, resource lending libraries, playgroups, training opportunities, and workshops.
- *Child development centres and Head Start programs.* These programs for "at risk" children help to prepare them for entry to school.
- *Emergency care.* These programs, which are to be used for no more than 72 hours per month, are for up to 12 children under three years of age or up to 25 children over three years of age.
- *Child-minding.* This type of service is for up to three hours of care for more than two days a week for children 18 months to entry into Grade 1. It can include up to 20 children if they are over three years.

- *Occasional centres.* These centres provide casual care for more than three infants or more than five preschoolers for less than 13–24 consecutive hours per week.
- *Kindergarten programs.* Programs for four- to five-year-olds, under the jurisdiction of the local school boards.

Across Canada, most of the parents or guardians of children aged three to five work outside the home, and 70 percent of these children are in unregulated care. Care in these cases may be provided by an extended family member (e.g., an aunt, grandparent, or cousin), an unregulated child-care provider, or a full-time nanny, while older children may be left alone without supervision. Either this care is in the home or the child is dropped off at the home of the caregiver.

> Organized ECEC services across Canada are in short supply or—like public Kindergarten—are not **labour-force sensitive**. Some—like regulated child care—are too costly for ordinary families or not always sufficiently high quality to be "developmental." Many young school-aged children are alone after school or attend recreational or other community programs that are not intended to provide "care." (Friendly, Beach, & Turiano, 2002b, p. 1)

Although the responsibility for setting the requirements of care is generally under the jurisdiction of the provinces and territories, there are some programs for which the federal government is responsible. These include child-minding programs for immigrant parents learning English, military family resource programs, Aboriginal early childhood education programs, and community action programs for children. Additionally, some of the funding for early childhood programs comes under federal jurisdiction, including child-care expense deductions and maternity/parental leave benefits.

labour-force sensitive
Term that applies to programs that meet the needs of working families; for example, half-day kindergarten programs require additional care for children for the other half day and, therefore, do not meet the needs of families who work full-time.

REGULATIONS

In every child-care centre across Canada, regulations have been established to set the standards for health and safety requirements for children. Some of these requirements include qualifications of staff and licensing criteria.

Web exercises

Qualifications

Regulations for child-care vary greatly across Canada. Regulations include requirements for licensing, monitoring and enforcement, staff qualifications, centre size, child-to-adult ratios and group size, parent involvement, accommodation of special needs, and funding. Regulations that are specific to various age groups will be covered later in the chapter.

One of the indicators of quality care for young children is the qualification of the caregiver. "Quality childcare employs graduates in early childhood education and care as primary care providers" (Mayer, 1994, p. 3). A child-care provider who has appropriate education will be able to apply skills and knowledge gained to his or her practice in order to provide better quality care to the children within the program. Some of these skills include

- sufficient knowledge of child development to know what materials to provide and how to set up the environment to maximize interactions (photo 10.1);
- knowledge and skill in observation to plan and implement appropriate learning experiences for children (photo 10.2);

Photo 10.2

Photo 10.3

Photo 10.4

- skill in interacting with children and adults (photo 10.3);
- skill in setting up an appropriate learning environment (photo 10.4); and
- skills to ensure health and safety of children (photo 10.5).

Qualifications of child-care providers vary greatly across Canada. Knowledge about qualification requirements will help early childhood educators to

- transfer jobs from one jurisdiction to another;
- advocate for more national training standards; and
- compare standards across Canada in order to advocate for the improvement of training standards in the individual's own jurisdiction.

As identified previously, child-care training is one of the dimensions that leads to greater quality in working with young children. The more knowledgeable a child-care provider is, the better that individual is able to meet the diverse needs of children and families. Table 10.1 provides information about training requirements across Canada.

Licensing Criteria

All provinces and territories specifically define what is needed to license a centre and how to maintain that licence. Requirements vary from jurisdiction to jurisdiction, but all identify the following criteria for licensing:

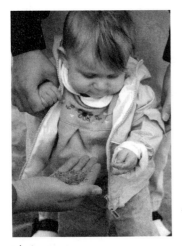

Photo 10.5

- Number of children in regulated care (see Tables 10.2, 10.4, 10.5, and 10.6 on pages 289–90, 295, 308, and 309).
- Number of children in unregulated care. Numbers vary from two jurisdictions that have no requirement specified to four jurisdictions that have a maximum of six children including caregiver's own children.
- Type and delivery of program for children.
- Health and safety requirements.
- Size of physical space. Size requirements vary throughout Canada. Some jurisdictions have no requirements listed, and some have 2 m^2 to 5 m^2 of indoor space per child and 4.5 m^2 to 5.6 m^2 of outdoor space per child. Size requirements may also vary for different age groups.
- Separation of space. Separation requirements vary throughout Canada—usually separation of space is required for different age groups in both indoor and outdoor play spaces.
- Evidence of liability insurance coverage.
- Administrative policies and procedures. These include record keeping, emergency procedures, health procedures, and staff requirements.

Child-Care in Canada Regulations—Staff Qualifications

Jurisdiction	Qualifications
Alberta	• Level 3—two-year ECE diploma from Alberta public college or equivalent or a four-year bachelor of education with a major in ECE • Level 2—one-year ECE diploma from Alberta public college or equivalent or a four-year bachelor of elementary education • Level 1—government orientation course or equivalent course of a minimum of 50 hours • Directors—level 3 or exemption • One in four staff members have level 2, and all other staff have level 1 • Family day homes—not licensed; no training required

British Columbia	• ECE basic—10 months training with 500 hours of supervised work
	• Specialization in infant/toddler care, and special needs
	• Ages of children determine the qualifications of staff (specialized training to work with infants, for example)
	• Regulated family child-care—caregiver must
	  – be at least 19 years of age
	  – have a first-aid certificate
	  – have completed one course in care of children or have relevant work experience

Manitoba	• ECE III—approved ECE III program and a recognized certificate program or an approved degree from an approved university • ECE II—approved diploma in child-care from recognized community college or completion of Child Care Competency-Based Assessment (CBA) program • Child Care Assistant (CCA)—not eligible for classification as ECE II or III • Two-thirds of full-time centre staff have ECE II or III • Director—ECE III and one year experience • All staff must be at least 18 years old and have first-aid and CPR training
New Brunswick	• Supervisor and one full-time staff—at least one year early childhood development diploma or university degree in child studies • Professional development—30 hours every three years • Director, designate, or one in four staff require one year early childhood training or equivalent • Staff between 16 and 19 years of age must be supervised by primary staff member who is at least 19 years old • All staff must have first-aid training
Newfoundland and Labrador	• Level 2—requires two-year diploma in ECE with certification for a particular age group • Level 1—requires one-year certificate in ECE with certification for a particular age group • Entry level—orientation course of 30–60 hours depending on age group staff is working with • Each centre must have two individuals with level 2 for particular age group and have two or more years of experience; one level 1 per age group; and all other staff must have minimum training • Professional development—30 hours every three years • Regulated family child-care • Entry-level certification

(cont'd)

Child-Care in Canada Regulations—Staff Qualifications

Jurisdiction	Qualifications

Northwest Territories	• Child-care staff members must
	  – be at least 19 years of age
	  – have a first-aid certificate
	  – have a clear criminal record
	• Regulated family child-care (same as child-care staff members)

Nova Scotia	• Director/supervisor and/or two-thirds of staff must have completed training in early childhood or equivalent
	• Staff members must have two years experience, one course, and 35-hour workshop on child development and curriculum
	• All staff must have current first-aid training
	• All staff must have up-to-date child abuse registry check
	• Regulated family child-care providers must
	  – be at least 18 years of age
	  – be screened through child abuse registry
	  – have a criminal reference check

Nunavut	• Child-care centre staff members must
	  – be at least 19 years of age
	  – have a first-aid certificate
	  – represent cultural backgrounds of children
	• Regulated family child-care providers must
	  – have a first-aid certificate
	  – represent cultural background of children

Ontario	• Supervisors must
	  – have a two-year ECE diploma from approved college of applied arts and technology (CAAT) or equivalent
	  – have two years experience with same aged children as daycare employing supervisor
	• One staff person with each group of children must have two-year ECE diploma from approved college program or equivalent
	• Educational requirements may be waived for directors and staff by Ministry Director
	• Regulated home child-care providers must
	  – be at least 18 years old
	  – have standard first-aid certificate if working with children with special needs
	  – receive training in early childhood education

Prince Edward Island	• Supervisor and one full-time staff in each program—must have at least a one-year early childhood development diploma or university child study degree
	• Professional development—30 hours every three years
	• Regulated family child-care providers must
	  – have a 30-hour training program
	  – have two letters of reference
	  – have a current first-aid certificate

Child-Care in Canada Regulations—Staff Qualifications

Jurisdiction	Qualifications
Quebec	• Two-thirds of staff under Centre de la petite enfance (CPE) have college diplomas or university degrees in ECE • Garderies—one-third of the staff working with the children must have a college diploma or university degree in ECE • Regulated family child-care providers must – have 45 hours in training for child development, health, safety issues, and organization and leadership in a "life environment" – have first-aid training
Saskatchewan	• ECE III—two-year diploma in ECE or equivalent • ECE II—one-year certificate in ECE or equivalent • ECE I—120-hour child-care orientation course (at community college) or equivalent • Directors must exceed ECE III qualifications • All staff working 65 hours or more per month must have at least ECE I • By Jan. 1, 2005, 30% of staff must have ECE II or equivalent • By Jan. 1, 2007, a further 20% of staff must have ECE III or equivalent • All staff must have first aid and CPR training • Regulated family child-care providers must – be at least 18 years old – complete orientation session – have first-aid and CPR training – complete 6 hours of professional development per year – complete a 40-hour Introduction to ECE course • In group family child-care homes, – all staff must have ECE III or must be committed to receive that designation within three years – assistants must have first-aid and CPR training – staff must have 6 hours of professional development course each licensing year
Yukon	• Child Care Worker III—must have two or more years training in early childhood development or equivalent from a recognized college or university • Child Care Worker II A—must have 1447 course hours in ECD • Child Care Worker II—must have one-year training in ECD or equivalent • Child Care Worker I A—must have 405 course hours in ECD • Child Care Worker I—must have 60-hour introduction to ECD or equivalent • 50% of staff must meet or exceed Child Care Worker I qualifications (implemented in 1997) • 30% of staff must meet or exceed Child Care Worker II qualifications (implemented in 1999) • 20% of staff must meet or exceed Child Care Worker III qualifications (implemented in 2000)

Source: Friendly et al., 2002a; and the official child-care legislation in each jurisdiction.

- Monitoring procedures. In most jurisdictions, this requires inspections conducted by a local or regional specialist. During an inspection, the specialists follow criteria as set out on a licensing checklist. Checks are also made for compliance with health inspection requirements, safety requirements, and fire safety inspections. Centres may have the following recommendations made after an inspection occurs:
  - All requirements met.
  - Some changes to be made (usually followed by a certain number of days in which these revisions must be made and submitted).
  - Failure to meet requirements—the centre receives a warning and timelines to make the required changes to meet required expectations.

  Centres that have received an unsatisfactory licensing review and have failed to make the required changes may face closure. Closure of the centre usually occurs if children are perceived to be in danger, or if the centre has been repeatedly noncompliant.
- Centre size. Each licensed daycare facility has a maximum number of children for whom the centre may be licensed. This again varies from jurisdiction to jurisdiction. Requirements range from no requirements specified to 90 children within one centre.
- Special needs. All jurisdictions in Canada advocate that children with special needs should be in inclusive settings. Variance in the delivery of services across the country are as follows:
  - Three jurisdictions have no written policies for dealing with children with special needs.
  - Training of individuals working with children with special needs ranges from no training required to resource consultant training, consisting of additional recognized post-secondary training.
  - Services may be provided on the basis of a referral or diagnosis of special needs.
  - Services are usually provided within regular daycare settings with resource consultant support, or increased funding to the centre to help with integration, or on a contract basis to help support inclusive care.

- Parent involvement. Parent involvement may be specified directly or may not be specified at all. If specified, parent involvement might be
  - Participation on child-care boards—requirement that one-fifth to two-thirds of the board members be parents.
  - Written plans to indicate how parents will be involved in the program.
  - Parent advisory committees.

In summary, policies for child-care in Canada have been varied and most often concerned the regulation of physical safety of young children. Over time, policies in the different jurisdictions have begun to change to include more quality issues, such as the education of caregivers. Note the changes in New Brunswick, Quebec, Saskatchewan, and the Yukon (see Table 10.1 on pages 283–85). It is critical to continue to advocate for changes across Canada. "The quality of ECEC services is absolutely critical in determining whether they are educational and enhance child development or are merely 'care' that supports parental employment. Indeed, 'the positive relation between child care quality and virtually every facet of children's development that has been studied is one of the most consistent findings in developmental science" (Shonkoff & Phillips, 2001, p. 313).

In addition to staff qualification and to licensing criteria, there are a number of regulations and guidelines in place for working with specific age groups (infants, toddlers, preschoolers, and school-aged children), and with multi-age grouping.

INFANT PROGRAMS

During the early years of development, there are a number of critical or sensitive periods. These periods provide windows of opportunity during which learning opportunities are maximized. With appropriate stimulation, the child's brain becomes "wired" to create stable long-lasting structures:

Web exercises

> In the first few months of life, the infant brain produces trillions of connections between neurons. By the age of two, a child's brain contains twice as many synapses or connections and consumes twice as much energy as the brain of a normal adult. Research has shown that by providing infants with appropriate cognitive, emotional, physical, and language stimulation, a "miraculous process of wiring their brain for a lifetime of learning" begins. (Watson et al., 2000, p. 27)

What Do Infants Need?

Consider the following:

- Nicole had been restless. Her grandfather picked her up. He interacted with her by holding her in front of him. He spoke to her, using soft language in higher tones and strong facial expressions. Nicole closely watched his face and cooed and laughed at him (photo 10.6). Infants need "key adults to respond to them promptly, consistently, and warmly, interacting with them, giving them language, face to face, so they can begin to understand the process of human communication" (Gestwicki, 1999, p. 69).

- Lauren was in a daycare that encouraged family members to participate whenever they could. Her father often used his lunch hour to visit Lauren. He interacted with her by providing interesting, safe choices for her to explore using all her senses—touching, listening, and reaching, grasping, and turning the toy around to look at it from all different perspectives and talking about the object (photo 10.7)—"It is soo soft"—when she held it up to her face. Infants flourish in environments that have warm and caring caregivers who are sensitive to the infant's and family's needs. These environments should provide opportunities for active participation for safe, **sensorimotor exploration** (learning by using all the senses—touching, grasping, moving, listening, and interacting with others).

sensorimotor exploration
Learning by using all the senses—including touching, grasping, movement, listening, and interacting with others.

Photo 10.6

Photo 10.7

trustworthy environment
An environment that is set up to encourage safe exploration, to meet all the infants' needs (cognitive, physical, emotional, motor, and communication), to provide flexible schedules, and to provide predictable routines.

Photo 10.8

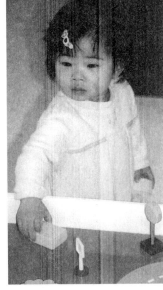

Photo 10.9

Photo 10.10

Photo 10.11

Photo 10.12

- Lara came to her daycare with a schedule in place—sleeping, waking, toileting, active play, eating. "Babies must not be required to fit into an arbitrarily drawn schedule; each child's daily schedule will be based on particular needs, temperament, and natural rhythms" (Gestwicki, 1999, p. 68). Lara had opportunities to practise similar skills in indoor and outdoor environments (photo 10.8).

In summary, infants need a **trustworthy environment** (safe to explore, meets the infant's needs and schedule, and has predictable routines) that has the following (Gestwicki, 1999):

- Separate spaces for sleeping, active play (both indoors and outdoors), and toileting (see Figure 10.1 on pages 292–93).
- Nurturing, caring caregivers who are well trained to provide experiences that enhance all areas of infant development—cognitive, social, emotional, physical, and language (photo 10.9).
- Sufficient adult-to-child ratios (see Table 10.2 on pages 289–90). The larger the number of infants a caregiver has to care for, the less likely it is that the infants will get the timely attention and care that are critical for building a trusting relationship.
- Learning areas that are developmentally appropriate for infants (photo 10.9).
- A system that coordinates communication with all partners. Providing a system of communication helps families gain perspective about their child's day and can provide an opportunity for discussion between caregivers and family members (see Table 10.3 on page 291).
- An environment that is predictable and familiar—avoid frequent major room changes.
- An environment that is safe to explore. It is necessary to have sturdy furniture and equipment that will not tip when used as support (photo 10.10) and is clear of sharp objects (photo 10.11); structures that are free from protruding parts and sharp corners (photo 10.12); toys that are safe to mouth and manipulate (photo 10.13); and an environment clear of obstructions to avoid such dangers as pinching of fingers or falling against sharp corners.

Infant Programs—Legislative Requirements in Canada

Jurisdiction	Adult-to-Child Ratios	Group Size	Other Considerations
Alberta	0–12 mos.—1:3 13–18 mos.—1:4	6 8	• Ratios are larger for drop-in centres (1:5) and group size is 10 • Infants must have separate crib in which to sleep • Outdoor play space not less than 2 m² per child
British Columbia	0–3 yrs.—1:4	12	• Specialized training to work with infants • Cribs are required for infants shorter than 90 cm or infants who are unable to climb out of crib unaided • Crib mattress not less than 7.5 cm thick
Manitoba	12 wks.–1 yr.—1:3 1–2 yrs.—1:4	6 8	• Infants younger than 12 weeks are only admitted with director approval • Written plan how space is to be used to meet infants' developmental needs for sleep and play • Infants must be put to sleep on back or side • Bathing facilities must be available for children under 18 months
New Brunswick	0–2 yrs.—1:3	9	• None identified
Newfoundland and Labrador	0–24 mos.—1:3	6	• Separate guidelines for program standards • Separate sleep room • No walkers or jumping apparatus • High chairs with safety belts • Separate cribs or cots • Identified diapering procedures • Individual eating/sleeping schedule • Staff required to have infant/toddler training course and minimum Level I
Northwest Territories	0–12 mos.—1:3 13–24 mos.—1:4	6 8	• Sleeping area separated from older children • High chair with safety harness for infants who cannot sit independently • Bathing facilities for children under 18 mos.
Nova Scotia	0–17 mos.—1:4	Not specified	• Separated from older age groups • Specification of daily record requirements • Must be on first floor • Separate sleeping area for infants • Cribs must comply with Hazardous Products Act • Strollers must have sun shades • Playpens, jolly jumpers, and walkers are not permitted • All staff required to have infant CPR course
Nunavut	0–12 mos.—1:3 13–24 mos.—1:4	6 8	• Sleeping area separated from older children • High chair with safety harness for infants who cannot sit independently • Bathing facilities for children under 18 mos.

Infant Programs—Legislative Requirements in Canada

Jurisdiction	Adult-to-Child Ratios	Group Size	Other Considerations
Ontario	0–18 mos.—3:10	10	• Separate play spaces indoors and outdoors • Separate sleep area • Cribs, cradles, and playpens meet standards of Hazardous Products Act
Prince Edward Island	0–2 yrs.—1:3	6	• Sturdy change table with disposable paper • Nap room with infant monitoring system • Separation from other age groups for 75% of day
Quebec	0–18 mos.—1:5	Not specified	• Barriers, carriages, and strollers must comply with Hazardous Product Act • A separate room for every 15 children, and separate rooms for sleeping and playing • Specific directions for routine care of infants • 4 m² of space per child
Saskatchewan	0–18 mos.—1:3	6	• 3.7 m² usable floor space per infant • At least 1.4 m² of sleeping space per infant • Sleeping area must be separate from other areas
Yukon	0–18 mos.—1:4	8	• Separation of space for sleeping • Safety harness must be used in high chair

Photo 10.13

Photo 10.14

• Comfortable furniture for adults and children. This will help to nurture attachment between infants and caregivers or other family members. Rachel, on one of her non-school days, came to visit the infant program to read to her brother and other children (photo 10.14).

• Knowledge of the various legislation requirements across Canada. This will help practitioners to

– ensure that licensing requirements have been met;
– identify what other skills they might need;
– provide information about what is needed to work in another jurisdiction; and
– advocate for changes to improve the quality of children's experiences by comparing requirements to other jurisdictions.

What Can You Do?

- In most instances there will be more than one caregiver in the room, as most programs will have two groups of infants. Often only one caregiver will be involved in a one-to-one interaction with an infant, leaving the second caregiver free to respond to the needs of another child. Establish careful teamwork to facilitate taking care of the needs of the infants.
- Arrange the room so that the adult can always see all of the infants. For example, Teresa, the infant caregiver, was giving Jamie his bottle. She noticed that Sarah, who was near her, was starting to become fussy. She looked at Sarah and said, "Sarah, I am giving Jamie his bottle. He is very hungry. Aren't you, Jamie?" As she talked, she shifted her attention from one child to the other. Sarah calmed down and listened to Teresa. Jonathan heard Teresa talking. He immediately crawled over to listen. Teresa changed her strategy to also include Jonathan.
- Ensure that you know the individual schedules of each infant, so that times of conflict can be avoided. The two caregivers can identify potential problems and plan strategies ahead of time to prevent problems.
- Make sure that all materials for all routines (toileting, eating, sleeping) are ready and easily accessible to minimize the time lost in locating necessary items.

■ TABLE 10.3

Communication System—Infants and Toddlers

Strategy	Description
Nutrition	<ul><li>Post weekly menus</li><li>Record child's nutritional intake on chart accessible to families and staff</li></ul>
Symptoms of ill health	<ul><li>Record any symptoms and action taken when child is not feeling well</li></ul>
Daily record	<ul><li>Record daily activities—activities engaged in, milestones reached, special interests, unusual behaviours</li><li>Record daily routines—sleep, bowel movements</li><li>Leave space for parent comments</li><li>Assign one part of chart for parents to record routines and activities at home</li></ul>
Posting of learning activities	<ul><li>Create interactive bulletin board to provide information about daily and weekly learning activities with room for family suggestions</li></ul>

Figure 10.1

Infant Play Room

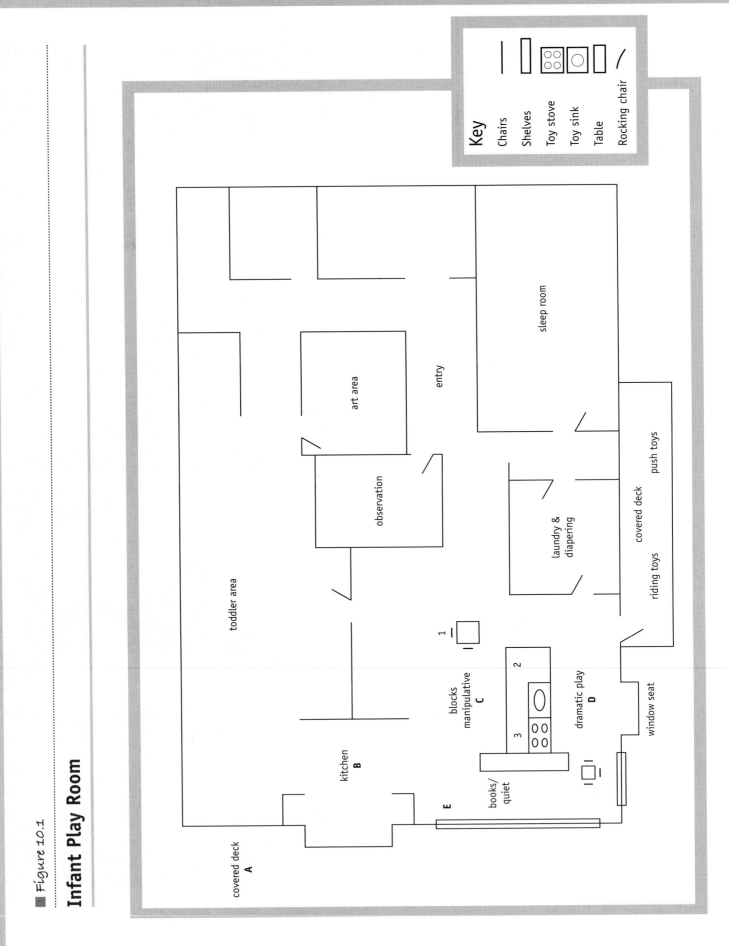

Key

Chairs	
Shelves	
Toy stove	
Toy sink	
Table	
Rocking chair	

covered deck
A

toddler area

kitchen
B

art area

observation

entry

sleep room

blocks
manipulative
C

books/
quiet
E

dramatic play
D

window seat

laundry &
diapering

riding toys

covered deck

push toys

1

2

3

■ **Figure 10.1** (continued)

Infant Play Room

Area A - Photo A
(Shared by infants/toddlers)
Outdoor - Deck area

Area D - Photo D

Area B - Photo B

Area C - Photo C

Area E - Photo E
Quiet area
Books

Photo 10.15

Photo 10.16

Photo 10.17

TODDLER PROGRAMS

Web exercises

Toddlers spend most of their waking hours walking, running, jumping, and being on the move (photo 10.15). Much of their play is imitative. They love to use equipment and toys they have observed others use—but in their own particular style (photo 10.16). Toddlers are intensely curious about the world around them. They are continually touching and examining items closely (photo 10.17). Toddlers use their developing manipulative skills to discover the properties of items they touch (photo 10.18). Toddlers have not yet learned to share and often declare that the things they have are exclusively theirs (photo 10.19). They often move from activity to activity—as soon as their attention is attracted, they move on to that activity.

Lara had been building and knocking towers down (photo 10.20). One of her blocks fell down and rolled toward the bookshelf. She went over to pick it up, but noticed a book lying on the floor. She promptly sat down and looked at the book. While she was looking at the book, she heard the children singing and pretending to jump into paper puddles taped to the floor. She promptly dropped her book and joined the children in the music activity. One of the teachers was reading a story to two children in another part of the room. At one point the toddlers excitedly clapped their hands and laughed loudly. Lara stopped and looked around. She went over to the activity, sat down, and listened to the story.

Toddlers spend about 16 percent of their time in social activities (White, 1995), alternating between seeking physical contact and attention from adults and resisting them. Yet, ambivalent as their social responses to loved adults are, toddlers resist and protest separation. Toddlers may show brief and transitory interest in peers, but mainly they use other toddlers as another vehicle for asserting self or conducting research. Toddlers may respond aggressively to others—biting, grabbing, hitting. Although they are not yet very verbal, they manage to express strong emotions both physically and loudly. (Gestwicki, 1999, p. 82)

Photo 10.18

Toddler Programs—Legislative Requirements in Canada

Jurisdiction	Adult-to-Child Ratios	Group Size	Other Considerations
Alberta	19–35 mos.—1:6	12	• Ratio for drop-in-centres is 1:8, and maximum group size is 16
British Columbia	0–3 yrs.—1:4	12	• Specialized training for this age group • Clean washable mattress at least 7.5 cm thick, or cot
Manitoba	1–2 yrs.—1:4 2–3 yrs.—1:6	8 12	• 2.3 m² space required per child • Separate sleeping space
Newfoundland and Labrador	0–24 mos.—1:3 25–36 mos.—1:5	6 10	• Staff training in infant/toddler orientation • Minimum of Level I
Northwest Territories	13–24 mos.—1:4 25–35 mos.—1:6	8 12	• Not specified
Nova Scotia	17 mos.–5 yrs.—1:7	Not specified	• Daily record requirements for routines and activities • Toddlers may not be above 2nd floor • Toys must be disinfected and checked for broken parts
Nunavut	13–24 mos.—1:4 25–35 mos.—1:6	8 12	• Similar requirements to those for the Northwest Territories (same act used for both jurisdictions)
Ontario	18 mos.–2 yrs.—1:5	15	• Separate play space both indoors and outdoors
Quebec	18 mos.–3yrs.—1:8	Not specified	• 2.75 m² space required per child • Rooms must be equipped with diaper-changing table of suitable height near a washbasin
Saskatchewan	18–30 mos.—1:5	10	• Minimum 3.25 m² of usable floor space per child
Yukon	18 mos.–2 yrs.— 1:6	12	• Minimum 2.75 m² of free usable space per child

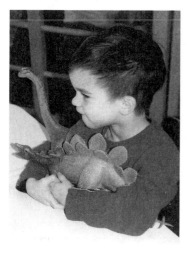

Photo 10.19

Photo 10.20

Photo 10.21

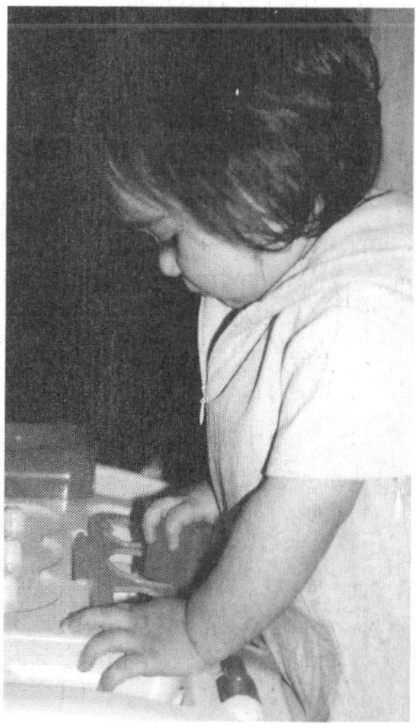

Photo 10.22

Photo 10.23

What Do Toddlers Need?

Toddlers, like infants, need a trustworthy environment to actively explore using all their senses and encourage their budding need for independence. Toddlers need

- An environment that supports their need to be independent—child-sized furniture, materials within reach of toddlers, and encouragement to make individual choices (photo 10.21).
- Separate areas for toileting, active play indoors, and outdoor play (see Figure 10.2 on pages 298–301).
- Caring caregivers who are well trained to provide experiences that enhance toddlers' need to be autonomous in all areas of development (cognitive, social, emotional, physical, and language; see Figure 10.2).
- Sufficient adult-to-child ratios (see Table 10.4 on page 295).
- Learning areas that are developmentally appropriate for toddlers (photo 10.22).
- A system that coordinates communication with all partners (see Table 10.3 on page 291).
- An environment that is predictable and familiar, with regular routines. Avoid frequent major room changes. Toddlers learn to know what to expect, and initiate self-help routines such as washing hands before meals or after toileting.
- A safe environment to explore. It is necessary to have sturdy furniture and equipment that will not tip (photo 10.23); play areas clear of clutter to avoid tripping or falling (photo 10.24); structures that are free from protruding parts and sharp corners (photo 10.25); toys and materials that encourage manipulation (photos 10.20, 10.21, 10.22, 10.24); and an environment clear of obstruction to avoid such dangers as pinching of fingers, falling against sharp corners, or tripping over items such as toys.

What Can You Do?

- Coordinate the efforts between you and your co-worker to be able to monitor the learning environment at all times. Some simple strategies include the following:
  - each adult is placed in such a way that the total learning environment can be scanned by the two individuals;
  - the body position of each adult always faces the group of children (backs never to the group); and
  - the adults listen to signals that might predict a problem, such as raised voices or sudden loud noises.
- When setting up the learning environment, provide more than one of each toy. Duplicate toys should be identical. Keep additional toys handy, so that you can quickly give a child the same toy if needed.
- Limit the number of choices in the environment. Toddlers get confused by too many choices. A toddler will tend to flit from activity to activity.
- Remember that toddlers like to "dump." Avoid large containers with lots of toys in them. These will be all over the floor.
- Keep storage of toys simple and accessible. Place them in clear containers, and provide labels with pictures and words.

- Comfortable furniture for both adults and children. This will help provide opportunities for quiet, relaxing times.

Legislative requirements about toddler environments give information to help early childhood educators provide

- a safe environment for toddlers;
- a smoother transition from one program to the next by comparing the environments to make viable adjustments; and
- an environment suitable for toddlers.

PRESCHOOL PROGRAMS

Photo 10.24

What are preschoolers like? They are beautifully confident creatures who have tested themselves out in toddlerhood and are now filled with enthusiasm to explore the world around them and the people in it. Hungry to learn how to live in a world, their awareness is moving from a strictly egocentric (that is, centered only on self) perspective to an outward perspective. They are like adventuring explorers who have an insatiable need to know and do more in the larger world around them. (Gestwicki, 1999, p. 97)

The preschool age range is much broader than the infant and toddler stages. It is, therefore, not surprising that the abilities of preschoolers vary greatly from a three-year-old, to a four-year-old, to a five-year-old. Compared to toddlers, preschoolers are much more autonomous, much less dependent on adults, and increasingly more interested in their peers.

Web
exercises

What Do Preschoolers Need?

Preschoolers need

- Opportunities to be involved in active play. Plan the learning environment and arrange materials to invite active play (see Figure 10.3 and photo 10.25).
- Activities that enhance coordination and agility (see photo 10.26 on page 302).
- Activities that encourage increased attention span or that require children to continue to work on the experience over more than one day. In one example, some of the children in the preschool had spent the weekend at the local flag festival. These children came into the room excited about what they had seen. They decided to make flags. They decided what materials to use—different-sized brushes, materials, cloth paint, and various materials for the pole, such as dowelling

Photo 10.25

■ *Figure 10.2*

Brite Beginnings Toddler Space

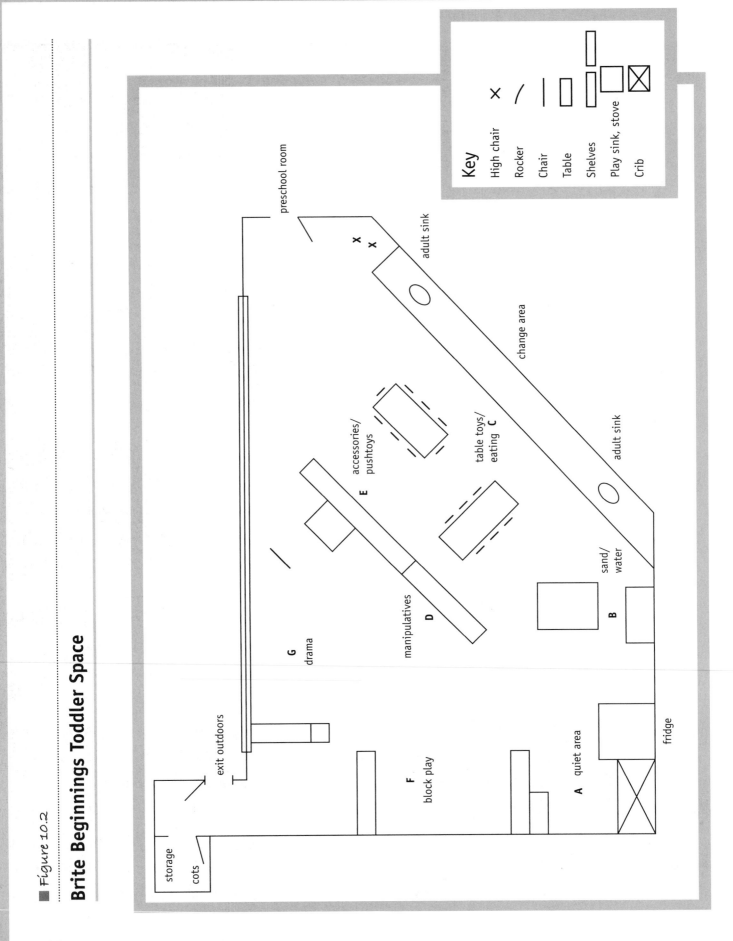

Key

✕	High chair
╱	Rocker
│	Chair
▭	Table
▭	Shelves
□	Play sink, stove
⊠	Crib

preschool room

exit outdoors

storage

cots

G drama

F block play

manipulatives **D**

E accessories/ pushtoys

table toys/ eating **C**

sand/ water

B

A quiet area

fridge

change area

adult sink

adult sink

Brite Beginnings Toddler Space

Area A - Photo A
Quiet reading area

Area B - Photo B
Sand
Water
Crib (one infant allowed within toddler group)
Adult sink

Area C - Photo C
Change area
Table toys
Eating area

Area D - Photo D
Manipulative bins

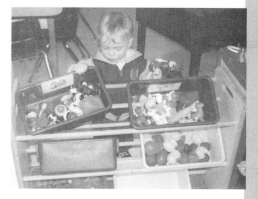

Area E - Photo E
Accessories
Push toys

Area F - Photo F
Block area
Manipulative materials
Accessories

Area G - Photo G
Dramatic play
Props
Kitchen area

■ *Figure 10.2 (continued)*

Brite Beginnings Outdoor Shared Space

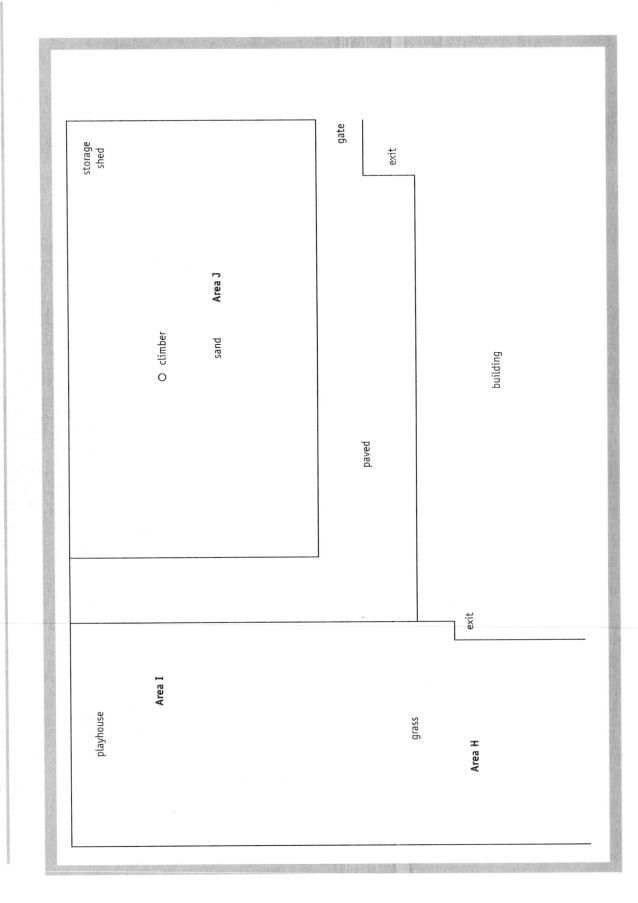

Brite Beginnings Outdoor Shared Space

Area H - Photo H

Area I - Photo I

Area J - Photo J

Photo 10.26

Photo 10.27

Photo 10.28

or cardboard rolls (photo 10.27)—and how to finally put the flags together (photo 10.28). The children worked on their flags for over three weeks.

- Decreased help from adults. Michael observed Kai as he clamped a piece of wood into the mitre box ready for sawing. Kai said that it was too loose. Michael asked him if he needed help. Kai nodded yes. Michael tightened the clamp. He asked Kai to check to see if the mitre box and wood were now tightly attached. Kai tried to move the wood. He smiled, turned to the shelf, and got out a saw. Every time Kai tried to cut, the saw jumped out of the groove. Kai said, "You do it." Michael said, "Let's see if I can help a bit." He encouraged Kai to cut while he kept his hand over the top of the saw to prevent it from jumping out of the groove (photo 10.29). Kai managed to cut the wood himself.

Photo 10.29

- Engagement in self-reflective activities. Yasmine had been painting at the easel. She suddenly noticed that she had a lot of paint on her hand. "Look, Jodi, my hand is covered in paint." Jodi asked her what she was going to do about it. Yasmine looked at her hand and at her paper. She said, "there's some fingerprints on my paper. I could paint my hand and make hand prints." Yasmine painted her hand with the brush, and then made several handprints on her paper. She looked at her hand and at the print that she had made, comparing them (photo 10.30). "I can see the front of my hand on the paper. I need to make the back of my hand too." After she had made several prints of the front of her hand and the back of her hand, Yasmine decided that she liked the back of her hand better because it was "Unusual!"
- Opportunities to work individually, in small groups, or in large groups. Rashawn needed time to carefully look at his dinosaur from every angle (see photo 10.17 on page 294), whereas Rachel and her brother shared a book together (see photo 10.14 on page 290). Aalasi, in contrast, had started to read a story to some of the preschoolers. She quickly had a large group in front of her listening to the story (photo 10.31).

- Opportunities to engage in imaginative play (photo 10.32).
- Opportunities to interact with adults and peers (photos 10.31 and 10.32).

Adult-to-child ratios and group sizes for preschoolers greatly impact on the ability of early childhood educators to interact appropriately with the children in their care. Table 10.5 (p. 308) shows the ratio and group size requirements across Canada. The larger the number of children per caregiver and the larger the age span, the harder it is to give individual attention to children. Knowing what the requirements are will give you the opportunity to think about and strategize how to work with this age group in a developmentally appropriate manner. It provides opportunities to dialogue with co-workers across Canada to

- identify strategies that work well in other jurisdictions;
- collaborate nationally to raise awareness of quality issues; and
- help advocate for better conditions within various jurisdictions.

Photo 10.30

What Can You Do?

- Coordinate with team members to take the responsibility of monitoring various learning areas of the room. Use strategies to make children aware that you are interested in what they are doing even if you are not directly with them. Some of these strategies might include
  - interacting with individual children from a distance using body language (facing them) and appropriate facial expressions such as smiles, or hand signals such as thumbs up;
  - expressing interest by using body language such as relaxed posture and warm facial expressions; and
  - interacting verbally as appropriate to indicate interest and express enthusiasm.

- Observe children to gain insight into when to leave the play alone or when to step in. Always step in if you perceive a potential problem. It is easier to solve a potential problem than to deal with the real problem.
- Encourage children to solve their own problems by using open-ended comments such as "I wonder what would happen if…"
- Provide a number of choices in the environment. Preschoolers need to engage in a wide number of learning experiences to enhance all domains. It is suggested in the ECERS (Harms, Clifford, & Cryer, 1998) that the learning area should include activities for reading, fine motor skills, art, music/movement, blocks, sand/water, dramatic play, nature/science, math/numbers, use of TV and/or computers, and promoting acceptance of diversity.
- Provide storage of materials that encourage independence. Use labelling with pictures and words.

Photo 10.31

Photo 10.32

Whispering Hills Floor Plan

■ *Figure 10.3*

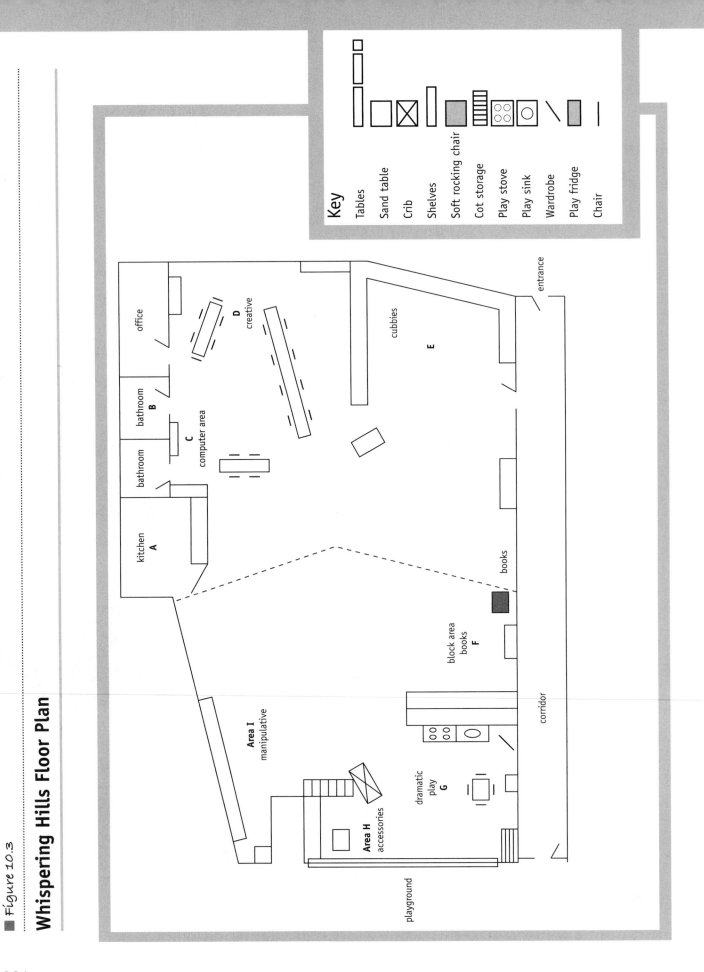

Key

Tables
Sand table
Crib
Shelves
Soft rocking chair
Cot storage
Play stove
Play sink
Wardrobe
Play fridge
Chair

office

creative
D

bathroom
B

bathroom

bathroom

kitchen
A

computer area
C

cubbies

E

entrance

books

block area
books
F

corridor

Area I
manipulative

dramatic
play
G

Area H
accessories

playground

Whispering Hills Floor Plan

Area A - Photo A

Area B - Photo B

Area C - Photo C
Computer area

Area D - Photo D
Creative area
Creative supplies
Eating area
Adult storage

Area E - Photo E
Cubbies
Adult storage

Area F - Photo F
Block area
Book area

Area G - Photo G
Dramatic play

Area H - Photo H
Accessories for dramatic play

Area I - Photo I
Manipulatives
Adult storage
Place to be alone

Figure 10.3

Whispering Hills Outdoor Space

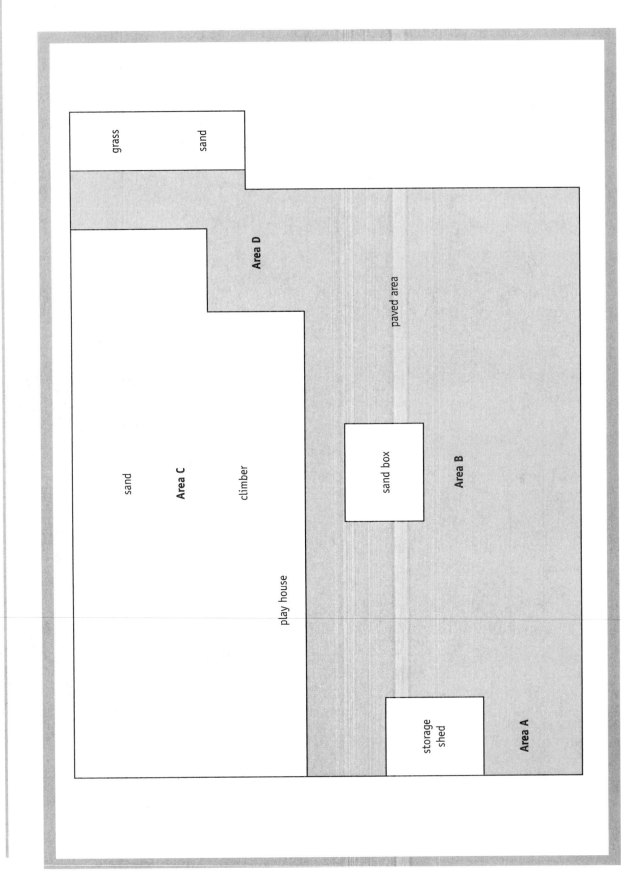

Whispering Hills Outdoor Space

Area A - Photo A

Area B - Photo B

Area C - Photo C

Area D - Photo D

Preschool Programs—Legislative Requirements in Canada

Jurisdiction	Adult-to-Child Ratios	Group Size
Alberta	3–5 yrs.—1:8 Ratio for drop-in-centres 1:12, with maximum group size of 24	16
British Columbia	1:15	20
Manitoba	3–4 yrs.—1:8 4–5 yrs.—1:9	16 18
New Brunswick	3–4 yrs.—1:7 4–5 yrs.—1:10	14 20
Newfoundland and Labrador	37–69 mos.—1:8	16
Northwest Territories	3 yrs.—1:8 4 yrs.—1:9	16 18
Nova Scotia	17 mos.–5 yrs. (full day)—1:7 17 mos.–5 yrs. (half day)—1:12	Not specified Not specified
Nunavut	3 yrs.—1:8 4 yrs.—1:9	16 18
Ontario	2–5 yrs.—1:8 3 yrs. 8 mos.–5 yrs.—1:10 (with director's approval)	16 20
Prince Edward Island	3–5 yrs.—1:10	Not specified
Quebec	4–5 yrs.—1:10	Not specified
Saskatchewan	30 mos.–6 yrs.—1:10	20
Yukon	3–6 yrs.—1:8	16

SCHOOL-AGED PROGRAMS

Web
exercises

School-aged programs are usually provided for children in need of care before the start and after the end of the elementary school program. Children whose family members work full-time may need care between 7:30 and 9:00 A.M. and 3:30 and 5:30 P.M. each day. There is a variety of options, both formal and informal, available (see Table 10.6). Knowledge about these options will help direct early childhood educators to the appropriate training options and also provide information about work-related choices.

■ TABLE 10.6

Options for School-Aged Care

Option	Description
In-home care	• One of the parents negotiated work schedule to be at home to care for child • A family member (e.g., aunt or grandparent) is at home to provide care • Individual is hired to come into the home to provide care
Regulated family child-care	• Children are part of a group with fixed ratios (see Table 10.7) • Children are cared for in a private home that is licensed and inspected regularly by a child-care agency
Unregulated family child-care	• Children are part of a group with fixed ratios (see Table 10.7) • Children are cared for by an individual within private home, often a neighbour
Neighbourhood school	• A child-care provider is hired to look after children within the school setting; often this is negotiated between an outside agency and the school—the school provides the space and the agency provides the staff • The school may provide its own services
Daycare setting	• Licensed daycare may offer after-school care within regular daycare operation for school-aged group of children • May be within separate room or with older preschoolers • Children may be bussed or delivered by taxi to the daycare or the school • If within walking distance, younger children will be picked up or dropped off at school under supervision of staff; older children arrive and depart independently
Community agency	• Some agencies (e.g., the YMCA) offer sport or other activity programs • Children may be bussed or delivered by taxi to the daycare • If within walking distance, younger children will be picked up or dropped off at school under supervision of daycare staff; older children arrive and depart independently
Kindergarten program	• Some daycares may offer a half-day program for kindergarten children who attend school for the other part of the day • Children may be bussed or delivered by taxi to the daycare • If within walking distance, younger children will be picked up and dropped off at school under supervision of staff

What Do School-Aged Children Need?

Many children have families who require care for their child both before and after school. This makes the day very long for the school-aged child. School-aged children need to be involved physically, socially, and emotionally and they need to be stimulated to use their cognitive abilities.

Ratios of adults to children vary across Canada (see Table 10.7 on the next page). School-aged children need to have understanding adults with whom to interact at the beginning or end of a long day. It is critical that caregivers have the time to spend with children individually or in groups as needed.

School-Aged Programs—Legislative Requirements in Canada

Jurisdiction	Ratios	Group Size
Alberta	5–6 yrs.—1:10 Drop-in-centres—1:15 with maximum group size of 30	20
British Columbia	6–12 yrs.—1:10–15	20–25
Manitoba	5–6 yrs.—1:10 6–12 yrs.—1:15	20 30
New Brunswick	5–6 yrs.—1:12 6–12 yrs.—1:15	24 30
Newfoundland and Labrador	57–84 mos. and attending school—1:12 85–144 mos.—1:15	24 30
Northwest Territories	5–11 yrs.—1:10	20
Nova Scotia	5–12 yrs.—1:15	Not specified
Nunavut	5–11 yrs.—1:10	20
Ontario	5–6 yrs.—1:12 6–10 yrs.—1:15	24 30
Prince Edward Island	5–6 yrs.—1:12 7+ yrs.—1:15	Not specified Not specified
Quebec	6–12 yrs.—1:20	Not specified
Saskatchewan	6–12 yrs—1:15	30
Yukon	6–12 yrs—1:12	24

Physical Needs

Children's physical needs include

- A snack and/or meal. Children may need breakfast in the morning. They may not have had time to eat or they may simply need a snack. Some children may require lunch (children in half-day programs). At the end of the day, it is important to have a snack available to tide children over until suppertime.
- Relaxation. Often children arrive in the morning without having had the appropriate amount of rest. These children may be irritable and cranky. At the end of the day, the child may need to unwind after a full academic day. The environment needs to include choices that encourage children to be by themselves or with others and to find

  - a comfortable, quiet place in which to relax (photo 10.33);
  - activities that encourage and maintain interest (photo 10.34); and
  - materials that offer opportunity for relaxation (photo 10.35).

Photo 10.33

Photo 10.34

- Opportunities to engage in activities to exert themselves both indoors and outdoors (photo 10.36). Some children need to exert themselves physically after a day of little physical activity.

Social and Emotional Needs

Children of this age group are usually very sociable. They need opportunities to form and maintain friendships in an environment that encourages active listening and active problem solving. They need opportunities to do the following:

- Play together or alone (photos 10.33 and 10.34).
- Interact in meaningful ways with adults and other children (photo 10.37).
- Solve their own problems. For example, Stephanie had come into the centre very quiet and withdrawn. When asked if she had a problem, she answered no, but that she felt like being alone for a while. She thought that she would like to sew by herself. She gathered the materials she wanted and moved to a solitary table by the window (photo 10.35). After working by herself for a while, she invited her friend to come and join her. She expressed, "I'm ready for company now."

Photo 10.35

What Can You Do?

- Acknowledge that many of the children may have had long and possibly stressful days, by providing opportunities to release energy through active participation, both physical and relaxing.
- Understand children's growing developmental abilities by encouraging children to solve their own problems.
- Create an environment that encourages active participation by providing a variety of choices—arts and crafts, music and movement, blocks and construction, drama and theatre, language and reading, math and reasoning, science and nature, cultural awareness, and gross motor activities (Harms, Vineberg Jacobs, & White, 1996).

Photo 10.36

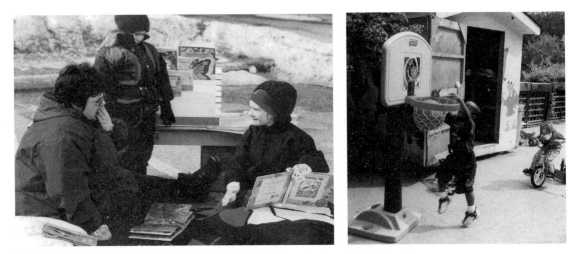

Photo 10.37   Photo 10.38

Cognitive Needs

To encourage cognitive development, school-aged children need to do the following:

- Engage in tasks that are challenging (photo 10.35). Stephanie cut out her own shapes, threaded her own needle, and sewed the shapes together to make a "purse."
- Use their imagination and growing skills to build and make working models (photo 10.34).
- Share their accomplishments with others (photo 10.37). Stephanie was able to read a book to her peer, Taylor, and to Kerri.

MULTI-AGE GROUPINGS

Mixed-aged groupings include children of various ages. The purpose of mixed-age groupings is to provide children with an experience that emulates family life more closely. The Ryerson Lab School has embraced and researched this approach: "Typically there are three infants, five toddlers, and eight preschoolers. Within this group, there may also be children with special needs. All are cared for by three teachers who rotate through the playroom" (Hart, 2000, p. 4). Multi-aged groupings are used across Canada, but group size and maximum number of children within the groups are varied.

Some of the critical elements of working with mixed age groups include

- *Flexibility*. Caregivers must be continually flexible to meet the needs of the various age groups. "Tremendous differences between children in a multi-age program requires that we constantly assess the nature of the needs and decisions about how the program can adapt to meet them" (Fortney, 2001, p. 30). For example, Jade, a toddler, was riding around on her tricycle. She was totally absorbed in what she was doing. Jonathan, one of the preschoolers, was playing basketball (photo 10.38). Norine noticed the potential problem. She encouraged the children to change their riding pattern to avoid the basketball area and ride around the other bike paths. This became a permanent adjustment to outdoor play.
- *Daily routines that adapt to individual needs*. Infants have individual eating schedules, while toddlers and preschoolers have more structured mealtimes. Infants can be included during mealtime if possible, but they have individual needs that need to be nurtured, as opposed to the group routine of eating together.

- *A wide range of materials.* "The multi-age physical environment offers a wide range of materials, furniture, and equipment to meet all interests and needs. This diversity creates a natural flexibility, because we are always able to offer, literally, something for everyone" (Fortney, 2001, p. 30). A group of children had built a platform to use as a stage. The younger children came to listen and dance to the music that the older children performed (photo 10.39).
- *Safety considerations.* "As well, for obvious safety reasons, certain materials need to be kept away from infants. In general, determining what can or cannot be used by children is a process determined by the child's skill rather than his/her age" (Fortney, 2001, p. 30). The environment needs to be organized to provide access for all children. Items more suitable for older children should be placed on higher shelves. Separate areas of the room can be created to protect nonwalkers from walkers.
- *Family considerations.* Children from same families (siblings or cousins) are not arbitrarily separated by age. This provides for closer and more natural linkages between home and the daycare. When in a home environment, children are part of the family unit and not separated. A multi-age model fosters more realistic family units.

Research Findings on Multi-Age Groupings

A comprehensive report on research about multi-age groupings (Bernhard et al., 2000) identified the following:

Photo 10.39

- *Language.* It is easier to preserve home language by keeping siblings together.
- *Attitudes.* Children had, overall, more positive attitudes toward school and themselves than children in single-age groups.
- *Play.* Placing children with special needs in multi-age groupings seems to be beneficial. Children seem to gain greater mastery during social play. Children's play behaviour had more positive interactions and showed more imitation, fantasy play, and verbal interactions.
- *Interactions.* Children are able to interact in a more realistic environment with peers of various ages and abilities. This may represent a more "home-like setting." As a result, children become more aware of various age groups and therefore more interested and responsive to them.
- *Sharing and cooperation.* Children are stimulated to learn with each other and from each other. Younger children have older siblings as role models, and older children have increased opportunities to become leaders and to help younger children in their activities and learning.
- *Families.* Family members can be assured that their children are learning in an environment that nurtures the family unit. Older siblings can help younger siblings cope with issues such as separation anxiety and thus help ease the trauma of separation of both child and family member.

There is, however, some conflicting research information. Some studies indicate that older children may develop more mature social skills, leadership skills, and better communication skills by looking after younger children. However, other studies have shown the opposite: "All together, the results do not support the idea

Chapter Ten   Regulation for Child-Care in Canada

that a large span encourages children's development. Instead the causal modeling indicates that a large age span either has a somewhat unfavorable effect on children's development or has no influence at all" (Bernhard et al., 2000, p. 91). The study conducted at the Ryerson Early Learning Centre clearly supports the first premise that children do make substantial developmental gains.

Children in the Ryerson Early Learning Centre were not at risk. "The notable difference between causes of accidents reported in the Public Health study and the ECL data also suggest that the multi-age program is having a significant impact on children's behaviour toward children generally. The observed high level of altruism and empathy is consistent with that reported in pilot data resulting from MROP [Multi-Age Relationship Observation Protocol]" (Bernhard et al., 2000, p. 126). It is important to recognize that the results of this study are positive because of a number of factors and cannot necessarily be generalized to other multi-age settings. The factors include

- the experience of staff with multi-age groupings;
- the ages of the children;
- group sizes;
- adult-to-child ratios;
- program practices and philosophy;
- resources available; and
- the facilities and learning environment.

KEY POINTS

REGULATIONS
- Canadian childcare options include preschool, centre-based full-day care, regulated family child-care homes, nonregulated family child-care homes, group family care, school-aged care, family resource centres, child development centres/Head Start programs, emergency care, child-minding services, occasional care, and kindergarten programs.
- Qualifications involve knowledge of child development, developmentally appropriate practices, and skill in observing, interacting, planning, and implementing healthy and safe learning experiences.
- Education for early childhood educators varies across Canada, and may require additional specialized education to work with various age groups or children with special needs.
- Licensing criteria relate to group size, adult-to-child ratios, program, size of learning environment, insurance, administrative policies and procedures, monitoring procedures, special needs, and family involvement.

INFANT PROGRAMS
- Infant programs require a trustworthy environment, separation of spaces, adequate adult-to-child ratios, nurturing caregivers, a communication system between all partners, developmentally appropriate learning areas, and predictable and familiar routines.

TODDLER PROGRAMS

- Toddler programs require caregivers who support growing independence in toddlers' interactions and in the organization of the environment, separate active play spaces, developmentally appropriate learning areas, safe environments for active exploration, and space for quiet relaxation.

PRESCHOOL PROGRAMS

- Preschool programs require opportunities for active play and activities to increase attention span, agility, coordination, creativity, decision making, problem solving, and independence. Toddlers also need the opportunity for self-reflection and to interact independently or in a group with peers or adults.

SCHOOL-AGED PROGRAMS

- Options for school-aged children include in-home care, regulated or unregulated family child-care, neighbourhood schools, daycare settings, community agencies, and kindergarten programs.
- These programs must meet

  - physical needs (relaxation, active play, food);
  - emotional needs (interacting with other children and adults or playing alone, solving their own problems); and
  - cognitive needs (challenges, using imagination and growing skills, and sharing accomplishments).

MULTI-AGE GROUPINGS

- Mixed-age groups include children of various ages, and thus emulate home life more closely.
- Elements include flexibility, adaptation of daily routines for various age groups, a wide range of materials, and safety considerations.
- Research has found that there are positive gains in retaining home language, increased positive attitudes, and enhanced play and interaction activities. Not all research, however, shows the same positive results. The research at Ryerson also shows that there is no risk associated with including infants within a multi-age grouping.

EXERCISES

1. In small groups, identify the various child-care options within your jurisdiction. Develop a questionnaire to identify quality components, such as ratios, group size, child guidance techniques, and schedule. Compare your results. Which would you use if you were a parent? Why?
2. Identify the qualifications needed in your jurisdiction to work with different age groups. Are they adequate? Explain your answer.
3. Using the chart on page 316, identify how more education might help you develop a better-quality program.
4. In a small group, discuss why licensing criteria are important.

   a) How does the licensing protect the child? The family?
   b) What other considerations should be included in licensing child-care?
   c) Why is inclusion of more quality within licensing requirements considerations difficult to implement?

CATEGORY	SKILLS GAINED
Child Guidance	
Child Development	
Developmentally Appropriate Practices	
Planning Learning Experiences	
Interacting with Families	

5. In a small group, summarize the licensing requirements for the various age groups (infants, toddlers, preschoolers, school-aged children) in your jurisdiction. Consider the following: ratios, group size, special age-group considerations, staffing patterns, size of learning environments, and safety considerations.

6. In a small group, look over the "What Can You Do?" box for one age group (infants, toddlers, preschoolers, or school-aged children). List some specific suggestions on what you might do to implement the strategies.

7. In a small group, define active learning. Discuss some strategies that you could use to create an active learning environment for one of the age groups (infants, toddlers, preschoolers, or school-aged children).

   a) How would you set up the environment?
   b) What learning activities would you include?
   c) What types of materials would you include?

8. In a small group, define multi-age groupings, and discuss the following:

   a) List at least three strategies of how you might ensure the physical safety of all children.
   b) What type of additional training do you think the staff might need?
   c) List the advantages of multi-age groupings.

REFERENCES

Bernhard, J., Pollard, J., Eggers-Piérola, & Morin, A. (2000). Infants and Toddlers in Canadian Multi-age Childcare Settings: Age, Ability and Linguistic Inclusion. *Research Connection Canada*, 79–185.

Fortney, J. (2001). Colouring Outside the Lines: A Metaphor for Flexibility in Early Education. *Interaction, 14,* 29–30.

Friendly, M., Beach, J., & Turiano, M. (2002a). *Early Childhood Education and Care in Canada.* Toronto, ON: Childcare Resources and Research Unit.

Friendly, M., Beach, J., & Turiano, M. (2002b). *Early Childhood Education and Care in Canada.* Toronto, ON: University of Toronto, Childcare Resources and Research Unit.

Gestwicki, C. (1999). *Developmentally Appropriate Practices* (2nd ed.). Scarborough, ON: Nelson Canada.

Harms, T., Clifford, R., & Cryer, D. (1998). *Early Childhood Environment Rating Scale* (revised ed.). New York, NY: Teachers College Press.

Harms, T., Vineberg Jacobs, E., & White, D. (1996). *School-Age Care Environment Rating Scale.* New York, NY: Teachers College Press.

Hart, L. (2000). The Dance of Emergent Curriculum in a Multi-Age Setting. *Interaction, 14,* 13–16.

Mayer, D. E. (1994). *National Statement on Quality Child Care.* Ottawa, ON: Child & Family Canada.

Shonkoff, J., & Phillips, D. (2001). *From Neurons to Neighborhoods: The Science of Early Childhood Development.* Washington, DC: National Academic Press.

Watson, L., Watson, M., Cam Wilson, L., & Crowther, I. (2000). *Infants and Toddlers* (1st Canadian ed.). Scarborough, ON: Nelson Thomson Learning.

White, B. (1995). *The New First Three Years of Life* (revised ed.). New York: Simon & Schuster.

PUTTING THE PIECES TOGETHER

"I started this book with the reflections about the magic of childhood. I feel it only fitting to try to tie together the concepts covered in this text by bringing back to the readers some of the magic I have personally observed as I have travelled from the Atlantic to the Pacific Ocean, from the far north to the far south, in search of Canadian perspectives on child-care. I have seen this magic reflected in the caregivers' eyes as they watch their children play, the children's eyes as they first catch sight of a wonderful new idea or experience, the families' eyes as they see their children happily interacting in their learning environments. Creating magic is not an easy task, but when you succeed, the rewards are reflected in the faces of our children."
—Ingrid Crowther, 2003

Chapter Outcomes

After reading this chapter, the reader will

1. Identify how child-care providers are providing quality care.
2. Describe the basic underpinnings of quality that exist in all programs, irrespective of the philosophical approach.
3. Identify how child-care providers have managed to bring "magic" into the lives of their children.
4. Identify how caregivers have created effective learning environments.
5. Describe how to create meaningful experiences for children.
6. Explain what children learn from their experiences in daycare.
7. Identify and describe caregiver interactions.

INTRODUCTION

The study entitled *You Bet I Care!* (Goelman et al., 2000) identified specific dimensions of quality—structural, contextual, adult work environment, safety and basic care, and process. This chapter will look at these dimensions in order to

- show that the basic dimensions of quality exist in all programs irrespective of the philosophical approach;
- identify various strategies used to ensure that quality dimensions have been addressed; and
- identify how child-care providers have managed to bring "magic" into the lives of their children.

PROVIDING QUALITY CARE

Structural Quality

The programs that have been described throughout the book and the children whom you have met are located in Ontario, Alberta, British Columbia, and Nunavut. All programs meet the minimum requirements as set out by the ministry requirements for that jurisdiction (see Chapter 10). In all areas,

- Adult-to-child ratios were appropriate for the age group of the children within the centre: notably, 1:3 or 1:4 for infants, 1:4 or 1:5 for toddlers, and 1:8 for preschoolers. In instances where ratios were higher for infants, the infants were not accepted into the program until they were one year old.
- Group sizes were appropriate for all age groups: 6 to 12 infants, 8 to 10 toddlers, and 16 to 20 preschoolers.
- All programs had larger than the minimum required play spaces indoors.
- All programs had large areas for outside play.

Contextual and Adult Environment Quality

Web exercises

All centres were large enough to support the appropriate number of early childhood educators on the floor and have a program supervisor or director. The qualifications of the staff and supervisors varied. In Ontario and British Columbia, all staff members

Salary Ranges

Province or Territory	Mean Average Hourly Salary of Staff	Mean Average Hourly Salary of Supervisor
Alberta	$8.36	$12.73
British Columbia	$13.28	$14.61
Nunavut	Untrained: $13.00 ECE certificate: $15.00 ECE diploma: $18.00	$20.00
Ontario	$13.48	$22.00

Source: Friendly, Beach, & Turiano, 2002.

had at least a two-year diploma in early childhood education. In Alberta and Nunavut, the supervisor or director of the centres was fully qualified. All staff had the minimum training requirements as set by the province or territory. Salary ranges varied dramatically (see Table 11.1).

The highest staff turnover rates were in centres that had low salaries and fewer qualified staff. The staff turnover rate ranged from 2 to 19 staff members in one year. Staff members who earned low wages and had not made the commitment to the field of early childhood education through specialized training had little incentive to stay. The average salaries for all job classifications in all jurisdictions, except for Nunavut, were higher than the average earnings in early childhood education settings. According to the BC Progress Board (BC Progress Board, 2001), ECE average hourly salaries ranged from $15.62 (Alberta) to $16.36 (BC) in 2001 (ranges did not include Nunavut). This meant that the opportunity to get a better-paying job with fewer responsibilities outside of ECE employment was high. In an informal observation based on asking graduates of early childhood programs across Canada why they no longer worked in the field, the answer was always the same—"I can earn more money and with less effort!" (Crowther, 2003).

Some of the staff and directors earned in excess of the average salaries listed. These individuals tended to work in unionized settings. Within these settings, employees received health-care and pension benefits and longer vacation periods. There was a low staff turnover reported in these centres. In one of these locations, one employee had worked in the same centre for 30 years.

In centres that had low staff turnover, the following was observed:

• stable routines and procedures;
• stable environment for children;
• high interaction among staff, children, and families; and
• greater cohesiveness of staff.

In centres that had high staff turnover, the following was observed:

• greater emphasis on health and safety practices;
• some staff had fewer interactions with children;
• staff were more likely to sit and observe children; and
• greater emphasis on large group activity.

■ TABLE 11.2

Comparison of Eleven Adult Physical Work Spaces

Characteristic of Adult Environment	Description
Space for personal belongings	• Five centres had hooks for coats near the children's area to hang personal belongings • All centres had lockable storage for personal belongings, usually in the drawer of a filing cabinet • Six centres had a separate staff room with appropriate hooks and filing cabinets for personal belongings
Adult-only space	• All centres had a small office space for the supervisor or director of the program • In five centres the supervisor's office doubled as space to hold private conversations • The remaining six centres had a separate adult office space for staff (photo 11.1)

Photo 11.1

Photo 11.2

Adult work environments were also very different (see Table 11.2). In six of the centres, staff members were encouraged to attend professional development activities each year. Professional development activities included conferences and workshops (paid for by the employer), access to magazines such as *Young Children* and *Interaction*, and time given to staff to meet to plan experiences for the children.

Safety and Basic Care Quality

All centres took great care to ensure that the children's physical safety was well looked after, and all centres ensured that the children's nutritional well-being was appropriate. Menus that were posted followed *Canada's Food Guide*.

Varying degrees of interactions were observed. There seemed to be a direct relationship between centre staff, degree of education, and the types of interactions initiated. When staff had higher levels of education and participated more in regular professional development activities, the following characteristics were observed:

- More individual or small group interactions took place. The environment was set up to support and encourage individual and group interactions. Comfortable furniture for adults and children was provided in various learning areas of the room (photo 11.2).
- Adults showed more interest and enjoyment in children's actions and discoveries. Emily had been delighted to find a "tiny, tiny, blue dinosaur" among the large dinosaurs. She showed it to Anna, who replied that it was indeed very tiny (photo 11.3).

Photo 11.3

Photo 11.4

- Adults responded more to signals of children and responded to these appropriately. Louise imitated the sounds that Lauren made (photo 11.4).
- Adults followed the children's leads more. Kaya picked up and dropped the requested shapes into the hat (photo 11.5).
- There was more of an open-door policy to encourage family members to participate within the program (photo 11.6).

In summary, there seemed to be a direct correlation between all the factors in the learning environment that led to more quality educational experiences for children. When early childhood educators received better pay and better benefits, there seemed to be greater program stability and less staff turnover. In addition, the greater the educational level of the staff, the more nurturing the interactions and the physical environments seemed to be. When greater attention was given to creating a more nurturing atmosphere, the adult environment and staff relations seemed to be more cohesive. All of these factors led to greater overall program quality for everyone—the children, their families, and the staff.

Photo 11.5

MAGIC IN THE LIVES OF CHILDREN

Children spend many of their hours in a daycare setting. When children look forward to their daycare day, to seeing the adults and other children, and to exploring their environments, they will establish healthy attitudes about themselves and about their learning experiences.

Young children are naturally curious and filled with a desire to learn. Environments that are set up to capture the children's imagination, to engage their sensibilities, and to empower them to engage in their own learning become naturally magical places.

Web exercises

PROCESS QUALITY

The last characteristic of creating quality environments—**process quality**—is probably most closely linked to the magical quality we just discussed. This characteristic of quality is elusive and very difficult to measure. Most of us can recognize it when we see it but have a hard time putting into specific words just what we mean. This is why most descriptions tend to be very general and therefore become quite subjective. For example, what does it mean to be nurturing and caring? When three different people were asked to define what they thought was meant by a nurturing, caring individual, these definitions were given:

- Early childhood educator: "The caregiver should consider all of the children's needs—to love all her children and consider all their needs, especially cultural needs. For example, some just shake hands, others hug. The caregiver should provide what the children need—music, soft toys, a blanket. The

Web exercises

process quality
"The nature of the child's experience; the daily interactions between the child and the teacher and among children themselves" (Goelman et al., 2000, p. 4).

Chapter Eleven   Putting the Pieces Together

Photo 11.6

family's judgment needs to be respected. The caregiver needs to follow through on what the family wants."

- Grandfather: "A warm and nurturing caregiver is someone who smiles a lot, is sensitive, and listens to the children. They shouldn't be too authoritarian. The caregiver needs to find things for children to do that are interesting and stay with them while they are involved. The children shouldn't be left alone to watch TV. The caregiver should stay with them and play with them."

- Early childhood education professor: "This is someone who listens to the child and responds to the message that was expressed appropriately. The caregiver should show his or her interest in what the child is doing by a relaxed body posture and a friendly, expressive face. The caregiver should observe the children carefully to know when to step in to interact or when to stay out of the situation and leave the children alone. Most importantly, the caregiver should have trust in the child's ability to direct his or her own learning."

All three definitions are similar, but not the same. Every person answered the question from a different perspective. If these three individuals were observing an early childhood educator in order to judge the capabilities of that person, would they all see the person in the same way? Would they all rate that individual at the same level? That is the quandary that needs to be faced when trying to evaluate the quality of child-care programs. How can personal characteristics be defined so that everyone will make the same quality judgment? It is far easier to look at measures such as structural quality, contextual quality, learning environments, safety, and basic care. These are very concrete—an adult-to-child ratio of 1:3 can be counted. Policies and procedures are developed and posted, and it is therefore easy to judge what is missing. Qualifications can be documented. So what are the characteristics that help to create some magic in children's lives?

Photo 11.7

Photo 11.8

According to the *You Bet I Care!* study, these qualities relate to "the nature of the child's daily experience, especially the daily interactions between the child and the teacher and among the children themselves" (Goelman et al., 2000, p. 4). Creating daily experiences that encourage positive interactions between all individuals and the learning environment depends on the adult's ability to create the appropriate physical environment and emotional atmosphere:

Process quality occurs when the children are engaged in developmentally appropriate activities and interactions in a supportive physical and human environment. While having wonderful learning materials in a child care room is of critical importance, it is of greater importance that the adults in that room provide dynamic "lived experience" in which the children use a variety of stimulating materials to help facilitate their intellectual, language, social, emotional, and physical growth. The use of developmentally appropriate learning and exploration is supported by a physical environment that is well organized and well implemented and supports children's independent learning. (Goelman et al., 2000, p. 4)

Creating a Learning Environment

Creating attractive learning environments takes a great deal of thought, time, and energy. It should involve everyone in the process—families and staff. This space can be created when the centre is first built, or it can be created after the centre is in operation. Consideration needs to be given to all spaces, inside and outside. It is important to remember that each part of the learning space gives a message by the way we use colour, arrangement, light, and what is in that space. The message should be one of welcome—to come in, to explore, to touch, to look at, to relax in, and to interact with others.

Photo 11.9

First Impressions

The outside of the building already influences how you feel about entering. You can do a variety of things to make the outside more welcoming. Imagine children's joy when they see

- Various levels of interest that have been created through benches that can be used to sit on or climb or balance on. Shaded areas can be created through the use of quick-growing trees and vines (photo 11.7). If you have a front yard, use it as part of your play yard.
- Flowers in flower boxes, hanging baskets, and planters. These can add natural colour to the environment, and can be seen as one enters the building and when the children look out of the window (photo 11.8). Children can help to plant and care for these items.

- Natural elements. Beauty was created by using the natural elements—in Iqaluit, the student carvers created beautiful carvings in natural rocks that were placed around walkways around the town and some directly across from the daycare (photo 11.9). Other areas have built an inuksuk (photo 11.10) in front of their buildings (Wallace, 2001). "An inuksuk, a powerful symbol of the Canadian Arctic, is a stone structure that resembles a human. Traditionally, inuksuit (plural) have been built by the Inuit to act in the place of a messenger" (Wallace, 1999). Similar beauty can be created using a variety of other sources that are prevalent in your area, such as snow, ice (Cole, Frankeny, & Jonath, 1999), or sand (Mitchell & Frankeny, 2000). Children can have great fun in helping to create lasting or passing mementos of their time in the centre.

Photo 11.10

- A warm and inviting entry into the child-care centre. Children's artwork, photos of children, and photos of families that are tastefully displayed could be used (see photo 8.16 on page 226). Softness can be created by adding mats, plants, interesting things to look at, tablecloths, and so on (see photo 8.15 on page 226).

Photo 11.11

- An attractive, well-organized cubby with room to sit to take off clothing, and room for personal items and clothing. Shelves should be labelled with the child's name. There should be room enough for several children to undress or dress at the same time. Placing benches in the centre of the room or around the outside of the space makes it easier for children to dress or undress and helps to avoid congestion.

Photo 11.12

Photo 11.13

Photo 11.14

Indoor Learning Spaces

Indoor spaces should reflect the children's environment, their learning, their activities, their accomplishments, and the interaction between children and adults. The first step is to create an aesthetically pleasing environment for adults and children through

- establishing a welcoming look—hanging plants, light, open spaces, and easy-to-see learning areas (photo 11.11);
- providing well-organized materials to optimize children's choices (photo 11.12);
- establishing well-defined interest areas that reflect children's interests (e.g., provide spill-out areas and soft areas, confine creative areas to be out of traffic flow with shelves, and arrange for easy supervision) (photo 11.13);
- creating clear, accessible, and well-organized storage of materials for rotation (photo 11.14). The more accessible and organized the materials are, the easier it is for staff to find relevant materials spontaneously or for planned purposes, and it also gives the caregiver the opportunity to react quickly to a child's request; and
- providing areas and materials that attract curiosity and interest (photo 11.15).

Outdoor Learning Spaces

Outdoor learning environments should be as aesthetically pleasing as indoor environments. Children should be able to engage in activities similar to those they do indoors, but should have additional opportunity to explore a variety of active gross motor activities—climbing, running, riding, sliding, swinging, and playing with equipment such as balls.

The outdoor play area at Kitsilano Area Childcare Society Daycare has been carefully planned and created with the help of staff, families, and the city of Vancouver. The result is an effort that has extended for over 30 years (see Figure 11.1).

The playground has a natural charm that is enhanced by many trees, plants, and flowers. Plants were carefully selected to represent the natural vegetation that children see in nature. This gives many opportunities to observe the natural cycle of living plants and to discuss natural growth. Some of the plants are grape vines. Children are able to watch the grapes grow over the season and eventually harvest them.

In many parts of the playground there are "magical places"—arbours to hide or rest under (see photo 7.18 on page 196), plants to walk among (photo 11.16), shaded areas in which to watch the sunlight flickering through the leaves (photo 11.17), and grassy areas to play or rest on (photo 7.18 on page 196). Children can help to grow

Figure 11.1

Outdoor Play Area of Kitsilano Area Childcare Society

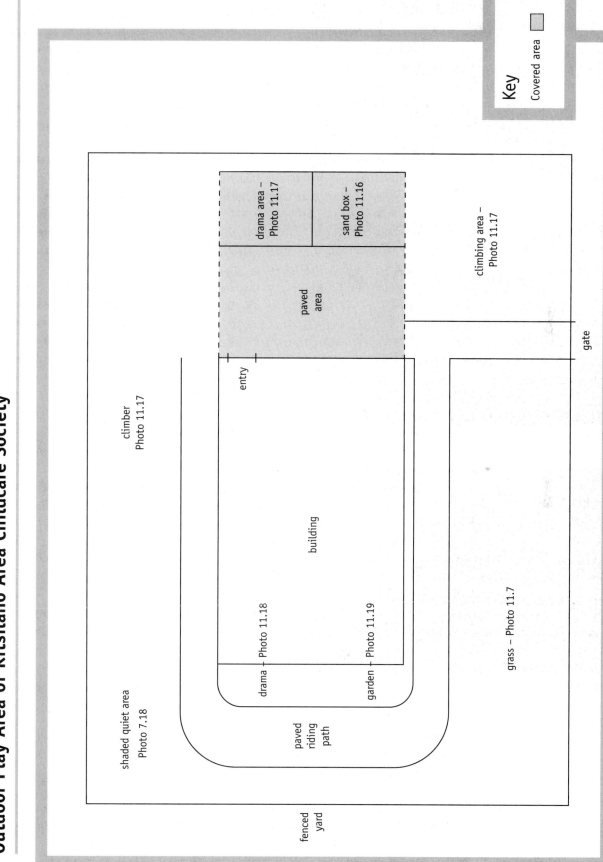

Key
Covered area

shaded quiet area
Photo 7.18

climber
Photo 11.17

fenced yard

paved riding path

drama – Photo 11.18

garden – Photo 11.19

building

entry

paved area

drama area – Photo 11.17

sand box – Photo 11.16

climbing area – Photo 11.17

grass – Photo 11.7

gate

Photo 11.15

and maintain a garden (photo 11.18). The produce is harvested and used to supplement lunches and snacks. Imagine the excitement of picking your own vegetables or fruit for lunch or a snack.

The playground offers many activities for the children to engage in:

- They can test their strength, endurance, and coordination (photo 11.19).
- They can solve problems together. Emily and Emmy had been using the tire swing. Erin heard them calling Anna, the early childhood educator, to help. Erin also went over. She heard the girls say that they needed a push. Erin volunteered to push the girls. Isabel was attracted by the activity. Anna anticipated a problem, so she leaned over and said, "I think Isabel wants to join you." Isabel beamed and nodded her head, and the other girls made room for her. Anna warned the girls that now they needed to be more careful because Isabel was younger (photo 11.20).
- They can relax and watch others (photo 11.21).
- They can participate in small groups or alone (photos 11.20 and 11.21).

Photo 11.16

Photo 11.17

Photo 11.18

The outdoor play spaces were well planned. The sandbox (photo 11.22) is totally enclosed with shutters, and a large doorway is closed when the area is not in use. The centre nestles in an older residential area in Vancouver. There are many cats that roam around in the area and other wild animals because of the many trees. The outdoor sand area is protected from animal feces and plant debris. Additionally, it can be used on rainy days as it is protected from the elements on all sides. The doorway to the sandbox is under a covered paved riding area.

The dramatic play area (see photo 7.17 on page 196) is adjacent to the sandbox and also a protected area from the elements. The general structure of both buildings is reminiscent of oriental architecture. Many of the children in Vancouver have an oriental background. Imagine the joy of seeing something familiar.

The whole area has been designed to fit into the neighbourhood of old, mature trees and pleasant gardens. The climbing structure is of natural wood. All aspects of the outdoor play area blend in together in harmony with the manufactured structures and the natural environment.

One of the challenges for the staff is to supervise the playground. Staff must always be positioned to be able to see at least two active play areas. All staff are outside with the children during outside play to maximize the supervision. Safety rules and safety reminders have been posted. The riding path that curls around the house is one-way only. Staff must work as a cohesive team, indicating to each other when they are going to interact with an individual child or with a small group and require someone else to take over the general supervision of the children.

MEANINGFUL EXPERIENCES

In all settings, children were empowered to make their own choices. Children make choices if materials are provided that reflect both their interests and their developmental levels. When children are able to make their own choices, they are able to take charge of their own learning. Experiences become much more powerful when the caregiver responds with warm and nurturing interactions (see Table 11.3 on pages 330–32).

Photo 11.19

CHILDREN'S LEARNING

Through these activities children were continually challenged, motivated, and valued for their contributions. Children took pleasure in their activities and enthusiastically participated to create their own learning opportunities. When children arrive with such enthusiasm, take such pleasure in their learning, and have their experienced valued, magical moments are created. Consider the following:

- Jacob could trust that his caregiver would notice what he was doing and enjoy it with him and provide more experiences to continue his interest (Example 1 in Table 11.3). He continually expanded his interests and learned new things about insects (camouflage, where to find them, and what they looked like), and his interest began to attract other children to participate in his activities. He was able to extend his interest from a one-time experience to many experiences over time—sorting insects, looking for grasshoppers, catching grasshoppers, looking at them closely, and learning to respect living things (Examples 2 and 3).

Photo 11.20

- Kacey had learned about the concepts of sinking and floating. She was able to expand on these concepts by discovering how to make things sink (Example 4).
- Michael was able to explore his interest in drawing. By working on a smaller surface (see photo 11.25 on page 334) he was able to refine his fine motor control. He had the freedom to create what he wanted. He was not required to complete a directed project, nor was he required to specify what had been created. He simply enjoyed the process of putting colours together in ways that pleased him (Example 5).
- Jordan developed pride in his ability to do tasks by himself (Example 6). Children were encouraged to be observant of others and to help each other solve problems (e.g., Autumn helped Jordan with his problem of stringing). Children's efforts were acknowledged and therefore valued. They could hang their beading up for others to see.

Photo 11.21

- Braelyn used the beading activity to engage in new sorting tasks by colour and shape and demonstrated her learning through the activity— counting, sorting, and identification of numbers and animals (Example 7).
- John was very comfortable with expressing his own feelings. He was not too happy when his mother left. He could choose the level of comfort he needed—holding his favourite blanket while waving goodbye. Through this experience, John learned that his feelings were acknowledged—when he felt sad he could control how he coped with his feelings (Example 8).
- Anya had a new baby at home. She was able to role-play something important to her—feeding her baby brother (Example 9).

Photo 11.22

Chapter Eleven   Putting the Pieces Together

Meaningful Experiences and Caregiver Interactions

Meaningful Experiences	Associated Adult Interaction
Example 1: Adult Follows Child's Lead	
Jacob had been fascinated by the insect he saw outside. The summer had brought out many flying grasshoppers. At first he was puzzled—he did not seem to be able to locate the sound he had heard. Once he located the insect, he would laugh with delight when he heard one flying though the air. He would chase the insect and always seemed to be disappointed when he lost sight of it. Once inside, the children drew and painted many pictures of the insects (see Figure 11.2 on page 333).	Saul noticed when Jacob first looked puzzled. He understood the cause and explained to Jacob that he had heard a grasshopper. He helped Jacob to locate the sound by pointing out to him where the grasshopper was. He shared in Jacob's delight by laughing with him and talking about what Jacob had experienced: "The grasshoppers are very quick. They are also very good at hiding. It is hard to see them. They are camouflaged." When the children went inside, Saul quickly retrieved the plastic insects and put them by the sandbox where Jacob often played.
Example 2: Provide Meaningful Materials Based on Experiences of Children	
After Jacob had undressed and gone to the washroom, he went to the sandbox. He immediately saw the insects. His face lit up. "Look, look, look, grasshoppers," he shouted. Jacob lined up all the insects on the edge of the sandbox (see photo 11.23 on page 334). When he had finished, he took the grasshoppers and flew them with his hand to land in the sandbox. The sandbox had several pieces of natural wood in it and a large trunk of a tree. After one of the grasshoppers landed on the tree, Jacob said, "Hard to see."	Saul was nearby, interacting with another child. He smiled and nodded at Jacob from a distance. Jacob smiled back and continued to play. Saul heard Jacob say that the grasshopper was hard to see. He indicated to him that yes, it was hard to see and that it was camouflaged. The next day, before they went outside again, Saul put some nets, collecting jars, and magnifying glasses outside.
Example 3: Encourage Children to Sustain Interest Over Time	
When Jacob went outside, he immediately again looked for the grasshoppers. Several other children got caught up in Jacob's excitement. One of the children noticed the nets. "Come quick," he shouted, "we can catch some grasshoppers." Soon seven children were involved in trying to catch grasshoppers. When one child caught one, he brought the insect over to Saul to show it to him. The children picked a plastic jar with holes in it and put some grass into the bottom "'cause grasshoppers like grass." The children looked at the grasshopper using a magnifying glass. Jamie said, "It grew." Some of the children laughed and said he was silly. After Jamie's comment, the children became intrigued by the concept. They all wanted to look at the grasshopper that looked like it grew but really didn't. When it was time to go, it was decided to let the grasshopper go, "'cause he doesn't like being locked up."	Saul watched the children and offered encouragement: "You almost caught that one." When one of the children finally caught a grasshopper, Saul talked to the children about it. When the children wanted to keep the grasshopper, Saul guided them through a respectful process: "How do you think we could do that? A grasshopper is alive." One of the children fearfully wanted to know if it had been hurt. Saul reassured the child that the grasshopper was all right but they had to take it out of the net carefully. Saul had heard the comment. He said, "It does look like he grew, doesn't it?"
Example 4: Provide Experiences That Involve All the Children's Senses	
Web exercises 🖑 Kacey had put things that float into the water centre. She poured water over the objects to see if she could make them sink (see photo 11.24 on page 334). When she succeeded, she would chuckle, look up at Simone, and chuckle.	Simone had noticed that children were trying to sink objects by pouring water on them. She provided a variety of floating objects to the children and several containers for pouring. She stood near Kacey as she poured water. When the object would sink, she would gasp and put her hand over her mouth as if in surprise.

Meaningful Experiences and Caregiver Interactions

Meaningful Experiences	Associated Adult Interaction
Example 5: Challenge Children's Creativity	
Michael loved to create small pictures. He loved to create his own designs. Often he would create something and then cut it out (see photo 11.25 on page 334).	Nancy had observed that some of the children liked to work with smaller pieces of paper. She provided a variety of resources for children with different skills and interests to use. The creative shelf was well stocked with markers; crayons; scissors; pencil crayons; paper of various colours, textures, and sizes; glue; tape; and a clear table at which to work. When Michael was finished, they discussed what they might do with his creation. He decided that he wanted to take it home and ran to put it in his locker.
Example 6: Encourage Children's Independence	
Jordan was fascinated with the beads, especially the animal beads. He could get the gimp into the hole of the bead (see photo 11.26 on page 334), but when he let go of the gimp to grab the end that had come through the hole, the gimp fell to the floor. He picked up the gimp and looked at the other children who were beading. A big smile came over his face and he put the end of the gimp on the table. He repeated the process. This time the gimp landed on the table. He tried again, with the same results. Autumn, one of his peers, noticed when the gimp fell on the table. She said. "You have to use a longer piece like this. See?" She showed Jordan how to feed a longer piece through her bead. Jordan smiled and tried again. This time he succeeded. His smile was huge. Jordan continued to bead until his string was full. He asked for help to tie a loop at the end so that he could hang it from the bead display hook.	Zofia had been careful to set up the beads to ensure maximum possibility of success. All beads were organized by type, such as bear or dog beads. They were in small clear containers, labelled with a picture and a word. For threading, a variety of colours and lengths of gimp and a variety of long pipe cleaners were in small baskets. Zofia had watched the whole episode. She did not interfere with Jordan's efforts. She did not feel that Jordan was getting frustrated. When he got his first bead on the gimp, she quietly said, "Good for you. You did it by yourself." She knew Jordan was very independent and liked to do things by himself. When Zofia looked over the displays of beads that the children had done, she noticed that some children were starting to sort beads by colour. The strings the children had created showed clumps of colours together—five red, three green, and six orange beads. She decided to put out an additional different arrangement in the bead area.
Example 7: Provide Additional Challenges	
When Braelyn decided she wanted to bead, she immediately noticed the sorting tray full of beads (see photo 11.27 on page 334). She started to bead. Braelyn matched beads first according to colour, and then she created a string of beads according to shape.	Zofia put out a sorting tray that had an assortment of animal beads of different colours in it. Zofia wrote down observations of Braelyn's efforts (see Figure 11.3 on page 334). She observed to see how many children were at the bead area and what types of tasks they were engaged in (see Figure 11.4 on page 335). She later transferred the information to the children's skill charts (see Figure 11.5 on page 335).
Example 8: Encourage Children to Choose the Level of Comfort They Need	
John at times still found it very hard to separate from his mother in the morning. He had his favourite blanket that he carried around with him for a few minutes, and he had the opportunity to wave goodbye to his mother (see photo 11.28 on page 336).	Nancy encouraged John to do what he felt comfortable doing by letting him decide how to handle the situation. *(cont'd)*

Meaningful Experiences and Caregiver Interactions

Meaningful Experiences	Associated Adult Interaction
Example 9: Take Safe Risks	
Colin was often found at the carpentry table. He was well aware of the safety procedures—clamping before sawing, wearing safety goggles, and so on. He also had heard the early childhood educators say to the children to stay clear of the person using tools (see photo 11.29 on page 336). Colin said to a child who wanted to get behind him, "Go away, 'til I am finished. You might get hurt."	The carpentry area was set up out of the high-traffic area. All tools were organized and stored appropriately (photo 11.29). A few simple rules had been set with the children and were reinforced as needed. *Rules* (posted with appropriate pictures) – Put tools away when finished. – Clamp wood when sawing or hammering. – Keep nails in bins. – Wait to use area until someone has finished sawing or hammering.
Example 10: Encourage Children to Have Opportunities to Role-Play Real Situations	
Anya loved to engage in caregiver types of role-play situations. In particular, she liked to care for and feed the baby (see photo 11.30 on page 336).	Appropriate props were available in various areas both indoors and outdoors. Children had the freedom to take the props to other locations.
Example 11: Work on Projects	
One of the children had been to Florida on a holiday. She brought back shells to leave in the classroom. The children became fascinated with the shells. They would place them in the water, observe them under a magnifying glass, and try to listen to the sound of the "waves" from the shell (see photo 11.31 on page 337).	The staff working in the preschool room had observed the children and had made notes about their interests—names of shells, more information about shells, sorting shells (broken and small), matching shells (same types), drawing shells, sequencing shells (small to big). The staff decided that enough interest had been expressed to try to further develop the project. They started to document the children's interest, photographed some of the activities, and collected some additional resources—more shells and books on shells.
Example 12: Encourage Family Involvement in Children's Learning Activities	
When the children saw the new shells and the new materials, a flurry of activities were observed. Families helped to organize a field trip to the beach to collect more shells.	The initial documentations were posted (Figure 11.6 on page 336). Additional shells were placed on the shell table and a variety of shell books and shell dictionary cards were put out (see Figure 11.7). The response of the families was tremendous. They took their children on shell-collecting outings, brought in books on shells from the library, brought in more shells, and brought in some shell products for display.

- Through the work on the shell project, children learned to
  - collaborate with each other;
  - collaborate with adults; and
  - reflect their interest in many ways—though drawings or paintings, through manipulation, by observing, by discussing, by reading, by collecting, in writing, and through continued documentation of their efforts.

Children's Drawings and Scribes

My grasshopper is hiding.

Grasshoppers flying and jumping all over.

A big flying grasshopper

A grasshopper in my hair. I'm happy not scared.

In summary, the children were all actively engaged. Their expressions of wonder, enthusiasm, creativity, and commentary made it very evident that indeed magical moments had been created for all of them.

CAREGIVER INTERACTIONS

The children's meaningful experiences give rise to a number of pertinent caregiver interactions. These interactions are a critical aspect of a quality learning environment. These interactions can be organized into the following categories:

- set-up of developmentally appropriate experiences;
- provision of "wonderful" materials;
- stimulation of children to facilitate their development in all domains (physical, social, emotional, cognitive, and language); and
- child–adult interactions.

Photo 11.23

Photo 11.24

Photo 11.25

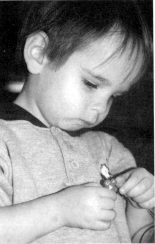
Photo 11.26

Photo 11.27

Setting Up Developmentally Appropriate Experiences

The adults ensured that the learning environments were aesthetically pleasing and that children learned through developmentally appropriate activities. Adults created a sense of excitement through developing an environment that encouraged children to look, touch, explore, and express their feelings in a variety of different ways—drawing, painting, discussing, planning, and collaborating. Environments were set up to be developmentally appropriate by

- ensuring that all aspects of the environment were welcoming;
- ensuring that the environment reflected the children's natural environment;
- ensuring that the environment reflected the children's right to play by providing a full range of interest/learning centres (see Figures 8.1, 8.3, 10.1, 10.2, and 10.3 on pages 220, 229, 292, 298, and 304);

■ **Figure 11.3**

Observation of Beading

Name of Child: Braelyn   **Activity:** Sorting

Setting: Bead Area

Circumstances: Using gimp and sorting tray filled with animal beads of same size but different colours.

Date	Observations	Interpretations
10/02	10 pi fish, 3 r giraffes, 4 bl cats, 2 g bears; named colours and animals	Sorts colour and shape; distracted from task
10/03	She looked at the previous string and picked out colours or shapes not used before: 5 o fish, 7 y rabbits, 8 pu fish, 8 bl cats	Used previous work to add to
	Second string—"I am going to sort animals by the real colour": 5 bl dogs, 7 wh cats, 10 y fish, 6 g elephants	Has knowledge of animals
	Went back and correctly counted by sorted animals—e.g., 10 p fish	

■ Figure 11.4

Interest in Beading

Date(s):   10/03

Children: Braelyn, Jordan, Jenna, Mathew, Michael, Damon

Activities: Beading using sorting tray or organized containers (organized by shape)

Circumstances: Using gimp to sort either colour or shape.

Observations

Random beading: //// ////
Colour sort: ///
Colour and shape: ////

■ Figure 11.5

Skills Set Observation

WORKING WITH NUMBERS

Name: Braelyn

Category	Counting Observed	Uses Counting in Everyday Experiences
Rote count		
Count to 3	////	Counts beads she strings
Count to 5	////	
Count to 7	////	Counts children at lunch table to
Count to 10	////	identify how many needed

WORKING WITH COLOURS

Key: pattern - pat, sequence - se, match - ma, sort – so, labels - la

Name: Braelyn

Category	Skill Observed	Times Observed	Comment
Black (b)	la, so	////	Sorting lacks consistency
Blue (bl)	la, so	///	
Brown (br)	la, so	////	
Grey (gr)	la, so	///	
Green (g)	la, so	//	
Orange (o)	la, so	/	
Pink (p)	la, so	////	
Purple (pu)	la, so	////	
Red (r)	la, so	//	
Yellow (y)	la, so	//	
White (w)	la, so	///	

- providing schedules that reflect the children's needs (see Figures 7.6 and 8.7 on pages 197 and 242);
- collaborating with parents as partners;
- observing children to base learning experiences and learning environments on their interests, skills, and abilities (see Figures 11.3 and 11.4 on page 334 and above); and
- documenting children's progress (see Figures 8.5a,b,c,d, and 11.5 on pages 233 and above).

Photo 11.28

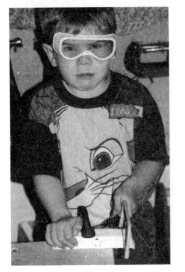

Photo 11.29

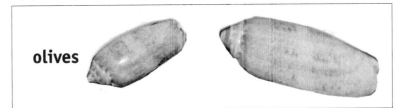

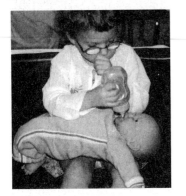

Photo 11.30

■ Figure 11.6

Initial Documentation

WE WANT TO KNOW:
the names of some of the shells
how shells are made
what shells are made of
where shells come from
why you can hear sounds

WE WANT TO:
go to find shells
make things with shells
make a display of shells
get more shells

CHILDREN WERE INTERESTED IN SHELLS
Liesl made a shell person.
Jacob found broken shells and whole shells.
Jacob found shells with sand in them and shells without sand in them.
Braelyn sorted shells into "teenie, weenie shells, in-between shells, and huge shells."

■ Figure 11.7

Ideas for Setup of Shell Project

1. **Sample Dictionary Cards**

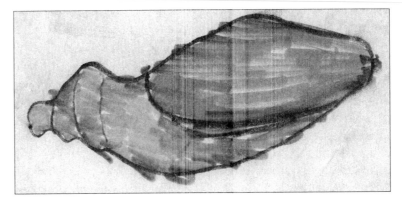

olives

These cards could be used in the following ways:

- Match shell to picture,
- Print the words, and
- Provide name of shell for everyone—adult, children

2. **Books on Shells**—Books to identify types of shells, identify parts of shells

3. **Pictures and Paintings**—Display drawings and paintings children had created (Example below had been placed in a small frame and hung in the area.)

4. **Displays of Shells**—Children and families brought in shell products—painted shells, shell figurines, shell boxes, shell jewellery and belt

Providing "Wonderful" Materials

"Wonderful" materials are magical. These materials inspire children to become curious (see photo 11.31), to become creative (see photo 11.25 on page 334), and to continue to explore new concepts (see photos 11.23, 11.24, and 11.27 on page 334). Too often adults think that children need the manufactured toys with which toy companies flood the market. In reality, children are as happy with the "wonderful" things in their environment. Think of the toddler joyfully exploring the environment by taking things out of the cupboards and using the items in his own special way (photo 11.32).

Children are fascinated with what adults are doing. They imitate behaviours previously seen (see photo 11.30 on page 336). It only makes sense to provide materials to them that are a child-sized reproduction of the "real thing" or the real thing. Children may actually get the wrong message. Plastic foods are a good example. If it looks like a banana, one should be able to eat it (photo 11.33). Instead, let children help prepare their own snack in the drama/kitchen area. They can emulate real life experiences by

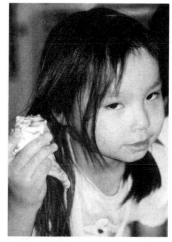

Photo 11.31

- setting the table;
- setting a "beautiful" table—with placemats, pretty dishes, sparkling glasses, and an attractive centrepiece;
- preparing their own snack (e.g., they can peel and cut up their own banana, add yogurt to fruit, pour their own juice, and so on); and
- cleaning up after themselves.

"Wonderful" materials surround us in our everyday lives. Children are naturally curious about what goes on around them. Nature provides many resources to spike curiosity and encourage learning (see photo 11.31 and Figure 11.8 on page 338).

The adult's role in providing "wonderful" materials can be described as

- setting up a collection process, brainstorming with children (see Figure 11.6 on page 336), and documenting learning (see Figure 11.7 on page 336);
- observing children (see Figures 11.3, 11.4, and 11.5 on pages 334 and 335);
- helping set up appropriate learning spaces (see photo 11.11 on page 325);
- organizing materials effectively for children and adults (see photos 11.1, 11.12, and 11.14 on pages 322 and 326);
- adapting and revising the learning area as needed (Example 7 in Table 11.3 on page 331); and
- displaying and documenting children's efforts appropriately (see Figures 11.2 and 11.8 on pages 333 and 338).

Photo 11.32

Stimulating Children to Facilitate Their Development

All individuals need stimulation. What we do every day becomes routine. How many times have you driven to work or school and not remembered stopping for a red light or passing a particular landmark? Boredom tends to set in when you are required to do the same thing over and over again.

Often adults do remember and apply this directly to the children's environments. I have observed environments that have total room changes every month. These room changes are thought to motivate and challenge the children. Often the changes do challenge the children, but not in ways that we necessarily desire. For example, the children may get confused about where things are or where they belong. The result is disorganization of space, materials, and the children's activity. Another problem can be that focus is placed on learning new routines and new organization, rather than learning or reinforcing skills.

Photo 11.33

Examples of Documentation

The documentation was mounted and hung in the hall. The children also created a book about what they learned about shells, using the same information that was posted on the documentation in the hall.

WHAT WE LEARNED ABOUT SHELLS

We learned that some shells are exactly the same. Jamie found two conch shells that are "identical."

We learned that some shells are different colours. Jessie found lots of white shells.

Jonas found broken shells. He thought that you could "Make stuff like necklaces or wind chimes."

Jerome said, "That some shells are big and some are small. You can put them in order of size."

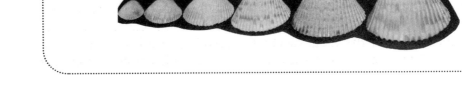

Examples of Documentation

Braelyn looked at Jessie's shells and said that one piece was a piece of white coral. "I don't really think it's a shell but it does come from the ocean."

Jonathan counted the white shells and said there were 7 shells and one piece of coral. "That makes eight," said Dillon.

Some shells are tiny and some are huge. Braelyn said, "I found itsy bitsy shells. They were very fragile. You have to hold them gently."

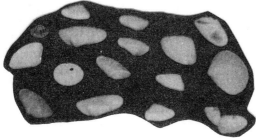

Gabrielle found "Great big shells, much bigger than Braelyn's, maybe 100 times more bigger."

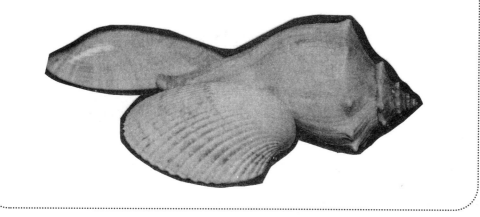

Children need to have consistency in their environment. They need to know where things are and where to find them. Imagine that you have been working on a carpentry project. Someone has decided that your organization is not appropriate, and this person has re-organized your space. When you come back to work on your project, you cannot find anything. How would you respond—with anger, confusion, frustration, or giving up?

I have also been in environments that are overwhelming in the number of choices that are available. I remember one dramatic area in particular. The children had everyday clothes, child-sized suits, aprons, child-sized dressy female clothes, and hats in one cupboard. A box of animal costumes sat on the floor. Role-playing costumes were kept in three drawers in a dresser, and fantasy clothes were hung in a corner behind black curtains. I observed one child acting out a "mother's role"—cooking in the kitchen. As she placed her pot on the stove, she saw the black fantasy curtain. She took off her apron, dropping it where she stood. She chose a "fairy costume." She tiptoed around the room touching everything with her magic wand. When she went back to the drama area, she noticed that three children were pretending to be pets. Off came the costume, again dropped at her feet. She immediately took all the costumes out of the box on the floor. She rummaged through them until she found a costume she liked. She joined the other three children in their role-play. A fourth child had observed the play. He decided to join. He sat on the floor and rummaged around to find a costume.

What was left in the drama area was a mess of clothes all over the floor. The children engaged in pet play had moved to a new area. No other children entered the area until clean-up time. Was it because this area was now so messy?

Stimulating children's interests means that the adults must do the following:

- Observe the children to decide what and when changes are needed. Zofia (Example 7 in Table 11.3) carefully observed the children before she made changes in their environment. She did not change the whole area—it was working the way it was set up. She adjusted the materials (bead organization) to reflect what children were doing (see Figure 11.4 on page 335). When we observe children's actions, we get a clue about what they are thinking and what they are learning (see Figures 11.3 and 11.5 on pages 334 and 335).
- Add extra materials that continue children's play and enhance their skills, such as the plastic insect for Jacob (Example 2 in Table 11.3) and adding pouring containers to the water table (Example 4).
- Provide alternative materials that will encourage children to transfer knowledge from one situation to another, such as small pitchers at the meal table to encourage children to pour drinks by themselves.
- Provide items that might encourage children's curiosity (e.g., animal beads, shells, or a vegetable garden).
- Provide ongoing displays, such as photos of children engaged in various activities, relevant pictures of current interest, artwork of famous artists, and new plants in the garden or outdoor environment.
- Observe the interactions of children within the environments to see whether interest is there. Adapt only based on the children's interest in activities. If the children are not interested in an area, then certainly it must be changed.

I observed one toddler setting over several days. On the first day, I noticed that although there was a quiet reading corner, the toddlers did not go into that area at all. I decided to look more closely at that area and made the following observations:

- there was no comfortable place to sit;
- all books except one were story books with more words than pictures;
- some books had covers only;
- most books were torn; and
- none of the books were attractive for toddlers—with pictures, hard covers, and topics of interest to toddlers.

As a result of my observations, I asked if I could bring in some books to encourage toddlers' interest in books. I was told that I was welcome to do this, but that I should understand that toddlers did not read. I should not be disappointed if it did not work. The next day I brought in a variety of books that I felt would interest the toddlers based on my limited observation of them. The consideration for choices included

- bright colours;
- foil backing on the pages of some of the books;
- large recognizable pictures;
- books that had sturdy, heavy cardboard covers or laminated pages; and

- topics such as animals, colours, objects, children, and songs (the children loved the "Itsy, Bitsy Spider" song).

I asked if I could move some of the big cushions into the area to provide comfort. The adults readily agreed. During the morning, one toddler noticed the area, sat down, and looked at one of the foil books. He got up, brought it to me, and asked me to read it to him. We talked about the book. Soon I had five toddlers with me. All nine of the toddlers visited the area that morning. The staff was astonished. One of the staff members admitted that she had learned about toddlers' interest in books in college, but thought it was perhaps one of the things that she had learned that "was not useful." The staff thanked me for making them aware of the potential of books. I was delighted when I next visited them to see the adaptations the staff had made to the book corner.

Child–Adult Interactions

One of the critical factors of quality is staff interactions. In order to provide the appropriate interactions, it is important to start with the same basic understanding. We all interpret messages differently (recall the adult interpretations of the statements made about warm nurturing characteristics). The National Statement on Quality Childcare (Canadian Child Day Care Federation, 1994) lists the characteristics of individuals working with young children and families. Table 11.4 lists the general categories along with the associated, specific behaviours that caregivers might demonstrate.

SUMMARY

This chapter was not intended to give you a prescriptive way of doing your work; rather, the intent was to open your eyes to a different way of looking at children, yourself, and the experiences you will provide for them. This last chapter should help you to reflect and discover and, in doing so, discover the "magic within ourselves, within children, and the environment which surrounds us all" (Lorie, 1989, p. 10).

KEY POINTS

PROVIDING QUALITY CARE
- Structural quality involves the following:
  - Adult-to-child ratios that are appropriate for the different age groups.
  - Appropriate group size for the different age groups.
  - Suitable adult environment with space for personal belongings. Some centres also had personal offices and shared spaces with the director's office.
- Contextual quality involves an appropriate level of staffing. High staff turnover is associated with lower levels of education and low salaries. Low staff turnover is linked to stable routines and environments, high interaction patterns, and greater staff cohesiveness. High staff turnover is linked to adults placing more emphasis on health and safety rather than quality learning activities for children, having fewer interactions, and placing greater emphasis on large group activities.
- Safety and basic care quality involves
  - all staff ensuring the health, safety, and nutritional well-being of all children.
  - higher educational levels, greater individual and small-group interactions, more interest in children, more responsiveness to children's signals, and more family involvement.

Adult–Child Interactions

Characteristic	Associated Behaviours
Warm	• Body language—get down to the child's level, have a relaxed posture, be in visible range of children, observe children, face children within the main group, and use hand gestures such as pointing, thumbs up, or waving (see photo 10.3 on page 282). • Facial expressions—have a friendly face, smile, use a variety of expressions to indicate your feelings such as joy, astonishment, and sadness (when appropriate) (see photos 2.1 and 10.6 on pages 29 and 287). • Learn about cultural variations: What is the personal space that the child is comfortable with? What body language and facial expressions are used by that culture?
Nurturing	• Respond to the child's signals immediately: when an infant cries, immediately check what he or she wants; if a child asks for attention, respond immediately either verbally or with a touch or facial expression (see photos 1.2 and 2.5 on pages 3 and 30). • Give the child the comfort needed—hug, touch, smile, verbal, body language (see photo 1.9 on page 4). • Learn about cultural variations (see photo 4.21 on page 106): what is appropriate—touch, hug, smile? • Respect the child's efforts, the child's unique way of approaching a task (such as trying to cut with either hand), the child's choices (such as painting more than one painting in a day); the child's help in displaying personal creative efforts (such as helping to create a corner in the room where all children can display their three-dimensional work) (see photo 7.3 on page 186).
Enjoy children and work	• Show enjoyment in body language and facial expressions (see photos 10.7, 11.3, and 11.4 on pages 287 and 323). • Verbalize your enjoyment—greet children and family members when they arrive (see photo 7.19 on page 196). • Talk positively about your experiences with children when in public: "I enjoy my work because …"
Flexible	• Adapt schedules to meet children's needs (see Figures 7.7 and 8.7 on pages 198 and 242). • Give children the time they need to complete individual or group projects.
Positive interactions/ guidance	• Observe children's play to identify potential problems. Nicola responded quickly to offer more materials to toddlers to prevent a dispute over a toy (see photo 6.18 on page 166). • Observe children to identify when children need support. Saul noticed that Jacob was puzzled because he could not identify the sound he heard. Saul helped him locate the source (Example 1 in Table 11.3). • Act as an intermediary between children to encourage problem solving. Angela noticed that Calla was upset because she was not allowed to play with the group. Angela guided children through a problem-solving situation (see photo 6.26 on page 169). • Redirect children only when needed. Jason, a four-year-old, arrived at daycare tired and cranky. His mother explained that he had not slept well during the night. When Jason went to the water centre he immediately took all the toys away and said, "These are MINE." Joel had observed the situation and walked over. Jason immediately ran away. Joel let him go but continued to observe him. Jason went to the block area and picked up a block. Joel noticed that Jason was going to throw the block. He stepped in, held his hand out, and said, "Let's build something together." The strategy worked.

Adult–Child Interactions

Characteristic	Associated Behaviours
Model behaviour	• Model language: provide unknown words such as *camouflage*; rephrase child's incorrect use of language (e.g., "I saw many mices." "Yes, you did. You saw a lot of mice.") • Model courtesy: hold doors open; ask for a toy; say "please," "thank you," and "excuse me." • Model appropriate health practices, such as blowing nose, washing hands, cleaning table before eating. • Model appropriate safety practices, such as holding scissors points down, sweeping sand off the floor, and wiping up spills. • Model personal hygiene, such as wearing appropriate clothes, having clean fingernails, brushing teeth after meals, and brushing or combing hair.
Encourage children's independence	• Observe children to see when to let them play alone or when you need to step in to help—John could handle his own feelings when his mother left (Example 8 in Table 11.3). • Observe the children to see what is needed to encourage them to take charge of their own learning. Beads were arranged in a different way to encourage different skills (Example 7 in Table 11.3). • Express pleasure in the child's attempt to complete tasks by him- or herself—Jordan was praised for his efforts (Example 6 in Table 11.3).
Offer realistic praise	• Telling children that everything is great, or wonderful, or beautiful takes away the meaning of the words. It may not be any of those things to the child. Are you going to tell everyone it is wonderful? Instead, praise their efforts: "You have worked hard." "Good for you. You did it by yourself." " I am proud of you for helping Amy." "Great job, you cleaned up the whole water centre by yourself." • Praise the child's accomplishment: "This is the first time you got all the way to the top. I took a picture of you so we can show your parents."
Assist in identifying feelings	• Children often do not yet know how they feel or how someone else feels. Use these opportunities to explain to children how someone else feels or label their feelings for them. Angela encouraged Calla to tell the other children how she felt (see photo 6.26 on page 169).
Involve children in planning, evaluating	• Children were encouraged to help decide what they wanted to keep of their old structures when their new daycare was being built (see photo 8.21 on page 228). Mackenzie helped to create the art room (see photo 8.24 on page 230). • Encourage children to reflect upon what they have done: "What else might we want to learn?" "What have you learned about ...?" "How else could we do this?"
Foster positive self-esteem	• Model appropriate respect—for example, documenting children's efforts (see Figure 11.8 on page 338). • Respect cultural differences—be aware of issues about personal space, provide photos of prominent cultures, and reflect children's background in their experiences (see photos 6.1, 6.14, and 6.15 on pages 151 and 164).

Process Quality

- Create an effective learning environment outdoors and indoors through levels of interest, plants, flowers, natural elements, artwork, projects, documentation, photos, labelled cubbies, and places for children and adults to sit.
- Indoor learning spaces can be made more inviting with plants, open areas, clearly defined interest centres, well-organized storage space, and points of interest.
- Outdoor learning spaces are enhanced through natural vegetation, shade (trees, shrubs, arbours), and various surfaces (grass and paved areas) for different types of play (such as gross motor activities that test strength, endurance, and coordination). There should also be places to relax, observe, and interact alone or in groups. Ensure outdoor safety by covering sandboxes, providing protection from elements, providing close supervision, and establishing safety rules.

Meaningful Experiences

- Follow children's lead.
- Provide materials based on children's experiences.
- Sustain children's efforts over time.
- Provide experiences that require use of all senses.
- Challenge children's creativity.
- Encourage children's independence.
- Provide additional challenges.
- Encourage children to choose own comfort level.
- Encourage safe risk taking.
- Encourage real situational role-play.
- Encourage work on projects.

Children's Learning

- Extend activities over time.
- Expand concepts and skills.
- Enjoy the process.
- Encourage children to become self-sufficient.
- Help children express and cope with their own feelings.
- Work through personal experiences through role-play activities.
- Collaborate with others.

Caregiver Interactions

- Set up developmentally appropriate experiences.
- Provide developmentally appropriate materials.
- Stimulate children's development.
- Observe interests and provide additional materials to continue building skills, alternative materials to transfer skills to new situations, materials to engage curiosity, and ongoing displays.
- In dealing with children, caregivers should exhibit the following characteristics:
  - Show warmth through body language, facial expressions, and sensitivity to cultural differences.
  - Be nurturing by responding to children's signals, providing comfort, and respecting children's efforts.
  - Show that you enjoy children and your work by using positive body language and facial expressions, verbalizing enjoyment, and speaking positively about personal child-care experiences.

- Be flexible on schedules and completion of tasks.
- Show positive interactions and provide guidance. Observe behaviour so that you know when to interact, when to provide support, when to act as an intermediary, and when to redirect behaviour.
- Model appropriate behaviour as it relates to language, courtesy, health practices, safety practices, and personal hygiene.
- Encourage independence. Know when to interact and when to provide support. Express pleasure in children's learning.
- Offer realistic praise of children's efforts and accomplishments.
- Assist children in identifying their feelings.
- Involve children in planning and evaluating.
- Foster positive self-esteem by modelling respectful behaviour and respecting cultural differences.

EXERCISES

1. Using a table like the one below, develop a comparative chart to identify how quality is met by the varying philosophical approaches.

Comparison of Approaches

QUALITY	HIGH/SCOPE	REGGIO EMILIA	MONTESSORI	HEAD START
Structural Quality				
Contextual Quality				
Adult Work Environment				
Safety and Basic Care				

2. In a small group, discuss and identify the various ways that individuals across Canada were able to create "magical" experiences for children by innovative adaptations to the physical environment—indoors and outdoors. Discuss what aspects could be implemented, and how, in a daycare setting you are all familiar with.
3. Why are first impressions so important? Visit at least three daycare centres. What is your first impression when you see the centre from the outside, when you enter the centre, when you see one of the children's rooms, and when you see the outdoor space? What general changes would you make?
4. In a small group, identify the elements that were used to create effective learning environments. Which do you think are particularly innovative? Which ones could you not use in the area in which you live? Explain your answers.

5. In a small group, describe how to make experiences for children meaningful. Suppose that your group has been hired to work in a preschool room in a day-care setting. The preschool is in a university in a large town. Most of your children come from students and about 20 percent of the children come from the faculty. You have many ethnic groups represented—Chinese, Japanese, Canadian, Mohawk, East Indian, and Mexican. The daycare is on the ninth floor of the social science building. The preschool area is made up of three large rooms. Each room has observation facilities attached. The outdoor play facility is a large rooftop area with climbers and riding paths. There is a deck over the area at one end. Each staff has an office space that is shared with one other person. How would you set up effective spaces both indoors and outdoors for this diverse group? Discuss materials and equipment that might be different from the normal materials you might see in a daycare. What additional information might you request from the families?

6. Describe how you might set up a project-based approach with a group of preschoolers. Base your project ideas on some of the possible activities in your area. What learning might you expect the children to gain from this activity?

7. In a small group, reflect upon the characteristics of quality caregiving as described in Table 11.4 (pages 342–43). Which are characteristics that you feel you do automatically already? Explain why. Which ones might you have to work on? Discuss some strategies that will help you in this process.

REFERENCES

BC Progress Board. (2001). Real Average Hourly Wages in BC and Canada, $1997. BC Progress Board [On-line]. Available: http://www.bcprogressboard.com/benchMkDocs/Page31.pdf.

Canadian Child Day Care Federation. (1994). *National Statement On Quality Child Care*. Ottawa, ON: Canadian Child Day Care Federation.

Cole, P., Frankeny, F., & Jonath, L. (1999). *Snowmen, Snow Creatures, Crafts, and Other Winter Projects*. San Francisco, CA: Chronicle Books.

Crowther, I. (2003). Informal Survey of Graduates of ECE Programs.

Friendly, M., Beach, J., & Turiano, M. (2002). *Early Childhood Education and Care in Canada*. Toronto, ON: Childcare Resources and Research Unit.

Goelman, H., Doherty, G., Lero, D., LaGrange, A., & Tougas, J. (2000). *You Bet I Care! Caring and Learning Environments: Quality in Child Care Centres Across Canada*. Guelph, ON: Centre for Families, Work and Well-Being, University of Guelph.

Lorie, P. (1989). *Wonder Child*. Switzerland: Labyrinth Publishing S.A.

Mitchell, P., & Frankeny, F. (2000). *Sandcastles—Great Projects: From Mermaids to Monuments*. San Francisco, CA: Chronicle Books.

Wallace, M. (1999). *Inuksuk*. Toronto, ON: Owl Books.

Wallace, M. (2001). *Make Your Own Inuksuk*. Toronto, ON: Owl Books.

GLOSSARY

achieved social status Status under the control of the individual (e.g., educational level, volunteer, or parent).

active listening Listening to the content and feelings expressed without bias or prejudice.

alert states Times when the infant is awake and ready to engage in activity.

anchored movements Movements through bending, twisting, rocking, or swinging arms or legs.

ascribed social status Status society has ascribed to the individual (e.g., sex, race, ethnicity, or socioeconomic status).

associative play Playing together, sharing materials and ideas, but engaged in individual activity.

babbling Stringing consonants and vowel sounds together in different intonation patterns—loud, soft, high, low, and so on.

childhood stress "[I]nvolves any unusual demand—something new or different—that forces children to draw on energy reserves that exceed what they would normally require for dealing with ordinary events in their lives" (Hart et al., as cited in Kostelnik et al., 2002, p. 147).

classification Arrangement of items into groups or subgroups using more than one attribute.

collaboration Working together in a diverse group (children, families, staff, community members, and other professionals) toward the common goal of best practices within a child-care program.

communication An interactive process that requires a message to be created (encoded), sent to someone else (verbally, physically, symbolically, or in writing), and understood by the receiver (decoded). The receiver then may respond to the message to continue the process.

communication boards Boards that are set up with symbols and pictures to encourage children to communicate by pointing.

competitive play Individual or group striving towards superiority in an activity; the products are superior or inferior; activities lead to winning or losing.

conflict resolution Solving interpersonal problems such as disputes or arguments independently.

constructive play Using materials, space, or objects to build or create specific ideas or structures.

cooperative play Two or more children working together toward a common goal.

creative representation Representing personal experiences from one situation to another.

critical periods Periods during which optimal development occurs; lack of stimulation in the critical period has resulting deficits that are not correctable at later stages of development.

culture "[T]he values, beliefs, and material objects that constitute a people's way of life" (Macionis et al., 1997, p. 637).

cumulative play Types of play that emerge in a predictable order, at a predictable age, and each type of play builds on the previous stage.

custodial care Care for the physical health and safety of children.

decoding Making sense of or understanding a message that has been sent.

deferred imitation Imitating an action or event that has been seen previously.

developmentally appropriate practices Practices "based on knowledge of how children develop and learn. All early childhood teachers must understand what occurs in the first eight years of life and how best to support growth and development" (Gestwicki, 1999, p. 6).

didactic Refers to something that instructs or teaches.

documentation board Photographs, drawings, and written descriptions of the children's activities that are mounted and displayed in a central location that all partners can view.

dramatic play Practising skills, roles, social interactions, and communication strategies.

dysfunctional families Families that do not function well together (e.g., they fail to solve problems together, fail to communicate adequately with each other, are emotionally neglectful, and may not function appropriately in their family roles).

economic family Any group of individuals sharing a common residence, related by blood, marriage, common-law, or adoption.

economic security An assured standard of living that can provide families with the level of resources and benefits necessary to participate economically, politically, socially, culturally, and with dignity in their community's activities (Hanvey, 2002, p. 16).

emergent curriculum A curriculum that is sensitive and responsive to all children.

emergent skills Skills that are beginning to appear.

encoding Creating a message (verbal, in writing, using body language, or in sign language) in order to start a communication interaction.

ethnicity A "shared cultural heritage. Members of an ethnic category may have common ancestors, language, and religion which, together, confer a distinctive social identity" (Macionis et al., 1997, p. 311).

expansion Adding more relevant detail to a verbal expression.

facilitator A person who sets the stage for learning to occur, observes and monitors the children's activity, provides additional resources when needed, and is sensitive to guide children's behaviour only when guidance is needed.

full-spectrum fluorescent lighting Fluorescent lighting that has the full spectrum of wavelengths of light; the closest match to sunlight.

functional play Repeated manipulation of an object.

imitate Copy an action, expression, idea, or symbol.

imitative play Copying a behaviour that is being observed exactly, or copying the behaviour to obtain a similar result.

inclusive setting A setting that provides children with special needs opportunities for active participation with children who are developing typically; includes support services and adaptations to the environment.

interest centres Core learning areas such as sand or blocks that are defined by children's current interests (e.g., building structures in sand or with blocks) and by common materials and learning experiences.

intrapersonal Refers to factors that are intrinsic and internal to the individual.

labour-force sensitive Term that applies to programs that meet the needs of working families; for example, half-day kindergarten programs require additional care for children for the other half day and, therefore, do not meet the needs of families who work full-time.

learning areas or interest centres Areas that are arranged for a common purpose such as building with blocks.

malnutrition A condition that occurs over a period of time. Individuals consume either too much of one food or too little of another.

master social status Social identity—usually based on occupation.

mission statement Statement of intent and philosophy of the program.

nonanchored movements Movements through running, jumping, hopping, skipping, marching, or climbing.

norms Rules or guidelines for social behaviour.

one-to-one-correspondence Forming sets of objects where one object is paired with another (e.g., one fork beside a plate).

onlooker or observer play Watching others without obvious personal involvement.

palmar grasp Using the whole hand to grasp the utensil to manipulate with; usually combined with movement of the whole arm to control the activity engaged in (see Figure 2.1 on page 34).

parallel play Playing beside another doing similar things with similar materials.

physical safety The "quality of children's natural environments and threats to their personal safety and well-being" (Hanvey, 2002, p. 20).

process oriented The play itself is rewarding; there may not necessarily be a product, or the product is not as important as the process in getting to the product.

process quality "The nature of the child's experience; the daily interactions between the child and the teacher and among children themselves" (Goelman et al., 2000, p. 4).

race A group of people sharing inherited physical characteristics such as skin colour, facial features, hair texture, and body shape.

reliability The consistency of the observations among different people.

repetitive play Play that is repeated over and over again.

sanctions Consequences associated with the breaking of social norms.

self-fulfilling prophecy Situation in which "we behave according to the expectations of others" (Mooney et al., 2001, p. 140).

sensitive periods Times during which learning, such as language development, occurs more easily.

sensorimotor activity Learning about the world through sight, touch, hearing, tasting, smelling, and motor movement.

sensorimotor exploration Learning by using all the senses—including touching, grasping, movement, listening, and interacting with others.

seriation Arranging things in order (e.g., large to small) or pattern (e.g., red, blue, red, blue).

social exclusion A seemingly socially acceptable mechanism for denying certain individuals the right to participate in the same activities that others participate in.

solitary play Play alone doing one's own thing.

sorting Putting things or ideas together based on a common characteristic—such as all the same size, all the same shape, or all the same colour.

symbolic play Using one thing to represent another, such as using a stick to represent an airplane.

task force A local group of individuals set up to look at a particular issue in the community (e.g., hunger, poverty, or increasing child-care spaces) in order to identify the need and develop recommendations to address the problem.

teachable moment Observing children and using the information gained by observing to spontaneously enhance or build on that skill (e.g., observing a child sign while reading or sitting with the child and signing what the child points to in the book).

transactional process Process in which the speaker and the listener both act as a speaker and a listener simultaneously.

trial and error Trying a task by manipulating objects such as puzzle pieces into various positions until the piece fits into the correct spot.

tripod grasp Grasping the utensil between forefinger and thumb, usually used to write or draw; the activity is controlled by wrist action with little whole arm movement (see Figure 2.2 on page 34).

trustworthy environment An environment that is set up to encourage safe exploration, to meet all the infants' needs (cognitive, physical, emotional, motor, and communication), to provide flexible schedules, and to provide predictable routines.

INDEX

Communication boards, 47
Communication network, 107–8
Community context, 60, 122–26
Community discussion panels, 111
Community functions, 77–78
Community members, collaboration with, 106
Community partnerships, 134–35
Community resource collection, 107
Competitive play, 35
Conciseness of observations, 92
Conflict resolution, 101
Constructive play, 34
Contextual quality, 263, 320–21
Cooke, K, 149, 156, 254
Cooperative play, 3–4, 8–9, 10, 11, 34, 35, 58–59
Counting, 48
Craig, G., 14, 36, 50
Crawling, 5, 30
Creative area, 207
Creative representation in High/Scope, 217
Critical periods, 38
Crowther, I., 4, 18, 28, 31, 40, 64, 65, 100, 182, 183, 190, 273, 274, 319, 321
Cultural diversity, 10–11, 12, 49–50, 97, 99, 130–32, 167–68, 272–73. See also Multiculturalism
Culture, 122, 124, 125, 126
  and programs, 167–68
  values, 164, 165
Cumulative play, 36
Curiosity, 3, 4, 5–6, 10, 32
Curriculum development, 215
Custodial care, 150

Dechillo, N., 60
Decoding, 85
Deferred imitation, 31, 33, 39
Depression, 15, 126
Developmentally appropriate practices, 37–40, 166
DeVito, J., 88, 89
de Waal, F., 39
Diapering area, 200
Didactic materials, 235
Digdon, N., 14
Directed activities, 273
Directed learning, 62–63
Diversity and inclusion, 195

Division of Childhood and Adolescence, 240
Documentation, 233, 234, 336, 338–39
Documentation board, 71, 72
Documentation panels, 232, 233
Doherty-Derkowski, G., 13, 65, 83, 166
Dramatic play, 34
Dramatic play area, 193
Duplicate materials, 6, 32, 84, 100, 158, 166, 296
Duyff, R., 15
Dysfunctional families, 15, 128

Early Childhood Environmental Rating Scales, 48
Early experiences, importance of. See Brain development
Early Learning Centre in Ontario, 273
ECE educator characteristics, 166, 342–43
Economic family, defined, 12
Economic security, factors involved, 16
Economic situation and quality experiences, 124
Educational system, 18
Edwards, C., 228
Elder, E., 254, 257
Emergency evacuation plan, 205
Emergent curriculum, 69
Emergent interests of children, 68, 330, 340
Emergent skills, 31
Emotional development, resources, 211–12, 213
Encoding, 85
Environment. See Learning environment
Epstein, H., 268
Ethnic diversity in Canada, 49, 131, 167–68
Ethnicity, defined, 123
Evaluation, 143–44, 153
Evans, R., 268
Exelby, B., 182, 190
Expansion, 87

Facilitator
  as a leader, 75–76
  as a learner, 66–67
  observing, planning, implementing, 68–72
  partnership with families (see Families)
  role in community, 76–78

role in learning environment, 58–59, 72–75, 332
role with children, 62–66
self-assessment, 74
Families
  in AHS program, 243
  diverse backgrounds, 12
  influences on children, 13–15
  as partners, 60–62, 67, 99, 106, 132–34, 138, 153, 159, 164, 170, 232, 332
  and public policies, 18
Family dynamics
  family functioning, 15, 127–28
  family health, 126–27
  parenting styles, 129
  recreation, 130
  support networks, 128
Family dynamics and young children, 158
Family stress, 270–71
Family support, 16
Family values, 50, 60, 99
Fanjoy, S.E., 157
Feeding infants, 203
Feelings in partnerships, 140
Fetus play, 29
Fine motor activities, 9, 38, 329, 334–35
Firlik, R., 85
Flexner, S., 76
Fortney, J., 312, 313
Framing a picture, 188
Frankeny, F., 325
Fraser, S., 105
Friendly, M., 60, 113, 254, 259, 261, 281, 316, 321
Friendships, 11
Full-spectrum fluorescent lighting, 188
Functional play, 31, 237
Funding as concern of program director, 153

Gallagher, J., 14
Gandini, L., 181, 182, 227, 232, 234
Gender differences, 50–51
Gestwicki, C., 3, 4, 13, 18, 19, 28, 29, 38, 40, 66, 68, 96, 106, 114, 135, 138, 151, 273, 287, 288, 294, 297
Goelman, H., 156, 157, 257, 262, 263, 266, 267, 320, 323, 324
Gordon, A., 95, 97
Government of Canada, 130

school-aged children, 10, 35
supportive conditions, 19–23
toddlers, 5–6, 32–33
Learning together, 5–6, 7, 8–9, 11, 66–67.
See also Communication;
Interactions
Lefrancois, G., 2, 14
Legislative requirements. *See* Regulations
in Canada
Lero, D., 254, 259, 261
Liberman, J., 183
Licensing criteria, 282, 286
Lilley, H., 183
Listening, 86, 88
Lorie, P., 1
Low-income families. *See* Poverty
Lunch, 202–3

Machado, J., 3
Macionis, J., 122, 123, 124, 126
"Magical" materials, 337
"Magical places," 323, 324, 326
Malaguzzi, L., 65, 67, 75, 226, 228
Malnutrition, 15
Marotz, L., 15, 205
Master social status, defined, 123
Math area, 193
Mathematics centre (Montessori), 236
Mayer, D.E., 281
McCain, M., 2, 3, 13, 15, 19, 38, 124,
127, 129, 156, 254, 255, 273
Mealtime routines, 196, 201–3
Mental health problems, 15, 126, 128
Mentoring, 135, 138
Miller, D., 100, 102
Mission statement, 154
Mitchell, P., 325
Mobile infants, 174
Monitoring procedures, licensing
requirement, 286
Montessori approach, 235–39, 267
Montessori, M., 236, 239
Montgomery, W., 74
Mooney, L., 12, 121, 122, 124, 128
Morrison, G., 237
Motivation, 22, 138
Motor skills. *See* Gross motor activities
Moving, effects on children, 14, 15
Moyer, J., 75
Multi-age groupings, 312–14

Multiculturalism, 167–68
resources, 178–79
See also Cultural diversity
Music, 191, 192
emotional development, 213
resources, 55
Mustard, F., 2, 3, 13, 15, 19, 38, 124, 127,
129, 156, 254, 255, 273
Mutual support in partnerships, 140

Nash, M., 2, 28, 29
National Association for Early Childhood
Educators (NAEYC), 38
Negative learning, 62–63
Networks. *See* Collaboration
Neural connections. *See* Brain development
Newborns, 29–30
Newsweek's special edition on Your Child, 156
Nilsen, B., 95
Nonanchored movements, 219
Nonliteral quality practices, 22
Nonmobile infants, 174
Norms, defined, 124
Nurturing, 15, 323–24
Nutrition, 14, 168, 243

Observation by children, 6
Observation skills, 89–95
criteria for, 90–93, 95
first step in planning, 68, 224, 225,
239, 340–41
interacting, 67, 92, 93, 224, 239
interpretation and use, 84–86, 95
knowledge of child development, 67,
93, 95
recording, 92, 95, 334, 335
tools and methods, 94
See also Communication
On-site program studies, 112
One-to-one-correspondence, 218–19
Onlooker or observer play, 32
Ontario Coalition for Better Child Care,
110
Ontario Early Years Centre, 245–46
Organization for Economic Co-operation
and Development, 150, 154
Organization of learning areas, 193
Ott, J., 183
Outdoor environments
infants, 41, 42

preschoolers, 44, 45, 306–7
school-aged, 44, 46
special needs, 46, 47
toddlers, 41, 43, 300–301
Outdoor spaces, 190, 194–95

Palmar grasp, 33, 34
Parallel play, 6, 32, 166
Parental health, 15, 126
Parental interactions, 13
Parent board, 102, 103
Parenting style, 129
Parents, involvement as licensing
requirement, 286
Parten, M., 36
Partners
communication among, 142–43,
288, 291
evaluation by, 143–44
families as (*see* Families, as
partners)
finding, 132–38
needs of, 138, 140–42
partnership climate, 138, 140
planning with, 143
Peer pressure, 39
Pendakur, R., 167
Perry Preschool Project, 240, 267
Pesticides, 17
Phillips, D., 286
Physical safety, 17, 18, 41
Pimento, B., 14
Planning, 69–72
and evaluating, 170–71, 172
observation first, 68, 224, 225,
239, 340
with partners, 143
Play
activities, 30
characteristics, 36–37
and the child with special needs, 35
cumulative levels, 37
and learning (*see* Learning through play)
materials, 32
supported, not directed, 62–66
Play, D., 36
Playground, 207–8, 219, 220, 326–28
Playing together, 3–4, 7, 8–9, 10, 11
Poisonous plants, 208
Political climate, 18, 124

Positive interactions, 15, 63–64, 166
Poverty, 15, 16–18
  effects on children (*see* Children in poverty)
  and social exclusion, 128–29, 257–59
  and stress, 268
  and well-being of children, 254–57
Prereading skills, 8
Preschool environments, 44, 45
Preschoolers, 7–10
  compared with school-aged children, 175
  learning environment, 304–7
  programs, 297, 302–3, 308
Pride in accomplishment (partnerships), 141–42
Problem-solving, 8, 12, 22, 101, 152, 225
Process-oriented play, 37
Process/product orientation, 21–22
Process quality, 267–68, 323–28
Professional contacts and resources, 138, 139
Professional development, 268, 322
Program directors, concerns, 153–54
Progress of Canada's Children, The, 13, 18
Project approach, 226, 232, 234, 332
  process of projects, 234
Psychological safety, 40, 41

Quality
  in Canada, 156
  considerations for children, 151–52
  defined, 150
  differences according to age group, 172
  early childhood educators, 152–53
  family considerations, 150–51
  interaction of perspectives, 155
  other professionals, 154
  program directors, 153–54
  studies, 156–57
Quality care, 262–68, 320–28
  adult work environment, 263, 266, 322
  contextual quality, 263, 320–21
  process quality, 267–68, 323–28
  safety and basic care, 266–67, 322–23
  structural quality, 262, 320
Quiet areas, 100, 340
Quiet spaces, 262
Quiet time, 4

Race, 123
Ratios. *See* Adult-to-child ratios
Read, M., 183
Real experiences and understanding, 20
Recording observations, 92, 95
Records, health, 169, 170, 171, 204
Recreational activities. *See* Play
Reggio Emilia approach, 226–34, 267
Regulations in Canada
  importance to educator, 113–14
  infant programs, 287–93
  licensing criteria, 282, 286
  preschool programs, 308
  qualifications, 281–82, 283–85
  structural quality and, 320
  toddler programs, 295, 297
Reliability of observations, 90–91
Religion, 124
Remuneration for ECE workers, 263, 266, 267, 321, 323
Repetitive play, 5, 31
Resource centres, 244–48
Resources, diversity, 212, 213
Respect for others, 102
Responding physically, 86
Responding verbally, 86
Responsiveness, 166
Roberts, R., 60
Robertson, P., 254, 257
Robinson, R., 2
Role models, 11
Role-play, 7, 34, 111–12, 329, 332
Roopnarine, J., 235, 240
Routines, 196–208
  feeding infants, 203
  greeting and dismissal routines, 196–97
  health practices, 204
  lunch, 202–3
  napping and resting, 203–4
  safety, 205–6
  schedules, 196, 197
  snack times, 201–2
  toddlers, 296
Rules, 22
Ryan, T., 108
Ryerson Early Learning Centre, 312, 314

Safe products, 207
Safety, 74, 100, 206–8, 332
  infants, 206
  physical, 41

playground safety, 207–8
  preschoolers, 207
  psychological, 40, 41
  routines, 205–6
  toddlers, 206–7, 295, 296
Safety and basic care, quality care, 266–67, 322–23
Safety practices, 169
Salary ranges, 321
Sample letter requesting materials, 136–37
Sanctions, 124
Sand area, 191, 192
Sawyer, W., 3
Sayre, N., 14
Schedules, 196, 197, 242, 288
Schickedanz, J., 2, 13, 50–51
School-aged children, 10–12
  compared with preschoolers, 175
  environments, 44, 46
  needs, 309, 310–11, 312
School-aged programs, 308–12
  options, 309
  regulations, 310
School readiness, 273–74
Schultz, F.E., 167
Schweinhart, L., 246, 267, 274
Scissors and knives, 207
Scribe centre, 192
Self-confidence, 3, 101, 329
Self-control, 100
Self-fulfilling prophecy, 128
Sensitive periods, 38, 237–39
Sensorial materials (Montessori), 235
Sensorimotor activity, 28
Sensorimotor exploration, 287
Seriation, 218
Setting the stage for learning, 64–65
Shapiro Kendrick, A., 168
Sharing, 6, 20, 32, 96–97, 100, 158
Sheridan Child Care Centre, 217–26
Shipley, D., 4, 18, 21, 39
Shonkoff, J., 286
Shore, R., 5, 255
Size requirements for licensed facilities, 286
Skills, 39
  discovering and developing, 7–8, 9, 10, 11
Skills and knowledge in partnerships, 141
Sleep schedules
  infants, 196, 203
  toddlers and preschoolers, 196, 204